DATE DUE

			PRINTED IN U.S.A.

Authors & Artists for Young Adults

ISSN 1040-5682

Authors & Artists for Young Adults

VOLUME 13

Kevin S. Hile
E. A. Des Chenes
Editors

 Gale Research Inc. • *DETROIT* • *WASHINGTON, D.C.* • *LONDON*

Kevin S. Hile and E. A. Des Chenes, *Editors*

Joanna Brod and Thomas F. McMahon, *Associate Editors*

Todd Ableser, Bruce Ching, Hazel K. Davis, Ronie-Richele Garcia-Johnson, Marian C. Gonsior, Helene Henderson, Janet L. Hile, Laurie Collier Hillstrom, Anne Janette Johnson, Diane Patrick, Tom Pendergast, Jani Prescott, Nancy E. Rampson, Megan Ratner, Susan M. Reicha, Tracy J. Sukraw, Sarah Verney, Barbara A. Withers, and Laura M. Zaidman, *Sketch Contributors*

Victoria B. Cariappa, *Research Manager*
Mary Rose Bonk, *Research Supervisor*

Reginald A. Carlton, Frank Vincent Castronova, Andrew Guy Malonis, and Norma Sawaya, *Editorial Associates*

Laurel Sprague Bowden, Dawn Marie Conzett, Eva Marie Felts, Shirley Gates, Sharon McGilvray, Dana R. Schleiffers, and Amy B. Wieczorek, *Editorial Assistants*

Margaret A. Chamberlain, *Picture Permissions Supervisor*

Pamela A. Hayes, Arlene Johnson, Keith Reed, and Barbara A. Wallace, *Permissions Associates*

Susan Brohman, *Permissions Assistant*

Mary Beth Trimper, *Production Director*
Catherine Kemp, *External Production Assistant*

Cynthia Baldwin, *Art Director*
Sherrell Hobbs and C. J. Jonik, *Desktop Publishers/Typesetters*
Willie Mathis, *Camera Operator*

∞™ The paper used in this publication meets the minimum requirements of American National Standard for Information Sciences—Permanence Paper for Printed Library Materials, ANSI Z39.48-1984.

Library of Congress Catalog Card Number 89-641100
ISBN 0-8103-8566-X
ISSN 1040-5682

10 9 8 7 6 5 4 3 2 1

Printed in the United States of America

Published simultaneously in the United Kingdom
by Gale Research International Limited
(An affiliated company of Gale Research Inc.)

I(T)P™

The trademark ITP is used under license.

Contents

Introduction

Authors and Artists for Young Adults is a reference series designed to serve the needs of middle school, junior high, and high school students interested in creative artists. Originally inspired by the need to bridge the gap between Gale's *Something about the Author,* created for children, and *Contemporary Authors,* intended for older students and adults, *Authors and Artists for Young Adults* has been expanded to cover not only an international scope of authors, but also a wide variety of other artists.

Although the emphasis of the series remains on the writer for young adults, we recognize that these readers have diverse interests covering a wide range of reading levels. The series therefore contains not only those creative artists who are of high interest to young adults, including cartoonists, photographers, music composers, bestselling authors of adult novels, media directors, producers, and performers, but also literary and artistic figures studied in academic curricula, such as influential novelists, playwrights, poets, and painters. The goal of *Authors and Artists for Young Adults* is to present this great diversity of creative artists in a format that is entertaining, informative, and understandable to the young adult reader.

Entry Format

Each volume of *Authors and Artists for Young Adults* will furnish in-depth coverage of about twenty to twenty-five authors and artists. The typical entry consists of:

— A detailed biographical section that includes date of birth, marriage, children, education, and addresses.

— A comprehensive bibliography or filmography including publishers, producers, and years.

— Adaptations into other media forms.

— Works in progress.

— A distinctive essay featuring comments on an artist's life, career, artistic intentions, world views, and controversies.

— References for further reading.

— Extensive illustrations, photographs, movie stills, cartoons, book covers, and other relevant visual material.

A cumulative index to featured authors and artists appears in each volume.

Compilation Methods

The editors of *Authors and Artists for Young Adults* make every effort to secure information directly from the authors and artists through personal correspondence and interviews. Sketches on living authors and artists are sent to the biographee for review prior to publication. Any sketches not personally reviewed by the biographees or their representatives are marked with an asterisk (*).

Highlights of Forthcoming Volumes

Among the authors and artists planned for future volumes are:

Ansel Adams	Linda Ellerbee	Patricia McKillip
Dave Barry	M. C. Escher	Andre Norton
Peter Benchley	Frank Frazetta	Joyce Carol Oates
James L. Brooks	Genaro Gonzalez	Stella Pevsner
Tim Burton	John Grisham	Joan Phipson
Brock Cole	James S. Haskins	Edgar Allan Poe
Barbara Corcoran	Stephen Herek	Chaim Potok
Frank Deford	Will Hobbs	Harold Ramis
Arthur Conan Doyle	Zora Neale Hurston	Rod Serling
Roddy Doyle	Dorothea Lange	Leslie Marmon Silko
Danny Elfman	H. P. Lovecraft	Timothy Zahn

The editors of *Authors and Artists for Young Adults* welcome any suggestions for additional biographees to be included in this series. Please write and give us your opinions and suggestions for making our series more helpful to you. Direct your comments to: Editors, *Authors and Artists for Young Adults*, Gale Research Inc., 835 Penobscot Building, Detroit, Michigan 48226-4094.

Authors
& Artists
for Young
Adults

Isaac Asimov

chemist at U.S. Navy Air Experimental Station, Philadelphia, 1942-45. *Military service:* Corporal in the U.S. Army, 1945-46. *Member:* Authors League of America, Science Fiction Writers of America, National Association of Science Writers, American Chemical Society, Zero Population Growth, Population Institute, National Organization of Non-Parents, Sigma Xi, Mensa.

■ Personal

Has also written under the pseudonyms Dr. A., George E. Dale, and Paul French; born January 2, 1920, in Petrovichi, Russia (formerly part of the U.S.S.R.); brought to United States, 1923, naturalized citizen, 1928; died of heart and kidney failure, April 6, 1992, in New York, NY; son of Judah (a candy store owner) and Anna Rachel (Berman) Asimov; married Gertrude Blugerman, July 26, 1942 (divorced November 16, 1973); married Janet Opal Jeppson (a psychiatrist), November 30, 1973; children: David, Robyn Joan. *Education:* Columbia University, B.S., 1939, M.A., 1941, Ph.D., 1948.

■ Addresses

Home—10 West 66th St., Apt. 33-A, New York, NY 10023.

■ Career

Writer. Boston University School of Medicine, Boston, MA, instructor, 1949-51, assistant professor, 1951-55, associate professor, 1955-79, professor of biochemistry, 1979—. Worked as a civilian

■ Awards, Honors

Guest of honor at the Thirteenth World Science Fiction Convention, 1955; Edison Foundation National Mass Media Award, 1958; Blakeslee Award for nonfiction, 1960; special Hugo Award for distinguished contributions to the field, 1963, for science articles in *The Magazine of Fantasy and Science Fiction;* special Hugo Award for best all-time science fiction series, 1966, for *Foundation, Foundation and Empire,* and *Second Foundation;* Hugo Award for best novel, 1973, for *The Gods Themselves,* and 1983, for *Foundation's Edge;* Hugo Award for best short story, 1977, for "The Bicentennial Man"; James T. Grady Award, American Chemical Society, 1965; American Association for the Advancement of Science-Westinghouse Award for science writing, 1967; Nebula Award, Science Fiction Writers of America, 1973, for *The Gods Themselves,* and 1977, for "The Bicentennial Man"; Glenn Seabord Award, International Platform Association, 1979; "Nightfall" was chosen the best science fiction story of all time in a Science Fiction Writers of America poll.

■ **Writings**

SCIENCE FICTION

Pebble in the Sky (novel; also see below), Doubleday, 1950.

I, Robot (short stories), Gnome Press, 1950.

The Stars, Like Dust (novel; also see below), Doubleday, 1951, published as *The Rebellious Stars* with *An Earth Gone Mad* by R. D. Aycock, Ace Books, 1954.

Foundation (also see below), Gnome Press, 1951, published as *The 1,000 Year Plan* with *No World of Their Own* by Poul Anderson, Ace Books, 1955.

(Under pseudonym Paul French) *David Starr, Space Ranger* (juvenile; also see below), Doubleday, 1952, reprinted under name Isaac Asimov, Twayne, 1978.

Foundation and Empire (also see below), Gnome Press, 1952.

The Currents of Space (novel; also see below), Doubleday, 1952.

Second Foundation (also see below), Gnome Press, 1953.

(Under pseudonym Paul French) *Lucky Starr and the Pirates of the Asteroids* (juvenile; also see below), Doubleday, 1953, reprinted under name Isaac Asimov, Twayne, 1978.

The Caves of Steel (novel; also see below), Doubleday, 1954.

(Under pseudonym Paul French) *Lucky Starr and the Oceans of Venus* (juvenile), Doubleday, 1954, reprinted under name Isaac Asimov, Twayne, 1978.

The Martian Way and Other Stories (also see below), Doubleday, 1955.

The End of Eternity (novel; also see below), Doubleday, 1955.

(Contributor) Groff Conklin, editor, *Science Fiction Terror Tales by Isaac Asimov and Others*, Gnome Press, 1955.

(Under pseudonym Paul French) *Lucky Starr and the Big Sun of Mercury* (juvenile), Doubleday, 1956, published under name Isaac Asimov as *The Big Sun of Mercury*, New English Library, 1974, reprinted under name Isaac Asimov under original title, Twayne, 1978.

The Naked Sun (novel; also see below), Doubleday, 1957.

(Under pseudonym Paul French) *Lucky Starr and the Moons of Jupiter* (juvenile), Doubleday, 1957, reprinted under name Isaac Asimov, Twayne, 1978.

Earth Is Room Enough: Science Fiction Tales of Our Own Planet (also see below), Doubleday, 1957.

The Robot Novels (contains *The Caves of Steel* and *The Naked Sun*; also see below), Doubleday, 1957.

(Under pseudonym Paul French) *Lucky Starr and the Rings of Saturn* (juvenile), Doubleday, 1958, reprinted under name Isaac Asimov, Twayne, 1978.

Nine Tomorrows: Tales of the Near Future, Doubleday, 1959.

Triangle: "The Currents of Space," "Pebble in the Sky," and "The Stars, Like Dust," Doubleday, 1961, published in England as *An Isaac Asimov Second Omnibus*, Sidgwick & Jackson, 1969.

The Foundation Trilogy: Three Classics of Science Fiction (contains *Foundation, Foundation and Empire*, and *Second Foundation*), Doubleday, 1963, published in England as *An Isaac Asimov Omnibus*, Sidgwick & Jackson, 1966.

The Rest of the Robots (short stories and novels, including *The Caves of Steel* and *The Naked Sun*), Doubleday, 1964, published as *Eight Stories from the Rest of the Robots*, Pyramid Books, 1966.

Fantastic Voyage (novelization of screenplay by Harry Kleiner), Houghton, 1966.

Through a Glass Clearly, New English Library, 1967.

Asimov's Mysteries (short stories), Doubleday, 1968.

Nightfall and Other Stories, Doubleday, 1969, published in England in two volumes, as *Nightfall One* and *Nightfall Two*, Panther Books, 1969, published as *Nightfall: Twenty SF Stories*, Rapp & Whiting, 1971.

The Best New Thing (juvenile; illustrated by Symeon Shimin), World Publishing, 1971.

The Gods Themselves (novel), Doubleday, 1972.

The Early Asimov: Or, Eleven Years of Trying (short stories), Doubleday, 1972.

(Contributor) Conklin, editor, *Possible Tomorrows by Isaac Asimov and Others*, Sidgwick & Jackson, 1972.

An Isaac Asimov Double: "Space Ranger" and "Pirates of the Asteroids", New English Library (London), 1972.

A Second Isaac Asimov Double: "The Big Sun of Mercury" and "The Oceans of Venus", New English Library, 1973.

The Third Isaac Asimov Double, New English Library/Times Mirror, 1973.

The Best of Isaac Asimov (short stories), Doubleday, 1974.

Have You Seen These?, NESFA Press, 1974.

Buy Jupiter and Other Stories, Doubleday, 1975.

The Heavenly Host (juvenile; illustrated by Bernard Colonna), Walker & Co., 1975.

The Bicentennial Man and Other Stories, Doubleday, 1976.

The Collected Fiction of Isaac Asimov, Volume 1: *The Far Ends of Time and Earth* (contains *Pebble in the Sky*, *Earth Is Room Enough*, and *The End of Eternity*), Doubleday, 1979, Volume 2: *Prisoners of the Stars* (contains *The Stars, Like Dust*, *The Martian Way and Other Stories*, and *The Currents of Space*), Doubleday, 1979.

Three by Asimov, limited edition, Targ Editions, 1981.

The Complete Robot (also see below), Doubleday, 1982.

Foundation's Edge (novel), Doubleday, 1982.

The Winds of Change and Other Stories, Doubleday, 1983.

(With wife, Janet O. Jeppson, writing as Janet Asimov) *Norby, the Mixed-Up Robot* (juvenile; also see below), Walker & Co., 1983.

The Winds of Change and Other Stories, Doubleday, 1983.

The Robots of Dawn (novel), Doubleday, 1983.

The Robot Collection (contains *The Caves of Steel*, *The Naked Sun*, and *The Complete Robot*), Doubleday, 1983.

(With Janet Asimov) *Norby's Other Secret* (juvenile; also see below), Walker & Co., 1984.

Robots and Empire (novel), Doubleday, 1985.

(With Janet Asimov) *Norby and the Invaders* (juvenile; also see below), Walker & Co., 1985.

(With Janet Asimov) *Norby and the Lost Princess* (juvenile; also see below), Walker & Co., 1985.

The Best Science Fiction of Isaac Asimov, Doubleday, 1986.

The Alternative Asimovs (contains *The End of Eternity*), Doubleday, 1986.

(With Janet Asimov) *The Norby Chronicles* (contains *Norby, the Mixed-Up Robot* and *Norby's Other Secret*), Ace Books, 1986.

Foundation and Earth (novel), Doubleday, 1986.

(Author of introduction) *Tales from Isaac Asimov's Science Fiction Magazine: Short Stories for Young Adults*, selected by Sheila Williams and Cynthia Manson, Harcourt, 1986.

(With Janet Asimov) *Norby and the Queen's Necklace* (juvenile; also see below), Walker & Co., 1986.

(With Janet Asimov) *Norby: Robot for Hire* (contains *Norby and the Lost Princess* and *Norby and the Invaders*), Ace Books, 1987.

Fantastic Voyage II: Destination Brain, Doubleday, 1987.

(With Janet Asimov) *Norby Finds a Villain* (juvenile; also see below), Walker & Co., 1987.

(With Janet Asimov) *Norby through Time and Space* (contains *Norby and the Queen's Necklace* and *Norby Finds a Villain*), Ace Books, 1988.

Azazel, Doubleday, 1988.

Nemesis, Doubleday, 1988.

Prelude to Foundation, Doubleday, 1988; with introduction by James Gunn and illustrations by Vincent DiFate, Easton Press, 1988.

(With Theodore Sturgeon) *The Ugly Little Boy/The Widget, the Wadget, and Boff* (also see below), Tor Books, 1989.

Franchise (juvenile), Creative education, 1989.

(With Janet Asimov) *Norby Down to Earth* (juvenile), Walker & Co., 1989.

All the Troubles of the World (juvenile), Creative Education, 1989.

(With Janet Asimov) *Norby and Yobo's Great Adventure* (juvenile), Walker & Co., 1989.

Sally (juvenile), Creative Education, 1989.

Robbie (juvenile; illustrated by David Shannon), Creative Education, 1989.

(Author of notes and commentary with Martin Harry Greenberg) *The New Hugo Winners: Award-Winning Science Fiction Stories*, Wynwood Press, 1989.

The Asimov Chronicles, edited by Greenberg, illustrated by Ron Lindahn and Val Lakey Lindahn, Dark Harvest, 1989.

The Asimov Chronicles, three volumes, Ace Books, 1990.

Invasions, New American Library, 1990.

(Author of foreword) *Why I Left Harry's All-Night Hamburgers, and Other Stories from Isaac Asimov's Science Fiction Magazine*, edited by Williams and Charles Ardai, Delacorte, 1990.

(With Janet Asimov) *Norby and the Oldest Dragon* (juvenile), Walker & Co., 1990.

Isaac Asimov: The Complete Stories, Doubleday, 1990.

Robot Visions, Penguin, illustrated by Ralph McQuarrie, 1990.

(With Janet Asimov) *Norby and the Court Jester* (juvenile), Walker & Co., 1991.

Forward the Foundation, Doubleday, 1993.

(With Robert Silverberg) *The Ugly Little Boy* (novel expanded from the short story "The Ugly Little Boy"), Bantam, 1993.

Also editor or co-editor of numerous science fiction and fantasy anthologies. Author of numerous works in the "Science Fiction shorts" series, published by Raintree.

MYSTERIES

The Death Dealers (novel), Avon Publications, 1958, published as *A Whiff of Death*, Walker & Co., 1968.

Tales of the Black Widowers, Doubleday, 1974.

Murder at the ABA: A Puzzle in Four Days and Sixty Scenes (novel), Doubleday, 1976, published in England as *Authorised Murder: A Puzzle in Four Days and Sixty Scenes*, Gollancz, 1976.

More Tales of the Black Widowers, Doubleday, 1976.

The Key Word and Other Mysteries, illustrated by Rod Burke, Walker & Co., 1977.

Casebook of the Black Widowers, Doubleday, 1980.

The Union Club Mysteries, Doubleday, 1983.

(Editor with Greenberg and Charles Waugh, and author of introduction) *Computer Crimes and Capers*, Academy Chicago Publishers, 1983.

Banquets of the Black Widowers, Doubleday, 1984.

The Disappearing Man and Other Mysteries, illustrated by Yoshi Miyake, Walker & Co., 1985.

The Best Mysteries of Isaac Asimov, Doubleday, 1986.

Puzzles of the Black Widowers, Doubleday, 1990.

Also editor, with others, of many mystery anthologies.

SCIENCE FACT; ADULT

(With William C. Boyd and Burnham S. Walker) *Biochemistry and Human Metabolism*, Williams & Wilkins, 1952, 3rd edition, 1957.

The Chemicals of Life: Enzymes, Vitamins, Hormones, Abelard-Schuman, 1954.

(With Boyd) *Races and People*, Abelard-Schuman, 1955.

(With Walker and Mary K. Nicholas) *Chemistry and Human Health*, McGraw, 1956.

Inside the Atom, illustrated by John Bradford, Abelard-Schuman, 1956, revised and updated edition, 1966.

Only a Trillion (essays), Abelard-Schuman, 1958, published as *Marvels of Science: Essays of Fact and Fancy on Life, Its Environment, Its Possibilities*, Collier Books, 1962, reprinted under original title, Ace Books, 1976.

The World of Carbon, Abelard-Schuman, 1958, revised edition, Collier Books, 1962.

The World of Nitrogen, Abelard-Schuman, 1958, revised edition, Collier Books, 1962.

The Clock We Live On, Abelard-Schuman, 1959, revised edition, 1965.

Words of Science and the History behind Them, Houghton, 1959, revised edition, Harrap, 1974.

Realm of Numbers, Houghton, 1959.

The Living River, Abelard-Schuman, 1959, published as *The Bloodstream: River of Life*, Collier Books, 1961.

The Kingdom of the Sun, Abelard-Schuman, 1960, revised edition, 1963.

Realm of Measure, Houghton, 1960.

The Wellsprings of Life, Abelard-Schuman, 1960, New American Library, 1961.

The Intelligent Man's Guide to Science, two volumes, Basic Books, 1960, Volume 1 published separately as *The Intelligent Man's Guide to the Physical Sciences*, Pocket Books, 1964, Volume 2 published separately as *The Intelligent Man's Guide to the Biological Sciences*, Pocket Books, 1964, revised edition published as *The New Intelligent Man's Guide to Science*, 1965, published as *Asimov's Guide to Science*, 1972, revised edition published as *Asimov's New Guide to Science*, 1984.

The Double Planet, Abelard-Schuman, 1960, revised edition, 1967.

Realm of Algebra, Houghton, 1961.

Life and Energy, Doubleday, 1962.

Fact and Fancy (essays), Doubleday, 1962.

The Search for the Elements, Basic Books, 1962.

The Genetic Code, Orion Press, 1963.

The Human Body: Its Structure and Operation (illustrated by Anthony Ravielli; also see below), Houghton, 1963.

View from a Height, Doubleday, 1963.

The Human Brain: Its Capacities and Functions (also see below), Houghton, 1964.

A Short History of Biology, Natural History Press for the American Museum of Natural History, 1964.

Quick and Easy Math, Houghton, 1964.

Adding a Dimension: Seventeen Essays on the History of Science, Doubleday, 1964.

(With Stephen H. Dole) *Planets for Man*, Random House, 1964.

Asimov's Biographical Encyclopedia of Science and Technology, Doubleday, 1964, 2nd revised edition, 1982.

A Short History of Chemistry, illustrated by Robert Yaffe, Doubleday, 1965.

Of Time and Space and Other Things (essays), Doubleday, 1965.

An Easy Introduction to the Slide Rule, Houghton, 1965.

The Noble Gasses, Basic Books, 1966.

The Neutrino: Ghost Particle of the Atom, Doubleday, 1966.

Understanding Physics, three volumes, Walker & Co., 1966.

The Genetic Effects of Radiation, U.S. Atomic Energy Commission, 1966.

The Universe: From Flat Earth to Quasar, Walker & Co., 1966, 3rd edition published as *The Universe: From Flat Earth to Black Holes—and Beyond*, 1980.

From Earth to Heaven (essays), Doubleday, 1966.

Environments out There, Abelard-Schuman, 1967.

Is Anyone There? (essays), Doubleday, 1967.

Science, Numbers and I (essays), Doubleday, 1968.

Photosynthesis, Basic Books, 1968.

Twentieth Century Discovery (essays), Doubleday, 1969, revised edition, Ace Books, 1976.

The Solar System and Back (essays), Doubleday, 1970.

The Stars in Their Courses (essays), Doubleday, 1971, revised edition, Ace Books, 1976.

The Left Hand of the Electron (essays), Doubleday, 1972.

Electricity and Man, U.S. Atomic Energy Commission, 1972.

Worlds within Worlds: The Story of Nuclear Energy, three volumes, U.S. Atomic Energy Commission, 1972.

A Short History of Chemistry, Heinemann, 1972.

(Contributor) *Physical Science Today*, CRM Books, 1973.

Today and Tomorrow and . . ., Doubleday, 1973.

The Tragedy of the Moon, Doubleday, 1973.

Asimov on Astronomy (essays), Doubleday, 1974.

Our World in Space, illustrated by Robert McCall, foreword by Edwin E. Aldrin, Jr., New York Graphic Society, 1974.

Asimov on Chemistry (essays), Doubleday, 1974.

Of Matters Great and Small, Doubleday, 1975.

Science Past, Science Future, Doubleday, 1975.

Eyes on the Universe: A History of the Telescope, Houghton, 1975.

The Ends of the Earth: The Polar Regions of the World, illustrated by Bob Hines, Weybright & Talley, 1975.

Asimov on Physics (essays), Doubleday, 1976.

The Planet that Wasn't (essays), Doubleday, 1976.

The Collapsing Universe, Walker & Co., 1977.

Asimov on Numbers (essays), Doubleday, 1977.

The Beginning and the End (essays), Doubleday, 1977.

Quasar, Quasar, Burning Bright (essays), Doubleday, 1978.

Life and Time, Doubleday, 1978.

The Road to Infinity (essays), Doubleday, 1979.

A Choice of Catastrophes: The Disasters that Threaten Our World, Simon & Schuster, 1979.

Visions of the Universe, preface by Carl Sagan, illustrated by Kazuaki Iwasaki, Cosmos Store, 1981.

The Sun Shines Bright (essays), Doubleday, 1981.

Exploring the Earth and the Cosmos: The Growth and Future of Human Knowledge, Crown, 1982.

Counting the Eons, Doubleday, 1983.

The Roving Mind, Prometheus Books, 1983.

The Measure of the Universe, illustrated by Roger Jones, Harper, 1983.

X Stands for Unknown, Doubleday, 1984.

The History of Physics, Walker & Co., 1984.

Isaac Asimov on the Human Body and the Human Brain (contains *The Human Body: Its Structure and Operation* and *The Human Brain: Its Capacities and Functions*), Bonanza Books, 1984.

The Exploding Suns: The Secrets of the Supernovas, illustrated by D. F. Bach, Dutton, 1985.

Asimov's Guide to Halley's Comet, Walker & Co., 1985.

The Subatomic Monster, Doubleday, 1985.

(With Karen Frenkel) *Robots: Machines in Man's Image*, Robot Institute of America, 1985.

Isaac Asimov's Wonderful Worldwide Science Bazaar: Seventy-Two Up-to-Date Reports on the State of Everything from Inside the Atom to Outside the Universe, Houghton, 1986.

The Dangers of Intelligence and Other Science Essays, Houghton, 1986.

Far as Human Eye Could See (essays), Doubleday, 1987.

The Relativity of Wrong: Essays on the Solar System and Beyond, Doubleday, 1988.

Asimov on Science: A Thirty Year Retrospective, Doubleday, 1989.

Asimov's Chronology of Science and Technology: How Science Has Shaped the World and How the World Has Affected Science from 4,000,000 B.C. to the Present, Harper, 1989.

The Secret of the Universe, Doubleday, 1989.

The Tyrannosaurus Prescription and One Hundred Other Essays, Prometheus Books, 1989.

Frontiers: New Discoveries about Man and His Planet, Outer Space, and the Universe, Plume, 1989.

Out of the Everywhere, Doubleday, 1990.

Atom: Journey across the Subatomic Cosmos, New American Library, 1991.

Asimov's Chronology of the World, HarperCollins, 1991.

Asimov's Guide to Earth and Space, Random House, 1991.

(With Frederick Pohl) *Our Angry Earth*, Tor Books, 1991.

SCIENCE FACT; JUVENILE

Building Blocks of the Universe, Abelard-Schuman, 1957, revised and updated edition, 1974.

Breakthroughs in Science, Houghton, 1960.

Satellites in Outer Space, illustrated by John Polgreen, Random House, 1960, revised edition, 1973.

The Moon, illustrated by Alex Ebel, Follett, 1966.

To the Ends of the Universe, Walker & Co., 1967, revised edition, 1976.

Mars, illustrated by Herb Herrick, Follett, 1967.

Stars, illustrated by Herrick, with diagrams by Mike Gordon, Follett, 1968.

Galaxies, illustrated by Ebel and Denny McMains, Follett, 1968.

ABCs of Space, Walker & Co., 1969, published as *Space Dictionary*, Scholastic, 1970.

Great Ideas of Science, illustrated by Lee Ames, Houghton, 1969.

ABCs of the Ocean, Walker & Co., 1970.

Light, Follett, 1970.

What Makes the Sun Shine?, Little, Brown, 1971.

ABCs of the Earth, Walker & Co., 1971.

ABC's of Ecology, Walker & Co., 1972.

Ginn Science Program, Ginn, intermediate levels A, B, and C, 1972, advanced levels A and B, 1973.

Comets and Meteors, illustrated by Raul Mina Mora, Follett, 1972.

The Sun, illustrated by Ebel, Follett, 1972.

Jupiter, the Largest Planet, Lothrop, 1973, revised edition, 1976.

Please Explain, illustrated by Michael McCurdy, Houghton, 1973.

Earth: Our Crowded Spaceship, John Day, 1974.

The Solar System, illustrated by David Cunningham, Follett, 1975.

Alpha Centauri, the Nearest Star, Lothrop, 1976.

Mars, the Red Planet, Lothrop, 1977.

Saturn and Beyond, diagrams by Giulio Maestro, Lothrop, 1979.

Venus: Near Neighbor of the Sun, illustrated by Yukio Kondo, Lothrop, 1981.

(Editor) David Lambert, *Planet Earth 200*, Facts on File, 1985.

Beginnings: The Story of Origins—Of Mankind, Life, the Earth, the Universe, Walker & Co., 1987.

Franchise, illustrated by David Shannon, Creative Education, 1988.

All the Troubles of World, illustrated by Shannon, Creative Education, 1988.

(With Frank White) *Think about Space*, Walker & Co., 1989.

Little Treasury of Dinosaurs, illustrated by Christopher Santoro, Crown, 1989.

Also author of many volumes in the "How Did We Find Out" series, Walker & Co., 1972—, and the "Isaac Asimov's Library of the Universe" series, Gareth Stevens, 1987—, and the "Ask Isaac Asimov" and "Isaac Asimov's Pioneers of Science and Exploration" series, G. Stevens Children's Books.

HISTORY

The Kite That Won the Revolution (juvenile), Houghton, 1963, revised edition, 1973.

The Greeks: A Great Adventure, Houghton, 1965.

The Roman Republic, Houghton, 1966.

The Roman Empire, Houghton, 1967.

The Egyptians, Houghton, 1967.

The Near East: Ten Thousand Years of History, Houghton, 1968.

The Dark Ages, Houghton, 1968.

Words from History, illustrated by William Barss, Houghton, 1968.

The Shaping of England, Houghton, 1969.

Constantinople: The Forgotten Empire, Houghton, 1970.

The Land of Canaan, Houghton, 1970.

The Shaping of France, Houghton, 1972.

The Shaping of North America from Earliest Times to 1763, Houghton, 1973.

The Birth of the United States, 1763-1816, Houghton, 1974.

Our Federal Union: The United States from 1816 to 1865, Houghton, 1975.

The Golden Door: The United States from 1865 to 1918, Houghton, 1977.

Futuredays: A Nineteenth-Century Vision of the Year 2000, illustrated by Jean Marc Cote, Holt, 1986.

(With White) *The March of the Millennia: A Key to Looking at History*, Walker & Co., 1990.

OTHER

Words from the Myths, Houghton, 1961.

Words in Genesis, Houghton, 1962.

Words on the Map, Houghton, 1962.

Words from Exodus, Houghton, 1963.

Asimov's Guide to the Bible, maps by Rafael Palacios, Doubleday, Volume 1: *The Old Testament*, 1968, Volume 2: *The New Testament*, 1969.

Opus 100 (selections from author's first one hundred books), Houghton, 1969.

Asimov's Guide to Shakespeare, illustrated by Rafael Palacios, two volumes, Doubleday, 1970, published as one volume, Avenel Books, 1981.

Unseen World, (teleplay), American Broadcasting Co. (ABC-TV), 1970.

(Under pseudonym Dr. A) *The Sensuous Dirty Old Man*, Walker & Co., 1971.

Isaac Asimov's Treasury of Humor: A Lifetime Collection of Favorite Jokes, Anecdotes, and Limericks with Copious Notes on How to Tell Them and Why, Houghton, 1971.

(With James Gunn) *The History of Science Fiction from 1938 to the Present*, (filmscript), Extramural Independent Study Center, University of Kansas, 1971.

More Words of Science, Houghton, 1972.

The Story of Ruth, Doubleday, 1972.

Asimov's Annotated "Don Juan," illustrated by Milton Glaser, Doubleday, 1972.

Asimov's Annotated "Paradise Lost," text by John Milton, Doubleday, 1974.

Lecherous Limericks, illustrated by Julien Dedman, Walker & Co., 1975.

"The Dream," "Benjamin's Dream," and "Benjamin's Bicentennial Blast": Three Short Stories, Printing Week in New York, 1976.

More Lecherous Limericks, illustrated by Dedman, Walker & Co., 1976.

Familiar Poems Annotated, Doubleday, 1977.

Still More Lecherous Limericks, illustrated by Mel Brofman, Walker & Co., 1977.

Asimov's Sherlockian Limericks, New Mysterious Press, 1978.

Animals of the Bible, illustrated by Howard Berelson, Doubleday, 1978.

(With John Ciardi) *Limericks Too Gross*, Norton, 1978.

Opus 200 (selections from the author's second hundred books), Houghton, 1979.

In Memory Yet Green: The Autobiography of Isaac Asimov, 1920-1954, Doubleday, 1979.

Extraterrestrial Civilizations (speculative nonfiction), Crown, 1979.

Isaac Asimov's Book of Facts, Grosset, 1979.

In Joy Still Felt: The Autobiography of Isaac Asimov, 1954-1978, Doubleday, 1980.

The Annotated "Gulliver's Travels," C. N. Potter, 1980.

In the Beginning: Science Faces God in the Book of Genesis, Crown, 1981.

Asimov on Science Fiction, Doubleday, 1981.

Change!: Seventy-One Glimpses of the Future (forecasts), Houghton, 1981.

(With Ciardi) *A Grossery of Limericks*, Norton, 1981.

Would You Believe?, illustrated by Sam Sirdofsky Haffner, Grosset, 1981.

(With Ken Fisher) *Isaac Asimov Presents Superquiz*, Dembner, 1982.

More—Would You Believe?, illustrated by Pat Schories, Grosset, 1982.

(Editor with George R. R. Martin and Greenberg) *The Science Fiction Weight-Loss Book*, Crown, 1983.

(Editor with Greenberg and Charles G. Waugh) *Isaac Asimov Presents the Best Horror and Supernatural of the Nineteenth Century*, Beaufort Books, 1983.

(Editor) *Thirteen Horrors of Halloween*, Avon, 1983.

(Editor with Greenberg and George Zebrowski; and author of introduction) *Creations: The Quest for Origins in Story and Science*, Crown, 1983.

(With Fisher) *Isaac Asimov Presents Superquiz 2*, Dembner, 1983.

Opus 300 (selections from the author's third hundred books), Houghton, 1984.

Isaac Asimov's Limericks for Children, Caedmon, 1984.

(Editor) *Living in the Future* (forecasts; illustrated by Lynn Williams), Beaufort Books, 1985.

The Edge of Tomorrow, T. Doherty, 1985.

(With James Burke and Jules Bergman) *The Impact of Science on Society*, National Aeronautics and Space Administration (NASA), 1985.

Isaac Asimov, Octopus Books, 1986.

(Editor with Greenberg and Charles G. Waugh) *Sherlock Holmes through Time and Space*, Bluejay Books, 1986.

The Alternate Asimovs, Doubleday, 1986.

Past, Present, and Future, Prometheus Books, 1987.

Robot Dreams, edited by Bryon Preiss, illustrated by Ralph McQuarrie, Berkley, 1987.

Other Worlds of Isaac Asimov, edited by Greenberg, Avenel, 1986.

(With Janet Asimov) *How to Enjoy Writing: A Book of Aid and Comfort*, illustrated by Sidney Harris, Walker & Co., 1987.

(Author of notes) *Asimov's Annotated Gilbert and Sullivan*, by William Schwenck Gilbert, Doubleday, 1988.

(Editor with Jason A. Schulman) *Isaac Asimov's Book of Science and Nature Quotations*, Weidenfeld & Nicolson, 1988.

Asimov's Galaxy: Reflections on Science Fiction, Doubleday, 1989.

Foundation's Friends: Stories in Honor of Isaac Asimov, edited by Martin H. Greenberg, T. Doherty Associates, 1989.

The Tyrannosaurus Prescription and 100 Other Essays, Prometheus Books, 1989.

(Compiler with Greenberg) *Cosmic Critiques: How and Why 10 Science Fiction Stories Work*, Writer's Digest, 1990.

(Contributor) *The John W. Campbell Letters with Isaac Asimov and A. E. van Vogt*, A. C. Projects, 1991.

Isaac Asimov Laughs Again, HarperCollins, 1991.

Also author of *The Adventures of Science Fiction*, Ameron Ltd. Author of "Science" column in *Magazine of Fantasy and Science Fiction*, 1958—. Contributor of stories to numerous science fiction anthologies, and to many science fiction magazines, including *Astounding Science Fiction, Amazing Stories, Fantastic Adventures, Science Fiction,* and *Future Fiction;* contributor of one short story under pseudonym George E. Dale to *Astounding Science Fiction.* Contributor of articles to numerous science journals and popular periodicals. Editorial director, *Isaac Asimov's Science Fiction Magazine.*

■ Adaptations

A sound recording of William Shatner reading the first eight chapters of *Foundation* was produced as *Foundation: The Psychohistorians*, Caedmon, 1976, and of Asimov reading from the same novel was produced as *The Mayors*, Caedmon, 1977; the film, *The Ugly Little Boy*, from a short story of the same title, was produced by Learning Corporation of America, 1977.

■ Sidelights

By the time of his death in 1992, Isaac Asimov was widely regarded as one of the most productive and versatile writers of all time. Asimov was best-known for his science-fiction novels and popularized accounts of science, but he worked in a number of other genres as well. Writing in the *New York Times*, Mervyn Rothstein asserted that "Mr. Asimov was amazingly prolific, writing nearly 500 books on a wide range of subjects, from works for pre-schoolers to college textbooks." Peter Stoler declared in *Time* that "Simenon may have written more thrillers, Chesterton more poetry and philosophy, Pulp Romance Writer Barbara Cartland more novels. But no single author has ever written more books about more subjects than Isaac Asimov."

Asimov's "usual routine," explained Rothstein, "was to awake at 6 A.M., sit down at the typewriter by 7:30 and work until 10 P.M." In order to maintain the necessary writing pace, Asimov typed his first drafts at a rate of ninety words per minute. *Detroit Free Press* writer Ellen Creager related that "once, interviewer Barbara Walters asked Asimov what he'd do if he was told he had only six months to live. 'I'd type faster,' he replied." He revised

each story only once, believing—as he said in *In Memory Yet Green*, the first volume of his autobiography—that "if after two typings the result proves unsatisfactory, it has always seemed to me it is better abandoned. There is less trouble and trauma involved in writing a new piece than in trying to salvage an unsatisfactory old one." He vacationed infrequently and claims never to have experienced "writer's block." He also maintained complete control over what he described, in his introduction to *The Bicentennial Man and Other Stories*, as "an absolutely one-man operation. I have no assistants of any kind. I have no agent, no business manager, no research aides, no secretary, no stenographer. I do all my own typing, all my own proof reading, all my own indexing, all my own research, all my own letter writing, all my own telephone answering. I like it that way. Since I don't have to deal with other people, I can concentrate more properly on my work, and get more done."

Childhood Science Fiction Interest

Asimov's interest in science fiction began when he first noticed several of the early s.f. magazines for sale on the newsstand of his family's candy store. Unfortunately the periodicals, like the candy, were forbidden to him. His father felt that young Isaac should spend his time in more serious pursuits than the reading of contemporary fiction. As a boy Asimov read, and enjoyed, numerous volumes of nonfiction as well as many of the literary "classics" (although, since modern fiction was off-limits, he claims that he had no way of knowing he was reading classical works); but he longed to explore the intriguing magazines with the glossy covers. His father, however, remained adamant, maintaining, as Asimov recalls, that fiction magazines were "junk! … Not fit to read. The only people who read magazines like that are bums." And bums, he explained, represented "the dregs of society, apprentice gangsters."

But in August of 1929, a new magazine, *Science Wonder Stories*, appeared on the scene. Asimov knew that as long as science fiction magazines had titles like *Amazing Stories*, he would have little chance of convincing his father of their worth. The newcomer, however, had the word "science" in its title, and he said in *In Memory Yet Green*, "I had read enough about science to know that it was a mentally nourishing and spiritually wholesome study. What's more, knew that my father thought so from our occasional talks about my schoolwork." When confronted with this argument, the elder Asimov capitulated. Soon Isaac began collecting even those periodicals that didn't have "science" in the title. He noted: "I planned to maintain with all the strength at my disposal the legal position that permission for one such magazine implied permission for all the others, regardless of title. No fight was needed, however; my harassed father conceded everything." Thus Asimov was allowed to feed his appetite for science fiction "pulp" and rapidly developed into an avid fan while, at the same time, gaining valuable experience in the genre which had yet to be labeled science fiction.

He Wrote Early and Often

Asimov wrote his first original fiction at the age of eleven. For some time he had been reading stories and then retelling them to groups of his schoolmates, adding a few personal embellishments in the process. In the fall of 1931 he decided to begin a series of books in the vein of some of the popular series of the 1920s: "The Rover Boys," "The Bobbsey Twins," and "Pee Wee Wilson." Asimov's series was called "The Greenville Chums at College," unashamedly patterned after the better-known "The Darewell Chums at College," and it grew to eight chapters before he abandoned it. Asimov, in *In Memory Yet Green*, described the flaw in his initial literary venture: "I was trying to imitate the series books without knowing anything but what I read there. Their characters were small-town boys, so mine were, for I imagined Greenville to be a town in upstate New York. Their characters went to college, so mine did. Unfortunately, a junior-high-school youngster living in a shabby neighborhood in Brooklyn knows very little about small-town life and even less about college. Even I, myself, was forced eventually to recognize the fact that I didn't know what I was talking about."

He made a similar mistake in 1934 when, in a high-school creative writing class, he attempted to write a descriptive essay about a spring day and chose, as a setting, not Brooklyn (with which he would have been familiar), but "a never-never pastoral land full of larks and daisies." To compound the error, he volunteered to read the finished work to the class; he had been writing, off and on, for several years and was eager to demonstrate his prowess to the teacher. As he tells it, "I had not read more than two paragraphs before Mr. Newfield could endure no more. 'This is shit!' he said, sending me back to my seat.... I never came closer in my life to giving up." But he kept writing, of course, and it was during the term of that same creative writing class that his first printed piece appeared. All the students were required to submit items for publica-

Young Asimov—pictured here in front of his family's candy store—first became interested in science fiction while reading the s.f. publications sold at the shop's newsstand.

tion in the school's literary semiannual, the *Boys High Recorder*, and Asimov wrote a humorous essay entitled "Little Brother" which was accepted, he says, because it was the only funny piece anyone wrote, and the editors needed something funny.

In the summer of 1934, Asimov had a letter published in *Astounding Stories* in which he commented on several stories that had appeared in the magazine. This was the first time any of his writing had appeared in a science fiction periodical, and it led to several other letters to the editor. His continuing activities as a fan brought him to the decision to attempt a science fiction piece of his own; in 1937, at the age of seventeen, he began a story entitled "Cosmic Corkscrew." It dealt with the notion of helical time, and in it the hero was able to travel through time to certain points determined by the shape of a helix. The procedure Asimov used to formulate the plot was, he said, "typical of my science fiction. I usually thought of some scientific gimmick and built a story about that." By the time he finished the story on June 19, 1938, *Astounding Stories* had become *Astounding Science Fiction* and was being edited by John W. Campbell, who was to influence the work of some of the most prominent authors of modern science fiction, including Arthur C. Clarke, Robert Heinlein, Poul Anderson, L. Sprague de Camp, and Theodore Sturgeon. Since Campbell was one of the best-known science fiction writers of the thirties and *Astounding* one of the most prestigious publications in its field at the time, Asimov was shocked by his father's suggestion that he submit "Cosmic Corkscrew" to the editor in person. But mailing the story would have cost twelve cents while subway fare, round trip, was only ten cents. In the interest of economy, therefore, he agreed to make the trip to the magazine's office, fully expecting to leave the manuscript with a secretary. Campbell, however, had invited many young writers to discuss their work with him, and when Asimov arrived he was shown into the editor's office. Campbell talked for over an hour and agreed to read the story; two days later Asimov received the manuscript back in the mail. It had been rejected, but Campbell offered extensive suggestions for improvement and encouraged the young man to keep trying. This began a pattern that was to continue for several years with Campbell guiding Asimov through his beginnings as a science fiction writer. Asimov is now generally considered to be one of the leading writers of science fiction's "Golden Age," which places him in the company of such luminaries as Heinlein, de Camp, Sturgeon, L. Ron Hubbard, and A. E. Van Vogt.

Laws for Robots

Asimov is credited with the introduction of several innovative concepts into the genre, not the least of which is the formulation of the "Three Laws of Robotics." He maintained that the idea for the laws was given to him by Campbell; Campbell, on the other hand, said that he had merely picked them out of Asimov's early robot stories. In any case, it was Asimov who formalized the three principles: "1. A robot may not injure a human being or, through inaction, allow a human being to come to harm. 2. A robot must obey the orders given it by human beings except where such orders would

conflict with the First Law. 3. A robot must protect its own existence as long as such protection does not conflict with the First or Second Laws." Commenting on the three laws of robotics, David N. Samuelson asserted in *Science-Fiction Writers* that "Asimov devised these control mechanisms to offset what he saw as a 'Frankenstein complex' in science fiction." Creager similarly noted that "Asimov in his science fiction created the concept of the humanistic, not evil, robot," and that the author's benevolent depiction of robots extended to his descriptions of alien species: "He also went against Campbell's wishes that aliens be inexorably evil. Asimov liked to think of his aliens as decent folk."

Asimov said of his three laws of robotics that he is "probably more famous for them than for anything else I have written, and they are quoted even outside the science-fiction world. The very word 'robotics' was coined by me." The three laws gained general acceptance among readers and among other science fiction writers; Asimov, in his autobiography, writes that they "revolutionized" science fiction and that "no writer could write a *stupid* robot story if he used the Three Laws. The story might be bad on other counts, but it wouldn't be stupid." The laws became so popular, and seemed so logical, that many people believed real robots, if they ever were invented, would be designed according to Asimov's basic principles.

The "Foundation" Series

Also notable among Asimov's science fiction works, in addition to the robot stories and the Three Laws, is the "Foundation" series, in which the inhabitants of Asimov's future worlds have forgotten Earth and owe allegiance to a crumbling Empire that has survived for over twelve thousand years. This group of short stories, published in magazines in the forties and then collected into a trilogy in the early fifties, was inspired by Edward Gibbon's *Decline and Fall of the Roman Empire*. It was written as a "future history," a story being told in a society of the distant future which relates events of that society's history. The concept was not invented by Asimov, but there can be little doubt that he became a master of the technique. *Foundation, Foundation and Empire,* and *Second Foundation* have achieved special standing among science fiction enthusiasts. In 1966, the World Science Fiction Convention honored them with a special Hugo Award as the best all-time science fiction series. Even thirty years after their original publication, Asimov's future history series remains popular, having sold in excess of two million copies.

Although some reviewers believe that traditional literary style, plot, and characterization in these books is scarce, James Gunn noted in his book *Isaac Asimov: The Foundations of Science Fiction,* "story in *The Foundation Trilogy* is plentiful. Events move on a grand scale, beginning with the approaching dissolution of a galactic empire." To those in power, all seems well, but all is not well. Gunn related the reasons: "According to the calculations of a psychologist named Hari Seldon, who has used a new science called 'psychohistory' for predicting mass behavior, the Empire will fall and be followed by 30,000 years of misery and barbarity. Seldon sets up two Foundations, one of physical scientists and a Second Foundation of psychologists . . . to

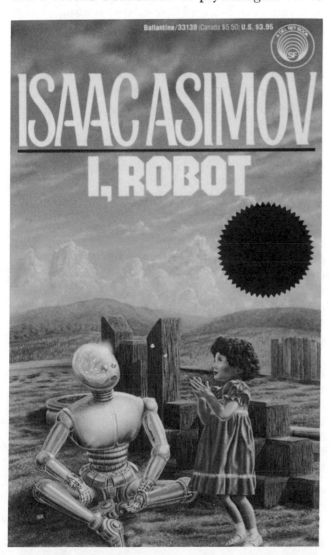

Ballantine/33139 (Canada $5.50) U.S. $3.95

ISAAC ASIMOV
I, ROBOT

Originally published in 1950, this is the first of Asimov's books in which robots must adhere to the "Three Laws of Robotics."

shorten the oncoming dark ages to only a thousand years."

In the psychohistorian's statistical forecasting and the unfolding of his thousand-year plan, Maxine Moore pointed out in her contribution to *Voices for the Future: Essays on Major Science Fiction Writers,* "the Foundation group deals overtly with the problem of Free Will in deterministic universe." Moore believes that "whereas [Asimov's] robot stories reveal individual man as mechanism, the Foundation group shows society as a mechanism."

What emerges from Asimov's study of this society at once guided and trapped by a grand scheme is, according to Gunn, the conviction that "rationality is the one human trait that can always be trusted. . . . Sometimes rational decisions are based on insufficient information and turn out to be wrong, or the person making the decision is not intelligent enough to see the ultimate solution rather than the partial one, but nothing other than reason works at all." Gunn asserted that this aspect of the "Foundation" trilogy reflects the nature of its author: "More than any other writer of his time (the Campbell era, as Asimov calls it) or even later, Asimov speaks with the voice of reason."

Asimov's achievement in writing the "Foundation" trilogy, maintained David A. Wollheim in *The Universe Makers,* rests in his application "to future history the lessons of past history. He brought to the attention of the science-fiction cosmos the fact that humanity follows patterns." Like conventional history, Asimov's "Foundation" stories are informed by the concept that "the rise of civilization follows a spiral that makes certain events seem to recur predictably but always on a new and vaster level," Wollheim suggested. And in the opinion of Jean Fiedler and Jim Mele in their book *Isaac Asimov,* "the successful transfer of this historical perspective to science fiction is, more than any other single element, one of Asimov's greatest fictional inventions."

The Best S.F. Story Ever?

Another of Asimov's science fiction masterpieces is a short story entitled "Nightfall." The idea for the story came from Campbell and was inspired by a quotation from Emerson's *Nature:* "If the stars should appear one night in a thousand years, how would men believe and adore; and preserve for many generations the remembrance of the city of God." Campbell wondered how men would react to the stars if they were visible only once every thousand years; he suggested the topic to Asimov

ISAAC ASIMOV
FOUNDATION

Ballantine
30899/$2.75

Book One of the *Foundation Trilogy,*
awarded the Hugo as Best Series Ever!

In 1966, the World Science Fiction Convention awarded the "Foundation" series—a trilogy that explores the history of a future society—with a special Hugo Award for best all-time science fiction series.

who began the story on March 18, 1941. At that time Asimov took stock of his position in the world of science fiction and realized, as he revealed in *In Memory Yet Green,* "It was a crucial moment for me. I had, up to that moment, written thirty-one stories in not quite three years. Of these I had, as of that time, sold seventeen stories and had published fourteen, with a fifteenth about to come out. Of those thirty-one stories, published and unpublished, sold and unsold, only three were what I would now consider as three stars or better on my old zero-to-five scale, and they were positronic robot stories: 'Robbie,' 'Reason,' and 'Liar!' My status on that evening of March 18 was as nothing more than a steady and (perhaps) hopeful third-rater.''

"Nightfall," written in twenty-one days by a twenty-one-year-old author, is considered by many people to be the best science fiction work of all time. Thirty years after its initial publication, in a poll conducted by the Science Fiction Writers of America, "Nightfall" finished in first place by a wide margin. It has done equally well in other polls by different organizations, and its popularity is confirmed by the numerous times it has been anthologized and reprinted. With the appearance of "Nightfall" in the September, 1941, issue of *Astounding,* Asimov was, as he stated, "no longer a minor writer, hovering about the fringes of science-fiction fame. Finally ... I was accepted as a major figure in the field." And yet he did not feel that the story is the best ever written; he didn't even think it's the best that he'd ever written. He listed three of his own short stories that he believed were better: "The Last Question," "The Bicentennial Man," and "The Ugly Little Boy." However, in response to an incident described in his autobiography in which he argues an interpretation of his work delivered by a lecturer, he stated, "it became clear to me that there might well be more in a story than an author was aware of."

In an interview with *Contemporary Authors,* Asimov made a similar comment when asked about critical reaction to his works: "It scares me a little, because they see a great deal more in my writing than I ever consciously put in. And it may even be they're correct; when I read their anlayses, it seems to me that they're very reasonable. And yet I don't remember putting it in it at all. In fact, I once wrote a little short story, very brief, about bringing Shakespeare back into the present through time travel, and he is astonished to discover that nearly four hundred years after his death, his plays are still being shown, and that there are college courses on his plays. So he took a course in Shakespeare, and of course, flunked it. And that's my own experience. When I read about what people have to say in analyzing my stories, I realize that if they were to give me a test in which they asked me to explain the stories from the light of these critical evaluations, I probably wouldn't do very well."

Non-Fiction Writings

Asimov's first nonfiction book was a medical text entitled *Biochemistry and Human Metabolism,* begun in 1950 and written in collaboration with William Boyd and Burnham Walker, two of his colleagues at the Boston University School of

Medicine. The project was Boyd's idea, and he asked Asimov, who was an instructor in biochemistry at the time, to be his co-author. Asimov, however, was working for Walker and was unable to take part in the project without his approval. When they approached Walker with the idea, he was sufficiently impressed to offer his assistance. Each of them wrote one-third of the 300,000-word text, and Asimov did the extremely detailed indexing. Although the book appears to have been fairly successful, Asimov was not terribly happy working on it, nor was he particularly satisfied with the text itself. "For one thing," he wrote in *In Memory Yet Green,* "Walker and I were antithetical in style. I wanted to be chatty, colloquial, and dramatic; Walker wanted to be terse, formal, and cold. More often than not, Boyd sided with Walker, and it was not long before it seemed to me the textbook was more trouble than it was worth." He also comments that "the fact is that the textbook was a distressing failure.... Just about the time it came out, two other new biochemistry texts appeared.... Each was longer and better than ours. And even if the two competitors had not appeared on the scene, ours just wasn't good enough."

It did, however, launch Asimov into the field of nonfiction. He had recognized his ability as an explainer early in life, and he enjoyed clarifying scientific principles for his family and friends; he also discovered that he was a most able and entertaining lecturer who delighted in his work as a teacher. The result is that Asimov was been phenomenally successful as a writer of science books for the general public. He invited his readers—adults and children—into the realms of chemistry, biology, physics, mathematics, astronomy, technology, and more in books such as *The Chemicals of Life, Only a Trillion, Great Ideas of Science, Quasar, Quasar, Burning Bright, Robots: Machines in Man's Image,* and *The Subatomic Monster. New York Review of Books* contributor Martin Gardner commended Asimov's "unfailing clarity, humor, informality, and enthusiasm. Like all top science-fiction writers he knows exactly where to draw the line between serious science and fantasy."

Fellow s.f. writer Theodore Sturgeon, in a *New York Times Book Review* article, declared that "Asimov has achieved a unique status, for not only is he admired and, by many, loved for his work in s.f. and his engrossing regular science column in the *Magazine of Fantasy and Science Fiction,* but he is equally respected by professionals in some 20-odd scientific disciplines. He has become the

perfect and the most inclusive interface between hard science (including math) and the layman, for he has a genius for bringing the obscure into the light." "Here and there ... [Asimov] fails to keep pace with contemporary research," Gerald Jonas observed in another *New York Times Book Review* article, but he then lauded Asimov by stating that "on the whole, however, he has probably done more than anyone else to give scientifically illiterate readers a feeling for the excitement and accomplishments of modern science."

Asimov's Later Science Fiction

In recent years, Asimov continued to produce science popularizations; he has also taken on the responsibility of editing several science fiction anthologies. Yet, perhaps more significant to his

Asimov blended elements of mystery and science fiction in this 1954 novel in which a robot sleuth is paired with a human detective to solve a murder.

numerous fans, he resumed writing science fiction novels after a ten-year break. During his hiatus, distanced from his imaginative worlds, the author was able to reconsider them and come to a new understanding of his fiction. "As Asimov has said," wrote Gene Deweese in the *Science Fiction Review*, "his robot series, his Empire stories and his Foundation series have, to his own surprise, turned out to be three parts of a single series." With this in mind, Asimov in his recent novels ventured to fill gaps and build bridges between his three major cycles and thereby unite his future history. Much of the critical debate surrounding his new work has focused on this unification attempt and whether or not it succeeds without damaging the integrity of his earlier works.

In this belated sequel to the "Foundation" trilogy, the two Foundation councils face a potentially disastrous threat from outside manipulators.

In *Foundation's Edge*, Asimov resumed his story of the two Foundations. One hundred twenty years have passed, and as E. F. Bleiler noted in the *Washington Post Book World*, "a crisis is at hand." Councilmen in each Foundation independently discover that "the Seldon Plan is working better than it theoretically should. This is disastrous, for it indicates the presence of outside manipulators, who must have their own aims and purposes," added Bleiler. From opposite ends of the galaxy, the two Foundations set out to prove the existence of a manipulative power. For a majority of the first Foundation council, however, Golan Trevize and his companion—a professor in search of man's mythical origin, Earth—are simply bait to lure the Second Foundation into the open to be destroyed.

"Like the trilogy," asserted Mary Ellen Burns in the *Nation*, "*Foundation's Edge* explores the nature of free will and the question of historical determinism." And it does so in Asimov's characteristic style. "In style [this novel] belongs to the 1940s— not simply to science fiction's 1940s but to Asimov's 1940s," commented James Gunn in the *Fantasy Newsletter*. "It is no novel of character . . . but a discursive novel of ideas, much like the rest of the Foundation stories."

Asimov's storytelling technique weakens *Foundation's Edge*, according to Brian Stableford in the *Science Fiction and Fantasy Book Review*: "Asimovian characters always spend a lot of time sitting around discussing their situation, but never before has their discussion been so obsessively concerned with the issue of whether things are as they appear and, if not, what might hypothetically lie hidden within the web of appearance." However, Donald M. Hassler offered a different perspective in another *Science Fiction and Fantasy Book Review* article, contending that in *Foundation's Edge* "all possibilities are carefully weighed, including the weighing of possibilities itself, before the next action is undertaken; and the whole piece orchestrates beautifully to hold the reader in suspense till the several strands of plot climax with a final question." Moreover, Gunn suggested that the characters' obsession with what is hidden behind appearances is crucial to the novel's development. He maintained that "the suspense of the novel is sustained by repeated examples of motivations within motivations, wheels within wheels." And finally, in his opinion, "the motivation-behind-motivation method is appropriate to the subject of the novel. When psychological control of people's actions and even of people's thought occurs, the hiding—and questioning—of motivation is natural."

A criticism often leveled against this sequel to the "Foundation" trilogy is that it does not complement its predecessors. "*Foundation's Edge* starts off promisingly . . . but ultimately loses itself in an overly elaborate plot," wrote Burns. In her estimation, Asimov "has tampered too much with his basic material; [this novel] destroys the harmony and balance of the theme the trilogy so elegantly set up and played out." Stableford went further, stating "it devalues by its existence the three books to which it is a belated sequel." Gunn also noted the differences between the sequel and the original series: "*Foundation's Edge* alters the message of the Trilogy—the message that rationality is the only human trait that can be trusted and that it will, if permitted to do so, come up with the correct solution. . . . In the new novel, however, Asimov has allowed to creep in (or purposefully has included) a significant element of mysticism."

On the other hand are critics who believe *Foundation's Edge* does live up to the standard Asimov set in the original books. In the opinion of Jonas in the *New York Times Book Review,* "[Asimov] writes much better than he did 33 years ago—yet has lost none of the verve that he brought to his series when he and the galaxy were much younger." Bleiler believes that not only has Asimov matched the accomplishment of the "Foundation" trilogy, he has surpassed it. "*Foundation's Edge* reveals many improvements over the earlier work," the reviewer wrote. "The ideas are better worked out; the plotting is better; the writing is superior; and Asimov has outgrown his tendency to trick endings that didn't always work. Instead of good guys and bad guys, we now find credible motivations like arrogance, ambition, suspicion, and feelings of insecurity—all of which take form in manipulation." "Rare is the author who can resume a story after a pause of three decades," concluded Stoler in *Time,* "but Asimov has never been predictable in anything but fecundity." Indeed, before his death, Asimov completed *Forward the Foundation,* an addition to the series.

The Robots of Dawn extends and expands Asimov's mystery robot novels—which began with *The Caves of Steel* and continued in *The Naked Sun*—toward the more distant future and toward his stories of the galactic empire. In *The Robots of Dawn,* Elijah Baley and his robot companion, R. Daneel Olivaw—the protagonists of the previous novels—travel to Aurora, the planet on which Daneel was created, to investigate the murder of

Using the First Law as their guide, two robots try to help the Settlers win an ongoing conflict with the Spacers in this 1985 novel.

his only robotic equal. As Stableford pointed out in another *Science Fiction and Fantasy Book Review* article, the novel also "deals with a pivotal point in history: will the empty galaxy be settled by men from Earth, who will crowd the worlds with their shortlived kind and keep their machines in their place; or will it be settled by humaniform robots . . . dispatched . . . to build utopias which men might later use?"

The Robots of Dawn is another novel of ideas. "Asimov is . . . addressing real problems about the interaction of humans with artificial intelligences," stated John Sladek in the *Washington Post Book World.* "He may even be raising real ethical and social questions which will need answers 20 years hence." However, Sladek claimed that "because [Asimov] chooses to bury it all in a humdrum whodunit, retrieving the message (if any) is just not worth it." Stableford believes that its flaws lie in that "much of what happens in it, and much of what is said and done by the characters, is not directed towards any internal purpose of the plot, but rather establishing coherency between this story and earlier robot stories, and between those stories and the Foundation series."

However, a positive analysis of the novel was given by a *Publishers Weekly* reviewer who admitted that "Asimov's narrative technique is more dependent than ever on dialogue, but his plotting is as ingenious as always. The mystery unravels with the polished logical precision of a robot's program." *Science Fiction Review* contributor Karl Edd agreed: "As usual with Asimov there are long passages of dialog ... and intellectual dissection of ideas, paradoxes ... and zero base contradictions.... Asimov's method is never boring, usually entertaining, and always thought-provoking." With *The Robots of Dawn*, Edd concluded, Asimov has "produced the proper blend—the humor of a Jewish elf, Yankee wit, word conundrums, mental boxing practice, a bit of mind-bending, a story and a learning experience."

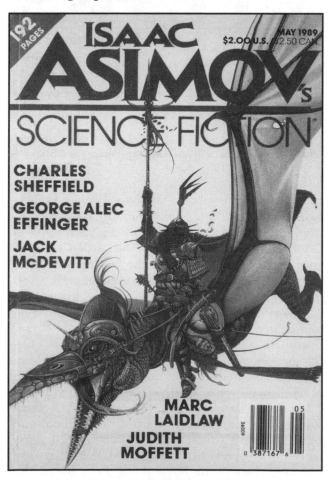

Asimov served as editorial director for this periodical which showcased many up-and-coming science fiction and fantasy writers.

Asimov's third science fiction novel of the 1980s provides a bridge between his near future and far future histories. As James and Eugene Sloam put it in their *Chicago Tribune Book World* review, "*Robots and Empire* ... extends and unites Isaac Asimov's Robot and Foundation trilogies, pushing robots to the forefront both as characters and as vehicles for asking philosophical questions." Central to the book are Daneel and his new companion, another robot called Giskard Reventlow. "This circumstance allows Mr. Asimov to examine, in greater depth than ever before, the strengths and limitations of his Three Laws of Robotics," observed Jonas in another *New York Times Book Review* article.

The growing tension between Spacers, the original galactic explorers, and the Settlers trekking out from Earth engages the attention of the two robots. They reach the conclusion that "in order to obey their elevated concept of the First Law enjoining robots to aid humans, they must manipulate the societies within their purview, so that the vital expanding Settlers can win the coming conflict, but peacefully," related John Clute in the *Washington Post Book World*. Building on this, observed Jonas, "Mr. Asimov [has] once again turned an ethical dilemma into the basis of an exciting novel of suspense." "The writing [in this novel] is typical smooth Asimov, in some ways his most visual and emotionally evocative novel yet," indicated Elton T. Elliott in the *Science Fiction Review*. Added Robert A. Collins in the *Fantasy Review*: "*Robots and Empire* is both entertaining and significant within the author's canon."

Asimov's future history series traces possible changes that might develop from a near future into a distant future. According to Marjorie Mithoff Miller, writing in her book *Isaac Asimov*, "one of the major functions of science fiction for Asimov is to accustom its readers to the idea of change." Asimov himself said to Schweitzer in *Science Fiction Voices 5* that contrary to the belief of some, science fiction "isn't intended to predict.... The only thing that [it] predicts is that the future is going to be different from the present, and that will always come true."

"In contemplating the possible futures presented in science fiction," said Miller, "the reader is forced to recognize and accept the idea that things will change, and he is helped to surrender some of his traditional human passion for the status quo. Asimov sees this as a real benefit to our society, as we try to plan and implement the changes that will do the most good for humanity." Two areas in

This special edition of *The Magazine of Fantasy & Science Fiction* celebrated Asimov's extensive contributions to fantastic literature.

which Asimov recently campaigned for change are population control and space exploration. Each, he believed, will influence significantly which future comes to pass. "My feeling is that the chance of our surviving into the twenty-first century as a working civilization is less than fifty percent but greater than zero," he told Charles Platt in *Dream Makers: The Uncommon People Who Write Science Fiction.* "There are several items, each one of which is sufficient to do us in. Number one is the population problem." One reason he advocated peaceful space colonization, he explained to Schweitzer, is that "we will have people living on a multiplicity of worlds so that if anything happens to any one of them, even to Earth, mankind will continue."

■ Works Cited

Asimov, Isaac, *The Bicentennial Man and Other Stories*, Doubleday, 1976.

Asimov, Isaac, *In Memory Yet Green: The Autobiography of Isaac Asimov, 1920-1954*, Doubleday, 1979.

Asimov, Isaac, interview with Jean W. Ross, *Contemporary Authors New Revision Series*, Volume 19, Gale, 1987.

Burns, Mary Ellen, review of *Foundation's Edge*, *Nation*, March 5, 1983.

Clareson, Thomas D., editor, *Voices for the Future: Essays on Major Science Fiction Writers*, Popular Press, 1976.

Clute, John, review of *Robots and Empire*, *Washington Post Book World*, August 25, 1985.

Deweese, Gene, in *Science Fiction Review*, spring, 1984.

Edd, Karl, review of *The Robots of Dawn*, *Science Fiction Review*, winter, 1985.

Elliot, Elton T., review of *Robots and Empire*, *Fantasy Review*, September, 1985.

Fiedler, Jean, and Jim Mele, *Isaac Asimov*, Ungar, 1982.

Gardner, Martin, article in *New York Review of Books*, September 12, 1977.

Gunn, James, *Isaac Asimov: The Foundations of Science Fiction*, Oxford University Press, 1982.

Gunn, James, review of *Foundation's Edge*, *Fantasy Newsletter*, April, 1983.

Hassler, Donald, review of *Foundation's Edge*, *Science Fiction and Fantasy Book Review*, December, 1982.

Jonas, Gerald, review of *In Memory Yet Green* and *Opus 200*, *New York Times Book Review*, February 25, 1979.

Jonas, Gerald, review of *Foundation's Edge*, *New York Times Book Review*, December 19, 1982.

Jonas, Gerald, review of *Robots and Empire*, *New York Times Book Review*, October 20, 1985.

Miller, Marjorie Mithoff, *Isaac Asimov: A Checklist of Works Published in the United States*, Kent State University Press, 1972.

Platt, Charles, *Dream Makers: The Uncommon People Who Write Science Fiction*, Berkley Publishing, 1980.

Review of *The Robots of Dawn, Publishers Weekly*, September 2, 1983.

Schweitzer, Darrell, *Science Fiction Voices 5*, Borgo Press, 1981.

Sladek, Jack, review of *Robots of Dawn*, *Washington Post Book World*, September 26, 1982.

Sloam, James, and Eugene Sloam, review of *Robots and Empire*, *Chicago Tribune Book World*, January 19, 1986.

Stableford, Brian, review of *The Robots of Dawn*, *Science Fiction and Fantasy Book Review*, November, 1983.

Stableford, Brian, review of *Foundation's Edge*, *Science Fiction and Fantasy Book Review*, June, 1983.

Sturgeon, Theodore, interview in *New York Times Book Review*, January 28, 1973.

Stoler, Peter, review of *Foundation's Edge*, *Time*, November 15, 1982.

Wollheim, Donald A., *The Universe Makers*, Harper, 1971.

■ For More Information See

BOOKS

Asimov, Isaac, *In Joy Still Felt: The Autobiography of Isaac Asimov, 1954-1979*, Doubleday, 1980.

Contemporary Literary Criticism, Gale, Volume 1, 1973, Volume 3, 1975, Volume 9, 1978, Volume 19, 1981, Volume 26, 1983.

Dictionary of Literary Biography, Volume 8: *Twentieth-Century American Science Fiction Writers*, Gale, 1981.

Greenberg, Martin H., and Joseph D. Olander, editors, *Isaac Asimov*, Taplinger, 1977.

Patrouch, Joseph F., Jr., *The Science Fiction of Isaac Asimov*, Doubleday, 1974.

Slusser, George E., *Isaac Asimov: The Foundations of His Science Fiction*, Borgo Press, 1979.

PERIODICALS

Chicago Tribune Book World, March 4, 1979.

Chicago Tribune Magazine, April 30, 1978.

Globe and Mail (Toronto), August 10, 1985.

Magazine of Fantasy and Science Fiction, October, 1966; September, 1980.

New York Review of Books, October 24, 1985.
New York Times, October 18, 1969, January 1, 1980, December 17, 1984, February 26, 1985.
New York Times Book Review, January 12, 1975.
Science Fiction Review, winter, 1982.
Time, February 26, 1979.
Times Literary Supplement, October 5, 1967, December 28, 1967.
Washington Post, April 4, 1979.
Washington Post Book World, April 1, 1979, May 25, 1980.

SOUND RECORDINGS

Isaac Asimov Talks: An Interview, Writer's Voice, 1974.

OBITUARIES:

PERIODICALS

Detroit Free Press, April 7, 1992, p. 1B
New York Times, April 7, 1992, p. B7.°

—*Sketch by Bruce Ching*

Francesca Lia Block

■ Personal

Born December 3, 1962, in Hollywood, CA; daughter of Irving Alexander (a painter) and Gilda (a poet; maiden name, Klein) Block. *Education:* University of California, Berkeley, B.A., 1986. *Hobbies and other interests:* Dance, film, and vegetarian cooking.

■ Addresses

Home—Studio City and Joshua Tree, CA. *Agent*—Julie Fallowfield, McIntosh and Otis Agency, 310 Madison Ave., New York, NY 10017.

■ Career

Writer.

■ Member

Phi Beta Kappa.

■ Awards, Honors

Shrout Fiction Award, University of California, Berkeley, 1986; Emily Chamberlin Cook Poetry Award, 1986; Book of the Year shortlist, American Library Association, for *Weetzie Bat* and *Cherokee Bat and the Goat Guys;* Best of the 1980's list, *Booklist,* for *Weetzie Bat;* YASD Best Book Award for *Weetzie Bat;* Recommended Books for Reluctant YA Readers list for *Weetzie Bat, Witch Baby,* and *Cherokee Bat and the Goat Guys;* Best Books citation, *New York Times,* and Best Fifty Books citation, *Publishers Weekly,* both for *Cherokee Bat and the Goat Guys.*

■ Writings

YOUNG ADULT NOVELS

Weetzie Bat, HarperCollins, 1989.
Witch Baby, HarperCollins, 1990.
Cherokee Bat and the Goat Guys, HarperCollins, 1991.
Missing Angel Juan, HarperCollins, 1993.
The Hanged Man, HarperCollins, 1994.

ADULT NOVELS

Ecstasia, New American Library, 1993.
Primavera, New American Library, 1994.

SCREENPLAYS

Author of screenplay for *Cherokee Bat and the Goat Guys;* also author (with James Edward Quinn) of screenplays *Luna and Rosa* and *Zeroes Journey.*

OTHER

Contributor of short stories to anthologies, including "Winnie and Tommy," *Am I Blue?,* edited by Marion Dane Bauer, 1994; and "Blue," *When I Was Your Age,* edited by Amy Ehrlich, 1994.

■ Work in Progress

Dangerous Angels.

■ Sidelights

Francesca Lia Block's first book, *Weetzie Bat,* "burst on the young adult book scene like a rainbow bubble showering clouds of roses, feathers, tiny shells and a rubber chicken," according to Patty Campbell in the *New York Times Book Review.* "Hardened critics," Campbell continued, "who thought they had seen all the possible variants of the coming-of-age novel, were astonished by the freshness" of Block's voice. While Block's success has everything to do with her own talents, the author owes much of her inspiration to the blond, spiky-haired punk princess wearing a pink, 1950's prom dress and cowboy boots she once saw hitching a ride in Laurel Canyon. Block thought she saw this apparition one more time: "A friend and I were rocking to KROQ, when we saw a pink Pinto with the license plates "WEETZIE," the author wrote in an article for the *Los Angeles Times Book Review (LATBR).* "There behind the wheel was the spiky-haired, blond pixie wearing big pink Harlequin glasses. Well, maybe she was a different girl. Or maybe we never really saw who was driving the Pinto. But as soon as I had the name, the character just evolved by herself." The four young adults novels that have grown around this character and her friends—*Weetzie Bat, Witch Baby, Cherokee Bat and the Goat Guys,* and *Missing Angel Juan*—have both captivated readers and incited controversy. For many critics, Block's use of colorful, if sometimes disturbing, themes, settings and characters is exactly what makes her work so important to the young adult canon.

Coming of Age in Los Angeles

"It is a striking literary irony that Block's work is perceived as fantasy," Campbell commented in *Horn Book.* "Although there are magical elements in her books and the tone is pure fairy-tale, I know of no other writer who has written so accurately about the reality of life in Los Angeles—or one of the many realities that make up this complex multicultural city." Block was born in Hollywood to a well-known painter and a poet; she grew up in Los Angeles and the San Fernando Valley. In this rich setting, Block's parents spent a lot of time both reading to their daughter and encouraging her to write.

As a student at North Hollywood High School, Block began to experience the more adult side of what she once termed the "fairy-tale magic" of Los Angeles. With her friends, Block explored Laurel Canyon, ate strawberry sundaes with marshmallow topping at Schwab's soda fountain in Hollywood, visited the stores on Melrose, and browsed through the "mirage" of the Farmer's Market. At night, Block and her friends ate hot dogs on the Sunset Strip, shopped at Tower Records, and slam-danced to the music of the Go-Go's and X. In her *LATBR* piece, Block remarked that she "wished I could write stories that made people react the way they do to music—sweating, dancing, crying."

Despite the fantastic charm of Los Angeles, Block told *LATBR* readers that "there was also a sense of encroaching darkness. My friends and I found ourselves confronted with punks wearing swastikas as fashion statements. People were beaten at concerts. There was the personal pain I was experiencing due to my father's illness. And there were the first terrifying signs of the disease that would later be named AIDS." In fact, Block would continue to be concerned about the social impact of the disease, a concern eventually reflected in her work. She told Campbell in *Horn Book* that she still tries "to imagine what it would be like to be a teenager now—to be thirteen or fourteen, and to not only be afraid of all the normal things, but AIDS, too."

College at Berkeley and the Manuscript for *Weetzie Bat*

When Block left Los Angeles to attend the University of California at Berkeley, she continued to draw pictures and make up stories about Weetzie, the "punk princess" she had seen in high school. Block's studies in English literature and poetry with Ron Loewinsohn and Jayne Walker allowed her to further her skills as a poet and minimalist short story writer (she wrote her senior thesis on Emily Dickinson and Hilda Doolittle). In her spare time, Block wrote the text which would become *Weetzie Bat.* The author told Diane Roback of *Publishers Weekly* that she "started working on *Weetzie Bat* for my own enjoyment. There are some things in it—the pop culture, the humor—that weren't in my other stories. It was closest to my own experience."

Although Block really didn't think much of her extra-curricular writing at the time, a family friend—artist Kathryn Jacobi—thought that Block's "Weetzie" pennings deserved wider attention. Eventually, Jacobi mailed a copy of the text Charlotte Zolotow at HarperCollins. Zolotow told Block, who had just graduated from college, that the publishing house wanted to print the novel for young adults. Despite the fact that Zolotow and Joanna Cotler (the book's co-editors) realized that the contents of *Weetzie Bat* might elicit some negative reactions, they decided against adding a disclaimer—*Weetzie Bat* was published as Block had written it. Sadly, Block's father, who died in 1986, did not get to see his daughter's first published work.

Weetzie Bat and Controversy

Weetzie Bat, as Anne Osborn related in the *School Library Journal*, is the story of a young woman who "wears a bleached-blond flattop and Harlequin sunglasses, covers her '50's taffeta dresses in glittery poetry, and sews fringe down the sides of her minis in sympathy with the plight of the Indian." At the beginning of the novel, Weetzie feels as if no one (especially her parents, who are divorced,) understand her. In high school, she meets Dirk, who takes her in his red '55 Pontiac to clubs to slamdance. Dirk, who is gay, understands Weetzie; eventually they develop a loving relationship. When Dirk's grandmother dies, she leaves her cottage to Dirk and Weetzie, who move in together.

Weetzie and Dirk go "duck-hunting," with great success. Weetzie finds a boyfriend, My Secret Agent Lover Man, and Dirk finds a lover in Duck. Weetzie's Dog Slingster brings home Go-Go Girl. The dogs have puppies, and it is not long before Weetzie gives birth to Cherokee. A baby born to Secret Agent Lover Man and the witch woman who seduced him is later left on the group's doorstep and completes the family. At the novel's end, Weetzie decides, "I don't know about happily ever after . . . but I know about happily."

Reviewers of *Weetzie Bat* appreciated the mystical quality of the novel. Betsy Hearne, a critic for the *New York Times Book Review*, wrote that *Weetzie Bat* "is full of magic, from the genie who grants Weetzie's wishes to the malevolent witch Vixanne [Witch Baby's birth-mother], who visits the family three times. There are beauties and beasts and roses, castles and Cinderella transformations." Critics also applauded the novel's setting. "In *Weetzie Bat*," wrote Roback in *Publishers Weekly*, "Francesca Block has created a technicolor love-song to Los Angeles, a 'land of skating hamburgers' with 'pink flamingo skies' with fountains 'that

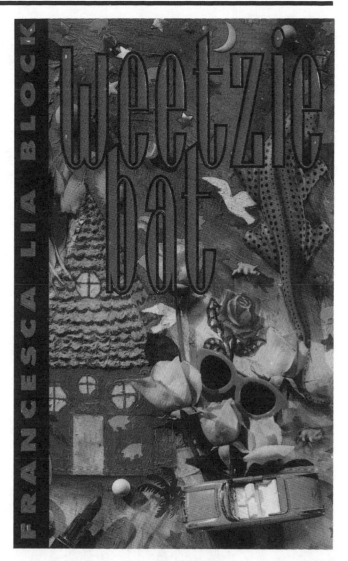

Block's controversial 1989 novel features a free spirit who finds companionship and love in a rather unlikely place.

turned tropical soda-pop colors,' a city 'hot and cool, glam and slam, rich and trashy, devils and angels.'" Other critics appreciated Block's use of language. Campbell, for one, noted in *Horn Book* that phrases from "clutch pig" to "lanky lizards" were not slang phrases which would date Block's work. (These phrases were invented by Block and her circle of friends to describe people and groups.)

Despite the praise Block received for her first novel, some of those who read *Weetzie Bat* did not approve of its content. Many adults felt that the novel was not suitable for young adult readers, that it did not belong in local libraries. One such critic, however, changed her mind after reading the book. According to Block, Frances V. Sedney, coordinator of children's services at the Harford

(Maryland) County Library, had been advised not to purchase the novel. After reading it, however, Sedney decided that *Weetzie Bat* "epitomizes the 'innocent' books where the reader's mind and experience make all the crucial difference.'" Patrick Jones wrote of the controversy caused by *Weetzie Bat* in *Horn Book:* "In the age of AIDS—whose ugly shadow appears—anything less than a 'safe sex or no sex' stance is bound to be controversial. The most controversial aspect of the books, according to most reviews, is the homosexual relationship between Duck and Dirk. Duck, Dirk, and Weetzie make a baby together, and it is valued as a good thing. This situation is hard for many adults to handle."

This sequel to *Weetzie Bat* continues the story of Weetzie's unorthodox family and its new addition—an angry abandoned baby.

Witch Baby's Story

With the encouragement of Zolotow, Block wrote a sequel to *Weetzie Bat. Witch Baby* is the story of the abandoned baby conceived by Secret Agent Lover Man and the witch Vixanne Wigg and later left on Weetzie's doorstep. Witch Baby feels alienated from her family and makes everyone miserable as she tries to understand "What time are we upon and where do I belong?" The girl with tilty purple eyes and tangled black hair gathers photos of her family which exclude her, collects news articles about disasters, pulls apart Cherokee Bat's kachina Barbies, and leaves home to search for her birth mother. Finally, Witch Baby returns to embrace the adoptive family which has never stopped loving her.

In her review of *Witch Baby* for *Horn Book*, Maeve Visser Knoth wrote: "An untraditional novel, *Witch Baby* is honest to the experience of many young adults, who use music, fads and material possessions to try to understand the world." Ellen Ramsay, writing for *School Library Journal*, was also enthusiastic about the work and its "superior" creator. She declared that "Block's writing features charming imagery, gently surreal characters and events, and the recurring theme of tolerance through love."

Cherokee's Band and Growing Up Responsibly

In her review of *Cherokee Bat and the Goat Guys* for *New York Times Book Review*, Campbell commented: "Ms. Block's distinctive style" takes on "breadth and sureness in a story that resonates with arcane animal symbolism and explores the dark power of unleashed sexuality." *Cherokee Bat* begins when Cherokee and Witch Baby are left alone by their parents, who decide to travel to South America to make a movie. Witch Baby pretends to be a seed and seeps herself in the mud in a shed as soon as they leave. Unable to cope with this problem on her own, Cherokee seeks the guidance of the family's Native American friend, Coyote. After Coyote gives Cherokee feathers of the wind, Cherokee makes wings for Witch Baby and plans a party for her. When Witch Baby sees her childhood friend, Angel Juan Perez, she emerges from the mud.

Along with Raphael Chong Jah-Love and Angel Juan Perez, the almost-sisters join to form a rock group. Coyote gives Cherokee goat wool after the group is threatened with failure; Cherokee makes goat-haunch pants for Raphael, whose resulting onstage performance makes the group a success.

In this 1993 work, Witch Baby's search for missing Angel Juan Perez takes her down some dark and dangerous Manhattan streets.

When Angel Juan becomes jealous of Raphel's dance, and Coyote denies Cheokee's request for totem antlers for Juan, Witch Baby steals the antlers and gives them to Juan. As the group revels in the magic possessed by Witch Baby, Raphael, and Angel Juan, Cherokee receives a pair of goat-hoove boots which give her the power to dance as they pain her feet. The four rockers indulge themselves with sex, drugs, and alcohol. As Gail Richmond of *School Library Journal* related, "everything begins to fly apart in wild and outrageous ways." It is not until Angel Juan slashes himself during a performance and Cherokee almost commits suicide that the four teenagers realize that they must give their gifts back to Coyote.

References to ancient Greek and Native American mythology are abundant in *Cherokee Bat and the Goat Guys.* Campbell pointed out in *Horn Book* that "Witch Baby is a raven; Cherokee is a deer; and Raphael is a dreaming obsidian elk." Campbell

also noted the significance of the antlers and the goat-haunch pants, a reference to the god Pan. As Block explained to Campbell, "I've always had a thing about fauns and satyrs.... My Dad would draw a lot of them, and talk about them. He told me Greek myths for bedtime stories."

Cherokee Bat and the Goat Guys was generally well-received by critics. Roback and Richard Donahue concluded in *Publishers Weekly* that the novel "provides yet another delicious and deeply felt trip" to her "wonderfully idiosyncratic corner of California." Knoth was a bit less enthralled with the novel, commenting that Block's "writing is strong and vivid, but her brief, readable story is more a moral tale than a developed novel." In *School Library Journal*, Richmond disagreed, musing that the "fairy-tale quality" of the novel and "its contemporary scene, and its modern language" would appeal to young adults.

Witch Baby's Search for Angel Juan

Block's fourth book based on the Weetzie group characters, *Missing Angel Juan*, focuses once again on Witch Baby. In this tale, a lonely Witch Baby leaves Los Angeles to search for Angel Juan Perez, who has moved to New York City to play his music on his own. When Witch Baby explores Manhattan, she realizes it is very different from her beloved Los Angeles. Weetzie Bat's father appears to Witch Baby as a ghost in his old apartment and guides Witch Baby in her travels around the city. Witch Baby's search for Angel Juan is fruitless; eventually she realizes that she must search for him underground, in the nightmarish tunnels of the subway. Michael Cart, writing in *School Library Journal*, perceives the references to the story of Orpheus's descent to the underworld in this book. He praises Block as a "brilliant visionary" describing *Missing Angel Juan* as "an engagingly eccentric mix of fantasy and reality ... magical, moving, mischievous ... marvelous."

A Fantastic Reality

If Block's works continues to create discussion, Campbell concludes, it is because they provide readers with "a deliciousness of detail, a deceptive smallness and lightness, a distilling of the style of a particular time and place, and a serious contemplation of life and death under the sparkling surface." Jones agreed: "As in most great literature, Block doesn't create pretty pictures; she presents mirrors in which readers may find reflections of their own emotional lives."

Block has a similar explanation for the success of her work. "I deal with young people, with their passions, fascinations, obsessions, longings. I use simple dialogue, often full of slang," she wrote in her *LATBR* article. "I believe that during adolescence we are powerfully in touch with two realms: Still close to our childhood, we are innocent enough to perceive the fantastic all around us—in the music we hear, the movies we see, the books we read, even the foods we eat and in our relationships with others, mostly when we fall in love for the first time. But we are also almost adults and very aware of the harsh world we are about to enter."

■ Works Cited

Block, Francesca Lia, *Weetzie Bat*, HarperCollins, 1989.

Block, Francesca Lia, *Witch Baby*, HarperCollins, 1990.

Block, Francesca Lia, "Punk Pixies in the Canyon," *Los Angeles Times Book Review*, July 26, 1992, pp. 1, 11.

Campbell, Patty, review of *Cherokee Bat and the Goat Guys*, *New York Times Book Review*, September 20, 1992, p. 18.

Campbell, Patty, "People Are Talking About ... Francesca Lia Block," *Horn Book*, January/February, 1993, pp. 57-63.

Cart, Michael, review of *Missing Angel Juan*, *School Library Journal*, October, 1983, p. 148.

Review of *Cherokee Bat and the Goat Guys*, *New York Times Book Review*, September 20, 1992, p. 18.

Hearne, Betsy, review of *Weetzie Bat*, *New York Times Book Review*, May 21, 1989, p.47.

Jones, Patrick, "People Are Talking About ... Francesca Lia Block," *Horn Book*, November/December, 1992, pp. 697-701.

Knoth, Maeve Visser, review of *Witch Baby*, *Horn Book*, January/February, 1992, p. 78.

Osborn, Ann, review of *Weetzie Bat*, *School Library Journal*, April, 1989, pp. 116-7.

Ramsay, Ellen, review of *Witch Baby*, *School Library Journal*, September, 1991, p. 277.

Richmond, Gail, review of *Cherokee Bat and the Goat Guys*, *School Library Journal*, September, 1992, p. 274.

Roback, Diane, "Francesca Lia Block," *Publishers Weekly*, December 22, 1989, p. 27.

Roback, Diane, and Richard Donahue, review of *Cherokee Bat and the Goat Guys*, *Publishers Weekly*, July 20, 1992, p. 251.

■ For More Information See

PERIODICALS

Booklist, August, 1992, p. 2004.

Bulletin of the Center for Children's Books, December, 1993, p. 115.

English Journal, December, 1990, p. 78; October, 1991, pp. 94-95.

New York Times Book Review, January 19, 1992, p. 24.

Publishers Weekly, March 10, 1989, p. 91.

Voice of Youth Advocates, December, 1993, p. 287.

—*Sketch by Ronie-Richele Garcia-Johnson*

Mel Brooks

■ Personal

Born Melvin Kaminsky, June 28, 1926, in Brooklyn, NY; son of Max (a process server) and Kate (a garment worker; maiden name, Brookman); married Florence Baum (a dancer), 1952 (divorced, 1959); married Anna Maria Italiano (an actress under name Anne Bancroft), August, 1964; children: (first marriage) Stefanie, Nicky, Edward; (second marriage) Maximilian. *Education*: Attended Virginia Military Institute, 1944; also attended Brooklyn College.

■ Addresses

Office—c/o Twentieth Century-Fox Studios, P.O. Box 900, Beverly Hills, CA 90213.

■ Career

Comedian, writer, actor, film director and producer. Worked as a stand-up comedian, handyman, musician, and social director, Grossinger's Resort, Catskills, NY, beginning c. 1945; sketch writer for Sid Ceasar on television shows *Broadway Revue*, National Broadcasting Company, Inc. (NBC-TV), 1949-50, *Your Show of Shows*, NBC-TV, 1950-54, *Caesar's Hour*, NBC-TV, 1954-57, and *Sid Caesar Invites You,* American Broadcasting Companies, Inc. (ABC-TV), 1957-58; writer of television specials starring Andy Williams, Jerry Lewis, Victor Borge, and Anne Bancroft, 1958-1970; film director, 1968—; founder, Brooksfilms production company, 1980. Creator (with Buck Henry) of television series *Get Smart*, NBC-TV, 1965, and (with John Boni, Norman Steinberg, and Norman Stiles) *When Things Were Rotten*, ABC-TV, 1975. Film directing credits include *The Producers*, 1968, *Blazing Saddles*, 1974, *High Anxiety*, 1977, *History of the World—Part I*, 1981, *Spaceballs*, 1987, *Life Stinks*, 1991, and *Robin Hood: Men in Tights*, 1993. Film acting credits include *Blazing Saddles, Robin Hood: Men in Tights*, and *To Be or Not to Be*, 1983. Producing credits include *The Elephant Man*, Paramount, 1980, *The Doctor and the Devils*, Twentieth Century-Fox, 1985, *The Fly*, Twentieth Century-Fox, 1986, *Solarbabies*, Metro-Goldwyn-Mayer/United Artists, 1986, and *84 Charing Cross Road*, Columbia, 1987. *Military service*: U.S. Army, combat engineer, 1944-46; served in Europe. *Member*: Directors Guild of America, Writers Guild of America.

■ Awards, Honors

Academy Award, best short subject, 1963, for *The Critic*; Emmy Award, outstanding writing achievement in variety, 1967, for *The Sid Caesar, Imogene Coca, Carl Reiner, Howard Morris Special*; Academy Award, best screenplay, and Writers Guild Award, best original screenplay, both 1968, for *The Producers*; Writers Guild Award, best original screenplay, 1975, for *Blazing Saddles;* Nebula Award for dramatic writing, and Writers Guild Award, both 1976, for *Young Frankenstein;* Academy Award nomination, best picture, 1980, for *The Elephant Man.*

■ Writings

PLAYS

(Contributor of sketches with Ronny Graham) *New Faces of 1952,* Royale Theatre, New York City, 1952.

(With Joe Darion) *Shinbone Alley,* Broadway Theatre, New York City, 1957.

All-American, Winter Garden Theatre, New York City, 1962.

SCREENPLAYS

New Faces, Twentieth Century-Fox, 1954.

The Critic (animated short), Pintoff-Crossbow Productions, 1963.

(And director) *The Producers,* Embassy Pictures, 1968.

(With Norman Steinberg, Andrew Bergman, Richard Pryor, and Alan Uger; and director) *The Twelve Chairs,* (based on a novel by Ilya Arnoldovich and Evgeni Petrov; also see below), UMC Pictures, 1970.

(With Bergman, Pryor, Steinberg, and Uger; and director), *Blazing Saddles* (also see below), Warner Bros., 1974.

(With Gene Wilder; and director) *Young Frankenstein,* (based on characters created by Mary Shelley), Warner Bros., 1974.

(With Ron Clark, Rudy DeLuca, and Barry Levinson; and director) *Silent Movie,* Twentieth Century-Fox, 1976.

(With Clark, DeLuca, and Levinson; and producer/director) *High Anxiety* (also see below), Twentieth Century-Fox, 1977.

(With Thomas Meehan and Ronny Graham; and producer/director) *History of the World—Part I* (also see below), Twentieth Century-Fox, 1981

(With Evan Chandler and J. David Shapiro; and producer/director), *Spaceballs,* Metro-Goldwyn-Mayer/United Artists, 1987.

(With DeLuca and Steve Haberman; and producer/director) *Life Stinks,* Twentieth Century-Fox, 1991.

(With Chandler and Shapiro; and producer/director), *Robin Hood: Men in Tights,* Twentieth Century-Fox, 1993.

FILM SCORES

The Twelve Chairs, UMC Pictures, 1970.

Blazing Saddles, Warner Bros., 1973.
High Anxiety (also see below), Twentieth Century-Fox, 1977.
History of the World—Part I (also see below), Twentieth Century-Fox, 1981.

TELEVISION SERIES AND SPECIALS

Your Show of Shows, NBC-TV, 1950-54.
Sid Caesar Invites You, ABC-TV, 1958.
Get Smart, NBC-TV, 1965-69, then Columbia Broadcasting System, Inc. (CBS-TV), 1969-70.
The Sid Caesar, Imogene Coca, Carl Reiner, Howard Morris Special, CBS-TV, 1966.

Also writer for *Broadway Review* and *Caesar's Hour.*

RECORDINGS

(With Carl Reiner) *2,000 Years,* Capitol, 1960.
(With Reiner) *2,000 and One Years,* Capitol, 1961.
(With Reiner) *At the Cannes Film Festival,* Capitol, 1961.
(With Reiner) *2,000 and Thirteen,* Warner Bros., 1973.
Music from High Anxiety, (soundtrack), Elektra, 1977.

BOOKS

Mel Brooks's History of the World—Part I, Warner Books, 1981.
(With Reiner) *The 2,000 Year Old Man,* (transcriptions of sound recordings), Warner Books, 1981.

■ Sidelights

Screenwriter, director, actor, producer and occasional Two-Thousand-Year-Old Man: no one title is encompassing enough to capture—let alone tame—Mel Brooks. He's like a comedic force of nature, whose brash, blunt and gleefully irreverent style has delighted, repulsed and entertained audiences since his early work on television during the 1950s. In a 1974 profile in *Saturday Review,* Brooks said: "My job as a humorist . . . is to take the audience and get it to look at something from the side instead of straight on. There are no schools for comic filmmakers. You're on your own and you must hope that what strikes you as funny also strikes a lot of others. The script is the raft you float on."

Among the "rafts" Brooks has written and directed are the movies *The Producers, Blazing Saddles,* and *Young Frankenstein.* His satires have been aimed at such off-limits subjects as racism, homosexuality, feminism, and religion. Writing in the *New York*

Brooks served as a writer for *Your Show of Shows*, a comedy-variety program which ran from 1950 to 1954 and starred Sid Caesar, Carl Reiner, and Imogene Coca.

Times, Peter Schjedahl dubbed Brooks "America's 'patron saint' of 'going too far,' a manic yuck-artist in the checkered tradition of burlesque, the Marx brothers, and *Mad* magazine." In a *Newsweek* story, Arthur Cooper remarked that "like a scrappy club fighter [Brooks] swings wildly with many punches but can knock you out with a series of jabs," adding that "what audiences are responding to are Brooks's anarchistic, zany tone and machine-gun tempo." Many critics credit the popularity of Brooks's style of humor—whose hallmark is often bad taste—with spawning an entire genre of "gross-out" comedy and numerous outrageous performers. Schjedahl claimed Brooks as the forerunner of the genre, the single artist who "brought to the screen a brand of convulsive comedy so completely original that it seems to have been dropped out of the sky." Writing in *Newsweek,* Paul D. Zimmerman commented that Brooks is "like the fool in *King Lear.* He is our jester, asking us to see ourselves as we really are, determined that we laugh ourselves sane."

Brooks was born the youngest of four sons in a Brooklyn family. When he was two-and-a-half, his father died. With the onset of the Depression, the Brooks family fell into a constant struggle with poverty. In a portrait of the director for in the *New Yorker,* Kenneth Tynan stated that the trauma of his father's early death left Brooks "with a sense of loss that persisted into adult life. For example, he recognizes that his relationship with Sid Caesar was that of a child clamoring for the attention of a father. When Brooks went into analysis in 1951, his purpose . . . was 'to learn how to be a father instead of a son.'"

As the baby of the family, Brooks was fussed over and adored (in interviews, he claims that he was so coddled that his feet didn't even touch the ground until he was six years old). Right from the start, Brooks was the performer in the family, making faces on command even when he was only a few months old. Growing up in the Jewish slums of Brooklyn, Brooks discovered that a quick wit and a penchant for comedy could save him from bullies. He clowned for relatives and friends when he was a child, and, according to Zimmerman, the "rejections of adolescence and the alienation of adulthood" gave his humor an additional "anarchic energy."

In his teens, Brooks worked at resort hotels in the Catskill mountains of New York state while learning to play the drums. According to Tynan, Brooks kept busy "washing dishes, keeping the tennis courts clean, and yelling things like 'Mrs. Weiss, your time is up!' at people in rented rowboats." The young man also "worked out a simple comedy routine, which, as a reward for good conduct, he was occasionally allowed to perform. Clad in a black overcoat and derby hat, and toting two suitcases, the fourteen-year-old Brooks would trudge out onto the diving board. Pausing at the edge, he would suddenly scream 'Business is terrible! I can't go on!' and plunge into the pool." Brooks's stage name—a shortened version of his mother's maiden name of Brookman—dates from these years.

World War II delayed Brooks's budding show business career. He enlisted in the army at seventeen and attended the Virginia Military Institute. Detailing this period to Zimmerman, Brooks noted that "they had us ride horses and cut down flags on bamboo poles. I was trained to become a Confederate officer." Brooks saw active duty on the European front following the Allied invasion in Normandy. "I was put in the combat engineers. We would throw up bridges in advance of the infantry but mainly we would just throw up," he told Zimmerman, who added that "the highlight of Brooks's war [was] when the Germans made a propaganda pitch over a loudspeaker after the Battle of the Bulge, [and] Brooks replied with an imitation of Al Jolson singing 'Toot Toot Tootsie.'"

Local Boy Makes Good: Writing for Sid Caesar

Brooks returned to the Catskills after the war. He eventually rose to the position of *tummler,* or social director, at various hotels. Spurred on by the comedians who performed on the Borscht Belt circuit, Brooks took to the stage himself, telling jokes, doing impressions and playing the drums. He was befriended by a young saxophonist who was eager to do comedy: Sid Caesar. Brooks would go on to work with Caesar for ten years, contributing to *Your Show of Shows* and *Caesar's Hour* (two comedy-variety shows of television's so-called "Golden Age" during the 1950s).

Caesar hired Brooks to write for him at fifty dollars a week. "I would have been a successful comic on my own ten years earlier if I hadn't met Sid,"

Brooks told Zimmerman, "but he was such a great vehicle for my stuff." The high level of talent Caesar managed to bring together in the script-room—his roster included then up-and-comers Woody Allen, Neil Simon, and Carl Reiner—fostered a keen sense of rivalry among the contributors. Each of the writers jostled for Caesar's attention. As Carl Reiner remembered for Tynan, Brooks would consistently come up with wild material: "Late one day, he started fooling with the word 'carrot.' Someone groaned, 'Not another one of those dumb eyesight jokes.' Mel was up against the wall but he was going to deliver the best carrot joke of all time. Finally, he blurted out, 'He ate so many carrots he couldn't go to sleep because he could see through his eyelids.' The joke was used on the show." In his book, *Method in Madness: The Comic Art of Mel Brooks,* Maurice Yacowar noted that Brooks's sketches typically began with "a closely detailed, persuasive fantasy" from which the viewer was abruptly withdrawn, left "stranded,

Secret agent Maxwell Smart, played by Don Adams, steers his Deskmobile through the streets in *The Nude Bomb,* a 1980 film based on characters that Brooks created for the 1960s television show, *Get Smart.*

embarrassed for having committed himself to the vision he was fed.''

The 2,000-Year-Old-Man, the Critic & Maxwell Smart

Things began to look up for Brooks with a some recordings that began life as an improvised party routine and late became known as the ''Two-Thousand-Year-Old-Man'' series. Reiner, who played straightman to Brooks's many characters in their recordings, explained to Tynan: ''We'd go to a party and I'd pick a character for him to play. I never told him what it was going to be, but I always tried for something that would force him to go into a panic, because a brilliant mind in panic is a wonderful thing to see. For instance, I might say, 'We have with us tonight the celebrated sculptor Sir Jacob Epstone,' and he'd take it from there.... There was no end to what he could be—a U-boat commander, a deaf songwriter, an entire convention of antique dealers.''

The duo's biggest hit was the opinionated, quarrelsome miracle of modern science—the Two-Thousand-Year-Old-Man. When interviewer Reiner questions him on his astonishing longevity, the Two-Thousand-Year-Old-Man offers a thickly Jewish-American accented response, ''Will t'Live.'' (further questioning reveals that this refers to the old man's physician, Dr. Will Talive.) The Methuselah-type character discloses that he developed physically at a very slow rate—''I breastfed for two hundred years''—and that he has seen and done it all. The Two-Thousand-Year-Old-Man was witness to the origin of religion; he saw a performance of *Antony and Cleopatra* ''with the original cast''; he was Joan of Arc's boyfriend; he fought in every war; and he is the father of more than forty-two thousand children—''and not one comes to visit me.''

''The single most striking characteristic of the old sage is that he's Jewish,'' wrote Yacowar. ''His Jewishness serves several functions. For one thing, it concentrates all his varieties of vulnerability. The Jewish comic figure—in Brooks as in [Franz] Kafka and Woody Allen—is helpless before hostile man as well as before nature and God.'' Brooks has pointed out that the old man speaks not in a Hebrew accent, but in an American-Jewish accent, recalling the immigrant voices Brooks heard in his childhood. Yacowar quoted the comedian as saying: ''Within a couple of decades there won't be any more accents like that. They're being ironed out by history, because there are no more Jewish

Two con men create an outrageous musical entitled *Springtime for Hitler* in the 1968 film *The Producers*, for which Brooks received an Academy Award.

immigrants. It's the sound I was brought up on, and it's dying.''

This success allowed Brooks to make his first solo foray into directing in 1963 with an animated short subject entitled *The Critic*. Brooks drew from his own experience for the movie, which presented on an elderly man's complaints about the lack of plot in an abstract film. Artist Ernest Pintoff supplied the abstract animation; the soundtrack of the film consists of Brooks's improvised reactions to the dots and lines hurtling randomly across the screen. (Brooks not only furnished the voice of the old grumbler, but those of several fellow viewers trying to silence him, as well.)

Brooks returned to the stability of television writing in 1965 when he and Buck Henry wrote the *Get Smart* series. At its core, the show spoofed James Bond thrillers. Bungling his way from one adventure to the next, Maxwell Smart—the extremely inept secret agent protagonist—managed to triumph over the powers of evil every week. The show enjoyed great popularity in the 1960s and has continued to entertain fans through years of syndicated reruns.

Becoming a Full-time Moviemaker

Brooks's leap from the small screen to a full-length feature came in 1967, when he wrote and directed *The Producers*. The film had begun life ten years earlier as an unpublished Brooks novel entitled *Springtime for Hitler*. According to Tynan, Brooks "had never thought of himself as a writer until 1950, when he saw his name on the credits of *Your Show of Shows*." Brooks stated: "I got scared and I figured I'd better find out what these bastards do. I went to the library, and read all the books I could carry—Conrad, Fielding, Dostoevski, Gogol, Tolstoy. I decided that Tolstoy was the most gifted writer who ever lived. . . . And I said to myself, 'My God, I'm not a writer, I'm a *talker*.' I wished they'd change the billing on the show so that it said 'Funny Talking by Mel Brooks.' Then I wouldn't feel so intimidated." Tynan notes that "before long, [Brooks] stifled his fears and embarked on his novel."

Once Brooks realized the visual possibilities of the story, the novel evolved from a play and into a film. In the movie, Zero Mostel and Gene Wilder play a pair of fraudulent producers who oversell shares in a "sure-fire flop" musical called *Springtime for Hitler*. When the show becomes a hit, the two conmen are thrown in jail.

The film unleashed a wide range of comments from critics at the time it was released. Renata Adler of the *New York Times* described it as a "violently mixed bag," while the *Village Voice*'s Andrew Sarris found Brooks's direction, with the exception of two or three scenes, "thoroughly vile and inept." Sarris added that *The Producers* "is in a class by itself as a movie that completely ignores the existence of women except as props, toys, or old bags." Regardless of such critical response, Brooks picked up his second Academy Award his *Producers* script.

In 1970, the writer-director released his second feature-length film, *The Twelve Chairs*. Based on the 1928 novel *Twelve Chairs* by Russian writers Ilya Ilf and Yevgeni Petrov, the film depicts a man's search for the family diamonds which his mother has sewn into a dining room chair during the Russian revolution. Writing in the *New Yorker*, Pauline Kael noted that "*The Twelve Chairs* was

bland and pokey, but Brooks himself was funny in it."

In 1974, Brooks enjoyed huge success with *Blazing Saddles*. Brooks spared none of the myths of the heroic Old West in his send-up. The film features the stock characters of traditional Westerns—the villain, the sheriff, the saloon chanteuse and assorted cowpunchers (one of whom actually knocks a horse out). In this saga, however, the scoundrel is a councilman—the "State Procurer"—who appoints a black sheriff to the frontier town of Rock Ridge in hopes of forcing the bigoted town residents to abandon the city and leave it open for his railroad to pass through. As Yacowar reports, Brooks said "he wrote berserk, heartfelt stuff about white corruption and racism and Bible-thumping bigotry. We used dirty language on the screen for the first time, and to me the whole thing was like a big psychoanalytic session. I just got everything out of me—all my furor, my frenzy, my insanity, my love of life and hatred of death."

The critical response to *Blazing Saddles* ran the gamut from esteem to disdain. Writing in the *New York Times*, Schjedahl noted that: "A film projector loaded with *Blazing Saddles* is a gag-firing machine. Some of the gags are priceless. . . . All of them, good and bad, come in a pell-mell torrent that leaves no time for reflecting on their quality. . . . But the final effect of *Blazing Saddles* is devastating. . . . The sheer wonder of its invention

Blazing Saddles, a 1974 film that satirized the Old West, featured Brooks in a dual role as Governor Lepetomane and Indian Chief.

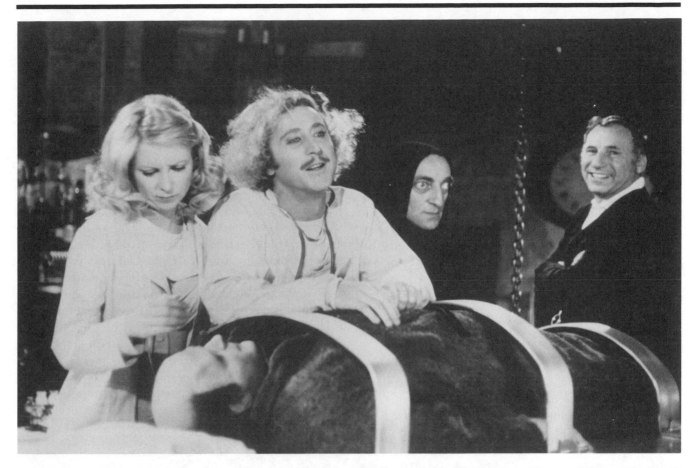

Brooks parodied the horror film genre in the 1975 film *Young Frankenstein*, starring Teri Garr, Gene Wilder, and Marty Feldman.

is really apparent only afterward, as one savors the moments of delight that flashed by in the theatre.'' The *New Yorker*'s Kael was less enthusiastic, noting that ''once again, [Brooks] demonstrates that he doesn't have the controlling vision that a director needs.''

Following the success of *Blazing Saddles,* Brooks parodied horror films in *Young Frankenstein. Newsweek*'s Zimmerman termed the film, ''an uproarious homage to the horror classic.'' Brooks paid close attention to detail in this effort, even managing to work with set designer Kenneth Strickfaden, who had designed Dr. Frankenstein's laboratory for the 1931 original. As Yacowar wrote: ''Technically, the film is a loving re-creation of the classic horror film style and mood.''

Brooks returned briefly to television in 1975 to create and contribute to *When Things Were Rotten,* a send-up of Robin Hood that included jokes with his unmistakable touch, including a crowd that obeys the edict to ''hold your tongues'' literally and a hero suffering from ''forest fatigue.'' The writer-director continued in the spoofing vein on the big screen with *Silent Movie,* compensating for

its nearly total lack of dialogue—the only word is spoken by mime Marcel Marceau—with plenty of sight gags and a simplistic plot. Next, the writer-director took on no less than Alfred Hitchcock with *High Anxiety.* This burlesque of several Hitchcock films, according to *Rolling Stone*'s Charles M. Young, ''transcends genre shtick enough so that you are glad when Brooks wins the fight, gets married to Madeline Kahn and lives happily ever after in the suburbs.''

Producing ''Un-Brooksian'' Movies and More Laughs

In 1980, Brooks founded a production company called Brooksfilms, Inc. Over the years, he has used it as a conduit to produce critically acclaimed films such as *The Elephant Man* and *My Favorite Year.* Responding to the apparent contradiction of Brooks's various undertakings, Margot Dougherty noted in *People* that Brooks ''is a connoisseur of [both] fine art and the exquisitely timed fart joke.'' Brooks has also acted in movies scripted and directed by others, including a cameo role as a mad German scientist in *The Muppet Movie* and a starring role, opposite second wife Anne Bancroft, in director Alan Johnston's 1983 remake of the classic farce, *To Be or Not to Be.*

In 1981, Brooks returned to filmmaking with *History of the World—Part I,* in which he presented various periods of history through vaudevillian sketches. The movie is peopled with characters such a "stand-up philosopher" in ancient Rome, a song-and-dance Torquemada during the Spanish Inquisition, and an utterly corrupt Louis XVI in revolutionary France. According to Jack Kroll of *Newsweek,* the movie "veers wildly between the Aristophanic and the Slobbovian." Critical reviews of the film were largely negative, with complaints about the director's sexist, racist, and scatological humor.

Returning to parodies in 1987, Brooks launched *Spaceballs,* a take-off on the George Lucas "Star Wars" series, with a few jabs at *Star Trek, Planet of the Apes* and *Alien* thrown in for good measure. Most of the film's characters are borrowed directly from the Lucas saga and given a Brooksian spin— the hero, Lone Starr, accompanied by his half-dog, half-man companion Barf, travels the galaxy in search of the love of his "Druish" princess. In order to reach her, he must fend off her chaperon, Dot Matrix, the slobbering Pizza the Hut, and the dastardly Dark Helmet. Assisting Lone on his quest is Yogurt, a cheeky midget played by Brooks himself, whose byword is "May the Schwartz Be With You."

The critics were uneven in their responses to Brooks's galactic lampoon. Richard Schickel noted in *Time* that: "A lot of the gags are pretty good.... It's not that Mel Brooks has lost his cunning ... What's missing is that zany old gang of his, ranging in size from Zero Mostel to Marty Feldman, in size from Madeline Kahn to Dom DeLuise (who does deliver the voice of Pizza the Hutt in *Spaceballs*)." Writing in *Newsweek,* David Ansen claimed that, "When it comes to jokes, Mel Brooks is the Reggie Jackson of comedy: he swings for the bleachers ... No Brooks film is without its knee-slappers. By my count *Spaceballs* has four or five bits (my favorite is a zany Pirandellian moment in which the videotape of the still-in-progress *Spaceballs* competes with the movie you're watching). But there are some

Brooks directed a send-up of the Robin Hood legend with the 1993 film, *Robin Hood: Men in Tights,* with Cary Elwes portraying Robin.

deep valleys and arid stretches between these peaks.''

In late 1989, Brooks moved from the entertainment news to the financial pages by announcing that he intended to go public with Brooksfilms, Inc. He justified the decision with the fact that the company needed to raise cash for movie and television projects. *Business Week* writers Ronald Grover and Susan Duffy quoted Brooks as saying that ''the studios give you a fee, and they own your work.... *Blazing Saddles* should have been mine, but I'm not going to cry over spilt celluloid.'' The venture had mixed success. Cameron Stauth reported in *American Film* that ''with an estimated 40 percent of the offering sold, the company halted sales indefinitely due to what it called 'general market skittishness.'''

Another Taboo Subject—Homelessness—& More Spoofing

Brooks returned to moviemaking in 1991 with *Life Stinks*. Never one to duck uncomfortable subjects, the director focused his comic eye on homelessness as the subject for this effort, in which he plays an immensely wealthy Los Angeles real estate magnate who agrees to spend thirty days living on the street. The executive endures this trial, only to discover that, because his erstwhile colleagues have conspired against him, he is now genuinely down and out. Defending Brooks against the critical digs he took for this film, Anne Billson of the *New Statesman & Society* remarked: ''Those of us who cherish Brooks as one of the unsung, underrated treasures of contemporary culture will hug this movie to our bosoms and squeeze for all we're worth.... For all its faults, *Life Stinks* is a move away from genre-spoof (now rapidly running out of gas) and a nod back towards the comedy of character.'' In *People*, Ralph Novak struck a more typical note. He wrote that ''coming from an accomplished movie satirist, [*Life Stinks*] approaches embarrassing levels of tedium.''

In 1993, Brooks again opted for a genre take-off with *Robin Hood: Men in Tights*. As with *Spaceballs*, Brooks's characters are borrowed directly from the original ''rob-from-the-rich-give-to-the-poor'' tale, with a few Brooksian additions—such as the Sheriff of Rottingham and Rabbi Tuckman—thrown in for good measure. The film's jokes offer a typical Brooks mix of the present-day with the past. In one typical example, The Club—a popular anti-theft car device—is used to secure a knight's horse. Acknowledging Brooks's role in creating a whole

category of genre spoof, the *New York Times*'s Caryn James commented that this film ''puts [Brooks] in the odd position of competing with his own unmatched reputation.''

Speaking to Dougherty, Brooks said that comedy ''is the vanguard of life. It's the joyous point of it all for me. It's the opposite of death—a protest and scream against death. I scream to the heavens, 'I'm alive! I'm alive! Listen, people are laughing! Listen!''' Brooks added: ''The image of a wacko is important to me, even though it's not really me. It's comforting for people who want to see a happy movie. And the real me takes comfort in it.... Every celebrity fights for anonymity. My anonymity is the serious Mel Brooks.''

■ Works Cited

Adler, Renata, review of *The Producers*, *New York Times*, March 19, 1968, p. 38.

Ansen, David, ''May the Schwartz Be With You,'' *Newsweek*, June 29, 1987, p. 66.

Billson, Anne, ''Bane of Buffs,'' *New Statesman & Society*, September 20, 1991, p. 36.

Cooper, Arthur, ''Mel Brooks: Chasing Rabbits,'' *Newsweek*, April 22, 1974, pp. 101-103.

Dougherty, Margot, ''May the Farce Be With Him: *Spaceballs* Rockets Mel Brooks Back Into Lunatic Orbit,'' *People*, July 20, 1987, pp. 38-40.

Duffy, Susan and Ronald Grover, ''Can the King of Yucks Bring in the Bucks?'' *Business Week*, January 15, 1990, p. 64.

James, Caryn, review of *Robin Hood: Men in Tights*, *New York Times*, August 1, 1993, p. 11.

Kael, Pauline, ''O Consuella,'' *Reeling*, Little, Brown, 1974, pp. 374-381.

Kauffmann, Stanley, ''Billionaires and Lesser Folk,'' *New Republic*, September 2, 1991, p. 26.

Kroll, Jack, review of *History of the World—Part I*, *Newsweek*, June 22, 1981.

Novak, Ralph, review of *Life Stinks*, *People*, August, 19, 1991

Novak, Ralph, review of *Robin Hood: Men In Tights*, *Newsweek*, August 9, 1993.

Sarris, Andrew, review of *The Producers*, *Village Voice*, March 28, 1968, p. 47.

Schickel, Richard, ''Lost in Space,'' review of *Spaceballs*,'' *Time*, July 13, 1987, p. 68.

Schjedahl, Peter, profile of Mel Brooks, *New York Times*, February 8, 1974.

Schjedahl, Peter, review of *Blazing Saddles*, *New York Times*, March 17, 1974.

Stauth, Cameron, ''Mel and Me,'' *American Film*, April, 1990, p. 100.

Travers, Peter, review of *Spaceballs, People Weekly*, July 13, 1987, p. 10.

Tynan, Kenneth, profile of Mel Brooks, *New Yorker*, October 30, 1978.

Yacowar, Maurice, *Method in Madness: The Comic Art of Mel Brooks*, St. Martin's Press, 1981.

Young, Charles M., "Seven Revelations about Mel Brooks: A Study in Low Anxiety," *Rolling Stone*, February 9, 1978, pp. 33-36.

Zimmerman, Paul D., "The Mad, Mad Mel Brooks," *Newsweek*, February 17, 1975, pp. 54-59.

■ **For More Information See**

BOOKS

Contemporary Literary Criticism, Volume 12, Gale, 1980, pp. 75-83.

PERIODICALS

Film Comment, March-April, 1975, p. 54.
Films and Filming, March, 1976, p. 39.
Monthly Film Bulletin, April, 1975, pp. 90-91.
Premiere, August, 1993, p. 22.
Time, December 11, 1989.°

—Sketch by Megan Ratner

Christopher Collier

James Lincoln Collier

Christopher and James Collier

■ Personal

Born in New York, NY; sons of Edmund (a writer) and Katharine (a teacher; maiden name, Brown) Collier.

Christopher Collier: Born January 29, 1930; married Virginia Wright (a teacher), August 21, 1954 (marriage ended); married Bonnie Bromberger (a librarian), December 6, 1969; children: (first marriage) Edmund Quincy, Sally McQueen; (second marriage) Christopher Zwissler. *Education:* Clark University, B.A., 1951; Columbia University, M.A., 1955, Ph.D., 1964. *Hobbies and other interests:* Trumpet playing, figure skating, ice hockey, water skiing, reading.

James Lincoln Collier: Born June 27, 1928; married Carol Burrows, September 2, 1952 (divorced); married Ida Karen Potash, July 22, 1983; children: (first marriage) Geoffrey Lincoln, Andrew Kemp. *Education:* Hamilton College, A.B., 1950. *Hobbies and other interests:* Music, reading, cooking, travelling, working on his country house.

■ Addresses

Christopher Collier: *Home*—876 Orange Center Rd., Orange, CT 06477. *Office*—Department of History, University of Connecticut, Storrs, CT 06269.

James Lincoln Collier: *Home*—South Quaker Hill Rd., Pawling, NY 12564. *Office*—c/o Oxford University Press, 200 Madison Ave., New York, NY 10016.

■ Career

Christopher Collier: Julian Curtiss School, Greenwich, CT, eighth grade teacher, 1955-58; Columbia University, Teachers College, New York City, instructor in history, 1958-59; New Canaan High School, New Canaan, CT, teacher of social studies, 1959-61; University of Bridgeport, Bridgeport, CT, instructor, 1961-64, assistant professor, 1964-67, associate professor, 1967-71, professor of history, 1971-78, chairman of department, 1978-81, David S. Day Professor of History, 1978-84; University of Connecticut, Storrs, professor of history, 1984—. Visiting lecturer, Yale University, 1977 and 1981, New York University, 1974; Columbia University Seminar on Early American History, chairman, 1978-79; Connecticut State Historian, 1985—; National Endowment for the Humanities Summer Institute for College Teachers, director, 1989. Consultant to numerous public and private organizations, including museums, historical societies, law firms, public utilities, and text, trade, and scholarly publishers. *Member:* American Historical Association, Organization of American Historians, Connecticut Historical Commission, Connecticut Committee for the Book, Historical Records Advisory Committee, Museum Advisory Committee, Connecticut Historical Society (member of board of trustees), Association for the Study of Connecticut History (co-founder). *Military service:* U.S. Army, 1952-54; trumpet player, Fort Hood, TX; became corporal.

James Lincoln Collier: Writer and jazz musician. Magazine editor, 1952-58. *Military Service:* U.S. Army, 1950-51; became private.

■ Awards, Honors

Newbery Honor Book Award, Jane Addams Honor Book Award, National Book Award finalist, all 1975, Phoenix Award, 1994, and American Library Association notable book citation, all for *My Brother Sam Is Dead; Jump Ship to Freedom* and *War Comes to Willy Freeman* were each named a Notable Children's Trade Book in the Field of Social Studies by the National Council for Social Studies and the Children's Book Council, 1981 and 1982, respectively; Christopher Award, 1987, for *Decision in Philadelphia: The Constitutional Convention of 1787.*

Christopher Collier: Pulitzer Prize nomination, and Award of Merit from Connecticut League of Historical Societies, both 1971, both for *Roger Sherman's Connecticut: Yankee Politics and the American Revolution;* Wilbur Cross Award, Connecticut Humanities Council, 1987.

James Lincoln Collier: Child's Study Association Book Award, 1970, for *Rock Star;* London *Observer* Book of the Year Award, and American Book Award nomination, both for *The Making of Jazz: A Comprehensive History;* National Foundation for the Humanities fellowship, 1982; Institute for Studies in American Music fellowship, 1985.

■ Writings

HISTORICAL NOVELS FOR CHILDREN AND YOUNG ADULTS WRITTEN TOGETHER

My Brother Sam Is Dead, Four Winds, 1974.
The Bloody Country, Four Winds, 1976.
The Winter Hero, Four Winds, 1978.
Jump Ship to Freedom, Delacorte, 1981.
War Comes to Willy Freeman, Delacorte, 1983.
Who Is Carrie?, Delacorte, 1984.
The Clock, illustrations by Kelly Maddox, Delacorte, 1991.
With Every Drop of Blood, Delacorte, 1994.

FICTION FOR CHILDREN AND YOUNG ADULTS BY JAMES LINCOLN COLLIER

The Teddy Bear Habit; or, How I Became a Winner, illustrations by Lee Lorenz, Norton, 1967.
Rock Star, Four Winds, 1970.
Why Does Everybody Think I'm Nutty?, Grosset, 1971.
It's Murder at St. Basket's, Grosset, 1972.
Rich and Famous: The Further Adventures of George Stable (sequel to *The Teddy Bear Habit*), Four Winds, 1975.
Give Dad My Best, Four Winds, 1976.
Planet Out of the Past, Macmillan, 1983.
When the Stars Begin to Fall, Delacorte, 1986.
Outside Looking In, Macmillan, 1987.
The Winchesters, Macmillan, 1988.
My Crooked Family, Simon & Schuster, 1991.
The Jazz Kid, Holt, 1994.

NONFICTION FOR CHILDREN AND YOUNG ADULTS BY JAMES LINCOLN COLLIER

Battleground: The United States Army in World War II, Norton, 1965.
A Visit to the Fire House, photographs by Yale Joel, Norton, 1967.
Which Musical Instrument Shall I Play?, photographs by Joel, Norton, 1969.
Danny Goes to the Hospital, photographs by Joel, Norton, 1970.
Practical Music Theory: How Music Is Put Together from Bach to Rock, Norton, 1970.

The Hard Life of the Teenager, Four Winds, 1972.

Inside Jazz, Four Winds, 1973.

Jug Bands and Hand Made Music, Grosset, 1973.

The Making of Man: The Story of Our Ancient Ancestors, Four Winds, 1974.

Making Music for Money, F. Watts, 1976.

The Great Jazz Artists, illustrations by Robert Andrew Parker, Four Winds, 1977.

CB, F. Watts, 1977.

Louis Armstrong: An American Success Story, Macmillan, 1985.

Duke Ellington, Macmillan, 1991.

FICTION FOR ADULTS BY JAMES LINCOLN COLLIER

Somebody up There Hates Me, Macfadden, 1962.

Fires of Youth, Penguin (London), 1968.

NONFICTION FOR ADULTS BY JAMES LINCOLN COLLIER

Cheers, Avon, 1961.

The Hypocritical American: An Essay on Sex Attitudes in America, Bobbs-Merrill, 1964.

The Making of Jazz: A Comprehensive History, Houghton, 1978.

Louis Armstrong: An American Genius, Oxford University Press, 1983.

Duke Ellington, Oxford University Press, 1987.

The Reception of Jazz in America: A New View, Institute for Studies in American Music, 1988.

Benny Goodman and the Swing Era, Oxford University Press, 1989.

The Rise of Selfishness in America, Oxford University Press, 1991.

Jazz: The American Theme Song, Oxford University Press, 1993.

Contributor to *The Fine Art of Swindling*, edited by W. B. Gibson, Grosset, 1966, and *Sex Education U.S.A.: A Community Approach*, Sex Information and Education Council of the United States, 1968. Contributor of more than six hundred articles to periodicals, including *Reader's Digest, New York Times Magazine, Village Voice*, and *Esquire*. Collier's manuscripts are held by the Kerlan Collection at the University of Minnesota.

HISTORICAL NONFICTION FOR ADULTS BY CHRISTOPHER COLLIER

(Editor and author of introduction) *The Public Records of the State of Connecticut, 1802-03*, Volume 11, State Library of Connecticut, 1967.

Roger Sherman's Connecticut; Yankee Politics and the American Revolution, Wesleyan University Press, 1971.

Connecticut in the Continental Congress, Pequot Press, 1973.

Roger Sherman: Puritan Politician, New Haven Colony Historical Society, 1976.

The Pride of Bridgeport: Men and Machines in the Nineteenth Century, Bridgeport Museum of Art, Science, and Industry, 1979.

(With wife, Bonnie Collier) *The Literature of Connecticut History*, Connecticut Humanities Council, 1983.

(Author of foreword) *Connecticut: A Bibliography of Its History*, University Press of New England, 1986.

(With James Lincoln Collier) *Decision in Philadelphia: The Constitutional Convention, 1787*, Random House, 1986.

Also author with wife, Bonnie Collier, of *An Essay Toward a Bibliography of Connecticut History for Teachers*, 1980. Contributor to *Words That Made American History*, W. C. Brown, 1967; *Lyme Miscellany*, edited by George Willauer, Wesleyan University Press, 1977; *Long Island Sound: The People and the Environment*, Oceanic Society, 1978; *Connecticut: A Bibliography of Its History*, edited by Roger Parks, University Press of New England, 1986; *The Constitution and the States: The Role of the Original Thirteen in the Framing and Adoption of the Federal Constitution*, edited by Patrick T. Conley and John P. Kaminski, Madison House and the Center for the Study of the U. S. Constitution, 1988; *The Fundamental Orders of Connecticut*, U.S. Bicentennial Commission of Connecticut, 1988; and *The States and the Convention*, edited by A. E. Dick Howard, Conference of Chief Justices of the National Center for State Courts, 1990. Editor, *Changing Connecticut: Thirteen Curriculum Units on Connecticut History* and *Curriculum Units on Connecticut History*, Yale Teachers Institute on Connecticut History, 1980-82; and *Monographs in British History and Culture*, 1967-72. Contributor to history, legal and educational journals. Editor, *Connecticut History Newsletter*, 1967-73.

■ Adaptations

My Brother Sam Is Dead has been adapted as a record, a cassette, and a filmstrip with cassette.

■ Work in Progress

James Lincoln Collier is working on various books for children; Christopher Collier is writing a young adult novel with Debrah Deford about academic freedom in high schools.

■ Sidelights

According to historian and teacher Christopher Collier, when he initially asked his older brother James to write a historical novel with him, his older sibling was reluctant. "I thought it would be great to teach history through novels," Christopher told Allen Raymond for *Teaching K-8*. But he told *AAYA* that his brother said he "was too busy with other things." James, on the other hand, wrote to *AAYA* that he "does not remember being as reluctant to undertake historical fiction as Christopher suggests. When Kit [Christopher] broached the idea underlying *My Brother Sam Is Dead*, I quickly saw the possibilities in it. At the time publishers believed that historical fiction for children did not sell well, but fortunately we had a sympathetic editor in Judith Whipple, who wanted to do the book." However the brothers first came to agree on writing historical fiction together, the immediate results quickly caught the attention of both critics and young audiences. "In *My Brother Sam Is Dead* ... the complexity of issues about the Revolutionary War ... is explored in ways perhaps unique in children's literature," stated Hughes Moir in *Language Arts*. Since then, the Collier brothers have become widely known for both their exploration of complicated issues and for creating interesting historical novels for children and young adults.

The Colliers' extended family was full of writers: their father, Edmund, worked as an editor and wrote cowboy stories for adults and biographies of Western heroes for teenagers; a cousin wrote for *Sports Illustrated*; their brother-in-law has won prizes for his short stories; and an ancestor was Anne Bradstreet, one of America's earliest poets. James and Christopher grew up in a family that believed in the old New England traditions of hard work and accomplishment, which James believes to be instrumental to his career. During the 1930s, the Collier family moved from Long Island to a small town in Connecticut, and the boys enjoyed an active, outdoor life before suburbs became the norm.

A Writer's Career

In the early 1950s, James graduated from Hamilton College, served in the Army during the Korean War, and married. He moved to Greenwich Village, intending to write, but instead became a magazine editor to support his family. After spending six years of writing in the evenings and on weekends, he turned to freelancing. "Upon the advice of his agent [James] began writing for children ... in order to make money, a choice he has never regretted," reports Moir. While James joked in *Speaking for Ourselves* about "not draw[ing] an honest paycheck" since starting out as a freelancer, he also added: "It has never been easy, especially as I had children to raise and educate, but the economic goal was critically important in teaching me that what I wrote had first of all to be interesting to real people."

James Collier's attitude toward writing is extremely practical. He has always been a prolific writer who doesn't believe in inspiration, and sees himself as a craftsman. "My best-liked books have always been those written not out of a fiery vision but as a professional, using sleights of hand that took me years to discover and develop," he said in *Speaking for Ourselves*. James's early training taught him how to write, regardless of how he felt. "There was a time, right after college," he told Raymond, "when I would write over 600,000 words in a year." When writing, he finds himself engrossed in his work: "The phone will ring, and I'll jump in alarm. When I'm writing I don't know whether the sun is shining outside."

A Historian's Career

Christopher Collier published his first article in the sixth grade. The first work of history he remembers reading was *They Also Ran*, by Irving Stone. While he enjoyed writing, Christopher eventually decided on a teaching career. (Christopher and James grew up during the Depression, and the younger Collier brother was interested in a regular paycheck.) He enjoyed music, and spent much of his time in the army playing in a band. Christopher received his bachelor's from Massachusetts' Clark University, earned his master's and doctoral degrees from Columbia University, and taught eighth American history for three years. At this point he decided history textbooks were too dull, and approached James with the idea of writing something of their own.

Christopher went on to teach history at the University of Bridgeport. He wrote several historical works, including *Roger Sherman's Connecticut*, which was nominated for the Pulitzer Prize. In 1984, he became a professor of history at the University of Connecticut. Christopher's love of the past extends into his personal life, as well. He lives with his second wife and college-age son in a house built in 1785 that has five fireplaces.

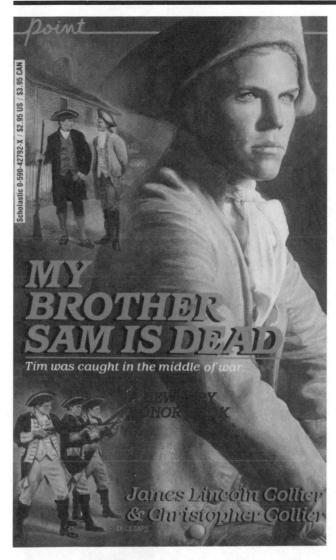

This 1974 novel, which focuses on one family's struggles during the Revolutionary War, was named a Newbery Honor book and National Book Award finalist.

Collaborating

James had published fifteen books and Christopher had written four when they collaborated on their first effort, *My Brother Sam Is Dead*. The duo specializes in the Revolutionary Era, since that is Christopher's area of expertise. "There are very few historians who can write for children, who can write for anyone," Christopher told Moir. While he has always enjoyed history texts, he also realizes that they often bore students. Christopher explained in *Horn Book* that writing about history without communicating the complexity of both the events and our perceptions of them teaches "nothing worth learning and [falsifies] the past."

"The Colliers have worked well together, with no serious conflicts in their writing relationship,"

commented Moir. Christopher establishes the historical theme, outlines the story, and researches the events. James receives the research and a synopsis, and then they discuss it over the phone or in a short face-to-face conference. James fashions the plot line and develops the characters. When he has completed the first draft, he sends it to his brother, who checks it for historical accuracy and thematic consistency. "Jamie is the one who makes the stories fun to read, interesting and exciting, sometimes funny," Christopher told Raymond. "Most of all, he gives the individuals in the books character and personality." To keep fact from fiction, all the Colliers' historical fiction contain an epilogue, "How Much of This Book Is True?"

My Brother Sam Is Dead

"*My Brother Sam* is obviously, at times very unsubtly, an antiwar novel," remarked *Washington Post Book World* reviewer Joyce Alpern. The book follows teenager Tim Meeker and his family through the American Revolution. Tim, who lives in a Tory village in Connecticut, is torn between his innkeeper father's love of peace and his older brother's zeal for independence. Tim "rubs elbows with historical luminaries ... under the war's demands," noted Alpern. He is "concerned more with his own problems and family in wartime than with issues or principles," added Zena Sutherland in the *Bulletin of the Center for Children's Books*.

"In a complex way [*My Brother Sam*] deals with why Americans did and did not become involved in the war," Christopher told Moir. The story deals with ideas that go beyond the stereotypes familiar to many children. "As a work conceived to present concepts related to the issues of war, *My Brother Sam Is Dead* portrays the Revolutionary War not as the good guys versus the bad guys, but rather as a *civil war* where families and communities were divided in public opinion," explained Moir. "With its sharp revelation of the human aspects of Revolutionary War life and its probing of political views and divided loyalties, this stirring and authoritative novel earns a place beside our best historical fiction," concluded a *Horn Book* contributor.

Bring Lesser-Known Events to Light

A more difficult book is *The Bloody Country*. "As they did in [*My Brother Sam*,] the Colliers focus on a small geographical area ... to explore the conflicting loyalties and abrasions between groups of [pioneers after the American Revolution]," a *Bulletin of the Center for Children's Books* reviewer commented. The story takes place near what is now Wilkes Barre, Pennsylvania. The main character is Ben, who, with his sister Annie, her husband, and Joe, the family slave, move from Connecticut and establish a flour mill. The Pennsylvanian Pennamites rely on the British and an Indian tribe to get rid of the new settlers. "*The Bloody Country* is ... dramatic, well-constructed ... [and] gives a vivid picture of the hard work and persistence so often needed by the successful pioneer," lauded Olivia Coolidge in *Washington Post Book World*. But Ruth M. Stein of *Language Arts* disliked its "honest look at brutal fighting and killing over land." As Christopher told *AAYA*, the intent of the more violent scenes was to "describe accurately the challenges and dangers of the pioneering life so many Americans lived."

The Winter Hero concerns another historical incident. Complaining of unfair taxation, Massachusetts farmers rebelled and had to face the state militia. The result was the Shays' Rebellion of 1786-87. The rebels were defeated, but learned they could exert more influence by electing representatives to the legislature. In *The Winter Hero*, fourteen-year-old Justin Conkey narrates the story, which "transcend[s] the urgent question of taxation in America and emphasize[s] the boy's desire to prove himself a hero," described Paul Heins in the *Horn Book*. "The political oppression and financial burdens suffered by Massachusetts citizens in 1787 ... are as vivid as [Justin's] descriptions of [military] confrontations," wrote Sutherland in the *Bulletin of the Center for Children's Books*.

The Arabus Family Saga and *The Clock*

The "past is not always a dusty place with mold growing in the corners, a fact born out by *Jump Ship to Freedom*," mused Stephen Krensky in *Christian Science Monitor*. The book is the second in the "Arabus" saga, which begins with *War Comes to Willy Freeman* and concludes with *Who Is Carrie?* Daniel Arabus and his mother are owned by Connecticut ship captain Thomas Ivers, even though Daniel's father earned his freedom by fighting against the British. But Jack Arabus has died, and his $600 in Continental notes is held by Ivers. Daniel reclaims the notes, but the unscrupulous Ivers loads him onto a ship bound for the West Indies to be sold. *New York Times Book Review* contributor Cynthia King found Dan almost too good to be true, "but his experience, credible or not, illuminates a historical time and place in fine detail." And a *Publishers Weekly* reviewer noted that the authors have combined fiction with "what

is known about real people of the time, and the result is an uncommonly rewarding creation."

War Comes to Willy Freeman follows Daniel's cousin, Willy. When British soldiers kill Willy's father and kidnap her mother, Willy dresses as a boy and sets out from New London, Connecticut, for New York City to find her. The girl eventually becomes involved in a legal case that frees hundreds of slaves. *School Library Journal* contributor Holly Sanhuber described Willy as "an endearing creature" and says "her exploits and daring ensure exciting reading." And *New York Times Book Review* contributor Marilyn Kaye praised the Colliers' accuracy, adding that "the authors' fictional interpretation is evocative and believable."

Ivers again becomes the villain in *Who Is Carrie?* Carrie, or "Nosy," as the servants sometimes call her, works in the kitchen at Sam Fraunces' tavern. The story follows Carrie's attempts to discover whether she is free or a slave. A subplot brings back Dan Arabus, who is debating whether to cash

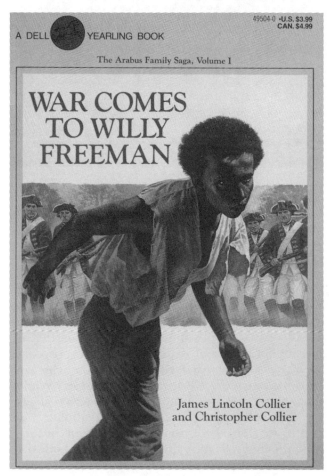

After her mother is kidnapped by British soldiers, Willy Freeman disguises herself as a boy and travels to New York to find her in this 1983 historical thriller.

in his Confederation bonds. "Carrie ... tells her story in a comic, moving fashion that creates empathy in the reader," wrote a *Publishers Weekly* contributor. And a *Bulletin of the Center of Children's Books* reviewer found that "the characters are believable, there is plenty of action to interest readers, and the outcome is satisfying."

The Clock concerns Annie, a fifteen-year-old in 1810, who must take a job spinning at the textile mill to pay off a debt incurred when father buys a clock. But when the mill's overseer makes advances, she collects evidence with the help of Robert, her neighbor. However, Robert is killed before she can press charges. "The novel thus succeeds not only as historical fiction, but also as a riveting story of the tragic romance and hard-won victory of one teenaged girl," wrote Diane Roback in *Publishers Weekly*.

Fiction by James Lincoln Collier

"Writing is a business. . . . It's not fun, but you can make yourself do it," James Collier told Moir. He has drawn comparisons between jazz improvisation and writing. "I find improvising jazz and writing fiction are very much the same. Both require me to *perform*," he said in *Speaking for Ourselves*. One of his early young adult novels, *The Teddy Bear Habit,* features a teenager who wants to be a professional musician. George "has been surreptitiously balancing out his classical voice training with rock'n roll lessons," explained *School Library Journal* contributors Lillian N. Gerhardt and Jean C. Thomson. But when George tries out the "wild world of television," according to Lavinia Russ in *Publishers Weekly*, he can't perform without seeing his teddy bear. When his guitar teacher stuffs the bear with stolen jewels, George's adventures start. *The Teddy Bear Habit* "develops into a heck of an exciting story, with a combination of humor and suspense," wrote *New York Times Book Review* contributor Jerome Beatty Jr.

The role of the outcast occupies many of James Collier's novels. In *It's Murder at St. Basket's*, an American friend tries to help a Pakistani boy abused by his English schoolmasters. A *Publishers Weekly* reviewer called the book "great escape reading." *When the Stars Begin to Fall* deals with the conflict faced by a boy when the local mill pollutes the town river, but the townspeople don't want to know about it. "This is a fast-paced story filled with action and excitement," declared Meryl Silverstein for *School Library Journal*. "Readers will be angered by Harry's treatment at the hands

Christopher and James Lincoln Collier relax in front of Christopher's home in Orange, Connecticut, with Frisbie.

of others, as well as enlightened by his intelligence, which comes shining through," claims a *Publishers Weekly* reviewer. *Outside Looking In* details the lives of another outcast family. Fergy's father, J.P., takes what he needs, since he feels society "owes" it to him. When he "reclaims" a van from a kindly family, Fergy runs away and his mother joins him. "Most of the characters in this novel are richly realized, especially Fergy, who longs for a normal life and schooling," wrote a *Publishers Weekly* reviewer.

Nonfiction

James has also written a number of nonfiction works. *Battleground: The United States Army in World War II*, features individual heroes from the war. *School Library Journal* contributor Robert Kinchen found the book "well written and factual." *The Hard Life of the Teenager* is a reassuring look at adolescent changes. *The Making of Man: The Story of Our Ancient Ancestors* teaches evolution from an adolescent's point of view. Sister M. Constance Melvin in *Best Sellers* argued with Collier's interpretation. He "presents his basic assumptions as if they were fact," she wrote. But *Appraisal* contributor Ronald J. Kley observed that "adolescent readers are certain to recognize many of their own characteristics, emotions, frustrations and motivations."

Many of James Collier's nonfiction books have dealt with music. *Practical Music Theory* is a "lucid, step-by-step exposition of musical theory for dedicated music students," wrote Loretta B. Jones in *School Library Journal*. *Inside Jazz* attempts to explain a form of music foreign to many teenagers. "Wisely Mr. Collier, a part-time jazz musician, reminds us in the first chapter just how difficult it is to translate musical sounds into words," warned Loraine Alterman in the *New York Times Book Review*. "Yet, he provides as good a verbal explanation as I've seen about jazz."

Collier's biography on *Louis Armstrong*, who was considered the world's greatest jazz artist before his death, "emphasizes the difficulties facing blacks of [Armstrong's] generation when they tried to build upon innate abilities," a *Publishers Weekly* contributor remarked. And *School Library Journal* reviewer Clarissa Erwin said the book "tells the story of [jazz] and the industry that surrounds it— an industry whose management excluded black performers while using their talent." *Benny Goodman* details life of the popular bandleader and details it with information about swing era music. The book contains "Collier's adroit analyses of dozens of significant recordings," praised Clarence Petersen in *Tribune Books*.

One of James Lincoln's most recent and unusual works for adults is *The Rise of Selfishness in America*. Collier draws on historical sources to show that Americans have changed their focus from duty to self-centeredness. The author claims that our Victorian forbears, in the years running from 1815-70, actually lived far better lives, in an moral and intellectual sense, than do their descendants. "As Mr. Collier sees it, Victorian America was, in many respects, 'a better society than this one,'" wrote Michiko Kakutani in the *New York Times*. "And it was so because—despite the hypocrisy—most people felt that they had duties and obligations to other people which came before their own gratification." While many critics have dismissed the work as moralistic, a *Publishers Weekly* critic found "this ringing, provocative jeremiad cuts a path through a haze of self-indulgent thought and action in the me-first society."

Overall, the interests of both Colliers in writing for young people was summed up in James Collier's interview with Moir: "The 'real' books today are written for children.... The author [of children's books] can deliver more than just a good read, but also a view of the world."

■ Works Cited

Alpern, Joyce, "Not a Bad Tory," *Washington Post Book World*, January 12, 1975, p. 4.

Alterman, Loraine, review of *Inside Jazz, New York Times Book Review*, December 30, 1973, p. 10.

Beatty, Jerome, Jr., review of *The Teddy Bear Habit, New York Times Book Review*, March 12, 1967, p. 28.

Review of *The Bloody Country, Bulletin of the Center for Children's Books*, Volume 30, number 4, December, 1976.

Collier, Christopher, "Johnny and Sam: Old and New Approaches to the American Revolution," *Horn Book*, April, 1976, pp. 132-138.

Collier, James Lincoln, interview in *Speaking for Ourselves*, National Council for Teachers of English, 1990, pp. 46-47.

Coolidge, Olivia, "The Founding Falters," *Washington Post Book World*, May 2, 1976, p. L3.

Erwin, Clarissa, review of *Louis Armstrong, School Library Journal*, October, 1985, pp. 169-170.

Gerhardt, Lillian N. and Jean C. Thomson, review of *The Teddy Bear Habit, School Library Journal*, April, 1967, p. 84.

Heins, Paul, review of *The Winter Hero, Horn Book Magazine*, Volume 55, number 1, February 1979, pp. 67-68.

Review of *It's Murder at St. Basket's, Publishers Weekly*, October 16, 1972, p. 49.

Jones, Loretta B., review of *Practical Music Theory, School Library Journal*, December, 1970, p. 58.

Review of *Jump Ship to Freedom, Publishers Weekly*, November 13, 1981, pp. 88-9.

Kakutani, Michiko, "How 'Oh No, After You' Became 'No, No, Me First'," *New York Times*, October 15, 1991, p. C17.

Kaye, Marilyn, review of *War Comes to Willy Freeman, New York Times Book Review*, May 8, 1983, p. 37.

Kinchen, Robert, review of *Battleground, School Library Journal*, October, 1965, p. 241.

King, Cynthia, review of *Jump Ship to Freedom, New York Times Book Review*, February 14, 1982, p. 28.

Kley, Ronald J., review of *The Making of Man, Appraisal*, Spring, 1975, p. 13.

Krensky, Stephen, "An Escape from Slavery," *Christian Science Monitor*, October 14, 1981, p. B10.

Review of *Louis Armstrong, Publishers Weekly*, July 5, 1985, p. 67.

Melvin, Sister M. Constance, review of *The Making of Man, Best Sellers*, June 15, 1974, p. 149.

Moir, Hughes, "Profile: James and Christopher Collier—More Than Just a Good Read," *Language Arts*, March, 1978, pp. 373-78.

Review of *My Brother Sam Is Dead, Horn Book*, April, 1975, p. 152.

Review of *Outside Looking In, Publishers Weekly*, March 13, 1987, p. 86.

Petersen, Clarence, "Paperbacks," *Tribune Books*, June 9, 1991, p. 6.

Raymond, Allen, "Jamie and Kit Collier: The Writer and the Historian," *Teaching K-8*, Volume 18, number 4, January, 1988, pp. 35-8.

Review of *The Rise of Selfishness in America, Publishers Weekly*, August 30, 1991, p. 73.

Roback, Diane, Review of *The Clock, Publishers Weekly*, January 1, 1992, p. 56.

Russ, Lavinia, review of *The Teddy Bear Habit, Publishers Weekly*, May 22, 1967, p. 64.

Sanhuber, Holly, review of *War Comes to Willy Freeman, School Library Journal*, Volume 29, number 8, April, 1983, p. 121.

Silverstein, Meryl, review of *When the Stars Begin to Fall, School Library Journal*, November, 1986, p. 98.

Stein, Ruth M., review of *The Bloody Country, Language Arts*, January, 1977, p. 83.

Sutherland, Zena, review of *My Brother Sam Is Dead, Bulletin of the Center for Children's Books*, March, 1975, pp. 108-09

Sutherland, Zena, review of *The Bloody Country, Bulletin of the Center for Children's Books*, December, 1976, p. 55.

Review of *When the Stars Begin to Fall, Publishers Weekly*, November 28, 1986, p. 77.

Review of *Who Is Carrie?, Bulletin of the Center of Children's Books*, May, 1984.

Review of *Who Is Carrie?, Publishers Weekly*, May 25, 1984, p. 59.

Review of *The Winter Hero, Bulletin of the Center for Children's Books*, February, 1979.

■ For More Information See

BOOKS

Children's Literature Review, Volume 3, Gale, 1978, p. 44.

Contemporary Literary Criticism, Volume 30, Gale, 1984, p. 70.

PERIODICALS

Bulletin of the Center for Children's Books, October, 1970, p. 23; October, 1981, p. 26.

Horn Book, April, 1975, p. 152; April, 1976, pp. 132-38; February, 1982.

School Library Journal, November, 1986, pp. 98-99.

—*Sketch by Jani Prescott*

Susan Cooper

■ Personal

Full name, Susan Mary Cooper; born May 23, 1935, in Burnham, Buckinghamshire, England; came to United States in 1963; daughter of John Richard (a railroad employee) and Ethel May (a teacher; maiden name, Field) Cooper; married Nicholas J. Grant (a college professor), August 3, 1963 (divorced, 1983); children: Jonathan, Katharine; (stepchildren) Anne, Bill, Peter. *Education:* Somerville College, Oxford, M.A., 1956. *Hobbies and other interests:* Music, islands.

■ Addresses

Office—c/o Margaret K. McElderry, Macmillan & Co., 866 Third Ave., New York, NY 10022.

■ Career

Writer, 1956—. *Sunday Times*, London, England, reporter and feature writer, 1956-63. *Member:* Society of Authors (United Kingdom), Authors League of America, Authors Guild, Writers Guild of America.

■ Awards, Honors

Horn Book Honor List citation for *Over Sea, under Stone; Horn Book* Honor List and American Library Association Notable Book citations, both 1970, both for *Dawn of Fear; Boston Globe-Horn Book* Award, American Library Association Notable Book citation, Carnegie Medal runner-up, all 1973, and Newbery Award Honor Book citation, 1974, all for *The Dark Is Rising;* American Library Association Notable Book citation, Newbery Medal, Tir na N'og Award (Wales), and commendation for Carnegie Medal, all 1976, all for *The Grey King;* Tir na N'og Award for *Silver on the Tree;* Christopher Award, Humanitas Prize, Writers Guild of America Award, and Emmy Award nomination, all 1984, all for adaptation of *The Dollmaker;* Emmy Award nomination, 1987, and Writers Guild of America Award, 1988, for teleplay *Foxfire; Horn Book* Honor List citation, 1987, for *The Selkie Girl;* B'nai B'rith Janusz Korczak Award, 1989, for *Seaward.*

■ Writings

"THE DARK IS RISING" SERIES

Over Sea, under Stone, illustrations by Margery Gill, J. Cape, 1965, Harcourt, 1966.
The Dark Is Rising, illustrations by Alan E. Cober, Chatto & Windus, 1973.
Greenwitch, Chatto & Windus, 1974.
The Grey King, illustrations by Michael Heslop, Chatto & Windus, 1975.
Silver on the Tree, Chatto & Windus, 1977.

JUVENILE

Dawn of Fear, illustrations by Gill, Harcourt, 1970.

Jethro and the Jumbie, illustrations by Ashley Bryan, Atheneum, 1979.

(Reteller) *The Silver Cow: A Welsh Tale*, illustrations by Warwick Hutton, Atheneum, 1983.

Seaward, Macmillan, 1983.

(Author of introduction) John and Nancy Langstaff, editors, *The Christmas Revels Songbook: In Celebration of the Winter Solstice*, Godine, 1985.

(Reteller) *The Selkie Girl*, illustrations by Hutton, Margaret K. McElderry Books, 1986.

Tam Lin, illustrations by Hutton, Margaret K. McElderry Books, 1991.

Matthew's Dragon, illustrations by Joseph A. Smith, Margaret K. McElderry Books, 1991.

The Boggart, Margaret K. McElderry Books, 1992.

Danny and the Kings, Macmillan, 1993.

PLAYS

(With Hume Cronyn) *Foxfire* (first produced at Stratford, Ontario, 1980, later Broadway at Ethel Barrymore Theatre, November 11, 1982; also see below), Samuel French, 1983.

TELEPLAYS

(With Cronyn) *The Dollmaker* (adaptation of novel by Harriet Arnow), American Broadcasting Companies, Inc. (ABC-TV), May 13, 1984.

Foxfire (adaptation of stage play), Columbia Broadcasting System, Inc. (CBS-TV), December 13, 1987.

Also author of *Dark Encounter*, 1976.

OTHER

(Contributor) Michael Sissons and Philip French, editors, *The Age of Austerity: 1945-51* (adult nonfiction), Hodder & Stoughton, 1963.

Mandrake (adult science-fiction), J. Cape, 1964.

Behind the Golden Curtain: A View of the U.S.A. (adult nonfiction; English Book Society alternative choice), Hodder & Stoughton, 1965.

(Editor and author of preface) J. B. Priestly, *Essays of Five Decades*, Little, Brown, 1968.

J. B. Priestly: Portrait of an Author (adult biography), Heinemann, 1970.

Also author of screenplays *The Cloud People* and *Dinner at the Homesick Restaurant*.

■ Adaptations

The Dark Is Rising was released as a two-cassette recording, Miller-Brody, 1979; *The Silver Cow* was adapted as a filmstrip, 1985, and recording, 1986, both Weston Woods; *The Selkie Girl* was adapted as a filmstrip and cassette, Weston Woods, 1988.

■ Sidelights

War changes people. It changes the soldiers who fight in the trenches, the doctors and nurses who struggle to save the wounded, and the refugees who flee as it approaches. It affects families who are uprooted from warm beds in the middle of the night by the call of the air raid siren. It also changes children, forever impressing upon them the fearful conflicts between right and wrong, good and evil, Light and Dark.

Susan Cooper is one of those wartime children who has taken her youthful experiences into adulthood. The age-old myths of Britain and Wales that she heard as a child in wartime England have found their way into her stories, along with a strong conviction that good can prevail over evil. "I'm really one of those authors who belong back in an age before labels, when all storytellers produced folktales—for folk, which meant everyone," Cooper wrote in *Speaking for Ourselves*. "I love being able to try to make a magic: to make you laugh, or cry, or experience what Aristotle called a catharsis—which means, in effect, feeling better even though a story has slugged you on the back of the head."

Cooper's books mine a rich vein of folktale and lore, most of the time presenting those ancient stories through the bizarre experiences of modern-day heroes and heroines. Her central characters may struggle with magic spirits, wield talismans, or travel through time, but they always recognize that such experiences are preparing them for conflicts that will occur throughout their so-called "normal" lives. In *Horn Book*, Margaret K. McElderry noted: "Old tales and legends, prose and poetry, theater and reality, imagination and intellect, power and control, a strong sense of place and people both past and present—all are part of the magic that has touched Susan Cooper.... Her journeys add great luster to the world of literature."

"A Noisy War"

Cooper was a four-year-old child living in Buckinghamshire, England when World War II began. For the rest of Cooper's childhood, the war raged, sometimes bringing danger right into her neighborhood. It is hard to imagine being instructed to dive into a ditch at the prompting of an air raid siren, but that is what she was told to do. As the

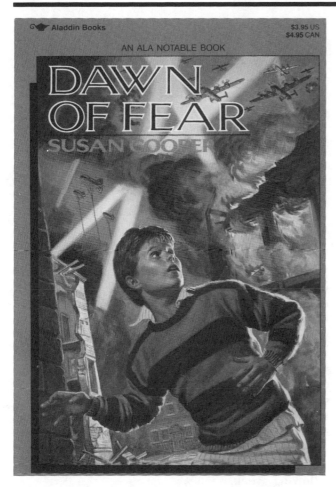

Cooper's memories of growing up in England during World War II were the basis for this 1970 novel.

German army bombed England indiscriminately, Cooper and everyone she knew had to take some-times drastic measures to protect their lives.

In an essay for *Something about the Author Autobiography Series* (*SAAS*), Cooper wrote: "It's a very long time since World War II, but I guess some things stick. I was four years old when the war broke out in Britain, and ten when it ended. I never came face-to-face with death, or with blood drawn by anything worse than broken glass, but it was a noisy war.... Once a German aeroplane swooped low, machine-gunning, as we ran; once, a house fifty yards away was blown to pieces; once, we went to school next morning to find a vast gaping hole in the playground." It was a terrifying time, even for a grade school child. In the first year of the war alone, more than 36,000 bombs were dropped on London and its suburbs; as a result, thousands of people were injured or killed.

The noise, confusion, and fear—as well as the sense of English patriotism and pride—all had lasting effects on Cooper. "A child raised in wartime is inevitably given a very strong sense of Us and Them, the good side (one's own, of course) against the bad," she noted in her autobiographical essay. "Though I wasn't thinking about Adolf Hitler and his night-bombing Luftwaffe when I began to write fantasies characterizing the forces of evil as the Dark, in the shadowy corners of my mind they probably weren't far away." One of Cooper's best-known books, *Dawn of Fear*, directly concerns the war's effect on a group of school-age boys. Many of the author's own wartime experiences found their way into that account as fiction.

In spite of the war, childhood was not uniformly bleak for Cooper. She was raised in a close and warm family, dominated by her stagestruck maternal grandfather. "Grandad carried off his older children to the theatre whenever he could, and they would sit in the cheapest seats high in the house, the 'gods,'" Cooper wrote in *SAAS*. "When the curtain fell, he would leap to his feet to applaud favoured performers, calling out in a great voice, 'Bravo! Bravo!', and the children would tug at his sleeve in anguished embarrassment and hiss: 'Dad! Dad! Sit down!'" Cooper herself was taken to the theater often from the time she turned three years old. In a *Horn Book* essay, she remembered her very first visit: "I sat there enchanted . . . and when it was all over and the curtain came down, I sat unmoving in my seat, and I howled and howled. All the others left on their legs, but they had to carry me out. I couldn't believe that this wonderful, magical new world, in which I had been totally absorbed, had vanished away. I wanted to bring it back again. I suppose I've been trying to bring it back again, in one way or another, ever since."

Cooper seldom went to the movies, but when she was twelve her grandfather took her to see a film—*A Matter of Life and Death*—that had a profound influence on the imaginative young girl. In the years since, Cooper has written for both the stage and screen, items ranging from song lyrics for the humorous Christmas Revels to serious stories about American life.

Cooper was always "a little afraid" of her grandfather, but she adored her maternal grandmother, who was born and raised in Wales. Many times Cooper and her family visited the small Welsh fishing village on the Dovey river where her grandmother had grown up and where many members of her extended family still lived. "Eventually, for a long time Aberdovey became my parents' home, and the lovely valley of the Dovey played a large part in my books because it has a large part of my heart," the author recalled in her autobiographical essay. "Perhaps I am a writer because of my grandmother's Welshness, the Celtic blessing that turns itself often into the words or melody of song. At any rate I am three-quarters English and one-quarter Welsh, by blood, and it is a lucky mixture."

Cooper's father was employed by England's Great Western Railway, just as his father and grandfather had been. The job was not terribly exciting, but it did allow the family to travel at reduced ticket rates. Cooper and her brother relished the chance to ride the crowded trains to some seaside destination in Cornwall or Wales, box lunches and books in their laps. Cooper's mother was a school teacher who encouraged her children to read and write. By the age of ten Cooper was writing original plays for a neighbor's puppet theater.

Few books for children were published during the Second World War, so Cooper read the works of Charles Dickens, H. G. Wells, Rudyard Kipling, and William Makepeace Thackeray. She also loved poetry and the rich tradition of mythology in both Great Britain and Wales. Like other youths of her generation, she tuned in to favorite weekly radio shows, among them the British Broadcasting Corporation's *Children's Hour.* There Cooper could hear some of her favorite stories dramatized for radio—a brilliant combination of the literature she loved and the drama she craved.

Cooper attended Slough High School, where she was encouraged to develop her writing talent. When she graduated from high school, she won a state scholarship that provided enough money for her to enroll at Oxford University. The author recalled in her autobiographical essay that she was stunned by her good fortune: "Oxford! I couldn't believe it. My mother said, smiling, 'Grandad would have been so pleased.'"

A Determined Journalist

At Oxford, Cooper studied English literature, enjoying what she called in *SAAS* "a calm stretch of such good fortune that I can hardly describe it." Her professors included C. S. Lewis and J. R. R. Tolkien, both of whom were busy writing fantasy novels in their spare time. Cooper wrote too, but her energies at the time were channeled into journalism. She began reporting stories for Oxford's student newspaper, *Cherwell,* and eventually became the newspaper's first female editor. Cooper's Oxford years were happy ones that confirmed her interests in writing and literature. In her essay, the author wrote: "On the last day of my last term,

I wrote a long elegiac piece about the end of a life at Oxford, and had the temerity to send it to the London *Times.* They published it, every word, and for a while I thought this was an immensely good omen; after all how could I earn my living as a writer except by writing for a newspaper? And where else should I go for a job but to the top?"

Unfortunately, London's top newspapers did not often hire people right out of college. Journalists were expected to train for several years at smaller newspapers in the provinces. Cooper did not want to do this. She liked London and felt she had the talent to work for one of the city's papers.

Soon after graduating, Cooper landed a short-term position with London's *Sunday Express,* filling in for reporters who were on summer vacation. At one point the *Express* sent her to get a story on newlyweds Arthur Miller and Marilyn Monroe, who were trying to avoid their celebrity status by hiding in a well-protected private home. When Cooper arrived at the house she found it surrounded by a high, glass-topped wall. The only gate was staffed by a policeman who had been directed to keep reporters away. Cooper could not get her story. When she returned to the *Express* office empty-handed, she was scolded for not having tried to scale the wall! She was "released" the following week.

Another opportunity arose for the young writer shortly after. The editor of the London *Sunday Times* invited Cooper to cover the annual National Rose Show. As she recalled it in her autobiographical piece, "I wandered among the glowing banks of flowers with names like Peace and Duet and Serenade, and the soft-spoken rose growers.... I drifted about, straining my ears, longing for one chance-heard line of the kind that can catch the attention of the casual newspaper reader. There was nothing. I was about to go home dejected, when beside me a little old lady whispered to one of the rose growers, 'How far apart should I keep my Passions?' The rose grower looked down at her gravely. 'Eighteen inches is a safe distance, madam,' he said. You can't invent an exchange like that. I used it happily."

The piece appeared in the *Sunday Times* and caught the eye of the paper's foreign manager, Ian Fleming. Fleming—who was also author of the "James Bond" novels—encouraged the *Sunday Times* editor to hire Cooper. Thus she began a seven-year association with the newspaper as a reporter and feature writer. One of her assignments was to write a regular column called "Mainly for Children" which allowed her to write about some of her favorite subjects: King Arthur, medieval castles, folklore, and trains. She never had to work for that small newspaper in the provinces after all.

"Journalism taught me some useful lessons," Cooper recalled in *SAAS*. "I learned how to tell the bones of a story in two hundred words or how to flesh it out in five thousand. I learned about all manner of subjects in hundreds of different parts of Britain; I met film stars and politicians and janitors and garbagemen. And like every journalist with a really insistent talent for writing, I learned the dissatisfaction that goes with the need for brevity, and I began to write books in my spare time."

"The Dark Is Rising" Series

In 1962 Cooper began—"almost by accident"—a novel for young adults. Prompted by a writing contest sponsored by an English publishing house, Cooper began to write a "family adventure story" about three youngsters on a holiday trip to Cornwall. The tale began as a realistic depiction of a seaside vacation, but then a strange thing happened. A tall, mysterious white-haired character named great-uncle Merry was introduced, and with him a whole world of supernatural and fantastic possibilities. Cooper forgot all about the writing contest and immersed herself in the story that would become *Over Sea, under Stone*.

In *Over Sea, under Stone*, the three Drew children—Simon, Jane, and Barney—find an old map in Cornwall and embark on a hunt for ancient treasure linked with King Arthur. With Great-Uncle Merry's help they find themselves searching for a mysterious chalice, but their search is impeded by sinister forces and strange, evil characters amongst the Cornish townspeople. The Drews come to realize that they are engaged in a centuries-old struggle between forces of ultimate good and evil, a struggle in which magic, myth, and history are all intertwined. "My subconscious mind, at any rate, knew very well what *Over Sea* was about," Cooper wrote in *SAAS*. "It, or I, had made myself a word of magical childhood possibilities to which, if I liked, I could return. In real life, childhood ends when we grow up, but I'd left a door open to this small world, in the way I'd ended the book." It was quite some time before Cooper realized that *Over Sea, under Stone* was not just a single volume, but the prelude to an adventure that would run through five full-length novels.

In the meantime, Cooper tried to find a publisher for the work. More than twenty publishing houses turned it down. Cooper was greatly disappointed, but she did not lose hope. She gave the manuscript to an acquaintance who worked for the publisher Jonathan Cape, asking for advice on how to improve it. The acquaintance read it, loved it, and recommended it to Cape. In her autobiographical essay, Cooper concluded: "The moral of this story may seem to be 'Have the Right Friends,' but I think it is really 'Be Persistent.'"

Soon after Cape accepted her manuscript, Cooper found that her real life took an unexpected turn. She was a successful journalist with a promising career writing fiction, and she had spent her whole life in England. At the age of twenty-seven, however, she married an American scientist with three

Three children find an ancient map and set out in search of the legendary Holy Grail in this 1965 novel, the first in Cooper's "The Dark Is Rising" series.

teenaged children. Cooper left behind job, family, friends and country, and moved to Massachusetts. The transition was very difficult, but gradually the author lessened her homesickness by writing pieces about America for her old employer, the *Sunday Times*.

By the mid-1960s, Cooper was busy raising two small children and writing books for adults. She finished one adult novel, which she called *The Camp*, but could not find a publisher. Her life then took another turn when she met and became friends with an American editor named Margaret K. McElderry. McElderry had overseen the American publication of *Over Sea, under Stone*. The editor/publisher informed Cooper that *The Camp* was really a *children's book;* once this fact was cleared up, McElderry's company released the novel as *Dawn of Fear*. A thinly-veiled autobiographical novel about World War II, Cooper's *Dawn of Fear* was the first of her works to win citations from the children's book services. Her confidence restored, the author began to contemplate future projects.

Again, almost by accident, Cooper began to think about *Over Sea, under Stone*—specifically the novel's ending. The author's ongoing fascination with the book's themes—and a vision of a young, magical boy in a snowy forest—led her back to her desk. Suddenly Cooper realized that *Over Sea, under Stone* was just a part of something larger, and she outlined a sequence of five books, each dealing with the struggle between the Light and the Dark. The second novel in the series, *The Dark Is Rising*, provided a title for the five-volume work.

In *The Dark Is Rising*, and its companion volumes *Greenwitch, The Grey King*, and *Silver on the Tree*, the Drew children are joined in their magical journey by Will Stanton, a descendent of the celebrated Old Ones, and by Bran, a strange Welsh boy with royal ancestry. The children are swept up in an adventure that takes them through time and pits them against enemies who are seeking to destroy the world. According to Dudley Brown Carlson in *Horn Book*, "One knows immediately which characters to cheer for; but whether their strength will be sufficient to overcome the enemy is in doubt until the very end."

Each of the five books took about a year to write (except for *Silver on the Tree*, which took two). As individual volumes appeared they were honored with awards both in America and abroad. "It was all quite marvelous, but it was all very public," Cooper recalled in *SAAS*. "I was no longer the

The Drew children and their companions confront evil forces that seek to destroy the world in this award-winning 1973 sequel to *Over Sea, under Stone*.

shadowy person at the typewriter, I was an *Author*. The sudden spotlight was unnerving.... It wasn't quite so easy to write as it had been before. I didn't have the wit to understand why."

Cooper was sure, however, of the value in fantasy literature for children. In a *Horn Book* essay, she wrote: "Fantasy, unlike real life, offers amazing adventures with no price tag; all you have to do is open a book. And afterwards, if one of its adventures does ever happen to overtake you, somewhere in your unconscious mind you will be equipped to endure or enjoy it.... Yes, we need outlets for the longing for mythic adventure, and we need mythic heroes."

As an author, Cooper relished the opportunity to create the fantasy, to be surprised herself where it led, and to get to know her fictitious "family" almost as well as her real husband and children. "I led a wonderfully peaceful life while I was writing the books of the 'Dark Is Rising' sequence," she noted in her autobiographical essay. "Once in a while I envy writers who have settled into the routine of a really long open-ended series; they work just as hard as the rest of us, but they have made themselves a lovely, if perilous, tranquility." When Cooper reached the final page of *Silver on the Tree*, she sat at her desk and cried. "I had just said good bye to my other family, with whom I had lived and struggled all these years, and I should never see them again," she wrote. "Yes, I should be able to meet my book people again as you do, by reading the books—just as I was always able to visit my parents, while they were alive, by crossing the Atlantic for a week or two, or three. But it's not

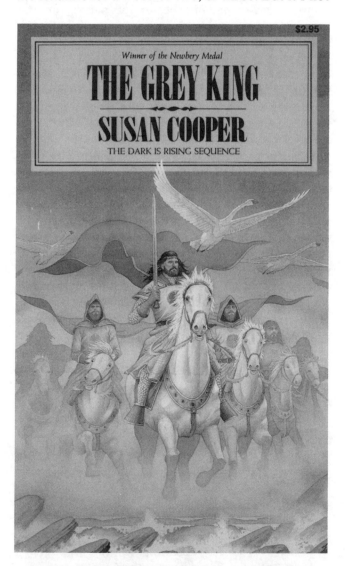

This 1975 fantasy novel—the fourth in a series about the Drew family and their time-traveling adventures—was awarded the Newbery Medal.

quite the same. Once you've left, you can't really go home again."

The Author at Work

The success of the "Dark Is Rising" series has enabled Cooper to pursue other, equally rewarding projects. While she was still at work on her fantasy novels, she met and became friends with Jessica Tandy and Hume Cronyn, well-known stage and film actors. Together Cooper and Hume Cronyn wrote a stage play called *Foxfire* that is based on the rugged life of Appalachian mountain folk. Cronyn and his wife Tandy starred in the production which eventually moved onto Broadway and from there onto television. In 1984, Cooper and Cronyn collaborated on the television adaptation of Harriet Arnow's novel *The Dollmaker*. Their script was filmed for ABC-TV with Jane Fonda in the starring role.

Writing plays gave Cooper a much-longed-for opportunity to work within the theater. Still, she did not neglect her fiction-writing. In 1983, coping with her parents' death and a divorce from her husband, she wrote *Seaward*, another fantasy for young adults, and a picture book called *Jethro and the Jumbie*. The picture book format appealed to her so much that in the mid-1980s she produced several more. Among these, *The Silver Cow* and *The Selkie Girl* are based on ancient folktales from Wales and Scotland, while *Matthew's Dragon* offers a simple tale of the friendship between a young boy and a dragon that escapes from one of his picture books.

In her *SAAS* essay, Cooper noted: "My friends in the world of children's literature say, from time to time, 'But when are you going to write another *real* book?' And I say, 'When it wants to be written.'" This is the author's recognition that fantasy cannot be forced, that it stems from dream and discovery and is as much a surprise for the writer as it is for the reader. "When working on a book which turns out to be a fantasy novel, I exist in a state of continual astonishment," Cooper wrote in *Celebrating Children's Books*. "The work begins with a deep breath and a blindly trusting step into the unknown; I know where I'm going, and who's going with me, but I have no real idea of what I shall find on the way, or whom I'll meet. Each time, I am striking out into a strange land, listening for the music that will tell me which way to go. And I am always overcome by wonder, and a kind of unfocused gratitude, when I arrive."

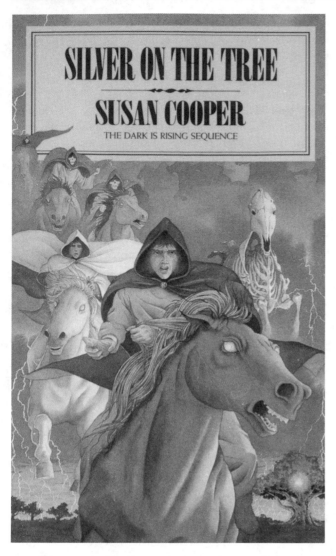

Cooper received her second Tir na N'og Award for this 1977 novel which concluded the five-volume "The Dark Is Rising" series.

In 1993 Cooper released a lighthearted fantasy novel called *The Boggart*. In that story, the Volnik family inherit an isolated Scottish castle filled with antiques—and inhabited by a mischievous boggart, a spirit that likes to play practical jokes. The boggart gets sent to Toronto inside an old desk and, released into a new, high-technology world, begins to wreak havoc in the lives of the two Volnik children. "The boggart is a fascinating character, sly, ingenious, and endearing—as long as he belongs to someone else," noted a *Horn Book* reviewer. The reviewer went on to commend Cooper's characters for their believability, concluding: "What is most admirable is Susan Cooper's seamless fusion of the newest technology and one of the oldest forms of wild magic."

Ideas and images for Cooper's stories come to her in dreams, or in waking reflections on a beautiful landscape, a childhood moment recalled in vivid detail, a wistful yearning for her home country and the people there. Fantasy, she wrote in *Horn Book*, appeals to the unconscious mind and draws its images from that "dark wonderland." Nevertheless, one of its recurring themes is concrete: the idea of a hero on an adventure. "All of us who write fantasy are creating, in one way or another, variations on a single theme," she noted. "We have a hero—or heroine—who has to cross the threshold from his familiar world into the unknown. In search of some person or thing or ideal, he has a series of adventures, undergoes trials, survives dangers and disasters, until he achieves his goal, his quest. And having achieved it, he comes home again a wiser person, better prepared for the longer journey which is now ahead of him, the adventure of living his life."

Life continues to be an adventure for Susan Cooper. She lives in Cambridge, Massachusetts but travels widely to visit schools and to give lectures on children's literature. Her own children and stepchildren are grown, giving her more time to devote to projects as diverse as fantasy novels, screenplays, and picture books. The author has said that she strives to retain that quality of childhood that enables boys and girls to "encounter delight" without skepticism. "The freshness of a child's vision of the world is what every artist strives to retain," she concluded in *Horn Book* "That's what we're all after, painters and poets and composers and the authors of certain kinds of books. If we can capture it, if we can make our audience catch its breath, create that great stillness that comes over a visible audience at moments of pure theater—if we can do that just a few times in our lives, then we've done what we were put here to do."

■ Works Cited

Review of *The Boggart, Horn Book*, May-June, 1993.

Carlson, Dudley Brown, "*A Second Look: Over Sea, under Stone*," *Horn Book*, October, 1976, pp. 522-523.

Cooper, Susan, "Nahum Tarune's Book," *Horn Book*, October, 1980.

Cooper, Susan, "Escaping into Ourselves," *Celebrating Children's Books: Essays on Children's Literature in Honor of Zena Sutherland*, edited by Betsy Hearne and Marilyn Kaye, Lothrop, 1981.

Cooper, Susan, autobiographical essay in *Something about the Author Autobiography Series,* Volume 6, Gale, 1988, pp. 67-85.

Cooper, Susan, essay in *Speaking for Ourselves,* National Council for Teachers of English, 1990, pp. 54-55.

Cooper, Susan, "Fantasy in the Real World," *Horn Book,* May-June, 1990, pp. 304-315.

McElderry, Margaret K., "Susan Cooper," *Horn Book,* August, 1976, pp. 367-372.

■ For More Information See

BOOKS

Children's Literature Review, Volume 4, Gale, pp. 41-49.

Roginski, Jim, editor, *Newbery and Caldecott Medalists and Honor Book Winners,* Libraries Unlimited, 1982.

PERIODICALS

New York Times Book Review, May 5, 1974; November 10, 1991.

Times Literary Supplement, December 5, 1975; March 29, 1985.

—*Sketch by Anne Janette Johnson*

Stephen Hawking

California Institute of Technology, 1974-75. *Member:* Royal Society of London (fellow), Pontifical Academy of Sciences, American Academy of Arts and Sciences, American Philosophical Society, Royal Astronomical Society of Canada (honorary member).

■ Personal

Full name, Stephen William Hawking; has also written under the name S. W. Hawking; born January 8, 1942; son of Frank (a research biologist) and E. Isobel (a secretary) Hawking; married Jane Wilde (a linguist), 1965; children: Robert, Lucy, Timothy. *Education:* Oxford University, B.A., 1962; Cambridge University, Ph.D., 1966.

■ Addresses

Office—Department of Applied Mathematics and Theoretical Physics, Cambridge University, Silver St., Cambridge CB3 9EW, England.

■ Career

Theoretical physicist. Cambridge University, Cambridge, England, research fellow at Gonville and Caius College, 1965-69, member of Institute of Theoretical Astronomy, 1968-72, research assistant at Institute of Astronomy, 1972-73, research assistant in department of applied mathematics and theoretical physics, 1973-75, reader in gravitational physics, 1977-79, Lucasian Professor of Mathematics, 1979—. Fairchild Distinguished Scholar at

■ Awards, Honors

Eddington Medal, Royal Astronomical Society, 1975; Pius IX Gold Medal, Pontifical Academy of Sciences, 1975; Dannie Heinemann Prize for mathematical physics, American Physical Society and American Institute of Physics, 1976; William Hopkins Prize, Cambridge Philosophical Society, 1976; Maxwell Medal, Institute of Physics, 1976; Hughes Medal, Royal Society of London, 1976; honorary fellow of University College, Oxford, 1977; Albert Einstein Award, Lewis and Rosa Strauss Memorial Fund, 1978; Albert Einstein Medal, Albert Einstein Society (Berne), 1979; Franklin Medal, Franklin Institute, 1981; Commander of the British Empire, 1982; honorary fellow of Trinity Hall, Cambridge, 1984; Royal Astronomical Society Gold Medal, 1985; Paul Dirac Medal and Prize, Institute of Physics, 1987; Wolf Foundation Prize for physics, 1988; named a Companion of Honour on the Queen's Birthday Honours List, 1989. Honorary degrees from various universities, including Oxford, 1978; Chicago, 1981; Leicester, Notre Dame, and Princeton, 1982; Newcastle and Leeds, 1987; and Tufts, Yale, and Cambridge, 1989.

■ Writings

A Brief History of Time: From the Big Bang to Black Holes, introduction by Carl Sagan, Bantam Books, 1988.

Black Holes and Baby Universes and Other Essays, Bantam Books, 1993.

ACADEMIC WRITINGS UNDER NAME S. W. HAWKING

(With G.F.R. Ellis) *The Large Scale Structure of Space-Time,* Cambridge University Press, 1973.

(Editor with Werner Israel) *General Relativity: An Einstein Centenary Survey,* Cambridge University Press, 1979.

Is the End in Sight for Theoretical Physics? An Inaugural Lecture, Cambridge University Press, 1980.

(Editor with M. Rocek) *Superspace and Supergravity: Proceedings of the Nuffield Workshop, Cambridge, June 16-July 12, 1980,* Cambridge University Press, 1981.

(Editor with G.W. Gibbons and S.T.C. Siklos) *The Very Early Universe: Proceedings of the Nuffield Workshop, Cambridge, 21 June to 9 July 1982,* Cambridge University Press, 1983.

(Editor with G.W. Gibbons and P.K. Townsend) *Supersymmetry and Its Applications: Superstrings, Anomalies, and Supergravity: Proceedings of a Workshop Supported by the Ralph Smith and Nuffield Foundations, Cambridge, 23 June to 14 July 1985,* Cambridge University Press, 1986.

(Editor with Werner Israel) *Three Hundred Years of Gravitation,* Cambridge University Press, 1987.

(Editor with G.W. Gibbons and T. Vachaspati) *The Formation and Evolution of Cosmic Strings; Proceedings of a Workshop supported by the SERC and held in Cambridge, 3-7 July, 1989,* Cambridge University Press, 1990.

OTHER

Author and editor of many articles for scientific journals. *A Brief History of Time: From the Big Bang to Black Holes* has been translated into over thirty languages.

■ Adaptations

Errol Morris directed a film version of *A Brief History of Time* for Anglia Television, 1991; *Black Holes and Baby Universes and Other Essays,* read by Simon Prebble, was adapted for audio cassette, Bantam, 1993.

■ Sidelights

"Where did the universe come from, and where is it going? Did the universe have a beginning, and if so, what happened *before* then? What is the nature of time? Will it ever come to an end?" These are the questions that absorb physicist Stephen Hawking, questions posed in his best-selling book, *A Brief History of Time.* Queries such as these drive the scientist towards his goal of helping to create a "Theory of Everything" (known to physicists as "TOE," or the "Grand Unification Theory," or "GUT"). Hawking believes that such an all-encompassing explanation may be worked out within the lifetime of many of his readers.

Hawking's parents decided that their child should be born in Oxford (largely because, during World War II, the British had an agreement with the Germans; they wouldn't bomb Heidelberg and Göttingen, and the Germans wouldn't bomb Oxford and Cambridge). After Hawking's birth, his family moved back to Highgate, the northern suburb of London they had left. Hawking was born, as he often likes to say, "exactly three hundred years after the death of Galileo," on January 8, 1942. As he writes in *Black Holes and Baby Universes,* "I estimate that about two hundred thousand other babies were also born that day. I don't know whether any of them were later interested in astronomy." Yet what some might call a portentous incident did take place shortly before Hawking's birth: his mother purchased an astronomical atlas.

The picture of Hawking as a lively, complex youngster emerges from memories of his family members and himself. The makers of the film version of *A Brief History of Time* interviewed Hawking's mother, siblings, school friends, and colleagues. Gene Stone compiled these interviews in *Stephen's Hawking's A Brief History of Time: A Reader's Companion (RC).* In *RC,* Isobel Hawking remembers a somewhat strange event from her son's childhood. She says that Hawking had "an imaginary house which he used to tell me was in a place called Drane. He used to have a tendency to try to leap onto buses to go there." On one occasion, the family visited Kenwood House in Hampstead Heath—the true location, according to young Hawking, of his imaginary home.

Hawking had two sisters—Mary, who was eighteen months younger, and Philippa, who was five years younger; Hawking's brother Edward was born when the physicist was fourteen. Mary jokingly recalls in *RC* that Hawking knew "eleven ways of getting into the house"—but then, she adds, "he was a much better climber." Apart from a strong interest in model trains, Hawking also loved games. Mary claims she stopped playing games with her brother when he was twelve. Around that age, he had begun to take his playtime "terribly seriously." He had adapted the Monopoly board to include railways and, tiring of that, he invented a game called "Dynasty" (which his mother and sister agree was horrible). In *Black Holes and Baby Universes*, Hawking writes that he invented many involved games with a school friend, Roger Ferneyhough. Dynasty was "a feudal game, in which each player was a whole dynasty, with a family tree." His mother called it "almost a substitute for living," in *RC*, but adds that "as much as anything it was the complication of it that appealed to him."

Like many future scientists and engineers, Hawking liked to take things apart to see how they worked (he was not fond, however, of putting them back together). He often built model airplanes and boats with a friend, John McClenahan. "I didn't care what they looked like," he writes in *Black Holes and Baby Universes*, "My aim was always to build working models that I could control." In 1957 or 1958, his mother tells Stone, Hawking and a group of friends built a computer: "We all went to see it at the school, where it was quite a sensation. As long as you asked the right questions, you quite likely got the right answers."

Hawking's father was a research biologist who took yearly trips to Africa to study his specialty, tropical medicine. Shortly after the family moved to St. Albans, the senior Hawking's trip was extended to four months, so his mother took the children to stay with a friend who was married to the poet Robert Graves. The couple lived in Majorca, a Spanish island in the Mediterranean. While living with the Graves, Hawking was tutored by a protege of professor Graves who assigned the children a chapter of the Bible to read each day. Hawking credits that experience with teaching him "not to begin a sentence with *And*," he recalls in *Black Holes and Baby Universes*.

Bet on the Future

Though Hawking was always recognized as being bright, he didn't learn to read until he was eight years old, and he didn't perform very well at school. His mother remembers her son's first year at St. Albans School (about the third grade in American public schools), when he ranked third from the bottom of the class. Hawking's parents

had just moved the family to St. Albans, so that young Hawking could eventually attend Westminster, a famous London school. (He was ill, however, when the entrance examinations were given, so he attended the less prestigious St. Albans). Hawking writes in *Black Holes and Baby Universes* that his "education there was as good as, if not better than, that I would have had at Westminster."

Whether Hawking had the childhood potential for a bright future seems to have been a point of contention among some of his friends. As he recounts with his typical wit in *Black Holes and Baby Universes:* "When I was twelve, one of my friends bet another friend a bag of sweets that I would never come to anything. I don't know if this bet was ever settled and, if so, which way it was decided." Two of these friends eventually exposed themselves as the bettors to Stone—Basil King, who believes he is entitled to a bag of sweets, and John McClenahan.

In 1962, Hawking graduated from Oxford University with First Class Honors.

Hawking made it to University College, Oxford, when he was seventeen years old. He wanted to study mathematics and physics. His father, on the other hand, wanted him to go into biology (the senior Hawking felt that teaching would be the only opportunity in his son's future if he studied math). So Hawking compromised, taking chemistry in addition to physics. In *Black Holes and Baby Universes*, Hawking notes that, though he is now a professor of mathematics, he had no "formal instruction in mathematics since I left St. Albans school. . . . I have had to pick up what mathematics I know as I went along." The problem with biology, Hawking felt, was that it was not an exact enough science, like physics or math. Besides, he writes in *Black Holes and Baby Universes*, "it also had a rather low status at school. The brightest boys did mathematics and physics; the less bright did biology."

Hawking estimates he did about one thousand hours of work during his three years at Oxford, "an average of an hour a day," he tells Stone. "I'm not proud of this lack of work, I'm just describing my attitude at the time, which I shared with most of my fellow students: an attitude of complete boredom and feeling that nothing was worth making an effort for." He didn't have many friends his first year or so; many of his classmates were older, having done national service before college. By his third year, though, Hawking was experiencing his happiest time at Oxford, discussing ideas and partying with friends and rowing for the boat club.

When it came time to choose an academic specialty, Hawking was sure it would be physics, but his interests within physics lay in cosmology and elementary particles—the very large and the very small. He finally decided on cosmology, since that field was governed by Einstein's "General Theory of Relativity" (there was no comparable theory in elementary particles). Eventually, Hawking would pull these interests together again with his renowned theory about black holes.

Along with choosing his specialty came the sticky business of where to pursue that specialty. At Oxford, the program of study was set up so that the only examination was at the end of a student's three years of study. Hawking did not do well on his test, scoring on the borderline between a first and second class degree. This put him in the unenviable position of having to undergo an interview with the examiners so that they could decide which he should get. At one point in the interview, Hawking says in *Black Holes and Baby Universes*, "they asked my about my future plans. I replied

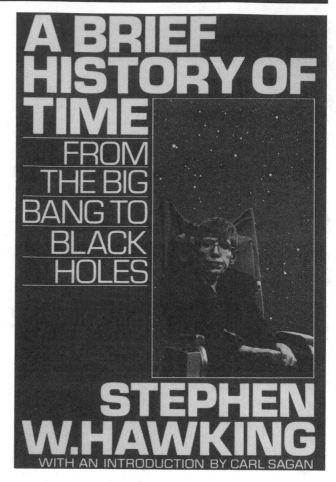

In his popular 1988 work, Hawking explores the mysteries of the universe and the nature of time.

that I wanted to do research. If they gave me a first, I would go to Cambridge. If I only got a second, I would stay in Oxford. They gave me a first."

Adversity Leads to a Reprieve

Having earned his bachelor's degree from Oxford, Hawking went on to Cambridge to study for his doctorate. He took a break, however, to visit Iran with a friend. His mother recalls for Stone that while Hawking was there, a severe earthquake struck between Tehran and Tabriz. At the time, Hawking was riding a bus to Tabriz. Apparently the ride was so bumpy that neither he nor his friend noticed the earthquake, and no one told them it had occurred. Hawking's family waited anxiously for three weeks to hear from him. "He had been ill well before" the trip, his mother recalls, but "when he finally came home he looked very much worse for wear."

During his last year at Oxford, Hawking remembers in *Black Holes and Baby Universes*, "I seemed to be getting clumsier, and I fell over once or twice for no apparent reason." While he was at Cambridge, his mother noticed his problems, and the family ended up at a specialist who put Hawking in the hospital for tests. He remembers: "They took a muscle sample from my arm, stuck electrodes into me, injected some radio-opaque fluid into my spine, and watched it going up and down with X-rays as they tilted the bed." The diagnosis was amyotrophic lateral sclerosis (ALS) or motor neuron disease, known in the United States as Lou Gehrig's disease (named after the New York Yankee player who died of the illness in 1941).

Hawking was given two and one-half years to live. He gradually lost the use of his body as it deteriorated. The long-term prognosis was grim: eventually, only his lungs and heart would work. His brain, however, would be totally unaffected to the end. At first, Hawking was extremely depressed. He spent a lot of time listening to classical music by Richard Wagner, a longtime family favorite, and sitting in his room. "But," he asserts in *Black Holes*

Because Hawking has lost his ability to speak, visitors to his office sit beside him and read his responses from a computer screen.

and Baby Universes, "reports in magazine articles that I drank heavily are an exaggeration." He also remembers having troubling dreams at that time. A couple of them made a tremendous impact on his outlook: "I dreamt that I was going to be executed. I suddenly realized that there were a lot of worthwhile things I could do if I were reprieved. Another dream that I had several times was that I would sacrifice my life to save others."

Just before being diagnosed, Hawking met Jane Wilde at a New Year's party. The two fell in love and got engaged. The scientist told Kitty Ferguson in *Stephen Hawking: Quest for a Theory of Everything* that "the engagement changed my life. It gave me something to live for. It made me determined to live. Without the help that Jane has given I would not have been able to carry on, nor would I have had the will to do so." After an engagement during which they commuted between London and Cambridge, the couple was married in July 1965 after Hawking won his fellowship to work at Gonville and Caius College at Cambridge. They eventually found a house conveniently located near the Department of Applied Mathematics and Theoretical Physics where Hawking would work. He lived by himself during the week, and Jane commuted on weekends to Cambridge until she finished her degree. Over the years, the Hawkings had three children—Robert, born in 1967; Lucy, born in 1970; and Timothy, born in 1979.

Hawking soon found that he needed a wheelchair to get around; he also required nursing care around the clock. When he contracted pneumonia in 1985, an operation was necessary to save his life; it also removed his voice. A computer programmer in California sent Hawking a program called Equalizer, which, Hawking says "allowed me to select words from a series of menus on the screen, by pressing a switch with my hand." When he has completed his statement, the computer attached to his wheelchair sends it to a speech synthesizer. "The only problem," says Hawking, "is that it gives me an American accent."

Black Holes

Before his impending marriage, Hawking realized he needed to finish his doctorate and get a job. He looked for a thesis topic. In Ferguson's *Stephen Hawking: Quest for a Theory of Everything*, Hawking says, "I started working hard for the first time in my life. To my surprise, I found I liked it. Maybe it is not really fair to call it work." His imagination was caught after reading Roger Penrose's ideas

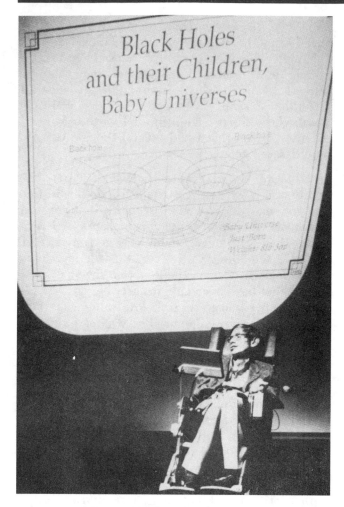

Using visual aids, Hawking presents a lecture on baby universes at Boston's Northeastern University.

about collapsing stars that turn into black holes, or singularities (tiny but incredibly dense points of mass in spacetime from which not even light can escape due to the immense gravitational pull). Hawking asked: if stars gradually burn out and collapse under their own gravity into singularities, what happens if one looks back in time, to the beginning of the universe? What if the universe began as a singularity and then exploded in what is called the Big Bang?

Hawking worked with Penrose to prove that there must be a singularity in spacetime if general relativity is correct and the universe contains as much matter as scientists have observed. This bit of information was not completely well received. Hawking says in *A Brief History of Time* that the opposition was "partly from the Russians because of their Marxist belief in scientific determinism [the idea that everything in the universe can be predicted], and partly from people who felt that the whole idea of singularities was repugnant and

spoiled the beauty of Einstein's theory." Now, Hawking's theory is generally accepted; as he put it, "one cannot really argue with a mathematical theorem."

Hawking Radiation

By the 1970s Hawking's work led him to study elementary particles in more depth, to see how they might contribute to an understanding of the cosmos. That study is now known as quantum mechanics, or the scientific theories dealing with the behavior of very small particles, such as photons and electrons, which make up larger particles, such as atoms. The basic rule of quantum mechanics is the uncertainty principle, formulated by the German physicist Werner Heisenberg. The uncertainty principle showed that some things in the universe just can't be predicted—in particular, the behavior of small particles. Heisenberg found, and many researchers have since confirmed, that one can never know both the position and speed, or velocity, of a particle. Scientists can measure one, but not the other. Hawking explains why in *Black Holes and Baby Universes:* "You had to use at least one packet, or quantum [of light] to try to measure the position of a particle. This packet of light would disturb the particle and cause it to move at a speed in some direction. The more accurately you wanted to measure the position of the particle, the greater the energy of the packet you would have to use and thus the more it would disturb the particle." The best scientists can do with these particles is to predict for them to be in a number of possible "quantum states" along the spacetime continuum.

In 1973, Hawking discovered that black holes appear to emit particles. In *A Brief History of Time,* he writes that he was surprised and annoyed, but every time he redid the calculations, he came up with the same result. Knowing that nothing can escape from a black hole, Hawking theorized that what must be happening is that the particles come from the space just outside the event horizon (the boundary of a black hole).

At first, Hawking told only a few close colleagues about his discovery. In *RC*, he remembers Roger Penrose calling him about it on his birthday. Penrose "was very excited and he went on so long that my dinner was quite cold. It was a great pity, because it was goose, which I'm very fond of." When Hawking presented his results to an audience at the Rutherford-Appleton Laboratory near Oxford, "people were flabbergasted. I remember someone getting up and saying, 'You must be wrong, Stephen. I don't believe a word of it'."

But physicists around the world began checking Hawking's findings on their own and, when they reached the same conclusions, they agreed he was correct. Hawking tells Stone that "Einstein never accepted quantum mechanics, because of its element of chance and uncertainty. He said, 'God does not play dice.' It seems that Einstein was doubly wrong. The quantum effects of black holes suggest that not only does God play dice, he sometimes throws them where they cannot be seen."

On God

Hawking is not known as a particularly religious man. He once commented on a BBC broadcast, *Master of the Universe: Stephen Hawking*, that "we are such insignificant creatures on a minor planet of a very average star in the outer suburbs of one of a hundred thousand million galaxies. So it is difficult to believe in a God that would care about us or even notice our existence." Yet the name comes up somewhat often in Hawking's writings and interviews. Tensions between science and the Roman Catholic church go back to Galileo's time. One of Hawking's experiences illustrates one reason why. He attended a cosmology conference at the Vatican in 1981 and gave a paper called, "The Boundary Conditions of the Universe," in which he proposed that space and time in the universe were similar to the earth's surface—finite in area but without boundaries or edges. Pope John Paul II granted the conference participants an audience. In his interview for Stone, Hawking recalls that the Pope "told us that it was all right to study the evolution of the universe after the big bang, but we should not inquire into the big bang itself because that was the moment of creation and therefore the work of God." He continues, "I was glad then that he did not know that subject of the talk I had just given at the conference was the possibility that space-time was finite but had no boundary, which means that it had no beginning, no moment of creation."

Hawking has made a number of provocative comments about the impact the current state of physics might have on the existence of God. In the chapter called "The Origin and Fate of the Universe" in *A Brief History of Time*, Hawking theorizes that "if the universe is really completely self-contained, having no boundary or edge, it would have neither beginning nor end: it would simply be. What place,

then, for a creator?" Some of the physicist's most well-known queries conclude the book: "Why does the universe go to all the bother of existing? Is the unified theory so compelling that it brings about its own existence? Or does it need a creator, and, if so, does he have any other effect on the universe? And who created him?" Hawking continues that if a unified theory is found, everyone will "be able to take part in the discussion of the question of why it is that we and the universe exist. If we find the answer to that, it would be the ultimate triumph of human reason—for then we would know the mind of God."

Michael D. Lemonick, writing in *Time*, notes that many *Brief History* readers have the impression that Hawking is trying to disprove the existence of God. Hawking responds, "You don't need to appeal to God to set the initial conditions for the universe, but that doesn't prove there is no God—only that he acts through the laws of physics."

Hawking mixes scientific and autobiographical essays in this 1993 work.

In this photo taken during the 1980s, Hawking and his wife Jane spend some quiet moments with their children, Robert, Timothy and Lucy.

A Brief History of Time

Though *A Brief History of Time* is certainly Hawking's most popular book, it was not his first. *The Large Scale Structure of Space-Time*, co-written with G.F.R. Ellis, deals with classical cosmological theory and is filled with equations. But Hawking wanted to write a book that would be sold at airport newsstands. He chose to submit his manuscript to Bantam, a publisher specializing in popular books, because "I wanted to explain how far I felt we had come in our understanding of the universe: how we might be near finding a complete theory that would describe the universe and everything in it.... I wanted it to get to as many people as possible," he writes in *Black Holes and Baby Universes*. Toward that end, his editor advised him that every equation he put in the book would halve the sales. Hawking managed with only $E=mc^2$.

In *A Brief History of Time*, Hawking gives an overview of the history of physics, relying heavily on pictorial diagrams and examples using everyday objects and ideas to explain the nature of space-time and imaginary time (which Hawking now wishes he had explained more thoroughly), general relativity, the uncertainty principle and elementary particles, black holes, the origin and possible future of the universe. In the process, he discusses his own theories and ideas on black holes, Hawking Radiation, the Big Bang, and the still elusive "Theory of Everything."

Jeremy Bernstein, writing in the *New Yorker*, compares *A Brief History of Time* to Steven Weinberg's *The First Three Minutes*. One problem in the book, he says, is some inaccuracy in Hawking's account of physicist George Gamow's work—Gamow's 1948 paper was on "The Origin of Chemical Elements," not microwave radiation. But Bernstein also points out that "very few active scientists ... actually take the trouble to read the papers of their early predecessors. A kind of folklore builds up which bears only a tangential relationship to reality." Martin Gardner spots a couple of other historical errors in the *New York Review of Books:* 1. That Newton believed in absolute time, not absolute space, and 2. That it was not Berkeley who believed that "'all material objects ... are an illusion'." In an aside, Gardner considers "The Origin and Fate of the Universe" chapter "the book's centerpiece."

Taking the book as a whole, Jeffrey Marsh of *Commentary* calls it "a concise, firsthand account of current scientific thinking," and A.J. Ayer, in the *London Review of Books*, writes that "Hawking gives a more lucid account than any that has yet come my way" of the complicated world of modern physics.

When producer Gordon Freeman and Hawking decided to make a film of *A Brief History of Time*, they went to Steven Spielberg for financing assistance. Errol Morris would direct, Gerald Peary would write the film, and Hawking would contribute to the narrative of the film and helped edit the final product. The movie was filmed in a studio made to resemble Hawking's office in Cambridge. Writer Peary interviewed director Morris for *Interview*. When asked if Hawking didn't like anything in the film, Morris replied that "he was always opposed to the chicken at the very beginning of the movie." Asked what brought Hawking the "most immediate pleasure" about the film, "he thanked me for making his mother into a movie star."

In a review of the film, *Time*'s Richard Schickel sees the "bottom line" as: "The real world and the theoretical universe of a physicist are explored with simplicity and elegance." The film is a series of short scenes focussing on Hawking, family members, Hawking, colleagues, old friends, Hawking—all having to do with Hawking's life and work in physics. Schickel writes that in watching the film "one begins to perceive a powerful analogy between Hawking's condition and the thrust of his thought. His disease seems to have affected him much as loss of energy affects a failing star."

All the reviews are not yet in for Hawking's latest book, *Black Holes and Baby Universes*, but critics who complained that the author did not reveal enough of himself in *A Brief History of Time* will not be disappointed. The first three essays in the book are autobiographical. The last chapter is a transcript of Hawking's appearance on BBC's *Desert Island Discs* program in 1992. And in between are more essays on cosmology and quantum mechanics. A reviewer in *Publishers Weekly* writes that Hawking "sheds light" on his personal life, and his "mind sparks in" the scientific essays that comprise the rest of the book. Michael D. Lemonick, writing in *Time,* quotes Hawking's answer to the question, "Why, when his days are already overcrowded with scientific meetings, lecture tours and the occasional sit-down with disabled kids, did he take the time to write a new book? 'I had to pay for my nurses.'"

"The uncertainty principle won't help you now, Stephen," asserts Einstein as he calls Hawking's bet. "Wrong again, Albert," smiles Hawking as he reveals the winning poker hand. Hawking, along with "Isaac Newton" and "Albert Einstein," made one of his most recent and popular public appearances on the television series *Star Trek: The Next Generation* in 1993. Since *A Brief History of Time* appeared in 1988, in fact, Hawking has had to deal as much with being famous as with his career. For example, coverage of an accident in which he was hit by a car and required thirteen stitches became a media event. Owners of a Chicago tavern start a "Stephen Hawking" fan club. Finally, although—and perhaps because—Hawking likes to forget about his illness, he has become a symbol of inspiration for many and spends time giving talks for the disabled.

Physicist Bernard Carr, who has known Hawking since graduate school, tells a story in *RC* about an incident that occurred while he and Hawking were at the California Institute of Technology in 1974. Hawking was visiting for a year as Sherman Fairchild Distinguished Scholar. One day, Carr says, the two were having a "discussion over lunch on the nature of fame, and [Hawking] came up with the definition that fame is when more people know you than you know. After lunch we were going back to the department when this guy walked past and said, 'Hi.' I had no idea who the guy was, so I said, 'Stephen, who was that?' Stephen looked at me—he could still speak then—and he said, 'That was fame.'"

■ Works Cited

Bernstein, Jeremy, "Cosmology," *New Yorker*, June 6, 1988, p. 117.

Review of *Black Holes and Baby Universes and Other Essays*, *Publishers Weekly*, November 1, 1993, p. 33.

Ferguson, Kitty, *Stephen Hawking: Quest for a Theory of Everything*, Bantam, 1992.

Gardner, Martin, "The Ultimate Turtle," *New York Review of Books*, June 16, 1988: 17.

Hawking, Stephen, *Black Holes and Baby Universes and Other Essays*, Bantam, 1993.

Peary, Gerald, interview with Errol Morris, *Interview*, September 1992: 126, 140.

Lemonick, Michael D., "Hawking Gets Personal," *Time*, September 27, 1993: 80.

Schickel, Richard, "The Thrust of His Thought," *Time*, August 31, 1992.

Stone, Gene, *Stephen Hawking's a Brief History of Time: A Reader's Companion*, Bantam, 1992.

■ For More Information See

BOOKS

White, Michael, and John Gribbin, *Stephen Hawking: A Life in Science*, Dutton, 1992.

PERIODICALS

Forbes, March 23, 1987, p. 142.

New Statesman & Society, June 24, 1988, p. 39.

Newsweek, June 13, 1988, p. 56.

People, September 11, 1989, p. 11.

Time, February 8, 1988, p. 58.

—Sketch by Helene Henderson

Mollie Hunter

Personal

Full name, Maureen Mollie Hunter McIlwraith; born June 30, 1922, in Longniddry, East Lothian, Scotland; daughter of William George (a motor mechanic) and Helen Eliza Smeaton (a confectioner; maiden name, Waitt) McVeigh; married Thomas "Michael" McIlwraith (a hospital catering manager), December 23, 1940; children: Quentin Wright, Brian George. *Education:* Attended Preston Lodge School, East Lothian, Scotland. *Politics:* Scottish Nationalist. *Religion:* Episcopalian. *Hobbies and other interests:* Theatre, music, physical exercise, traveling to new places. "Like dogs (useful ones only) and places without people. Company preferred—children."

Addresses

Home—"The Shieling," Milton, near Drumnadrochit, Inverness-shire 1V3 6UA, Scotland. *Agent*—A.M. Heath & Co. Ltd., 79 St. Martin's Ln., London WC2N 4AA, England; McIntosh & Otis, Inc., 475 Fifth Ave., New York, NY 10017.

Career

Writer, 1953—. May Hill Arbuthnot Lecturer in the United States, 1975, and in 1976 toured New Zealand and Australia lecturing under the joint auspices of the British Council, the International Reading Association, and the education authorities for New Zealand and Australia; Dalhousie University, Halifax, Nova Scotia, writer-in-residence, 1980, 1981; 29th Anne Carroll Moore Spring Lecturer, 1986; Aberlour Summer School for Gifted Children, teacher of creative writing, 1987, 1988; organized and taught in writer's workshops for both adults and children. *Wartime service:* Performed volunteer services in a Serviceman's canteen during World War II. *Member:* Society of Authors (past chairman, Society of Authors in Scotland).

Awards, Honors

Child Study Association of America's Children's Books of the Year citations, 1968, for *The Ferlie*, 1970, for *The Walking Stones*, 1971, for *The Thirteenth Member*, 1972, for *A Sound of Chariots* and *The Haunted Mountain*, 1974, for *The Stronghold*, 1975, for *A Stranger Came Ashore*, 1976, for *Talent Is Not Enough*, 1977, for *A Furl of Fairy Wind*, and 1987, for *Cat, Herself; Book World's* Children's Spring Book Festival honor book citation, 1970, for *The Lothian Run; New York Times* Outstanding Book of the Year citations, 1972, for *The Haunted Mountain* and *A Sound of Chariots*, and 1975, for *A Stranger Came Ashore;* Children's Book Award, Child Study Association of America,

1973, for *A Sound of Chariots*; Scottish Arts Council Award, 1973, for *The Haunted Mountain*; Carnegie Medal for Children's Book of Outstanding Merit, British Library Association, 1974, and Silver Pencil Award (Holland), 1975, both for *The Stronghold*; *School Library Journal* Best Children's Book citation, 1975, and *Boston Globe-Horn Book* Award Honor Book, 1976, both for *A Stranger Came Ashore*; *School Library Journal* Best Book for Spring citation, and Scottish Arts Council Award Book, both 1977, both for *The Wicked One*; New York Public Library Books for the Teen Age citation, and Notable Children's Trade Book in the Field of Social Studies, National Council of Social Studies and Children's Book Council, both 1982, both for *You Never Knew Her as I Did!*; American Library Association Best Books for Young Adults citation, and *School Library Journal* Best Books for Young Adults citation, both 1986, both for *Cat, Herself*.

■ **Writings**

JUVENILE FANTASY NOVELS

Patrick Kentigern Keenan, illustrated by Charles Keeping, Blackie & Son, 1963, published in United States as *The Smartest Man in Ireland*, Funk, 1965.

The Kelpie's Pearls, illustrated by Keeping, Blackie & Son, 1964, illustrated by Joseph Cellini, Funk, 1966.

Thomas and the Warlock, illustrated by Cellini, Funk, 1967, illustrated by Keeping, Blackie & Son, 1967.

The Ferlie, illustrated by Cellini, Funk, 1968, illustrated by Michal Morse, Blackie & Son, 1968, published as *The Enchanted Whistle*, illustrated by Morse, Methuen, 1985.

The Walking Stones: A Story of Suspense, illustrated by Trina Schart Hyman, Harper, 1970, published in England as *The Bodach*, illustrated by Gareth Floyd, Blackie & Son, 1970.

The Haunted Mountain: A Story of Suspense, illustrated by Laszlo Kubinyi, Harper, 1972, illustrated by Trevor Ridley, Hamish Hamilton, 1972.

A Stranger Came Ashore: A Story of Suspense, Harper, 1975.

The Wicked One: A Story of Suspense, Harper, 1977.

A Furl of Fairy Wind: Four Stories (includes "A Furl of Fairy Wind," "The Enchanted Boy," "The Brownie," and "Hi Johnny"; also see below), illustrated by Stephen Gammell, Harper, 1977.

The Knight of the Golden Plain (also see below), illustrated by Marc Simont, Harper, 1983.

The Three-Day Enchantment (sequel to *The Knight of the Golden Plain*; also see below), illustrated by Simont, Harper, 1985.

The Brownie, illustrated by Christopherson, Byway Books, 1986.

The Enchanted Boy, illustrated by Christopherson, Byway Books, 1986.

A Furl of Fairy Wind, illustrated by Christopherson, Byway Books, 1986.

The Mermaid Summer, Harper, 1988.

The Day of the Unicorn (sequel to *The Three-Day Enchantment*), Harper, 1994.

JUVENILE HISTORICAL NOVELS

Hi Johnny, illustrated by Drake Brookshaw, Evans, 1964, Funk, 1967, illustrated by M. Christopherson, Byway Books, 1986.

The Spanish Letters, illustrated by Elizabeth Grant, Evans, 1964, Funk, 1967.

A Pistol in Greenyards, illustrated by Grant, Evans, 1965, Funk, 1968.

The Ghosts of Glencoe, Evans, 1966, Funk, 1969.

The Lothian Run, Funk, 1970.

The Thirteenth Member: A Story of Suspense, Harper, 1971.

The Stronghold, Harper, 1974.

You Never Knew Her as I Did!, Harper, 1981, published as *Escape from Loch Leven*, Canongate (Edinburgh), 1987.

YOUNG ADULT NOVELS

A Sound of Chariots (also see below), Harper, 1972.

The Third Eye, Harper, 1979.

The Dragonfly Years (sequel to *A Sound of Chariots*), Hamish Hamilton, 1983, published in United States as *Hold on to Love*, Harper, 1984.

Cat, Herself, Harper, 1985, published in England as *I'll Go My Own Way*, Hamish Hamilton, 1985.

NONFICTION

Talent Is Not Enough: Mollie Hunter on Writing for Children, Harper, 1976.

Flora MacDonald and Bonnie Prince Charles (juvenile), Methuen, 1987.

The Pied Piper Syndrome, and Other Essays, Harper, 1991.

PLAYS

A Love-Song for My Lady (one-act; produced at Empire Theatre, Inverness, Scotland, 1961), Evans, 1962.

Stay for an Answer (one-act; produced at Empire Theatre, 1962), French, 1962.

OTHER

Contributor of articles to numerous newspapers and magazines, including *Scotsman* and *Glasgow Herald*; contributor to anthologies. Hunter's papers will eventually be housed in the collection of the National Library of Scotland.

■ Adaptations

A number of Hunter's books have been serialized on BBC-Radio programs, including *The Kelpie's Pearls*, *The Lothian Run*, and *The Enchanted Whistle*; *A Stranger Came Ashore* has been read in serial form on Swedish radio; the four stories in *A Furl of Fairy Wind* are published in cassette form in the United Kingdom; *The Walking Stones* and *The Wicked One* have been featured on Yorkshire TV's *Book Tower* program.

■ Work in Progress

Continuing research into Scottish history and folklore, with emphasis on Celtic folklore; a fantasy, and a picture story book.

■ Sidelights

"The idea of herself as a small flame stubbornly burning brought a smile to her face. The dragonfly years, she thought, all those past years of loosing her flight of big and bright ideas into the air and then trying to capture them all again on one small sheet of paper each time she sat down to write; those years hadn't really been wasted! They had been practice, instead, for shaping all the tales still moving in her mind, for making perfect the patterns of lovely words still stored there. And her flame now would at least be a clear one!"

Hunter (far left), who grew up in Scotland, is shown at age nine with her sisters and brother.

Mollie Hunter's flame burns as brightly as the spark of her adolescent heroine Bridie McShane in *The Dragonfly Years*. As a young child struggling to overcome her father's death, Hunter turned to writing. And several years later she relived this time of loss and discovery through the character of Bridie in *A Sound of Chariots* and its sequel *The Dragonfly Years*. In the meantime, however, Hunter's clear flame made her one of Scotland's most celebrated writers for children and young adults. Viewed as a storyteller in the traditional sense, Hunter portrays her native Scotland in both historic and modern times and often infuses her tales with elements of the supernatural. "Mollic Hunter is by general consent Scotland's most distinguished modern children's writer," maintains Peter Hollindale in *Children's Literature in Education*. And Patricia Dooley contends in the *Children's Literature Association Newsletter* that "in her books it is the highroad of story, carrying the reader back and forth between past and present, that is illuminated by Mollie Hunter's imagination."

Born in a small house in southeast Scotland in 1922, Hunter found herself the daughter of a strong ex-soldier and a gentle and lively storyteller. Along with her three sisters and one brother, Hunter inherited a flair for the dramatic, and the house often rang with their improvisations of the stories, songs, and poems told by their mother. Reading was another indoor enjoyment, as well as tales and plays created from the combined imaginations of all the McVeigh children. The majority of activity took place outside the house, though, in the village of Longniddry and in a part of the Scottish countryside so fertile that it's been known for centuries as "the garden of Scotland."

Ghosts of Past Generations

"The village street was our playground," remembers Hunter in an essay for *Something about the Author Autobiography Series* (SAAS), "especially in the long twilight that ends each summer day in our northern clime—'the gloaming,' as we call it—when we would play the kind of games that involved much running and chasing and hiding, along with ritual calling back and forth. From end to end of the village cries would echo, sounding thin and eerie in that mysterious half light which has always seemed to me to be the ghost of the day that has passed. And listening from whatever hiding place I had chosen for myself, I would sometimes have the strangest feeling that I was hearing the voices of ghost children calling, calling.... It was a feeling that could often send me into what we call a 'dwam,' a state of mind so much like a trance that the outside world seems barely to exist. Or even matter, supposing one did recall it."

This tendency to be easily distracted often caused Hunter problems, especially on the way to school; she was regularly late because she couldn't resist stopping at the smiddy's to watch him work. School itself was something she viewed as worthwhile only for the English language courses which enabled her to write essays and indulged her pleasure in the sounds and meanings of words. This love of language made Hunter a great talker, but she could also wander off alone and become silently enchanted with various parts of the natural world. "I had an instinctive sense of past generations, too, in my constantly-wondering gaze at the various ancient buildings dotting our rural landscape," explains Hunter in *SAAS*. There was always something within her that responded to old customs and beliefs. "Without my having the least awareness of what was happening, in fact, that childhood environment of mine was nurturing a whole range of feelings so essentially part of my nature that they were quite inevitably destined to become also an integral part of my writing," asserts Hunter in *SAAS*, adding: "But even so, what I did realise in those childhood years, was that I revelled, literally revelled, in being what I was then—partly a little country savage, but partly also an exalted dreamer finding total fulfillment in a world where (metaphorically speaking, at least) the sun always shone."

Loss Leads to Aspirations

The day the sun of Hunter's childhood stopped shining was the day her father died. Only nine years old at the time, Hunter later attempted to come to terms with her grief through her novel *A Sound of Chariots*. In this tale, Bridie McShane is also her father's special daughter and must deal with his death at the young age of nine. Through the loss of her father Bridie gains a sudden awareness of death and begins to see each passing minute as bringing her closer to her own end. Over the next four years, though, she comes to terms with the passing of time and begins writing as a means of expressing her emotions. By the end of the novel, Bridie has grown into an aware young woman on her way to maturity.

"*A Sound of Chariots* is a tough yet tender, humorous yet tragic, sometimes horrific yet always gentle and compassionate autobiographical (surely) novel," describes a *Times Literary Supplement*

Bridie McShane, the heroine of Hunter's semi-autobiographical 1972 novel, loses her father at age nine and comes to terms with her grief through her writing.

contributor. Geraldine DeLuca, writing in the *Lion and the Unicorn*, contends that *A Sound of Chariots* is "absolutely uncontrived" and "captures the mind of a young adolescent the way few adolescent novels do." And Eleanor Cameron concludes in the *New York Times Book Review*: "Whether it is a reliving or not, this is the most memorable of Miss Hunter's books, the distinguished account of a child's traumatic experiences and her struggle to gain the realization of selfhood."

Hunter's own loss and traumatic experience proved to be a turning point in her young life. "In all that I thought and did from then on, I realised, there was an even keener awareness of both myself and the world around me—so keen, sometimes, that I could hardly bear the experience," recalls Hunter in *SAAS*. "I began to take with me on my lonely expeditions a pencil and notebook—the notebook that held my previous attempts to express myself in some original form of words. And gradually, out of all this came one further realisation that embraced all the others. I was going to be a writer." Now that her goal was clear, Hunter had to face her first obstacle—getting a proper education. The Depression years, however, forced Hunter to leave school at the age of fourteen (the earliest age possible) and search for a job.

This too was not as simple as it appeared. When her daughter was unable to find a job locally, Hunter's mother eventually swallowed her pride and asked her Edinburgh family to take Hunter into their business. So began Hunter's routine that had her travelling to Edinburgh to work in one of her grandfather's flower shops six days a week. At the same time, she attended night school four nights a week and spent the other two studying and doing research at the National Library of Scotland. Night school eventually enabled Hunter to acquire a job in the Civil Service as a clerk, and her many hours at the library led to her first studies of magic, superstition, and folklore. And this course of study soon overlapped and flowed into the study of Hunter's own country—Scotland. "It was impossible for the library staff to guess, of course, that these two interests would remain with me lifelong," Hunter relates in *SAAS*. "And I've no doubt that they found it peculiar to see me sitting there night after night—myself so young and all the books I drew from the stacks concerned with matters so ancient!"

A Marriage of Poetry and Love

Despite these interests, though, poetry remained Hunter's writing love. At the same time, romantic love began to overwhelm her emotions, and near the beginning of her eighteenth year Hunter met the young man who became the great and true love of her life. This blissful courtship was cut short,

This 1959 photo shows Hunter with her husband, Thomas, and two sons, Quentin and Brian.

though, when Thomas was drafted into the Navy for World War II. At the end of his year of training, with ten days leave before sailing, he and Hunter got married. These years of war and separation found Hunter returning to her library studies and doing volunteer work in a canteen. And of course there were the occasional visits from her husband that never lasted long enough. "Separated again, we wrote constantly to one another," relates Hunter in *SAAS*. "Most of my writing during those years, in fact, was in my letters to him, most of the thoughts that would otherwise have been expressed in poetry went into those letters instead—although in the kind he wrote to me in return, I sometimes had the feeling that he was a better poet than I was!"

Once the war ended and her husband returned home to her, Hunter and he set about the business of building a family. After losing their first child the couple was told that there would be no more, and it took several years to prove the doctor wrong. In the time that passed before Hunter had her two sons she occupied herself with helping her husband further his career. "He was so much in sympathy with my writing urge, however, that he took the first chance he could to buy me a typewriter—a battered old thing, but still the only one he could lay hands on during those post-war years of machine scarcity," recounts Hunter in *SAAS*. "And it was his encouragement, too, that was responsible for my writing my first book."

After moving around a bit, Hunter found herself living in the north of Scotland in a mountainous region called the Highlands. She had resumed her historical research, was frequently having newspaper feature articles published, and was experimenting with the short story when her husband suggested she use all her knowledge to write a novel. Although she gaped at the idea at first, Hunter decided she had nothing to lose in utilizing her folklore knowledge to write a book. "There had been so many marvellous stories in the stuff I had read! The one that had always intrigued me most, also, was one that centered around a mystery of identity—and it was the possible solution of this mystery that had been the subject of the research findings I had published! I had been a great fool, I thought, not to have realised that I had already given myself the bones of a book by doing so; and straight away I sat down to my typewriter."

Favorite Stories Retold

Two years later Hunter had a very long novel which she then spent a year revising before making a few vain attempts to publish it. The manuscript was put away in a bureau, where it still lies to this day. These three years were not wasted, however, and Hunter discovered this through the help of her two sons. "Both out of doors and indoors, too, I entertained the boys as my mother had entertained me—with songs, poems, and stories, but especially with stories," explains Hunter in *SAAS*. "And, of course, they had favourites among the stories I made up for them, particularly those I wove around a boastful Irishman I had invented, and whom I called Patrick Kentigern Keenan. He had flashed complete in my head, this Patrick, on a day when my elder son was only a tiny baby." When this same son was ten years old, he asked Hunter why she didn't make a book out of the Patrick stories so he could read them for himself instead of waiting for her to tell them.

Once again, Hunter thought, why not? The one style of storytelling that had always fascinated her was the Celtic folktale and its poetic language. So, Hunter made a deal with her sons—she would write a part of the book every day if they would follow certain household rules. Both sides of the bargain were kept and Hunter sent the finished book, *Patrick Kentigern Keenan* off to a publisher. An editor at the firm who had previously enjoyed two of the original "Patrick" tales had the book published, which succeeded beyond everyone's expectations. And when the editor cried for more Hunter was ready. "I was well away, by then, into the work of writing another kind of book for my children. And by then also, I was fully realising that *nothing* of either the study or the writing I had done up till that time, had been in any way a waste of effort."

Fantasy and history quickly became Hunter's specialties as she entered the most productive period of her writing career. "My feeling for poetry, finally, had been the spur to writing that first fantasy; and so what I had been doing, in effect, was to serve a long and thorough apprenticeship in two forms of writing—that of fantasy, and the historical novel. For both forms, my research work had laid down a fertile seedbed of ideas." And the thread that connects these two, and all the genres Hunter writes in, is Scotland; almost all her books are set here, and her stories are rooted in Scottish folklore and history. But Hunter is a national, not a regional writer, assures Hollindale, adding that "it is in her work that children can find the fullest recent expression of the legend and history which make Scots culture distinctive."

An old man known as the Bodach and his young companion use ancient magical rites to prevent the electric company from flooding his valley in this 1970 fantasy novel.

Scottish Sprites and Spirits

It is Scottish legend and folklore that bring alive such fantasies as *Thomas and the Warlock*, *The Ferlie*, *The Bodach*, and *A Stranger Came Ashore*. "In this group of stories," maintains Hollindale, "which take as their theme the relationship between humankind and the many supernatural beings of Celtic myth, we find a narrative form under immaculate, almost flawless control." In all of these fantasies it is a child or adolescent who plays the crucial role and possesses insights not open to adults. And this understanding of things, both natural and supernatural, requires the young hero or heroine to have resolute courage. "Natural rhythms of youthful strength and aged weakness, of growth and decay, co-exist in the stories with the unearthly everlastingness of the nonhuman world," continues Hollindale.

In both *Thomas and the Warlock* and *The Ferlie* humans cross the line between the real world and the fairy world, and it is the wisdom and courage of youth that save them. Thomas Thomson, the local blacksmith and a well-known poacher, must face the wrath of the evil warlock Hugo Gifford after venturing too close to the Goblin Ha'. Thomas has allies to help fight the warlock, though, the most important being his young son, Alexander, who is the only one who knows the fairy rhyme that will tell his father what to do. Margery Fisher, writing in *Growing Point*, observes that *"Thomas and the Warlock* is a very open, active and lively tale; its magic is brisk rather than mysterious." *The Ferlie* similarly pits the young orphan Hob Hazeldene against a ferlie. Hob is obsessed with a sweet music he hears in his dreams, and is delighted when he is able to make a whistle upon which he can play it. The music, however, is that of a ferlie, and Hob must resist its efforts to lure him into the fairy world. In her *Growing Point* review of the book, Fisher describes *The Ferlie* as "a brilliant, clear-cut, robust story." And Polly Goodwin concludes in the *Washington Post* that Hunter "puts a dramatic climax on a well-told tale touched with magic."

The Bodach and *A Stranger Came Ashore* are also filled with otherworldly magic, and both have older characters sacrificing their lives for young heroes. Set in the Scottish Highlands, *The Bodach* (known in the United States as *The Walking Stones*) is the tale of an old man's fight to stop the electric company from flooding his valley. Skilled in ancient Druidic rites, the Bodach and his young pupil Donald use their magic to stop the water from coming for as long as they can. "Unreal? Not in Mollie Hunter's crisply told tale," states Jane Yolen in the *Washington Post Book World*, adding: "Readers, fantasy and fact lovers alike, will be caught up in the reality of unreality." And a *Kirkus Reviews* contributor concludes that *The Bodach* is "as graceful an unhurried talespin as ever you please or a silver-tongued Bodach could match." In *A Stranger Came Ashore*, Hunter explores the legend of the Selkie Folk, seals that live in the water around the Shetland islands. The narrative, recounted by bride-to-be Elspeth's young brother Robbie, focuses on who will be the bridegroom— Elspeth's love Nicol Anderson, or Finn Learson, who appears mysteriously from the sea one night. Robert Bell, writing in the *School Librarian*, finds Hunter's style effective in conveying the tension of the story, and adds that "the language is direct, commanding and evocative." Ann Thwaite concludes in the *Times Literary Supplement* that *A*

Stranger Came Ashore contains plenty "to attract and hold a young reader, and Mollie Hunter's love of the Shetlands and their selkie-legends is pervasive."

In Hunter's fantasies, the supernatural world is so close to the real world that the two often overlap. "The matter of these stories accords completely with the manner of their telling," observes Hollindale. "The narrative comes essentially from a *speaking* voice of distinctive quality. It is matter-of-fact and brisk, daring the reader (or listener) to find anything implausible in its strange tales; it is confidential and intimate; but it is also spare and economical, almost bardic in its adroit and dignified simplicity; and it is full of humour and full of music, not least the music of Gaelic idiom and sentence-forms. These diverse qualities merge, with remarkable consistency and control, to express a wide span of moods and emotions within a taut narrative structure."

Courageous Youth

In an interview with M.K. for *Top of the News*, Hunter explains that she gets a different kind of satisfaction from the various genres in which she writes—"partly because each calls for a technique that's specific to itself and partly because each indulges some aspect of my own nature. In the fantasies, for instance, I'm indulging the dreamy, mystical side of my nature, the side that has always relied on intuition rather than on any reasoning process and that has, consequently, always been attracted to the supernatural. . . . I also have a very practical side to my nature, and this comes out in the plot structuring required for my historical novels."

In such historical novels as *A Pistol in Greenyards*, *The Ghosts of Glencoe*, and *The Stronghold*, Hunter brings to life past events through young characters who have conflicting loyalties and who must show bravery and courage in the face of powers stronger than themselves. The tragedy of the Highland Clearances is told through the eyes of Connal Ross in *A Pistol in Greenyards*. Connal's father is in one of the Highland regiments fighting for England when the crofters are evicted from his valley after a doomed resistance in which Connal takes part. Hunter "is a fine story-teller, able to shape a plot without loss of historical integrity," describes a *Times Literary Supplement* contributor. Judith Aldridge, writing in *Children's Book Review*, points out that Hunter presents "a range of strongly-drawn characters" and "gives the book an intensity of focus which adds greatly to its strength." In *The Ghosts of Glencoe* Hunter provides a fictional account of the brutal massacre of 1692 through the use of an eyewitness involved with both sides—the Campbells and the Macdonalds of Glencoe. A *Times Literary Supplement* contributor contends that Hunter's "portraits of the principals on both sides are brilliantly done." And a *Junior Bookshelf* reviewer observes that Hunter succeeds in "presenting a piece of history as a novel that is convincing as a novel without distorting the facts."

Hunter's Carnegie Medal-winning novel, *The Stronghold*, contains similar themes to her other historical works; there are opposing loyalties, the realities of power and weakness, and courageous young characters. Set in a primitive community on an Orkney island during Roman times, the novel provides a hypothesis for the origins of the wondrous circular stone defense towers known as the "brochs." Because the tribe is constantly threat-

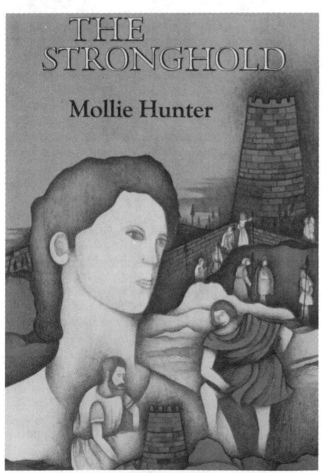

This 1974 historical novel—winner of Great Britain's Carnegie Medal—concerns a young member of a primitive tribe whose plans to defend his island against invading forces meet with opposition from tribal leaders.

ened by neighbors, the young physically handicapped Coll designs the towers and stands firm against the resistance of the dominating Druid priests. It is only after a sacrifice is made to appease the gods that Coll is able to persuade the tribe to build an experimental broch. The broch saves the community from an attack and also saves the tension-filled relationship between the island's leading Druid-priest and the warrior-chief. *The Stronghold* is "a tumultuous yet clearly conceived and tautly constructed novel, narrated in one evoking scene after another," describes Cameron in the *New York Times Book Review*. Fisher, in her *Growing Point* review of the novel, maintains: "A close, detailed reconstruction of the past in practical terms ... helps to establish a brilliantly imagined picture of an ancient society which we can only know now through conjecture."

Birth of a Stronger Voice

After the publication of *The Stronghold*, Hunter's writing progressed to a different level; she found another voice for her novels, a voice she discovered through the character of Bridie McShane in *A Sound of Chariots*. "I was still writing the historical and the fantasies, of course, but I was also beginning to find an altered perspective for my imagination in terms of realising that there were other and different types of books to be gleaned out of the experiences of my own life rather than from the material of my study," explains Hunter in *SAAS*. From these experiences Hunter wrote a number of her young adult novels, including *The Third Eye*, *The Dragonfly Years*, and *Cat, Herself*. "All the female characters I had created both before and after her [Bridie's] time had been as strongly drawn as I could make them; yet still, none of them had been the protagonist of a book," continues Hunter in *SAAS*. "But now, in these young adult novels, I *was* speaking through female protagonists. And by doing so, it seemed to me, I was finding a furtherance of the release that Bridie had given me—and so also confirming in myself a specific *kind* of voice through which to tell each of these stories."

This voice is given life through the character of Jinty Morrison in *The Third Eye*. The youngest of three girls, Jinty and her family reside in Ballinford, Scotland during the Depression. Having a psychic sensitivity makes Jinty more aware of the problems and troubles of people around her. The pasts and secrets of other characters are revealed through a series of flashbacks and through Jinty as she ponders local gossip and community activities. "Mollie Hunter works out her plot so expertly and directs her narrative so firmly that we are drawn completely into the book, getting to know the characters in the slow, partial manner of real life," asserts Fisher in *Growing Point*. *The Third Eye*, concludes M. Crouch in the *Junior Bookshelf*, is "a book to savour, to read slowly and then to read again noting how beautifully every episode is dovetailed into the main structure."

Returning to her first female protagonist, Bridie McShane, Hunter published *The Dragonfly Years* (also known as *Hold on to Love*) in 1983. Bridie is still residing in Edinburgh, where she takes evening classes and works as a florist's apprentice in the time just before World War II. As she develops a friendship with another evening class student, Peter McKinley, Bridie also develops her political awareness and her writing. The relationship between Bridie and Peter grows closer to love, but is nearly destroyed because of an argument. Peter stubbornly joins the Navy just before war breaks out, and it is only after this that Birdie is able to admit her love for him. Mary Hoffman points out in the *Times Educational Supplement*: "Despite the mushy ending, the book makes a powerful point: it is only with the victory of independence that you recognize your necessary involvement with the rest of humankind."

Although Bridie gave Hunter the voice to tell her young adult tales, it was the story of Catriona McPhie that gave this voice its full strength. "It was when I wrote the present-day story of *Cat, Herself* . . . that I found this voice speaking out on the loudest and clearest note I could summon for it; and speaking, too, in a way that enabled me to use aspects of my own life more fully than had ever before been the case with me," recalls Hunter in *SAAS*. A member of one of Scotland's many travelling families, also known as tinkers, Cat McPhie possesses many characteristics similar to Hunter herself. "Through this girl, I could recreate all the halcyon days of my own childhood, making her as physically hardy as myself, giving to her all my own love of freedom, all my own sensuous pleasure in the colours, the shapes, the smells, the very *feel* of the countryside I have always so passionately loved," reveals Hunter. Cat is also very independent, which enables her to break the traditional work roles of tinkers and eventually find a husband who allows her to be herself. Hunter "depicts the caravan life of tinkers with authority and captures the flavor of their folklore and customs during their travels through the Scottish countryside," observes Ethel R. Twichell in *Horn Book*. *Cat, Herself* "is as finely crafted as we have come to expect from Mollie Hunter," concludes *School Librarian* contributor Christine Walker.

"So, also, the wheel on which my life had been turning came full circle at last," continues Hunter in *SAAS*. "Or in a manner of speaking, at least, that was so; because there have been other books since that girl's story was written, other books that have taken me back to the medium of fantasy that started it all. And why? Because now I have grandchildren, along with whom has come a renewal of the childhood demand for the story. And that, it seems to me, is the most delightful of all renewals for one who, at heart, has never really been other than just a storyteller!"

Storytellers and Listeners

Also included as part of the turning wheel of Hunter's life and writing career are essays in which she discusses and examines the craft to which she is most dedicated—storytelling. "Passing on stories is the endeavor to which Mollie Hunter is most deeply committed," points out Janet Hickman in *Language Arts*. This commitment and Hunter's sense of responsibility to her children readers are evident in her book of essays, *Talent Is Not Enough*. Based on a series of Hunter's lectures, the five essays collected in *Talent Is Not Enough* reveal the author's theories on good writing and storytelling. "The whole collection of essays is an extraordinary combination of various patterns of thought and expression," states Paul Heins in the introduction. *Talent Is Not Enough*, concludes Mary M. Burns in *Horn Book*, is "enhanced by the wit and felicitous style which is characteristic of [Hunter's] novels" and "should be required reading for all who would write or evaluate books for children—and for adults."

Hunter goes on to examine the meeting point between writers and readers in her most recent collection of essays, *The Pied Piper Syndrome, and Other Essays*. In order for this meeting to take place, Hunter contends that children must be respected and viewed as individuals. "In these essays, one of Hunter's most important recurring themes is the invaluable gift of imagination," maintains Susan A. Burgess in *School Library Journal*, adding: "By revealing her own thoughts so generously and articulately, Hunter demonstrates how all of us who work with children and books can understand each other better."

Hunter's critical acclaim and popularity among children themselves suggest that she both understands and connects with her audience. And she does this by putting so much of herself, including her experiences and her emotions, into her books. "At its lowest, then, what I am trying to achieve with my writing is just to entertain," relates Hunter in her *Top of the News* interview, adding: "At it's highest, my writing is an attempt to create form and beauty and maybe a grain or so of truth out of my personal chaos. Usually I fall between two stools and succeed only in producing a readable story. That's not much to achieve, it's true; but if it gives some lasting pleasure to any reader, anywhere, I'll not quarrel with it."

■ Works Cited

Aldridge, Judith, review of *A Pistol in Greenyards*, *Children's Book Review*, summer, 1975, pp. 67-68.

Bell, Robert, review of *A Stranger Came Ashore*, *School Librarian*, March, 1976, p. 50.

Burgess, Susan A., "Connecting with Readers," *School Library Journal*, March, 1993, p. 136.

Burns, Mary M., "Of Interest to Adults: *Talent is Not Enough: Mollie Hunter on Writing for Children*," *Horn Book*, December, 1976, pp. 637-38.

Cameron, Eleanor, "At Her Back She Always Heard," *New York Times Book Review*, November 5, 1972, p. 6.

Cameron, review of *The Stronghold*, *New York Times Book Review*, July 21, 1974, pp. 8, 10.

"Casualties of Change," *Times Literary Supplement*, May 25, 1967, p. 447.

Crouch, M., review of *The Third Eye*, *Junior Bookshelf*, August, 1979, p. 221.

DeLuca, Geraldine, review of *A Sound of Chariots*, *Lion and the Unicorn*, fall, 1978, pp. 92-96.

Dooley, Patricia, "Mollie Hunter," *Children's Literature Association Newsletter*, autumn, 1978, pp. 3-6.

Fisher, Margery, review of *Thomas and the Warlock*, *Growing Point*, May, 1967, p. 920.

Fisher, review of *The Ferlie*, *Growing Point*, December, 1968, p. 1239.

Fisher, review of *The Stronghold*, *Growing Point*, September, 1974, p. 2455.

Fisher, review of *The Third Eye*, *Growing Point*, November, 1979, p. 3595.

Review of *The Ghosts of Glencoe*, *Junior Bookshelf*, April, 1967, p. 123.

"The Gift of the Gab," *Times Literary Supplement*, September 28, 1973, p. 1113.

Goodwin, Polly, review of *The Ferlie*, *Washington Post*, November 3, 1968, p. 16.

Heins, Paul, "Introduction," in *Talent Is Not Enough*, by Mollie Hunter, Harper, 1976, pp. ix-xiii.

Hickman, Janet, "The Person behind the Book—Mollie Hunter," *Language Arts*, March, 1979, pp. 302-06.

Hoffman, Mary, "No Longer an Island," *Times Educational Supplement*, June 17, 1983, p. 28.

Hollindale, Peter, "World Enough and Time: The Work of Mollie Hunter," *Children's Literature in Education*, autumn, 1977, pp. 109-19.

Hunter, Mollie, *The Dragonfly Years*, Hamish Hamilton, 1983, published in the United States as *Hold on to Love*, Harper, 1984.

Hunter, in an interview with M.K. for *Top of the News*, winter, 1985, pp. 141-46.

Hunter, in an essay for *Something about the Author Autobiography Series*, Volume 7, Gale, 1989.

Review of *A Pistol in Greenyards*, *Times Literary Supplement*, December 9, 1965, p. 1147.

Thwaite, Ann, "Fey, Fi, Fo, Fum," *Times Literary Supplement*, September 19, 1975, p. 1053.

Twichell, Ethel R., review of *Cat, Herself*, *Horn Book*, July/August, 1986, p. 455.

Walker, Christine, review of *I'll Go My Own Way*, *School Librarian*, March, 1986, p. 73.

Review of *The Walking Stones*, *Kirkus Reviews*, August 1, 1970, p. 800.

Yolen, Jane, review of *The Walking Stones*, *Washington Post Book World*, November 8, 1970, p. 8.

■ For More Information See

BOOKS

Blishen, Edward, editor, *The Thorny Paradise: Writers on Writing for Children*, Kestrel Books, 1975, pp. 128-39.

Children's Literature Review, Volume 25, Gale, 1991.

Contemporary Literary Criticism, Volume 21, Gale, 1982.

PERIODICALS

Children's Literature in Education, summer, 1986, pp. 112-25.

Horn Book, January/February, 1989, p. 70; May/June, 1993, pp. 346-47.

Publishers Weekly, June 27, 1986, pp. 93-94; June 10, 1988, p. 81.

School Librarian, June, 1978, pp. 108-11.

School Library Journal, January, 1986, p. 58; June/July, 1988, p. 105.

—*Sketch by Susan M. Reicha*

Hadley Irwin

■ Personal

Ann Irwin: Born Annabelle Bowen, October 8, 1915, in Peterson, IA; daughter of Benjamin (a farmer) and Mary (a teacher; maiden name, Rees) Bowen; married Keith C. Irwin (in business), May 29, 1943; children: Jane Irwin Croll, Ann Irwin Bauer, Rees, Sara. *Education:* Morningside College, B.A., 1937; University of Iowa, M.A., 1967.

Lee Hadley: Born October 10, 1934, in Earlham, IA; daughter of Oren B. (a farmer) and Pearle Hadley. *Education:* Drake University, B.A., 1956; University of Wisconsin-Madison, M.A., 1961.

■ Addresses

Ann Irwin: *Home*—Lake View, IA, 51450.

Lee Hadley: *Home*—R.R. 1, Madrid, IA 50156. *Office*—Department of English, Iowa State University, 307 Ross Hall, Ames, IA, 50011.

■ Career

Ann Irwin: Writer. High school English teacher, 1937-67; Buena Vista College, Storm Lake, IA, instructor in English, 1967-68; Midwestern Col-

lege, Denison, IA, instructor in English, 1968-70; Iowa State University, Ames, associate professor of English, 1970-1985 (Retired emeritus).

Lee Hadley: Writer. Younkers of Des Moines (department store), Des Moines, IA, copy writer, 1955-58; De Soto, IA, high school English teacher, 1959-60; Monmouth, NJ, high school English teacher; Ocean County Community College, Toms River, NJ, instructor of English, 1965-68; Iowa State University, Ames, assistant professor, 1969, associate professor of English, 1980, professor of English, 1992.

■ Awards, Honors

Honor Book Award, Jane Addams Peace Association, 1981, for *We Are Mesquakie, We Are One;* Society of Midland Authors Award, 1982, for *Moon and Me;* Notable Children's Trade Book in the Field of Social Studies Award, joint committee of the National Council on Social Studies and Children's Book Council, 1982, for *What About Grandma?,* and 1985, for *Abby, My Love;* Best Young Adult Book Award, American Library Association, 1982, for *What About Grandma?,* and 1985, for *Abby, My Love;* Children's Choice Book Award, and Children's Book Award, joint committee of Children's Book Council and International Reading Association, 1986, for *Abby, My Love;* Children's Books of the Year list, Library of Congress, 1987, for *Kim/Kimi.*

Ann Irwin: Children's Books of the Year selection, Child Study Association, 1973, for *One Bite at a Time.*

■ Writings

NOVELS FOR YOUNG ADULTS

The Lilith Summer, Feminist Press, 1979.
We Are Mesquakie, We Are One, Feminist Press, 1980.
Bring to a Boil and Separate, Atheneum, 1980.
Moon and Me, Macmillan, 1981.
What About Grandma?, Atheneum, 1982.
I Be Somebody, Macmillan, 1984.
Abby, My Love, Macmillan, 1985.
Kim, Kimi, Macmillan, 1987.
So Long at the Fair, Macmillan, 1988.
Can't Hear You Listening, Macmillan, 1990.
The Original Freddie Ackerman, Macmillan, 1992.
Jim-Dandy, Macmillan, 1994.

Hadley Irwin's novels have been translated into numerous languages, including German, Swedish, French, and Spanish.

NON-FICTION

(With Jeannette Eyerly), *Writing Young Adult Novels*, Writer's Digest Books, 1988.

FOR YOUNG ADULTS; BY ANN IRWIN

(With Bernice Reida) *Hawkeye Adventure*, Graphic Publishing, 1966.
(With Bernice Reida) *Hawkeye Lore*, Graphic Publishing, 1968.

JUVENILE; BY ANN IRWIN

One Bite at a Time, F. Watts, 1973.
(With Bernice Reida) *Moon of the Red Strawberry*, Aurora, 1977.
(With Bernice Reida) *Until We Reach the Valley*, Avon, 1979.

ONE ACT PLAYS; BY ANN IRWIN

And the Fullness Thereof, Pioneer, 1962.
Pieces of Silver, Eldridge Publishing, 1963.

■ Adaptations

The Lilith Summer was released with a teaching guide by Aims, 1984; *Abby, My Love* was adapted as a "CBS Schoolbreak" presentation, 1988.

■ Work in Progress

Sarah-with-an-H.

■ Sidelights

Ann Irwin and Lee Hadley have been writing books together as Hadley Irwin since 1979. The duo noted in the *ALAN Review* that Hadley Irwin is "over a hundred and twenty-five years old" and has "taught for 75 or 80 years, everything from kindergarten through graduate school." Irwin and Hadley told *Something about the Author Autobiography Series* (SAAS) that Hadley Irwin "knows that she's lived long enough to have something to say and cares enough to try to say it as well as possible."

Ann Irwin

Ann Irwin was born in October to a proud, Welsh farming family in Iowa, but, as she explained in *SAAS*, her "life began one hot September day" when her mother enrolled her in the first grade at Peterson Consolidated School. "Any memory I retain of my life prior to that eventful day is fleeting, based mainly on smells." Irwin insists that she "never recovered from what Peterson Consolidated School did" to her—she has spent her life as a pupil, teacher, and professor. Irwin did, however, overcome one aspect of her formal education: she retained her ability to imagine not only with her eyes closed, but without her eyes. According to the writer, she began making up stories before she went to school, and even before she learned to write.

Words, Irwin explained to *SAAS*, have always been important to her. "Our farm home was full of books and magazines and music and laughter. I can't remember when words—the looks and sounds of them—were not a part of my life. As a toddler, I traced the bright letters on our kitchen stove: M-O-N-A-R-C-H . . . My mother, a teacher, probably to keep me out from under her feet, taught me to read before I went to school."

Eventually, Irwin began to express herself through words. She related in *SAAS* that she kept a diary from the time she was nine until the ninth grade when she "gave up in frustration. My younger brother, Wid, discovered where I hid my diary and to tease me memorized some rather poignantly romantic passages and proceeded to recite them aloud at the dinner table that evening. I took to writing letters after that—to anyone I could think of that lived over a mile from our farm." Irwin did not limit herself to letter writing. She was just in ninth grade when she sent a short story to a magazine for adults (which rejected the story).

In high school, Irwin began her intellectual exploration of history, literature, botany, and algebra. She went on to Morningside College, where she received a bachelor's degree. At twenty-one, she held her first job as a teacher in a small town in

Iowa. As she became a wife and mother of four, she continued to teach various grades of elementary and secondary school. "Nights and weekends and summers I went back to college to complete the graduate degree I had started at Columbia University, before I was married, and never finished," Irwin wrote in *SAAS*.

As full as her life was, Irwin found the time to write entries to jingle contests and thus express the fact that, as she related in *SAAS*, "Words continued to fascinate" her. "I became a Contest Enter-er ... I not only sharpened my skills of expression, but also won among various things a boat, riding lawn mower, set of luggage, portable typewriter (most welcome), and the ultimate biggie, a Rambler station wagon full of groceries." Irwin gained more than promotional prizes from her time as a "Contest Enter-er." She told *SAAS* that she "learned two valuable lessons from those years of entering contests: 1) to discard my first ten ideas and go in search of the new and fresh and original, and 2) to keep in mind that less is often more in forming a good sentence."

Irwin began to write seriously again after Bernice Reida told her that there were no up-to-date history books available for the junior high school children Irwin was teaching. Irwin suggested that she and Reida write an Iowa history book. Her career, from that point, began to blossom. "After the history text," she explained in *SAAS*, "I began tentatively to submit some of my writing for publication. I began with one-act plays, went on to magazine articles, short stories, and finally a young adult novel, *One Bite at a Time*."

By this time, Irwin had earned her master's degree at the University of Iowa. She began to teach first in a small college, and then in the English department at Iowa State University. After many years, she received tenure and the title of Associate Professor. It was at Iowa State that Ann Irwin met Lee Hadley.

Lee Hadley

Like Ann Irwin, Lee Hadley also grew up on an Iowa farm. Hadley, however, was born in the midst of the Great Depression, in a year when the only other thing produced on the family farm was a heifer calf. Hadley was an inquisitive child who was delighted (as was Irwin) to be able to romp around the countryside. She told *SAAS*, "In my memory, the scenes of childhood are caught in a forever-summer, each event evoking the sights and scents and sounds of an Iowa farm in late July."

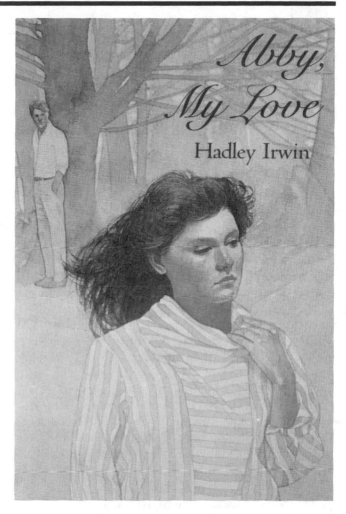

In this 1985 work, a teenage boy learns that his friend Abby has been the victim of sexual abuse by her father.

Hadley's mother drove her children to the library every Saturday, and Hadley would comb the shelves for "whatever looked inviting." "Mother," she recalled in *SAAS*, "a voracious reader herself, never scolded me for being awake at midnight, but hundreds of times must have turned off the light when I fell asleep holding an open book." Throughout her high school years, Hadley enjoyed her writing assignments, writing a column for the school paper, working for the yearbook, and attending football and basketball games, plays, and proms.

Hadley's college years at Drake University in Des Moines, Iowa are now (she related in *SAAS*) "a collage of fragmented experiences." The English major worked as a copy-writer in a department store's advertising department. Upon graduation, she spent a year in Europe. "London, Paris, Rome, Vienna, Athens turned into scraps of time recorded on bits of napkins, backs of menus, in tattered notebooks . . . Why I was putting words on paper—sketches, poems, bits of dialogue, descriptions—I didn't understand at the time. Now I know. The written word holds the ability to recreate what memory must inevitably lose: the scent, the taste, the sound, the presence of a particular moment. I knew I had to write; I didn't know that I would become a writer," Hadley wrote in SAAS.

When Hadley returned to the United States, she became a teacher, attended graduate school at the University of Wisconsin in Madison (where she spent a year writing poetry), and then worked for nine years in New Jersey at the Monmouth Regional High School and a community College in Toms River. In the late 1960s, Hadley returned to Iowa. She explained this decision in SAAS: "Then with Robert Kennedy lying in a pool of blood in a hotel kitchen, and young men still dying in an endless war, and Blacks still struggling for equality, and women just beginning to talk of it, life seemed to me more fragile than it had before." Hadley wanted to spend time with her parents, who were "getting older." Once again in the quiet of Iowa, Hadley recalls in SAAS, she had "no excuse for not writing, except for my teaching job at Iowa State University!" She did not write because "(a) I was scared, (b) I was lazy." Hadley knew that she had to start writing soon.

Hadley Irwin Is Born

Irwin and Hadley were professors in the English Department at Iowa State University when they were assigned to work together to arrange a summer workshop. Although the project did not emerge as it was supposed to, Irwin and Hadley developed a friendship as they prepared a report about their efforts to plan the workshop. When summer came, the pair went their separate ways. "We lived, at that point, about a hundred miles apart and only met when we were teaching. So we didn't see each other often," Hadley said in ALAN Review.

Despite this separation, the pair had similar thoughts upon seeing a photo of an elderly woman who had just been told that plans for new highway would not force her to leave her home in the Des Moines Register. Both women were inspired by the photo of "strength, beauty, triumph," as Hadley described it in ALAN Review: "Ann saw it, and I saw it. When we got back together, we thought: isn't there something there that could be turned into a book? And then we started what turned into a collaboration."

Irwin and Hadley began to write the text that was to become The Lilith Summer. Each weekend, the women would write portions of the story, and, during the week, each would read and edit the other's work. "We finally got something that kind of looked like a book," remembered Hadley in ALAN Review, and then the writers decided that they needed to write together. It was at this point that they developed the technique that they would continue to use as they created books together. One woman would sit down at the typewriter, and the two would contribute words, phrases, and sentences to the text.

Finding a publisher for a book about a twelve-year old girl and a seventy-seven year old woman, The Lilith Summer, was not an easy task. Ann Irwin, who had written several books for young adults with Bernice Reida and had won an award for a book she had written herself, had an agent in New York. The agent, however, insisted that the Hadley Irwin book was for adults, and reminded the writers that she dealt only with books for young adults. The writers then sent a letter and the first chapter of the book to the Feminist Press, which decided that the book was for young adults, and they were only interested in adult books. Finally, the Feminist Press began to publish young adult books and published The Lilith Summer.

The Lilith Summer received a favorable review in the New York Times Book Review. According to Natalie Babbit, the "story is warm and the writing exemplary." Mary M. Burns, writing for Horn Book, concluded that the novel was "readable and engaging narrative" which "represents a promising collaboration." In Book Worm, Michele Slung remarked that the novel "radiates empathy." The Gray Panthers praised the work, and the Book-of-the-Month Club chose the book that Christmas as a selection.

We Are Mesquakie, We Are One and a Jane Addams Association Honor Book Award

Irwin and Hadley decided to write another book together. Ann Irwin had been reading a history book and was struck by the story of the Mesquakies of Tama, Iowa. The Mesquakie resisted assimilation by the federal government and saved money received from government payments to buy back the Iowa land they had been forced to leave. "I got to thinking what it would have been like if you were an eight-year-old Mesquakie back in 1837 or so," when the government decided that the Mesquakies had to leave their land, she remarked in

ALAN Review. Hadley Irwin then began a summer of research and writing on the lake where Annabelle lived. Sitting together, they read through every document they could find about the Mesquakies. They "ended up throwing them against the wall because most of them were written by either missionaries or military men who regarded the Mesquakies as something less than human. We couldn't use *them*, but we could reverse the facts and come out very nicely," Hadley recalled.

Irwin and Hadley were very careful as they wrote *We Are Mesquakie, We Are One*: "We have to be very careful [writing cross-culturally] because we are not black or Mesquakie or Japanese," the authors commented in *ALAN Review*. The pair asked a Mesquakie woman, Adeline Wanatee, to read the book. Wanatee assured them that the book was authentic, and the book was published.

We Are Mesquakie, We Are One is the story of Hidden Doe, a young Mesquakie girl who is taught by her grandmother, Gray Gull, and her father, Chief Great Bear, that the Mesquakie are one people who must retain their language and religion. As Hidden Doe becomes a young woman, the white settlers immigrating to Iowa force the Mesquakie to move to Kansas. Hidden Doe remembers the lessons of her childhood and preserves her culture. Along with some other Mesquakie people, she buys back some of the old Mesquakie land in Iowa. At the end of the novel, she gives birth to her first child.

Cynthia L. Beatty, a critic for *Voice of Youth Advocates* (VOYA), wrote that Hadley Irwin "give a detailed picture of what a Mesquakie childhood was like." In *School Library Journal*, Gale Eaton concluded that "the historical predicament" of the Mesquakie was "portrayed with more sorrow than bitterness," and that this "gives the book impact."

Writing about the Trials of Teenagers

After the success of *We Are Mesquakie, We Are One*, Hadley Irwin decided to try something different—a book about divorce. *Bring to a Boil and Separate.* begins when thirteen-year-old Katie Wagner's parents, both veterinarians, separate. Katie has difficulties understanding the divorce and coping with the emotions her family's situation has evoked. When her friend Marti returns from summer camp, Katie becomes preoccupied with her friendship and the changes adolescence brings. Cyrisse Jaffee noted the book's "lively writing, likable characters," and "realistic situation" in *School Library Journal*.

When her friend Stanley's behavior becomes erratic, Tracy confronts the troubled teen about his drinking and drug use.

Hadley Irwin's next book, *Moon and Me*, was inspired by a scene the writers saw one day after speaking to 7th graders in a gymnasium. At a locker, two girls were having an argument. According to Lee Hadley in *ALAN Review*, "One girl was saying, 'He is not my boyfriend. He's just a friend who happens to be a boy.' We looked at each other and said, 'There's a book.'"

In What About Grandma?, sixteen-year-old Rhys forgoes the usual summer with her father to help her mother Eve care for her grandmother Wyn. Wyn is too frail to stay home alone, and she cannot bear the nursing home; she has decided to spend her last days with her family at home. The three women, however, find getting along difficult. The relationships they share become increasingly strained when Rhys falls in love with Lew, who is ten years older than herself. Eve begins to compete with Rhys for Lew's attention. It is not until Rhys learns a secret that her grandmother has kept and

Eve condones Rhys relationship with Lew that Wyn can enjoy the last days of her life with the women she loves. Geneveve Stuttaford, in a review for *Publishers Weekly*, described the story in *What About Grandma?* as "touching." Sari Felman concluded that "This novel is wonderful ... The authors ... have done a superb job portraying Wyn's last days at home," in *VOYA*.

Hadley Irwin would continue to write about the serious issues (from divorce to drug abuse) that young people face. She explained in *SAAS* that she writes about these issues because "those things do exist and, unfortunately, many of my readers are directly involved with them. I think you may have noticed by now that no matter how terrible an event may be, the rest of the world goes right on functioning in its usual absurd way and that funny

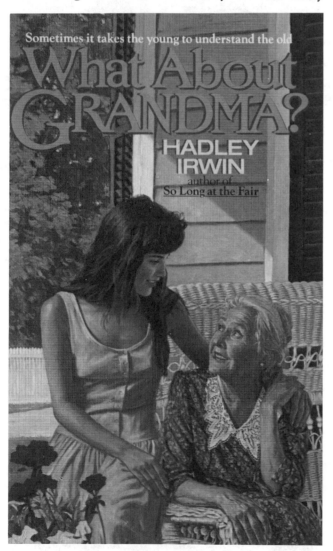

Sixteen-year-old Rhys spends a tumultuous summer helping her mother care for Rhys's ailing grandmother in this 1982 novel.

things do happen when we least expect them. What is there to do except to laugh and get on with our lives?"

Another Historical Novel

Irwin and Hadley found themselves in the roles of researchers once again as they prepared to write *I Be Somebody*. Although they had to drive to Clear View, Oklahoma, to see what kind of trees grew in the town and create the setting for the book, much of the research for the plot had been compiled by Charles C. Irby, a professor of ethnic and women's studies at California State Polytechnic University. The historical background (1910-1913) for *I Be Somebody* is based on Irby's notes. Set in this context, ten-year-old Anson J. Davis struggles to understand the treatment of his people in Oklahoma's black community.

A Sensitive Subject

Abby, My Love, Hadley Irwin's seventh novel, was written to confront a sensitive subject that the authors had been wanting to address since a teenage girl who had been sexually abused wrote to them. The authors neglected the project for a couple of years. When one of their adult students told the women that her father had molested her from the time she was just four years old, they realized that they wanted to write the book. They were encouraged when they understood that the book was needed for victims of incest as well as for the friends of a victim. According to the writers, one librarian told them, "'There's always a best friend who has a sense that something is wrong but doesn't know what. And if the friend did know would want to help but doesn't know how.'"

In *Abby, My Love*, Chip Martin grows to love Abby, who lives in his neighborhood. Abigail is intelligent and pretty, yet she sometimes seems remote and tells Chip little about her family. Chip thinks it strange that Abby is so careful when she watches her little sister, Pete, and that Abby's father doesn't like to let her leave the house. Finally, when Chip and Abby are in high school, Abby tells Chip a terrible secret. During all the years that she has known Chip, she had been raped and sexually abused by her father. Chip confides this secret to his mother, who ensures that Abby and her sister are removed from the situation. The love between Abby and Chip blossoms, and Abby becomes the valedictorian at her high school graduation.

Abby, My Love was well received by critics who felt the need for books which addressed this sensitive issue. Maria B. Salvadore concluded that, "This is an important book that adults and young adults should be aware of in terms of subject matter and quality" in *School Library Journal*.

A Novel About Cultural Heritage

Kim, Kimi was Hadley Irwin's next project. As the writing team stated in *ALAN Review*, they realize that, as they are "not black or Mesquakie or Japanese," they must work with great care when writing cross-culturally. Irwin and Hadley explained the development of *Kim/Kimi* in *SAAS*: "Hadley Irwin received an invitation from Barbara Hiura, a *sansei* (third-generation Japanese-American), and her real-life husband, Ernie, a second-generation Chinese-American, who provided us time and place and information needed to find what Kim would eventually discover in the book. It also furnished the names of two characters and left us with a permanent appreciation of Japanese food."

Kim/Kimi is the story of a Japanese-American girl who attempts to find out about her father, who died before she was born, and her Japanese heritage. Fifteen-year-old Kim Andrews, or Kimi Yogushi, lives with her loving Irish-American mother, stepfather, and young half-brother in Iowa. Although she has friends, she knows she is different from others in the Midwestern town, and she has many questions about her father. When her parents leave town one spring break, Kim flies to Sacramento, California to find her father's family, even though she knows they disowned him when he married her mother. A helpful Japanese-American family guide her in her search for her father's family, and she tours the Lake Tule Japanese internment camp where many of her relatives spent a year during World War II. When she finally finds her grandmother and aunt, the family is not immediately receptive. Nevertheless, Kimi is satisfied at her return to Iowa—she has taken the first step towards understanding her father's life and family, her heritage, and her identity. In the process, Kimi realizes that the teenage romance novels that so engaged her before her California trip do not reflect her reality, and they lose their charm.

Ai-Ling Louie pointed out that the character of Kim in *Kim/Kimi* reinforces the stereotype of the Asian woman as "helpless" and "indecisive." She wrote in the *Journal of Youth Services in Libraries*

A PUFFIN BOOK

Kim / *Kimi*
Hadley Irwin

Kim feels like her friends on the inside, but looks different— where does she fit in?

A fifteen-year-old Japanese American girl, whose father died before she was born, travels to California to seek answers about his—and her own—life and heritage.

that "Daydreaming, ineffectual little Kim is contrasted with the Caucasian, nearly six-foot Jav, who is decisive, brave, and a true friend ... It is Jav whom the reader ends up admiring, not Kim." Irwin and Hadley have discussed the problems they encounter and mistakes they make as cross-cultural writers. They acknowledged in *ALAN Review*, "We knew we would be criticized for attempting such [cross-culturally written] books. Even though you do your homework and do your research and have all these good feelings, it is so easy to make a mistake that you don't realize is a mistake."

Irwin and Hadley illuminated these "good feelings" in *SAAS*: "Actually, she's [Hadley Irwin's] in love with diversity. 'The exciting part of living is sharing this universe with other people. I've always responded to color—people of color, I mean. They make the world so much more beautiful. The various shades we come in are like ice-cream flavors. I've always been bored with plain vanilla. It's so bland, don't you think?'"

Two More Novels About Serious Issues: Suicide and Alcohol and Drug Abuse

Lee Hadley explained Hadley Irwin's motivation for writing so long at the fair was *So Long at the Fair* in *ALAN Review:* "I don't know where you're from, but in Iowa so many high school kids are committing suicide.... After *Abby, My Love,* we decided, okay, why don't we try, a book about suicide." Irwin and Hadley were determined to write a book that neither explained the "how" or "why" of suicide; they wanted to focus on the impact of suicide on loved ones left behind. The suicide that haunts the main character of *So Long at the Fair* does not occur in the book itself.

The book begins when Joel Wendell Logan III, a young man who has everything (intelligence, looks, and wealth) attempts to stop thinking about Ashley. Ashley had been his good friend; like Joel, Ashley had "everything." Yet Ashley was not content to enjoy her good fortune. At every opportunity, she struggled to help others. While her suicide was a mystery to many people, it makes Joel begin to question his upperclass life. He decides to live and work for a while at the state fair in the guise of a drifter, Joe Logan. When Joel is able to remember Ashley again, he cannot help but think of all of the things he could have done to further their emerging love. Finally, as a result of his week as Joe Logan, he learns to live with the best of his memories of Ashley and face his future instead of his past.

Bev Robertson, a critic for *VOYA*, reported that Hadley Irwin "has presented a thought-provoking picture of the frightening and near-epidemic problem of teen suicide." In *The Five Owls,* Cathryn M. Mercier called *So Long at the Fair* a "poignant story of an aching adolescent challenged to muster the inner strength necessary to cope with the unfair complexities of living and caring." And Susan H. Williamson, in *School Library Journal,* stated that the "quality work of literature" was "well-written."

After another speaking engagement, Irwin and Hadley were approached by a man who thought that they could help teenagers understand the serious issue of drug and alcohol abuse. The man's son, who had been heavily involved with alcohol and drugs, burned to death in a car accident at the age of twenty-one. Irwin and Hadley invited the man to lunch to talk. Lee Hadley spoke in *ALAN Review:* "So we did [sit down and talk], and we used it in the book. We dedicated the book to his son. He said, 'At least his life has done something. I can go to high schools and talk about drugs, alcohol. Kids won't listen to me, but, if they read something in a book of fiction, maybe they'll believe.'"

The book, *Can't Hear You Listening,* is about a sixteen-year-old young woman, Tracy Spencer, her relationship with her separated parents, and her friend Stanley. Stanley begins to upset her when she realizes that his behavior is abnormal. As his alcohol and drug use intensifies, Tracy struggles to decide what she can do for her friend. Stanley is no help—he threatens to tell about her participation in a few rum and Coke parties when she tries to

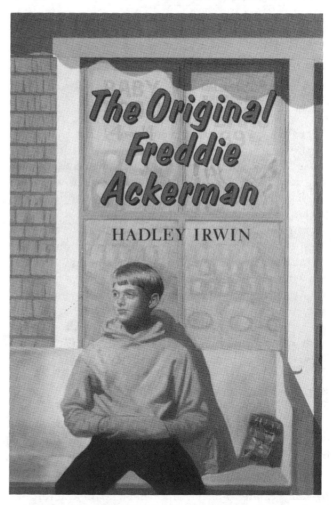

In this 1992 novel, Trevor Freddie Ackerman finds adventure and romance in an unlikely spot: the isolated island off the coast of Maine where he lives.

talk to him about his emerging problem. Ultimately, Tracy makes the important decisions she had been evading. Valerie Mead of *VOYA* reviewed *Can't Hear You Listening* and concluded that, while "Irwin accurately portrayed the socially limited life teens often experience in our modern-day suburban environment," the difference between "experimental" and "problematic" drinkers could have been "given more emphasis."

A Lighter Novel for the Younger Crowd

The Original Freddie Ackerman is set on an island off the coast of Maine. There, Trevor Freddie Ackerman overcomes the feeling that no one in his family cares about him. While Trevor is bored by the pace of life on the island initially, he is caught up in the adventures his great-aunts (with whom he lives) have contrived. Throughout the book, Trevor develops love for Ariel, who is also stuck on the island. Jacqueline Rose, a critic for *School Library Journal*, praised *The Original Freddie Ackerman* as a "fine book.... Irwin effectively conveys a sense that magic, adventure, and love might be found in unexpected places."

Hadley Irwin will continue to write salient works of fiction for young people. The team spoke of their combined identity fondly in *SAAS:* "She is our dearest friend, our harshest critic, and a total task-monster. Though she remains invisible to everyone but us, she is a much better writer than either Lee Hadley or Ann Irwin."

■ Works Cited

Babbit, Natalie, review of *The Lilith Summer, New York Times Book Review*, January 27, 1980, p. 24.

Burns, Mary M., review of *The Lilith Summer, Horn Book*, April, 1980, p. 174.

Review of *Can't Hear You Listening, New York Times Book Review*, March 10, 1991, p. 29.

Eaton, Gale, review of *We are Mesquakie, We Are One, School Library Journal*, January, 1981, p. 62.

Feldman, Sari, review of *What About Grandma?, Voice of Youth Advocates*, August, 1982, p. 32.

Irwin, Hadley, dialogue between Ann Irwin and Lee Hadley, *ALAN Review*, Fall 1992, pp. 3-7.

Jaffe, Cyrisse, review of *Bring to a Boil and Separate, School Library Journal*, April, 1980, p. 111.

Louie, Ai-Ling, "Growing Up Asian American: A Look at Some Recent Young Adult Novels," *Journal of Youth Services in Libraries*, Winter 1993, pp. 115-127.

Mead, Valerie, review of *Can't Hear You Listening, Voice of Youth Advocates*, October, 1990.

Mercier, Cathryn M., *review of So Long at the Fair, Five Owls*, March/April, 1989, pp. 61-2.

Robertson, Bev, review of *So Long at the Fair, Voice of Youth Advocates*, December, 1988.

Rose, Jacqueline, review of *The Original Freddie Ackerman, School Library Journal*, August, 1992, p. 156.

Salvadore, Maria B., review of *Abby, My Love, School Library Journal*, May, 1985, p. 102.

Slung, Michele, review of *The Lilith Summer, Book World*, September 9, 1979.

Stattaford, Genevieve, review of *What About Grandma?, Publishers Weekly*, February 13, 1987, p. 95.

Williamson, Susan H., review of *So Long at the Fair, School Library Journal*, November, 1988, p. 125.

■ For More Information See

PERIODICALS

Publishers Weekly, October 31, 1984, p. 436.
New York Times, October 4, 1987.
School Library Journal, March, 1992, p. 164.

—*Sketch by Ronie-Richele Garcia-Johnson*

Jamaica Kincaid

■ Personal

Born Elaine Potter Richardson, May 25, 1949, in St. John's, Antigua, West Indies; daughter of a carpenter/cabinet maker and Annie Richardson; married Allen Shawn (a composer and teacher at Bennington College); children: Annie Shawn and Harold. *Education:* Studied photography at the New School for Social Research in New York; attended Franconia College, NH. *Religion:* Methodist.

■ Addresses

Home—284 Hudson, New York, NY, and Bennington, VT. *Office*—*New Yorker*, 25 West 43rd St., New York, NY 10036.

■ Career

Writer. *New Yorker*, New York City, staff writer, 1976—. Lecturer, Bennington College, VT.

■ Awards, Honors

Morton Dauwen Zabel Award, American Academy and Institute of Arts and Letters, 1983, for *At the Bottom on the River;* Lila Wallace-Reader's Digest Fund annual writer's award, 1992.

■ Writings

At the Bottom of the River (short stories), Farrar, Straus, 1983.
Annie John (novel), Farrar, Straus, 1985.
A Small Place (essays), Farrar, Straus, 1988.
Annie, Gwen, Lilly, Pam and Tulip, illustrations by Eric Fischl, Knopf and Whitney Museum of American Art, 1989.
Lucy (novel), Farrar, Straus, 1990.

Contributor to periodicals.

■ Sidelights

"Everyone thought I had a way with words, but it came out as a sharp tongue. No one expected anything from me at all. Had I just sunk in the cracks it would not have been noted. I would have been lucky to be a secretary somewhere," Jamaica Kincaid told Leslie Garis in the *New York Times Magazine*. Garis continued Kincaid's story: "In 1966, at the age of 17, with no money, no connections and no practical training, Elaine Potter Richardson left the West Indian island of Antigua, bound for New York and a job as an *au pair*. She did not return until she was 36. By then she was Jamaica Kincaid, a respected author of fiction and a staff writer for *The New Yorker* magazine whose prose is studied in universities and widely anthologized."

A Young Girl Grows Up in Antigua

Kincaid was born and raised in Antigua, a West Indian island once under British rule. Kincaid's father was a carpenter and her mother kept house, occupations typical for the island's inhabitants. "I grew up on an island in the West Indies which has an area of a hundred and eight square miles," the author recalled in the *New Yorker*. "On the inland were many sugarcane fields.... There were cotton fields, but there were not as many cotton fields as there were sugarcane fields. There were arrowroot fields and tobacco fields, too, but there were not as many arrowroot fields and tobacco fields as there were cotton fields."

Young Kincaid attended government schools on Antigua. As a student, she was considered a bright troublemaker. "I was sullen," she recalled for Garis. "I was always being accused of being rude, because I gave some back chat. I moved very slowly. I was never where I should be. I wasn't really angry yet. I was just incredibly unhappy."

As Kincaid grew into early adolescence, her internal anger was also cultivated. Through a love a reading, however, the author found expression. She told Garis: "When I was a child I liked to read. I loved *Jane Eyre* especially and read it over and over. I didn't know anyone else who liked to read except my mother, and it got me in a lot of trouble because it made me into a thief and a liar. I stole books, and I stole money to buy them.... Books brought me the greatest satisfaction. Just to be alone, reading, under the house, with lizards and spiders running around."

A New Life in a New Country

Even though she did not know precisely what it was she longed for, Kincaid was overwhelmed by a desire to escape life as she knew it. "I thought, if only I can get out of here, I will live forever," she told Emily Listfield in an interview for *Harper's Bazaar*. "I believed I could handle anything other than the life that was expected of me."

With the agreement of her parents, Kincaid left her native Antigua at the age of sixteen find a new life for herself in New York City. When she arrived, Kincaid found a job with an affluent family in the northern suburb of Scarsdale, but soon left to be an au pair for another wealthy, white couple on the upper East Side. Although she had hoped to attend college at night, the author found out—to her dismay—that her educational background was insufficient. She took up photography instead at the

New School for Social Research and, eventually, won a scholarship to study photography at Franconia College (a degree program Kincaid never completed). Referring to her ill-fated attempts to obtain a college diploma, Kincaid told Patricia T. O'Conner in the *New York Times Book Review*: "College ... was such a dismal failure. I just educated myself, if that's possible."

Becoming a Writer

In an interview with Selwyn R. Cudjoe for *Caribbean Women Writers*, Kincaid discussed her early education and how she discovered writing: "We were taught to read from Shakespeare and Milton when I was five. They were read to us while we sat under a tree." Because of this emphasis on long-dead authors, Kincaid admitted that she "didn't know that people were still writing. I somehow thought that writing had been this great "thing" and that it had stopped. I thought that all the great writing had been done before 1900. Contemporary writers just didn't exist.... I never wanted to be a writer because I didn't know that any such thing existed."

Kincaid told Cudjoe that she changed her name because she "had always hated [it] and wanted to change it, but it was only when I started to write and actually started to sign my name to things that I decided I just couldn't do this. Since my family disapproved of my writing, it was easy for me to change names." As to the name "Jamaica," the author admitted: "It wasn't really anything meaningful. By the time I decided to change my name, that part of the world had become very remote to me. It was a kind of invention: I wouldn't go home to visit that part of the world, so I decided to recreate it. 'Jamaica' was symbolic of that place. I didn't come from Jamaica. I changed my name before Jamaica became fashionable—at least, before I was aware of it.... [Kincaid] just seemed to go with it."

Kincaid eventually began to submit articles to various magazines; two of her pieces were published in 1975. After her name appeared in a "Talk of the Town" column written by her friend George Trow, Kincaid was invited to meet the magazine's editor, William Shawn. "They took me to lunch at the Algonquin," she recalled for Listfield in *Harper's Bazaar*. "I was very poor, and I ordered the most expensive dish on the menu. At the end of lunch, Mr. Shawn suggested I give writing a try myself." Kincaid composed an article about a West Indian parade that she and Trow had seen. To the author's great shock, the story was accepted for publication with no editing. Kincaid told Garis, "When I saw [the article], and it was just what I had put on paper, that is when I realized what my writing was. My writing was the thing that I thought. Not something else. Just what I thought." Since this first piece appeared, Kincaid has been a regular contributor to the *New Yorker*.

Along with the articles for the "Talk of the Town" column in the *New Yorker*, Kincaid began to write fiction. She vividly recalled that early experience for Listfield: "I was living in a house on Hudson Street; I remember how the light was on the building next door. The afternoon light was a light purple, mauvish pink. One Sunday afternoon I just sat down at the typewriter and wrote 'Girl,' and it was just my mother's voice. I showed it to my husband and he said, 'This is great.' But I didn't care if it was great. I just knew that was what I would write. Suddenly, I knew how to say what I wanted to say. It hadn't always been so."

At the Bottom of the River

"Girl," published in the *New Yorker*, became the first of ten "stories" or "fictional narratives" that were eventually published together under the title *At the Bottom of the River*. The book established Kincaid as an "instant literary celebrity." "Girl" is a series commands from a mother to her daughter: "Wash the white clothes on Monday and put them on the stone heap/Wash the color clothes on Tuesday and put them on the clothesline to dry/Don't walk barehead in the hot sun/Cook pumpkin fritters in very hot sweet oil/On Sunday try to walk like a lady, and not like the slut you are so bent on becoming." Anne Tyler, in her review for the *New Republic*, declared that this passage provides "the clearest idea of the book's general tone; for Jamaica Kincaid scrutinizes various particle of our world so closely and so solemnly that they begin to take on a nearly mystical importance." Ike Onwordi wrote in the *Times Literary Supplement*: "Jamaica Kincaid uses language that is poetic without affectation. She has a deft eye for salient detail while avoiding heavy symbolism."

Another story in *At the Bottom of the River* also illustrates Kincaid's ability to observe and record the mundane aspects of life that she so well expressed in "Girl." The main character in "The Letter from Home" recounts daily chores: "I milked the cows, I churned the butter, I stored the cheese, I baked the bread, I brewed the tea." This "singsong style," wrote Suzanne Freeman in *Ms.*,

"is . . . akin to hymn-singing or maybe evening chanting" and produces "images that are as sweet and mysterious as the secrets that children whisper in your ear." Barney Bardsley, commenting on Kincaid's style in the *New Statesman*, said, "Jamaica Kincaid can seem pretentious. She repeats words and phrases in biblical monotone . . . but then she comes back, to express something fundamental about the way we live."

Henry Louis Gates, Jr., a critic and black studies scholar, told Listfield in *Harper's Bazaar* that he feels comfortable comparing Kincaid's work to that of Tony Morrison and Wole Soyinka: "There is a self-contained world which they explore with great detail. Not to chart the existence of that world, but to show that human emotions manifest themselves everywhere." Gates believes that an important contribution of Kincaid is that "she never feels the necessity of claiming the existence of a black world or a female sensibility. She assumes them both. I think it's a distinct departure that she's making, and I think that more and more black American

This 1983 collection of short stories celebrates the joys of everyday life and examines relationships between mothers and daughters.

"Coming of age in Antigua—so touching and familiar...
it could be happening to any of us, anywhere, any time, any place."
—NEW YORK TIMES BOOK REVIEW

PLUME
FICTION

Annie John

BY

JAMAICA KINCAID

Annie John, a seventeen-year-old from Antigua, leaves her native land to begin a nursing career in England in this 1985 work.

writers will assume their world the way that she does. So that we can get beyond the large theme of racism and get to the deeper themes of how black people love and cry and live and die. Which, after all, is what art is all about."

A number of themes emerge in these stories that continue to be explored in later works. Tyler focused on two dominant themes in her review of *At the Bottom of the River* in the *New Republic.* "The first is the wonderful, terrible strength of a loving mother. 'My mother can change everything,' a narrator says, and she fantasizes about spending the rest of her days with a woman who 'every night, over and over, ... will tell me something that begins, "Before you were born."'" The second theme is the mysteriousness of ordinary life ... [it] describes the most mundane events as if they were dreams. 'Either it was drizzling or there was a lot of dust in the air and the dust was damp,' she tells us. 'I stuck out my tongue and the

drizzle or the damp dust tasted like government school in.' Is this a dream, or is it real life? Come to think of it, are the two all that different," concluded the reviewer.

Annie John

These types of themes are also evident in Kincaid's second book, *Annie John,* which contains interrelated stories about a young girl growing up in Antigua. Jacqueline Austin wrote in *Voice Literary Supplement:* "Ten-year-old Annie John lives in a paradise: a back yard in Antigua overseen by a benevolent goddess—her mother.... Into this Eden come twin serpents: death and separation from the mother." The daughter of a carpenter, Annie John relates her life story from the age of ten to seventeen. She experiences her first menstruation, buries a friend, has a love-hate relationship with her mother from whom she separates to establish an independent life. After recovering from a serious illness, she goes to England to become a nurse.

Critically acclaimed as a coming-of-age novel, *Annie John* was praised by a number of reviewers for expressing qualities of growing up that transcend geographical locations. "Her work is recollections of childhood," Paula Bonnell remarked in the *Boston Herald.* "It conveys the mysterious power and intensity of childhood attachments to mother, father and friends, and the adolescent beginnings of separation from them." Susan Kenney, writing in *The New York Times Book Review,* noted Annie John's ambivalence about leaving behind her life in Antigua and declared that such ambivalence was "an inevitable and unavoidable result of growing up." Kenny concluded that Kincaid's story is "so touching and familiar ... so inevitable [that] it could be happening to any of us, anywhere, any time, any place. And that's exactly the book's strength, its wisdom, and its truth."

John Bemrose added in *Maclean's* that Kincaid "knows her way around the human heart. [She] gradually shows that Annie's personality is too large for the society in which she lives. Being a good student and a virtuous girl is simply too easy and too boring. She abandons her friendship with her school mate Gwen for a rebellious ragamuffin she calls the 'Red Girl,' because of her red hair. The two meet secretly to fondle each other with the clumsy urgency of adolescents. In the same story Annie takes up the "boys only" game of marbles, an activity that spells the end of her private Eden by bringing her into violent, hateful opposition to her mother.''

Lucy

Kincaid's second novel, *Lucy,* a first-person narrative in which nineteen-year-old Lucy expresses not only feelings of rage, but struggles with separation from her homeland and especially her mother. *Lucy* is about a young woman from Antigua who comes to an unnamed American city to work as an au pair girl. She is employed by a wealthy, white couple—Mariah and Lewis—and takes care of their four young daughters. In the *Washington Post Book World,* Susanna Moore commented: "Lucy is unworldly. She has never seen snow or been in an elevator.... Written in the first person, [the novel] is Lucy's story of the year of her journey—away from her mother, away from home, away from the island and into the world." Richard Eder mused in

This 1990 work—a coming-of-age novel that mirrors Kincaid's own adolescence—follows a young Antiguan girl who travels to the United States to work as an au pair for a wealthy family.

the *Los Angeles Times Book Review* that "The anger of Lucy . . . is an instrument of discovery, not destruction. It is lucid and cool, but by no means unsparing. Eder calls Mariah "a romantic environmentalist."

Derek Walcott, a West Indian poet, talked with Garis in the *New York Times Magazine* about Kincaid's identification with issues that thread through all most people's lives: "That relationship of mother and daughter—today she loves her mother, tomorrow she hates her, then she admires here—that is so true to life, without any artificiality, that it describes parental and filial love in a way that has never been done before. [Kincaid's] work is so full of spiritual contradictions clarified that it's extremely profound and courageous."

The novel ends with Lucy writing in a journal given to her by Mariah, the woman for whom she works, weeping over the very first line: " 'I wish I could love someone so much that I would die from it.' And then as I looked at this sentence a great wave of shame came over me and I wept and wept so much that the tears fell on the page and caused all the words to become one great blur." Eder ends his review saying, "she will turn the page and go on writing."

Thulani Davis, writing in the *New York Times Book Review,* said, "Ms. Kincaid is a marvelous writer whose descriptions are richly detailed; her sentences turn and surprise even the bare context she has created, in which there are few colors, sights or smells and the moments of intimacy and confrontation take place in the wings, or just after the door closes.... Lucy is a delicate, careful observer, but her rage prevents her from reveling in the deliciousness of a moment. At her happiest, she simply says, 'Life isn't so bad after all.' "

Other Works

Kincaid wrote a nonfiction essay entitled *A Small Place,* which continued her focus on Antigua. This time, however, the author's focus was on tourism, not individual personalities. Alison Friesinger Hill, writing in the *New York Times Book Review,* had a mixture of both praise and criticism for the book: "*A Small Place* is strongest when Ms. Kincaid is concrete in her grievances, or when she indulges in her wily, wonderful descriptions. Often, however, the writing is distorted by her anger, which backs the reader into a corner.... Consequently, both writer and reader are left unsatisfied."

In one of a series of books published by the Whitney Museum pairing authors and artists, Jamaica Kincaid and Eric Fischl collaborated to create *Annie, Gwen, Lilly, Pam and Tulip,* the story of five girls growing into womanhood. "Kincaid's text is so appealing ... that it yearns to be read aloud repeatedly by both children and adults. Fischl's lithographs illustrate the mysteries, fears, and revelations of the five young women as they share some time musing about love, life, and their futures," wrote Jean Keleher in *Library Journal.*

Davis assesses Kincaid's three works of fiction with these comments: "With the passage of time her first book, *At the Bottom of the River,* a collection of gorgeous, incantatory stories of young life in Antigua, can now be viewed as the sketchbook from which was drawn her more conventional coming-of-age novel, *Annie John....* *Lucy* could be construed as a kind of sequel to Annie John, but ... the two books are like night and day in style and structure: one lush and descriptive, moving chronologically and underscoring its major themes with imagery and metaphor; the other narrative sparse and seemingly scattered, meandering in and out of situations rather than resolving or coming to conclusions, perhaps, more like life."

Kincaid's unusual blending of theme and technique brought forth these comments from Walcott: "The simplicity of her sentences is astounding. As she writes a sentence, the temperature of it psychologically is that it heads toward its own contradiction. It's as if the sentence is discovering itself, discovering how it feels. And that's astonishing, because it's one thing to be able to write a good declarative sentence; it's another thing to catch the temperature of the narrator, the narrator's feeling. And that's universal, and not provincial in any way."

Garis, at the end of her article, takes the reader from the present back to the young girl in Antigua. Garis noted, "Off [Kincaid's] living room is a small space stuffed haphazardly with books. They seem to tumble off her desk and rise up from the floor in wondrous piles of disorder. She tells me that no matter how hard she tries, her study looks exactly like the stash of stolen books under her house when she was a little girl. What an odyssey her life has been."

■ Works Cited

Austin, Jacqueline, "Up from Eden, *Voice Literary Supplement,* April 1985.

Bardsley, Barney, *New Statesman,* September 7, 1984.

Bemrose, John, "Growing Pains of Girlhood," *Maclean's Magazine,* May 20, 1985.

Bonnell, "*Annie* Travels to Second Childhood," *The Boston Herald,* March 31, 1985.

Cudjoe, Selwyn, "Jamaica Kincaid and the Modernist Project: An Interview," *Caribbean Women Writers: Essays from the First International Conference.* Callaloo, 1990.

Davis, Thulani, "Girl-Child in a Foreign Land, *New York Times Book Review,* October 28, 1990.

Eder, Richard, "Third-World Person Singular, *Los Angeles Times Book Review,* October 21, 1990.

Freeman, Susanne, review of *At the Bottom of the River, MS.,* January 1984.

Garis, Leslie, "Through West Indian Eyes," *New York Times Magazine,* October 7, 1990.

Hill, Alison Friesinger, *New York Times Book Review,* July 10, 1988.

Keleher, Jean, *Library Journal,* December 1, 1989.

Kenney, Susan, *New York Times Book Review,* April 7, 1985.

Kincaid, Jamaica, *At the Bottom of the River,* Farrar, Straus, 1983.

Kincaid, Jamaica, *Lucy,* Farrar, Straus, 1990.

Listfield, Emily, article about Jamaica Kincaid, *Harper's Bazaar,* October, 1990.

Moore, Susanna, "A Journey of Self-Discovery, *Washington Post Book World,* October 7, 1990.

O'Conner, Patricia T., *New York Times Book Review,* April 7, 1985.

Ike Onwordi, "Wising Up," *Times Literary Supplement,* November 29, 1985.

Tyler, Anne, "Mothers and Mysteries," *Republic,* Volume 189, No. 27, December 31, 1983.

■ For More Information See

BOOKS

Black Literature Criticism, Volume 2, Gale, 1991.

Contemporary Literary Criticism, Volume 68, Gale, 1987.

Dance, D. Cumber, editor, *Fifty Caribbean Writers,* Greenwood, 1986.*

—Sketch by Barbara A. Withers

Mercedes Lackey

■ Personal

Full name, Mercedes R. Lackey; born June 24, 1950; daughter of Edward George and Joyce (a housewife; maiden name, Anderson) Ritche; married Anthony Lackey, June 10, 1972; married Larry Dixon (science fiction/fantasy artist) December 10, 1990. *Education:* Purdue University, B.S., 1972. *Politics:* "Esoteric." *Religion:* "Nontraditional." *Hobbies and other interests:* Music, falconry, and scuba diving.

■ Addresses

Home and office—207 South Harvard, Tulsa, OK 74112. *Agent*—Russell Galen, 845 Third Ave., New York, NY 10022.

■ Career

Fantasy writer. Artist's model in and near South Bend, IN, 1975-81; Associates Data Processing, South Bend, computer programmer, 1979-82; CAIRS (survey and data processing firm), South Bend, surveyor, layout designer, and analyst, 1981-82; American Airlines, Tulsa, OK, computer programmer, 1982-1990. *Member:* Science Fiction Writers of America.

■ Awards, Honors

Best Books for Young Adults citation, 1987, for *Arrows of the Queen.*

■ Writings

"QUEEN'S OWN" SERIES

Arrows of the Queen, DAW Books, 1987.
Arrow's Flight, DAW Books, 1987.
Arrow's Fall, DAW Books, 1988.
Sacred Ground, Tor Books, 1994.

"VOWS AND HONOR" SERIES

Oathbound, DAW Books, 1988.
Oathbreakers, DAW Books, 1989.

"DIANA TREGARDE INVESTIGATIONS" SERIES

Burning Water, Tor Books, 1989.
Children of the Night, Tor Books, 1990.
Jinx High, Tor Books, 1991.

"LAST HERALD-MAGE" SERIES

Magic's Pawn, DAW Books, 1989.
Magic's Promise, DAW Books, 1989.
Magic's Price, DAW Books, 1990.
By the Sword, DAW Books, 1991.

"MAGE WINDS" SERIES

Winds of Fate, DAW Books, 1991.
Winds of Change, DAW Books, 1993.
Winds of Fury, DAW Books, 1993.

"BARDIC VOICES" SERIES

The Lark and the Wren, Baen, 1992.
The Robin and the Kestrel, Baen, 1993.

"SERRAted EDGE" SERIES

(With Larry Dixon) *Born to Run*, Baen, 1992.
(With Mark Shepherd) *Wheels of Fire*, Baen, 1992.
(With Holly Lisle) *When the Bough Breaks*, Baen, 1993.

COLLABORATIONS

(With C. J. Cherryh) *Reap the Whirlwind*, Baen, 1989.
(With Ellen Goun)*A Knight of Ghosts and Shadows*, Baen, 1990.
(With E. Goun) *Summoned to Tourney*, Baen, 1992.
(With E. Goun) *Freedom Flight*, Baen, 1992.
(With Joseph Sherman) *Castle of Deception*, Baen, 1993.
(With Andre Norton) *The Elvenbane: An Epic High Fantasy of the Halfblood Chronicles*, Tor Books, 1993.
(With Ru Emerson) *Fortress of Frost and Fire*, Baen, 1993.
(With Piers Anthony) *If I Pay Thee Not in Gold*, Baen, 1993.
(With M. Shepherd) *Prison of Souls*, Baen, 1993.
(With Marion Zimmer Bradley) *Rediscovery: A Novel of Darkover*, DAW Books, 1993.
(With Anne McCaffrey) *The Ship Who Searched*, Baen, 1993.
(With L. Dixon) *The Black Gryphon*, illustrated by Dixon, DAW Books, 1993.

Also author (with Shepherd) of *Prison of Souls*.

OTHER

Contributor of stories to numerous anthologies and periodicals, including "Stolen Silver," *Horse Fantastic*, edited by Martin Greenberg, DAW Books; "Werehunter," *Tales of the Witchworld*, edited by Andre Norton, DAW Books; "Skitty," *Catsfantastic*, edited by Norton, DAW Books; "Fiddler Fair," *Magic in Ithkar*, edited by Robert Adams and Norton; "Deathangel," *Merovingen Nights, Festival Moon;* "Don't Look Back" and "Friends Like These," *Merovingen Nights, Divine Right;* "Turnabout," *Fantasy Book*, September, 1985; and "The Last One of the Season," *American Fantasy*, winter, 1987. Has also written music and lyrics for cassette release.

■ Work in Progress

(With Norton) *Elvenblood* (sequel to *Elvenbane*); *Triangle Park* (sequel to *Jinx High*); *Arcanum 101* (a

"Diana Tregarde Investigations" book), *Chrome Circle* (a new *SERRAted Edge* novel); and (with Sherman) *A Cast of Corbies: A Novel of Bardic Choices*, all expected in 1995; and a third *Bardic Voices* novel.

■ Sidelights

Animals communicate with people, who also coexist with elves and gryphons, psychic abilities are taken for granted as talents, like singing, and magic is recognized as particular manipulations of earthly and human energy—welcome to the worlds of Mercedes Lackey. A self-confessed addict to fantasy/science fiction, Lackey began writing her own stories as a child, when Andre Norton "wasn't turning out books at a fast enough rate to suit me." Lackey describes those early stories to Bradley Sinor in *Starlog* as "Andre Norton pastiches." Years later, however, she found herself returning to her childhood hobby and writing a novel with her early favorite as an award-winning author of fantasy fiction.

Lackey was born in Chicago and grew up in Indiana. She became hooked on fantasy and science fiction early on, beginning with Ruthven Todd's "Space Cat" books when she was eight or nine years old. She soon discovered Andre Norton and other authors whose works are aimed at adult audiences. Lackey used to save her allowance "to order [Norton's books] directly from Ace," she told interviewers Rebecca Taylor, Gayle Keresey, and Margaret Miles in *Voice of Youth Advocates* (*VOYA*).

In 1972, Lackey graduated from Purdue University with a degree in biology, but worked as an artist's model around South Bend, Indiana, where she eventually landed a job in computer programming at Associates Data Processing. In 1982, Lackey moved to Tulsa, Oklahoma, and found a computer programming job with American Airlines. She remained there until her writing began to fully support her in 1990.

Lackey began writing stories for science fiction/fantasy fan magazines while working at American Airlines. "Whenever I wasn't at work, I was bored out of my mind and needed something to do," she told Sinor. Known as "zines," the publications usually feature stories written by fans of well-known worlds created by authors who sometimes, but not always, sanction these fan-produced additions to their original creations. Lackey wrote for *Fortune and Glory, Shadowstar* (which frequently publishes stories related to "Star Wars" themes and characters), and *Dragonlore*. The first "Diana Tregarde" stories appeared in *Shadowstar*.

In addition to writing for the magazines, Lackey attended science fiction fan conventions. It was at one such convention that she met writer C.J. Cherryh, who encouraged her to move her work into the professional arena. Lackey told Sinor that "at that time, I had sold one story to a professional market, one of Marion Zimmer Bradley's *Darkover* anthologies." In 1985 she attended the North American Science Fiction Convention and met with Betsy Wollheim at DAW Books.

Wollheim told Lackey that DAW was considering buying her books. As Lackey told Sinor, Wollheim was also "feeling me out to find out if I was going to act hysterically when she said there were rewrites that they wanted." But Lackey confides she would only have gotten anxious if they had to be done on a typewriter (she has a type of dyslexia that makes typing very difficult). Over time, Lackey has developed self-discipline in checking her work. In addition, working on the computer she bought in the meantime has made corrections much easier to do.

In 1987, DAW Books published Lackey's first novel, *Arrows of the Queen*. It was dedicated "to Marion Zimmer Bradley and Lisa Waters who kept *telling* me I could do this." According to the Sinor interview, when Cherryh read the manuscript for *Arrows of the Queen* in 1984, she told Lackey to "commit trilogy." Lackey responded a bit skeptically, but continued *Arrows of the Queen* with *Arrow's Flight* the same year and *Arrow's Fall* in 1988.

Until Lackey was able to quit her full-time job, she decorated her work area with her book jackets. She told Sinor that she had "a very good boss who got a big kick out of the fact that I was a published writer." Finally, in 1990, she had so many contracts to write books that her writing alone was able to support her. And she loves it. "Working eight-to-five was killing me. Now, I can go back to being a vampire," Lackey told Sinor.

Night Work

Certainly a little moonlight doesn't hurt when weaving tales of fantasy worlds. Yet Lackey's work involves at least as much discipline as magic. According to Sinor's article, she writes "at least ten pages . . . [and] has been known to push for as many as 20" a night. Lackey described for Sinor a system involving first, character development—"for me,

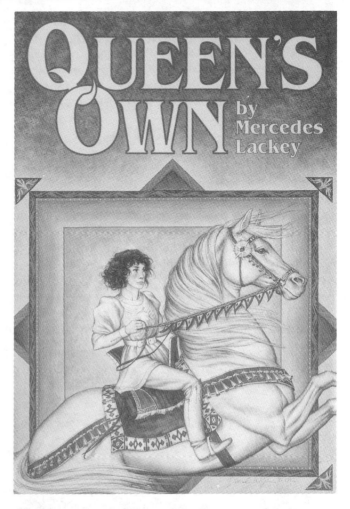

This 1987 work follows the adventures of Talia, a runaway who becomes special advisor to the Queen of Valdemere.

everything in storytelling starts from the characters." Next, Lackey creates a fairly detailed outline of the book's action, a task requiring anywhere from two weeks to a month, then the rest of the story is gradually filled in, night after night.

Certain images recur throughout Lackey's work. Birds, in particular, have a way of finding important niches in the novels. Lackey and her husband are "federally-licensed bird rehabilitators, specializing in injured hawks, owls, and falcons," Dixon told *VOYA*. Music is another element Lackey incorporates into her work again and again. She writes lyrics for songs, sometimes making it part of the novel-writing process. Some of her lyrics appear as an appendix to *Arrow's Fall*. She once commented: "I frequently will write a lyric when I am attempting to get to the heart of a crucial scene. . . . When I write the 'folk music' of these peoples, I am enriching my whole world, whether I actually use the song in the text or not." Lackey is known as a leading songwriter in the filk genre ("filk" is folk music set in science fiction or fantasy worlds). Her own musical preferences are varied, ranging from the Eurhythmics and Queen to Steeleye Span and Gold Bough to Alan Hovaniss and Tchaikovsky to Davis Lanz and Spencer Brewer.

The Valdemar Books

Magic or no, Lackey's first novel grew out of a dream she had in 1981. In the dream, she tells the *VOYA* interviewers, she was Talia, 'Chosen' by her Companion and meeting with the Queen. *Arrows of the Queen* develops the story of Talia, a thirteen-year-old girl from a "solemn and straight-laced Hold" family living in the ultra-conservative Borderlands of Valdemar. Unlike most Holdgirls, Talia rebels; she manages to read, her only escape from a life of unending chores and obedience to male members of the family. When she is confronted by

In this 1993 novel, the second book in "The Mage Winds" fantasy trilogy, the magician Darkwind and his clan must combat the sinister Mornelithe Falconsbane.

the women of the family with the very near prospect of marrying, she flees the house to wander a nearby road and seriously contemplates running away. But before she can make a decision, she encounters a Companion, one of the magical, intelligent, and clairvoyant beings in horse form who choose those who will be Heralds, respected and admired administrators of justice throughout Valdemar. Unaware that she has been Chosen, since Holderkin do not believe in educating their children about the Heralds, she learns about her new life as not only a Herald but also special advisor to the Queen, Queen's Own. Her position requires that she learn to trust men (Holderkin men proved to be very hurtful to her in the past) and train her special powers of empathy.

In *Arrow's Flight*, Talia has graduated from her classes and become a full Herald. The story follows her on her first tour of duty through a region of Valdemar. Accompanied by Kris, a more experienced Herald, she faces the challenges presented by a less than complete training of her gift of empathy. Together, with the help of her Companions, she gradually learns to control it. Along the way, she faces ethical problems related to her gift: is she unwittingly manipulating people? are there ever circumstances when doing so may be the right thing? *Arrow's Fall* concludes the trilogy. In this novel, Talia investigates a marriage proposal for the Queen's daughter, Elspeth, from Prince Ancar of a neighboring kingdom. She discovers there is an evil magic in his kingdom and must prevent the marriage.

A reviewer in *Publishers Weekly* felt *Arrows of the Queen* was "agreeable if sentimental," and perceived the novel as an "uncritical embodiment of adolescent wish fulfillment." But James T. Crawford in *Fantasy Review* called *Arrows of the Queen* "absorbing," and admired its themes of "personal growth and discovery." In *Booklist*, Roland Green, reviewing *Arrow's Fall*, forecasted Lackey as a potential "major figure in the field" of fantasy literature.

The "Mage Winds" trilogy begins where *Arrow's Fall* leaves off. In the first book, *Winds of Fate*, Elspeth, heir to the throne, has become a Herald. Prince Ancar is causing more magical trouble and she urges the court that Valdemar needs to relearn the magic power it has lost, since the shields placed around the kingdom by Vanyel are weakening. She volunteers herself to go in search of an Adept mage who can train them in protecting the kingdom. Eventually she finds Darkwind of the Tayledras Clan in k'Sheyna who, for his part, feels that his

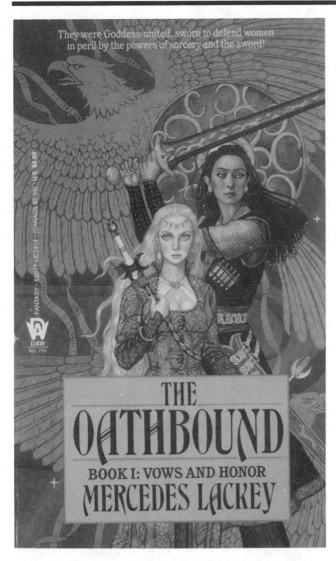

They were Goddess-united, sworn to defend women in peril by the powers of sorcery and the sword!

THE OATHBOUND

BOOK I: VOWS AND HONOR
MERCEDES LACKEY

This 1988 novel, part of the "Vows and Honor" series, features a sorceress and swordswoman who are sworn by oath to fight evil as they wander the world together.

people have misused magic to serve their needs and has renounced his own powers, until he meets Elspeth and learns her troubles. But Darkwind's clan has their own evil enemy. They team up with others to combat Mornelithe Falconsbane in *Winds of Change*. In the final novel of the series, *Winds of Fury*, Elspeth and Darkwind travel to Valdemar to take care of the threat Prince Ancar presents.

In this series Lackey presents a number of non-human characters in addition to the Companions. Gryphons, changechildren, and hertasi share this world with human characters in interesting ways. Taylor and Miles noted that Lackey "excels in making [them] ... sympathetic, complex, and believable." Many reviewers note the coming-of-age theme in the series; referring to Lackey's "essential themes," Taylor and Miles put it this way:

"Becoming an adult is scary, hard work; finding the right person to share your life with is never as simple as it seems; and honesty and honor are the best one can strive for."

Filling in Valdemar's History

The "Last Herald-Mage" series depicts people and events in Valdemar about 600 years before those in *By the Sword*, and *The Mage Winds* trilogy (which are set in the same period). At fifteen, Vanyel is heir to the throne in Valdemar and the last of the Herald Mages, but would rather be a Court Bard, a musician for one of the Great Courts of Valdemar, than a warrior. His disappointed father sends him to live with his Aunt Savil, a Herald at Valdemar's High court. There he discovers his mage gift and trains it until he becomes the most powerful mage in Valdemar. He faces the challenge of his homosexuality; by the third book, *Magic's Price*, his parents finally accept it. And throughout the trilogy he is haunted by dreams of his own death, which also occurs in the third book. Ironically, from the point of view of the first novel, *Magic's Pawn*, he dies heroically, defending Valdemar by holding off the Dark Servants' approach. Of *Magic's Promise*, Green wrote that Lackey's storytelling skills here are of a "high order." Carolyn Cushman of *LOCUS* acknowledges the depth of Lackey's characterizations in her review of *Magic's Promise*. Vanyel's "brutal" father is also an "unintelligent, confused man trying to do his misguided best," while the "sadistic arms instructor becomes an ally."

Lackey's second series consisted of the "Vows and Honor" novels, *The Oathbound* and *Oathbreakers*. The protagonists, the Shin'a'in swordswoman Tarma and the sorceress Kethry, first appeared in Marion Zimmer Bradley's *Sword and Sorceress* volumes. Their story continues as the wandering oathbound pair battles demons real and human. Tarma and Kethry inhabit the same world depicted in the "Last Herald-Mage" series, *By the Sword*, and the "Mage Winds" series.

By the Sword tells the story of Kerowyn, granddaughter of Kethry of *The Oathbound* and *Oathbreakers* and arms instructor of Elspeth in the "Mage Winds" trilogy. After tragedy strikes her family, Kerowyn leaves home to learn the trade of a mercenary. Eventually, she joins a company known as the Skybolts, becomes their captain, and leads them into a reputation as the best mercenary group in Valdemar. She also represents a long tradition of magic in conflict with the Heralds' tradition of using only mind magic, or psychic powers. Taylor pointed to this novel as potentially difficult for those unfamiliar with either of the series it connects, while Cushman considered it to be "complete in itself." Both critics agree, however, that here Lackey has crafted a suspenseful story. Cushman finds that Lackey's greater emphasis on action and strategy and Kerowyn being "less taken up in internal struggles" than other Lackey characters to be major strengths of this novel.

On the SERRAted Edge and Other Worlds by Lackey

Many of Lackey's books center around young people who've been abused, or, as she put it in her *VOYA* interview, "misunderstood, outsiders." So it's not surprising that she has involved herself in the *SERRAted Edge* series, a group of novels dealing with what faces kids who are abused or run away from home. She gives publisher Jim Baen "a world of credit" for backing this collaborative project.

Set in the United States, SERRA is a acronym for South Eastern Road Racing Association, a group of elves who add their own special gifts to the cars they race. The last page of each novel contains 800 numbers to three agencies. Two help to locate missing children; the third is a hotline available to abused children to get help. As the Epilogue at the end of *Wheels of Fire* reads: "You don't need elves or magic to get a start on helping a child in a desperate situation-you don't even need a quarter."

With the "Diana Tregarde Investigations" series, Lackey moves quite a bit closer to the "real" world. Diana Tregarde is an investigator who writes to pay the bills. She also happens to be psychic, so her specialties tend to be cases involving the supernatural. In *Burning Water*, she helps solve a series of ritualistic murders committed by workers of dark magic. *Children of the Night* involves Diana with vampires. The latest, *Jinx High*, has Diana helping some "very real kids involved in some very unreal and very scary things," as Taylor put it.Lackey told Sinor that she modeled Diana Tregarde after Diana Rigg and other people she knows, including her sister-in-law, and started writing the series because "I needed an outlet for some otherwise unchannelable aggressions."

In the "Bardic Voices"—her most recent solo series—Lackey takes us to a decidedly medieval type of world dominated by the Church. Fourteen-year-old Rune works in a tavern with her unmar-

ried mother, whose main concerns are marrying the recently widowed innkeeper and making sure Rune performs her large share of chores. Rune happens to be a gifted fiddler and grows increasingly frustrated with the total lack of support for nurturing her talent. Subjected to ridicule by the other teenagers in town and attempted rape by some of the males, one night she boasts that she will run off to play her fiddle for the Ghost of Skull Hill. No one has ever returned from a night trip to Skull Hill before, and neither does Rune. She plays for the Ghost who leaves her at sunrise with a bag of silver. She decides to run away to find a tutor to prepare her to face the Bardic Guild's annual trials for admission.

Traveling in disguise as a boy for safety reasons, she finds musician jobs and a tutor along the way. Eventually she makes it to the competition, wins, and is beaten and thrown out when the judges discover she is a girl. At that point she is cared for and "adopted" by the Free Bards, a group of wandering musicians who either could not or would not join the Guild. They are led, she discovers, by Master Bard Gwydain aka Talaysen aka Wren, one of the greatest Bards in the Guild, who left the Guild and went underground when he realized all the disadvantages to belonging. The Free Bards confront and negotiate with wily elves and deal with an evil priest who turns Gwyna into a bird. The next book in the series, *The Robin and the Kestrel*, follows two of the Free Bards who marry at the conclusion of *The Lark and the Wren*, Gwyna aka Robin and Kestrel aka Prince and heir to the throne of Birnam.

Partnerships in Fantasy

Mercedes Lackey has written many novels in collaboration with other authors. On writing novels with others, she says that "now that I have my 'own' style, [I can] chameleon anyone" she works with, in order to blend styles in the work so that the novel itself is what grabs the reader's attention. Some works are based on video and computer games. *Freedom Flight*, written with Ellen Guon, is based on the video game *Wing Commander*, while *Castle of Deception*, written with Josepha Sherman, is based on the *Bard's Tale* computer game.

One of the most well-known collaborations Lackey has done is *The Elvenbane: An Epic High Fantasy of the Halfblood Chronicles*, written with Andre Norton. Elves are in control of this world, and human beings are their slaves, until Shana, a half-breed, along with her half-brother and allied dragons leads a revolution against the elves. Lackey and Norton plan on a sequel, tentatively entitled *Elvenblood.*

One of Lackey's newest collaborations, *The Black Gryphon,* was done with her husband, Larry Dixon. Dixon told Miller that he has worked with his wife on her novels since *Magic's Price,* but that he's "not about to steal any of Misty's thunder." Events in *The Black Gryphon* predate the foundation of Valdemar and center around a group of gryphons led by Skandranon.

TANSTAFL

(Or, there ain't no such thing as a free lunch)

That's how Lackey terms the guiding tenet of her creations of other worlds. She once commented that "in my worlds, magic is paid for, and the cost to the magician is frequently a high one." Responsibility and social consciousness are significant themes in Lackey's work. Her inventions of non-human intelligent beings to populate her worlds with humans and how they do and don't get along seem evocations of ethnic problems in our own world. Her protagonists more often than not are abused children and adolescents finding ways to live better lives. Of potential criticism for dealing with controversial issues, such as homosexuality, she told Taylor that she'd "considered borrowing the disclaimer from the game *Stalking the Night Fantastic*—If anything in this book offends you, please feel free to buy and burn as many copies as you like. Volume discounts are available."

Lackey often describes herself as a storyteller ("That's what I see as 'my job'"). She once remarked that "in everything I write I try to expound the creed I gave my character Di Tregarde in *Burning Water*–there's no such thing as 'one, true way'; the only answers worth having are the ones you find for yourself; leave the world better than you found it. Love, freedom, and the chance to do some good—they're the things worth living and dying for, and if you aren't willing to die for the things worth living for, you might as well turn in your membership in the human race."

Lackey bridged her worlds with her readers' in the dedication to *Winds of Change:* "To the Tayledras and Heralds of our world: police, firefighters, and rescue workers everywhere, whose accomplishments in everyday life outdo anything in fiction."

■ Works Cited

Review of *Arrows of the Queen, Publishers Weekly,* February 13, 1987, p. 87.

Crawford, James T., "Bringing Up Brat," *Fantasy Review,* March, 1987, p. 46.

Cushman, Carolyn, review of *Magic's Promise, LOCUS,* January, 1990, p. 23.

Cushman, Carolyn, review of *By the Sword, LOCUS,* March, 1991, p. 31.

Green, Roland, review of *Magic's Promise, Booklist,* January 15, 1988, p. 831.

Green, Roland, review of *Arrow's Fall, Booklist,* January 1, 1990, p. 895.

Lackey, Mercedes, *Arrows of the Queen,* DAW Books, 1987.

Lackey, Mercedes, *Winds of Change,* DAW Books, 1993.

Lackey, Mercedes, and Mark Shepherd, *Wheels of Fire,* Baen, 1992.

Sinor, Bradley H., "Mage of Winds," *Starlog,* December, 1991, pp. 52-56.

Taylor, Rebecca Sue, review of *By the Sword, Voice of Youth Advocates,* June, 1991, p. 110.

Taylor, Rebecca Sue, and Margaret Miles, review of *Winds of Fate, Voice of Youth Advocates,* February, 1992, p. 384.

Taylor, Rebecca, Gayle Keresey, and Margaret Miles, "Interview with Mercedes," *Voice of Youth Advocates,* October, 1992, pp. 213-217.

■ For More Information See

PERIODICALS

Fantasy Review, March, 1987, p. 46.

Library Journal, June 15, 1988, p. 71; October 15, 1991, p. 126; September 15, 1992, p. 97.°

—Sketch by Helene Henderson

Harper Lee

Personal

Born Nelle Harper Lee, April 28, 1926, in Monroeville, AL; daughter of Amasa Coleman (a lawyer) and Frances Finch Lee. *Education:* Attended Huntingdon College in Montgomery, AL, 1944-45, and the University of Alabama, 1945-49; also attended Oxford University for one year. *Religion:* Methodist. *Hobbies and other interests:* Music and golf.

Addresses

Home—Monroeville, AL. *Agent*—c/o McIntosh & Otis, Inc., 18 East 41st Street, New York, NY 10017.

Career

Novelist and essayist. Eastern Air Lines and British Overseas Airways, New York City, airline reservations clerk, early 1950s. *Member:* National Council on Arts, 1966-72.

Awards, Honors

Pulitzer Prize for fiction, 1961, for *To Kill a Mockingbird;* Brotherhood Award, National Conference of Christians and Jews, 1961; Alabama Library Association Award, 1961; Paperback of the Year award, *Best Sellers,* 1962, for *To Kill a Mockingbird.*

Writings

To Kill a Mockingbird, Lippincott, 1960.

OTHER

Contributor of essays to periodicals, including "Love—In Other Words," *Vogue;* and "Christmas to Me," *McCalls. To Kill a Mockingbird* has been translated into over ten languages and a large print edition.

Adaptations

To Kill a Mockingbird was adapted as a film by Horton Foote, starring Gregory Peck and Mary Badham, Universal, 1962; and as a London stage play by Christopher Sergel, 1987.

Sidelights

As a child, Harper Lee was "a rough 'n' tough tomboy.... She had short, cropped hair, wore coveralls, went barefoot, and could talk mean like a boy," according to Marianne M. Moates in *A Bridge of Childhood: Truman Capote's Southern Years.* Known as Nelle to her family and friends in the small town of Monroeville, Alabama, Lee lived

The setting for *To Kill a Mockingbird* was taken from Lee's memories of her hometown, Monroeville, Alabama, seen here in a 1932 photograph.

next door to the Faulks—spinster sisters Jenny, Sook, and Callie, and brother Bud; writer Truman Capote lived with the Faulks for several childhood summers, as well (and may have been the model for Dill, Scout and Jem's "summer" friend). In many ways, Moates's description of young Lee mirrors that of Scout in the author's only completed novel, *To Kill a Mockingbird*. The striking similarities between Lee and her fictional counterpart are also reflected in the parallels between the fictional setting of the novel and Lee's hometown. At times, Lee's use of autobiographical elements gave rise to controversy. Amid all the hoopla for Lee's winning the Pulitzer Prize was gossip that her friend Truman Capote had actually written the book for her. According to Moates, there was also a rumor that one Monroeville family threatened to sue the author because the book's heroic, reclusive Boo Radley too closely resembled someone in their family. Moates, who attended some of the social events honoring Lee's early celebrity, observes: "When [Lee] had enough, she reminded people that her book was fiction, zipped her lips shut, and caught the next plane back to New York."

Lee's lips have stayed shut, for the most part, since the mid-1960s. A fairly reclusive author, Lee was

initially surprised by reader reaction to her book. Since *To Kill a Mockingbird*'s publication, she has given few interviews and, for all intents and purposes, seems to have "faded from view." Lee's sister Alice—an attorney practicing in Monroeville—filled in some gaps when she told *Authors and Artists for Young Adults* that her sister currently divides her time between New York City and Monroeville. Neither Lee sister, however, cares to discuss the novel written more than thirty years ago because they consider it "old news."

Lee's Claim to Fame

Whatever the reasons behind for Lee's failure to publish another book, *To Kill a Mockingbird* remains very popular with young adult readers; it is also a frequent selection in high school and college English classes. In the three-plus decades since its release, *To Kill a Mockingbird* remains one of the most studied novels in modern American literature, in large part because its themes and characters have a timeless appeal. According to Dorothy Jewell Altman in the *Dictionary of Literary Biography*, Lee's place in American letters is assured because this "regional novel with a universal message . . . combines popular appeal with literary excellence."

According to Altman, Lee spent several years writing her novel. She did not, however, begin her writing career with *To Kill a Mockingbird* in mind. In the early 1950s, Lee worked as an airline reservations clerk in New York City, writing essays and short stories in her off hours. Encouraged by her literary agent to expand one of her stories into a novel, Lee quit her airline job. With the financial support of some friends, she spent several years revising her manuscript before submitting it to Lippincott in 1957. When editors criticized Lee's initial plot structure as being too disjointed and fragmentary, the author made some revisions, making her final—and accepted—submission in early 1960.

A young girl and her brother learn about prejudice, courage, and dignity in this Pulitzer Prize-winning 1960 work.

To Kill a Mockingbird is "quite an ambiguous title," states R. A. Dave in *Indian Studies in American Fiction*, leaving one "guessing whether it is a crime-thriller or a book on bird-hunting." In truth, the book is about a young girl's coming of age in an era of social and political upheaval. Jean Louise Finch (also known as Scout)—the novel's narrator—lives with her bother Jem and widowed father Atticus in the small fictional town of Maycomb, Alabama during the 1930s. Told from the perspective of a grown-up Scout, the novel traces the circumstances that lead Atticus to take on the case of Tom Robinson, a black man falsely accused of raping a white woman. In the three years surrounding the trial, Scout and Jem witness the unjust consequences of prejudice and hate, while at the same time experiencing the value of courage and integrity through the example of their father. Through the course of the book, readers come to know the residents of Maycomb—good and bad—as well as the misunderstandings and long-held beliefs that lead to the book's tragic climax.

The novel's colorful characters have long been a draw for young readers. Aside from independent Scout, there is stalwart Jem and mischievous Dill Harris, whose antics and wild plans often get the trio into "worlds of trouble." Calpurnia, the Finch's black housekeeper, helps keep the children in line; she also exposes them to Tom Robinson's world via a trip to her church for Sunday services. Arthur "Boo" Radley—perhaps the most tragic figure in the tale—is the town recluse. As the novel progresses, Scout, Jem, and Dill come to see Boo as less of a scary, shadowy figure, and more of a feeling human being. Through all the book's turmoil, Atticus Finch remains the voice of reason and restraint. While obviously disturbed and dismayed by the nature of Tom Robinson's trial, the lawyer nevertheless takes great pains to explain to his children why his participation, as well as their understanding, is necessary.

Initial critical response to Lee's story was mixed. Harding LeMay, writing in the *New York Herald Tribune Book Review*, praises the author's "grace of writing and honorable decency of intent." "Miss Lee's problem has been to tell the story she wants to tell and yet stay within the consciousness of a child, and she hasn't consistently solved it," observes Granville Hicks in *Saturday Review*. Dave, in a more supportive vein, claims that in the novel "there is a complete cohesion of art and morality. And therein lies [*To Kill a Mockingbird*'s] success. [Lee] is a remarkable storyteller. The reader just glides through the novel abounding in humor and pathos, hopes and fears, love and hatred, humanity and brutality—all affording him a memorable human experience of journeying through sunshine and rain at once.... The tale of heroic struggle lingers in our memory as an unforgettable experience."

Setting and Characterization: The Old Vs. the New South

Aside from Lee's depiction of various Southern character "types," the unique setting of her novel has engendered a great deal of commentary. Fred Erisman of the *Alabama Review* argues that Lee's novel reflects the possibilities of a new, revitalized South, moving "from the archaic, imported romanticism of its past toward the more reasonable, pragmatic, and native romanticism of a Ralph Waldo Emerson." Erisman remarks that Lee establishes the stagnant "Old South" setting by describing Maycomb of the early 1930s as "an old town," "a tired old town," and "an ancient town." He

points to Lee's description of the Maycomb County courthouse, which dominates the town square, as symbolizing the South's being mired in the past: "Greek revival columns clashed with a big nineteenth-century clock toward housing a rusty unreliable instrument, a view indicating a people determined to preserve every physical scrap of the past."

Erisman offers two specific examples to show Maycomb's affinity with the past, the first being Jem's reading of Sir Walter Scott's romantic classic *Ivanhoe* to the dying Mrs. Henry Lafayette Dubose (described in the text as an "indomitable Southern lady"). Again connecting setting to characterization, Erisman contrasts Atticus and his class-conscious sister Alexandra. While Alexandra "reveres and protects" class distinctions between the upper class (the Finches) and the lower class (the Cunninghams), Atticus presents a more benevolent Southern face. He is the one man the town *knows* is incorruptible and honorable, a man who will not be

The 1962 film adaptation of *To Kill a Mockingbird*, starring Mary Badham and Gregory Peck, captured two Academy Awards.

swayed by public opinion. This becomes clearer in passages such as the one in which the attorney explains to Scout his opinion about the townspeople's prejudice against Tom Robinson: "They're certainly entitled to think that, and they're entitled to full respect for their opinions ... but before I can live with other folks I've got to live with myself. The one thing that doesn't abide by majority rule is a person's conscience."

Many critics have tried analyze the characters in *To Kill a Mockingbird* by looking at Lee's childhood. Altman notes that Lee claims the novel is not autobiographical; the author also admits, however, that a writer "should write about what [he or she] knows and write truthfully." Moates is one of several writers who find obvious similarities between fiction and reality in the text. According to Moates, Lee grew up the youngest of three children in a strictly segregated town. In her novel, she uses her mother's maiden name for her fictional family, and makes Atticus a lawyer like her father Amasa. Lee's mother Frances Finch was eccentric, often rising in the middle of the night and "banging out tunes that in the summer months could be heard all the way to the downtown square," writes Moates. In *To Kill a Mockingbird*, Scout reveals that her mother died from a sudden heart attack when she was two, so she never felt her mother's absence and does not miss her.

Moates goes on to describe Lee's father, Amasa Coleman Lee, as an attorney preoccupied by work who nevertheless tried to spend time with his family (much the same as the fictional Atticus). Scout has this to say about her father Atticus: "Jem and I found our father satisfactory: he played with us, read to us, and treated us with courteous detachment."

Monroeville and Maycomb: Merging Fact and Fiction

Stories about Lee's childhood—as it meshed with writer Truman Capote—have long been part of the mystique surrounding the author's novel. Lee's real-life youthful adventures with young Capote are in many ways similar to those enjoyed by Scout and Jem with Dill. According to Moates, Lee was Capote's "pal, confidante, and, at times, sparring partner." The duo—together with one of Lee's brothers—played together constantly. They conspired in Nelle's backyard tree house, swam in the creek, and staged a Halloween party. When Moates moved to Monroeville in 1961, she walked by the town's grammar school, knowing that "one of the big oak trees on the school grounds was the tree where Boo Radley had hidden trinkets for Scout and Jem" and that nearby in the center of town "stood the tired red-brick courthouse, supposedly where Atticus Finch defended a wronged black man." She also describes the Lees's and Faulks' homes, separated by a hedge through which the children slipped back and forth to visit.

Along with these tales about Lee's family and neighbors, Moates suggests some other possible origins for the novel's characters. For example, Lee's next-door neighbor Callie Faulk, a former schoolteacher, read to a blind neighbor while the neighborhood children listened from the sofa. When Lee writes about Scout's frustrations in school—most notably being so far ahead of her peers in reading that she was bored—Moates speculates that Lee might have been thinking of Capote's having "to sit through slow, dreary lessons when he had been reading since age five," thus transferring Capote's predicament to Scout's: "If I didn't have to stay [in school] I'd leave. Jem, that damn lady says Atticus's been teaching me to read and for him to stop it." Furthermore, Callie's oldest sister, Sook, is described by Moates as a "childlike woman who probably suffered from agoraphobia, an abnormal fear of being in public places" and who became a recluse hiding in the house's shadows. "If a stranger came," Moates writes, "she ducked out of sight." Sook and the children, however, shared a very close emotional bond: they cleaned the house, baked tea cakes and other special delights, read comic books, worked jigsaw puzzles, and rocked on the back porch.

Another reclusive person lived in Lee's neighborhood—the son of the Boular family who lived down the street. Moates speculates that this man may have inspired the characterization Boo Radley, since young Boular stayed hidden away in the house, eventually becoming the neighborhood "bogeyman" in impressionable children's imaginations. In Lee's novel, Jem describes the creature he has never seen: "Boo was about six-and-a-half feet tall, judging from his tracks; he dined on raw squirrels and any cats he could catch, that's why his hands were bloodstained—if you ate an animal raw, you could never wash the blood off. There was a long jagged scar that ran across his face; what teeth he had were yellow and rotten; his eyes popped, and he drooled most of the time." While Monroeville's Boular (and Boo Radley, for that matter), did not fit this description, it is rather easy to see how such a person might ignite a writer's—and a child's—imagination.

The interior of the Monroe County Courthouse in Monroeville served as the model for the courtroom in *To Kill a Mockingbird.*

Narrative Point of View: Child's Eyes, Adult's Heart

Readers see all the people and events of *To Kill a Mockingbird* through Scout's eyes—the "structural *forte*" of the novel, asserts William T. Going in *Essays on Alabama Literature.* Going claims that many early reviewers of the novel either misunderstood or misinterpreted the way Lee tells her story. For instance, *Atlantic Monthly* reviewer Phoebe Adams refers to the narrative point of view as "frankly and completely impossible, being told in the first person by a six-year-old girl with the prose and style of a well-educated adult." Richard Sullivan of the *Chicago Tribune* is similarly puzzled by Lee's narrator: "The unaffected young narrator uses adult language to render the matter she deals with, but the point of view is cunningly restricted to that of a perceptive, independent child, who doesn't always understand fully what's happening, but who conveys completely, by implication, the weight and burden of the story." Going, however,

concludes that the narrator's "evolving perception of the social milieu is handled through a "well-conceived" point of view which combines "child eyes and mature heart."

Theme: Chasing Away "Gray Ghosts"

Connected to the issue of the South's racial conflict are several other themes that capture many critics' attention. For example, Edgar H. Schuster, writing in *English Journal,* points to Scout and Jem's psychological growth, the Maycomb "caste system," and education versus superstition as themes which help explain the novel's theme and structure. Jem and Scout learn a great deal from the people and events around them during the three years of the story; in particular, they learn to replace fear and ignorance with security and knowledge, asserts Schuster. When Dill dares Jem to touch Boo Radley's spooky house, he wagers his book *The Gray Ghost* against two Tom Swift books. Schuster points out that two of the children's neighbors—Mrs. Dubose ("gray" in age and the unknown) and Radley (in a "gray" house)—are "'ghosts' in the sense that the children do not know them; fear and prejudice and superstition surround both homes."

As the story progresses from the first chapter to the last, Lee demonstrates how the children's contacts with the *real* Dubose and Radley have dispelled their *gray ghosts*—superstitions, prejudices, and fears. Schuster remarks, "The achievement of Harper Lee is not that she has written another novel about race prejudice, but rather that she has placed race prejudice in a perspective which allows us to see it as an aspect of a larger thing; as something that arises from phantom contacts from fear and lack of knowledge; and finally as something that disappears with the kind of knowledge or 'education' that one gains through learning what people are really like when you 'finally see them.'" Schuster concludes that the theme and structure unify to show the children's becoming educated to the ways of the world. He praises the novel's astute "rendering of a child's perspective through an adult's evaluation as among the most technically expert in contemporary literature."

When no second novel appeared thirty years after Lee's initial phenomenal success, many readers and critics began to question the reasons why. Associated Press writer Nancy Shulins speculates in *Item* that Lee had joined writers such as J. D. Salinger "who relinquish the spotlight at the height of fame" but "leave an indelible mark on the audiences they abandon." Shulins quotes a 1961 *Newsweek* article that promises a forthcoming novel: "Snowed under by fan letters, Harper Lee is stealing time from a new novel-in-progress to write careful answers." Except for some short pieces in popular women's magazines, however, Lee never published again. Like the reclusive Boo Radley, she has consistently declined to come out and speak. Critics can only speculate as to whether this reticence was caused by Lee's disillusionment with celebrity status, or perhaps, that the ideas for writing ceased to come. Even without a second novel however, the author's reputation seems secure. As Lee herself once said: "Writing is the hardest thing in the world ... but writing is the only thing that has made me completely happy."

■ Works Cited

Adams, Phoebe, review of *To Kill a Mockingbird*, *Atlantic Monthly*, August, 1960, pp. 98-99.

Altman, Dorothy Jewell, "Harper Lee," *Dictionary of Literary Biography*, Volume 6: *American Novelists since World War II*, Gale, 1980, pp. 180-183.

Dave, R. A., "*To Kill a Mockingbird:* Harper Lee's Tragic Vision," *Indian Studies in American Fiction*, Macmillan, 1974, pp. 211-323.

Erisman, Fred, "The Romantic Regionalism of Harper Lee," *Alabama Review*, April, 1973, pp. 122-136.

Going, William T., "*Store* and *Mockingbird:* Two Pulitzer Novels about Alabama," *Essays on Alabama Literature*, University of Alabama Press, 1975, pp. 9-31.

Hicks, Granville, "Three at the Outset," *Saturday Review*, July 23, 1960, 15-16.

Lee, Alice, in a phone interview with Laura M. Zaidman for *Authors and Artists for Young Adults*, November, 1993.

Lee, Harper, *To Kill a Mockingbird*, Lippincott, 1960.

LeMay, Harding, "Children Play: Adults Betray," *New York Herald Tribune Book Review*, July 10, 1960, p. 5.

Moates, Marianne M., *A Bridge of Childhood: Truman Capote's Southern Years*, Holt, 1989.

Schuster, Edgar H., "Discovering Theme and Structure in the Novel," *English Journal*, October 1963, pp. 506-511.

Shulins, Nancy, "Letting Go," *Item*, March 3, 1991, p. 24.

Sullivan, Richard, "Engrossing First Novel of Rare Excellence," *Chicago Sunday Tribune*, July 17, 1960, p. 1.

■ For More Information See

BOOKS

Contemporary Literary Criticism, Gale, Volume 12, 1980, pp. 340-343, Volume 60, 1990, pp. 239-250.

PERIODICALS

America, May 11, 1991, pp. 509-511.
Commonweal, December 29, 1960, p. 289.
English Journal, December, 1964, pp. 656-661.
New Statesman, October 15, 1960, p. 580.
New York Times Book Review, July 10, 1960, pp. 5, 18.
Times Literary Supplement, October 28, 1960.°

—Sketch by Laura M. Zaidman

Sonia Levitin

■ Personal

Has also written under maiden name Sonia Wolff; born August 18, 1934, in Berlin, Germany; emigrated to the United States, 1938; naturalized U.S. citizen, 1944; daughter of Max (a manufacturer) and Helene (Goldstein) Wolff; married Lloyd Levitin (a business executive), December 27, 1953; children: Daniel Joseph, Shari Diane. *Education:* Attended University of California, Berkeley, 1952-54; University of Pennsylvania, B.S., 1956; San Francisco State College (now University), graduate study, 1957-60. *Religion:* Jewish. *Hobbies and other interests:* Hiking, piano, Judaic studies, travel, history, painting.

■ Addresses

Home—Southern California. *Agent*—Toni Mendez, Inc., 141 East 56th St., New York, NY 10022.

■ Career

Writer and educator. Junior high school teacher, Mill Valley, CA, 1956-57; adult education teacher, Daly City, CA, 1962-64; Acalanes Adult Center, Lafayette, CA, teacher, 1965-72; teacher of crea-

tive writing, Palos Verdes Peninsula, CA, 1973-76, and University of California, Los Angeles Extension, 1976—; University of Judaism, instructor in American Jewish literature, 1989—. Founder of STEP (adult education organization) in Palos Verdes Peninsula. Has performed volunteer work, including publicity, for various charities and educational institutions. *Member:* Authors League of America, Authors Guild, PEN, Society of Children's Book Writers, California Writer's Guild, Moraga Historical Society (founder and former president).

■ Awards, Honors

National Jewish Book award in children's literature and American Library Association (ALA) Notable Book citation, both 1970, both for *Journey to America; Who Owns the Moon?* received an ALA Notable Book citation, 1973; *The Mark of Conte* received the Southern California Council on Literature for Children and Young People Award for fiction, 1976, and was nominated for California Young Readers Medal award in the junior high category, 1982; Golden Spur Award from Western Writers of America, and Lewis Carroll Shelf Award, both 1978, both for *The No-Return Trail;* Southern California Council on Literature for Children and Young People award, 1981, for a distinguished contribution to the field of children's literature; National Jewish Book Award in children's literature, PEN Los Angeles Award for young adult fiction, Association of Jewish Libraries Sydney Taylor Award, Austrian Youth Prize, Catholic Children's Book Prize (Germany), Dorothy

Canfield Fisher Award nomination, Parent's Choice Honor Book citation, and **ALA** Best Book for Young Adults citation, all 1988, all for *The Return;* Edgar Allan Poe Award from Mystery Writers of America, Dorothy Canfield Fisher Award nomination, and Nevada State Award nomination, all 1989, all for *Incident at Loring Groves; Silver Days* was named a 1989 Sydney Taylor Book Award Honor Book; *Roanoke: A Novel of the Lost Colony* was nominated for the Dorothy Canfield Fisher Award, the Georgia Children's Book Award, and the Mark Twain Award; *Journey to America* and *The No-Return Trail* were both Junior Literary Guild selections.

■ **Writings**

FOR YOUNG ADULTS

Journey to America (first novel in "Platt Family" trilogy), illustrated by Charles Robinson, Atheneum, 1970.

Roanoke: A Novel of the Lost Colony, illustrated by John Gretzer, Atheneum, 1973.

The Mark of Conte, illustrated by Bill Negron, Atheneum, 1976, published without illustrations, Collier Books, 1987.

Beyond Another Door, Atheneum, 1977.

The No-Return Trail, Harcourt, 1978.

Reigning Cats and Dogs (nonfiction), illustrated by Joan Berg Victor, Atheneum, 1978.

The Year of Sweet Senior Insanity, Atheneum, 1982.

Smile Like a Plastic Daisy, Atheneum, 1984.

A Season for Unicorns, Atheneum, 1986.

The Return, Atheneum, 1987.

Incident at Loring Groves, Dial, 1988.

Silver Days (second novel in the "Platt Family" trilogy), Atheneum, 1989.

The Golem and the Dragon Girl, Dial, 1993.

Annie's Promise (third novel in the "Platt Family" trilogy), Atheneum, 1993.

Escape from Egypt, Little, Brown, 1994.

PICTURE BOOKS FOR CHILDREN

Who Owns the Moon?, illustrated by John Larrecq, Parnassus, 1973.

A Single Speckled Egg, illustrated by Larrecq, Parnassus, 1976.

A Sound to Remember, illustrated by Gabriel Lisowski, Harcourt, 1979.

Nobody Stole the Pie, illustrated by Fernando Krahn, Harcourt, 1980.

All the Cats in the World, illustrated by Charles Robinson, Harcourt, 1982.

The Fisherman and the Bird, illustrated by Francis Livingston, Houghton, 1982.

The Man Who Kept His Heart in a Bucket, illustrated by Jerry Pinkney, Dial, 1991.

OTHER

Rita, the Weekend Rat (fiction), illustrated by Leonard W. Shortall, Atheneum, 1971.

Jason and the Money Tree (fiction), illustrated by Pat Grant Porter, Harcourt, 1974.

(Under name Sonia Wolff) *What They Did to Miss Lily* (novel for adults), Harper, 1981.

(Author of introduction) Yale Strom, *A Tree Still Stands: Jewish Youth in Eastern Europe Today,* Putnam, 1990.

Adam's War (for children), Dial, 1994.

Feature columnist for Sun Newspapers, Contra Costa, CA, and *Jewish Observer of the East Bay,* Oakland, CA. Contributor to periodicals, including *Christian Science Monitor, Ingenue, Parents', The Writer, Reform Judaism,* and *Smithsonian.*

■ **Work in Progress**

A Piece of Home, "a picture book about a Russian immigrant boy who comes to America," to be published by Dial; *Nine for California,* "a picture book about the early West, centered on a wild stage coach ride with Mama and five young 'uns"; and "a YA book about the West in 1861, involving the Pony Express and the 'Underground Railroad.'"

■ **Sidelights**

Imagine belonging to a group whose members are being deliberately killed off by another group. Now, imagine being unable to defend yourself because the group carrying out the killings is the government of the country in which you live. Scary? You bet. It might sound like a plot from a novel, or even a futuristic spy thriller. But this scenario was reality to the millions of Jews living in Germany during the 1930s, when extermination of the Jewish people was a matter of public policy. Author Sonia Levitin was one of those who escaped from Germany and the horror of the Holocaust—the name for the systematic destruction of Jews initiated by Nazi party leader Adolf Hitler—but the horror of what she and her family experienced has never left her.

"To be born a Jew in Germany in 1934," Levitin writes in her *Something about the Author Autobiography Series (SAAS)* essay, "was to be born into crisis. From earliest childhood I knew that if Hitler had had his way, I would have been killed along with millions of other Jews." Turning adversity into opportunity, Levitin used her recollections and those gathered from other members of her family to write a personal memoir of the struggles of those German Jews who were able to escape from Hitler's reign of terror and the hardships they faced as refugees dreaming of coming to the United States. Her compilation of memories, originally planned as a remembrance for her children, became Levitin's first published book, the highly-acclaimed *Journey to America*. The memories of these early years are always with her, for the major themes to which she returns again and again were born in the intolerance of Nazi Germany. While some of her books for young adults are pure fun, the bulk of her work centers on her Jewish heritage, mutual respect among all races and religions, and each person's moral obligation to look out for his or her fellow human beings.

The Platt Family Trilogy

The most profound picture of the effect of the early years of Levitin's life on her work is seen in *Journey to America* and her two novels that continue the story of the Platt family, *Silver Days* and *Annie's Promise*. In many ways *Journey to the America* is one of Levitin's most important works, not only because of its high approval rating from critics, but also because it helped establish Levitin as an author. Wanting desperately to be a writer of fiction, but having only a few stories published in magazines to show for her efforts, Levitin worked on what would become *Journey to America* for several years before feeling it was ready for publication. She recalls the novel's difficult birth in *SAAS*: "I submitted it, cold, to an editor, and subsequently to eleven more, meanwhile rewriting, until *Journey to America* took on a tighter shape and moved from third to first person. After five entire rewrites, I sold the book to Atheneum, the publisher that had seen it first!"

More than a novel, *Journey to America* is in a very real sense an autobiographical portrait of Levitin, her family, and their own journey to America. Being only four at the time of her arrival in the United States, Levitin understandably chose to tell the story from an older child's point of view. In *SAAS* Levitin calls Lisa Platt, the twelve-year-old narrator of the story, "a fictionalization of my sister Eva." Like Lisa, Levitin had two sisters, although Levitin was the youngest in her family and Lisa is the middle child. The Platt girls' father is a designer and manufacturer of women's clothing,

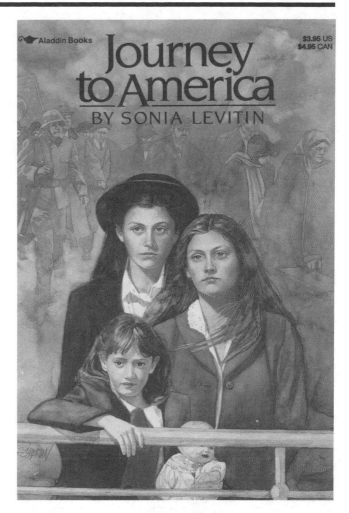

A Jewish family flees Nazi Germany in this 1970 novel that was inspired by Levitin's childhood memories.

just like Levitin's father. The novel opens in the year 1938 just as Papa is about to leave Berlin for America. His departure begins a year of nearly unbearable hardships for Mama, Lisa, and her sisters, Ruth and Annie. Increasing Nazi violence forces them to flee to Switzerland with only a few belongings and little money. There the family is separated briefly as Mama is forced to send Lisa and Ruth to a camp for refugee children and then to live in separate foster homes. Through courage and determination, the family eventually reunites with Papa in America.

Journey to America won the 1970 National Jewish Book Award for juvenile literature and was named an American Library Association notable book for that year. Critics celebrate both the story of how the family bravely responded to misfortune and what Gloria Levitas calls in the *New York Times Book Review* Levitin's "direct, unsentimental prose." Levitas asserts that while Levitin includes details of Nazi mistreatment of the Jews in her story, those who read the novel will find it to be "more thrilling than terrifying." In the *Bulletin of Children's Books* Zena Sutherland hails it as "well-written and perceptive," while in a *Commonweal* review, Elizabeth Minot Graves declares the work to be a "warm, moving story of kindness and courage." The reception the book received was just the inspiration Levitin needed to continue in her hoped-for profession. "With *Journey to America*," she writes in *SAAS*, "I felt that my career was launched, and that I had found my niche. I loved writing for young people."

In the late 1980s and early 1990s, autobiography again became important to Levitin as she returned to the story of her family's early days in America in her continuation of the Platt family saga. The second book in the series, *Silver Days*, takes up the story where *Journey to America* left off. With Papa's prodding the family soon leaves New York for Los Angeles looking for a better life, just as Levitin's family had done. The story is again told through the middle sister Lisa's eyes, sometimes through the pages of her diary. The girls adjust to their new life: Ruth decides she wants to be a nurse; Lisa returns to her dancing lessons. Racial prejudice again causes the family to suffer when they learn that their next-door neighbors, who are Japanese, must go to an internment camp as the United States reacts to Japan's entry in the war. As the novel closes, Mama has received the dreaded news that her mother who stayed behind in Germany has been sent to the camp at Auschwitz and has probably perished there. Out of her despair, Papa and the others realize that they should pay closer attention to their Jewish roots. "Our future," he says, "must have room in it for the past."

In Levitin's third novel about the Platts, *Annie's Promise*, the point of view shifts to that of Annie, who is now thirteen, and the year is 1945. Like Levitin in real life, Annie goes to a summer camp run by Quakers for refugee children. At "Quaker Pines" Annie comes to terms with a lot of difficult issues like how to deal with jealousy, feelings of revenge, and getting along with people of different backgrounds. She can't believe it when her parents refer to Tallahassee, a black girl who is her best friend at camp, as a "nigger." She stuns them back by calling them Nazis. All the girls show signs of growing up: Ruth waits for her soldier boyfriend to come back from the war, and Lisa moves out of the family house. The summer concludes with the end of the war and Annie returning to Quaker Pines for

a second session, this time on a scholarship at the request of the co-director.

Reviewers have written generally positive comments about *Silver Days* and its sequel. In their reviews of *Silver Days*, both a *Publishers Weekly* contributor and *Horn Book*'s Hanna B. Zeiger admire Levitin's portrayal of America during the World War II. "Levitin's novel," notes the *Publishers Weekly* reviewer, "offers a brief look into America of the '40s from an unusual perspective." Zeiger maintains that through the novel Levitin "has given us insight into the special problems of a young woman growing up as a refugee in America during World War II." In *School Library Journal*, Renee Steinberg finds *Annie's Promise* "a realistic, honest coming-of-age story" and calls Annie a "likeable heroine whose sensitivity and intelligence are keenly felt." In the *New York Times Book Review* Perri Klass comes to nearly the same conclusion about Annie, calling her a "tough-mind-

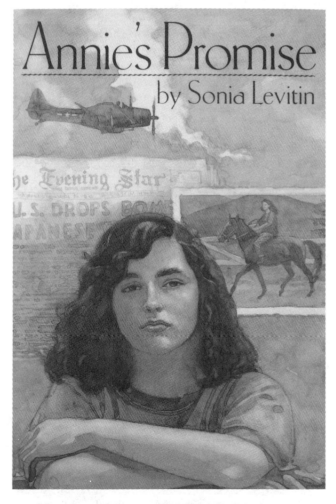

In this 1993 conclusion to the "Platt Family" trilogy, a young girl learns to deal with prejudice and intolerance at a Quaker summer camp.

ed and highly likeable heroine." Klass also notes the typical moral overtones of Levitin's book. He maintains that the novel "is in part a story of Annie's search for her own moral absolutes, and her gradual understanding of how her tolerance and forgiveness can ultimately be extended to include her family."

History and Mystery

Levitin's work encompasses more than just autobiographical fiction, however. The historical novel is another genre she has tackled successfully. *Roanoke: A Novel of the Lost Colony,* her first contribution to the field, took nearly ten years for Levitin to finish, but the end result was a novel that she considers one of her favorites. In the story, Levitin attempts to explain what has long been one of the great mysteries of American history: what happened to a group of colonists who attempted to establish a colony on Roanoke Island off the shore of Virginia in 1587. They were left there by their leader John White while he returned to England for more supplies, but when he returned in 1590 the group had completely disappeared. Levitin's fictional account follows William Wythers, a sixteen-year-old runaway apprentice, as he grows in maturity and wrestles with the injustice of the way his fellow colonists deal with the "savages" they encounter in the New World. In his *Horn Book* review of the book, Beryl Reid refers to it as a "substantial, well-researched novel."

A few years later, Levitin published the award-winning novel *The No-Return Trail,* which is based on an event from the history of the American West. This time Levitin chose for her subject seventeen-year-old Nancy Kelsey, the first white woman to make the treacherous trip across the country to California. As with *Roanoke,* Levitin strove to make the book as historically accurate as possible, adding only the fictional elements necessary to flesh-out the story. The novel begins as Nancy and her husband, Ben, make plans to join the wagon-train that leaves Sapling Grove, Missouri, in 1841. Although the group of pioneers is small, they are all determined to discover for themselves the riches they have heard exist in California. Little by little, their confidence is deflated as disease, skirmishes with Native Americans, and weariness overtake many of them and the expedition breaks up. Eventually, only Nancy, Ben, their baby, and a few others are left to cross the steep mountain peaks that separate them from their longed-for destination.

Levitin based this 1978 work on the life of pioneer Nancy Kelsey, the first white woman to travel across the United States.

Although *The No-Return Trail* won the Western Writers of America Golden Spur Award for the best juvenile western of 1978 and the Lewis Carroll Shelf Award, critical response was somewhat mixed. *School Library Journal* contributor George Gleason calls the book "only modestly interesting," while a *Kirkus Reviews* essayist finds Levitin's characterization of Nancy Kelsey "oddly bland." On the positive side, in her *Booklist* review of the novel, Denise M. Wilms maintains that the book is "absorbing, if conventional, historical fiction." In *Best Sellers* Tony Siaulys praises Levitin for presenting the story in a way to catch the interest of her audience: "The novel is not a droll account of people, places, and things. More often than not, the chapters end on a pivotal situation, just begging the reader to go further."

In 1977, Levitin became interested in the paranormal and wrote *Beyond Another Door,* a book that was reissued in 1994. About this work, Levitin said in a letter to *AAYA*: "I think this book was ahead of its time, dealing with two topics of current interest—the single parent family and psychic phenomena. My heroine, Daria, discovers, through extrasensory perception, that she is a 'love child,' which leads to confrontation with her strange new psychic abilities, her past, and her mother, who has lied to Daria about the circumstances of her birth. Researching this book took me into such diverse areas as psychic phenomena, reincarnation, and even sorcery. The research included interviews with psychics, past-life readers, and two magicians. A great motivation for me when writing a novel is to delve into new areas that intrigue me, and then to render them in a realistic and exciting way for the reader, always keeping a good psychological and moral perspective. Thus, Daria is able at last to use her gift toward a good purpose, and she and her mother become reconciled to their differences."

The Golem and the Dragon Girl, which also contains elements of the spiritual and mysterious, addresses the issue of reconciling people from different backgrounds. Levitin draws upon her Jewish heritage to discuss the need for understanding between cultures. The dual figures in the title allude to the two central characters in the novel, Laurel Wang and Jonathan Weiss. Laurel is a Chinese-American girl just entering junior high who has quite a few concerns, among them her grandparents' imminent arrival from China and the sale of her family home in which she believes the spirit of her great-grandfather resides. Her most prized possessions are two golden dragons sent to her by her great-grandfather before he died. For the Chinese, dragons are symbols of protection and guardians against evil. Jonathan is about the same age as Laurel, of Jewish descent, and with worries of his own, especially the way his mother has changed since meeting Steve, his new step-father. Jonathan's prized possessions are his models of monsters, including his latest favorite, Mogul the Muscle Man, to whom he whispers one night, "Get rid of Steve." Laurel and Jonathan get to know each other after the boy and his family move into Laurel's old house, and she visits with the intention of luring her great-grandfather's spirit away. But her plan goes awry and a series of mysterious happenings must be dealt with before both families are once again happy with their living arrangements.

Developing her story line around two young people of such distinct backgrounds allowed Levitin to incorporate in the novel a wealth of fascinating information about the Chinese and Jewish cultures. Critics have praised Levitin's ability to include so much factual material in a fictional piece. "The characters are well developed," states *School Library Journal* contributor Sharon Grover, "and the cultural information is presented in an interesting, nondidactic fashion." And, while in Ilene Cooper's *Booklist* review the critic wonders if it was wise for Levitin to cover so many different thematic elements in one novel, she concludes that in the work "Levitin shows off her writing skill, and despite the tumult, she keeps readers entertained."

Incident at Loring Groves

In a much more down-to-earth mystery, Levitin explores the importance of taking moral action in her award-winning *Incident at Loring Groves.* Like many of Levitin's novels, *Incident at Loring Groves* features a plot based on an actual event. The trouble begins when a group of teens from Loring Groves High get together after a school dance and continue partying at an old abandoned summer house. Their celebrating soon turns to horror when they come across the body of a missing classmate. Not wanting to implicate themselves in the murder—or admit to trespassing on private property or using marijuana and alcohol—the teens all vow to put the incident behind them. But Cassidy Keaton and Ken Farquar, one of the school's most popular couples, can't forget what happened. Their guilty consciences impel them to work together to uncover enough clues to expose the murderer. What they do with the information might be one of the most difficult decisions they will ever have to make.

Incident at Loring Groves is one of Levitin's most critically acclaimed novels, winning for its author the coveted Edgar Allan Poe Award from the Mystery Writers of America. Critics have commended her ability to create a realistic setting for her novel. "This is a disturbing and all too believable look at teenagers growing up today," writes Elizabeth Mellett in the *School Library Journal.* The critic also applauds the author for the moral questions raised in the story, calling the novel "a thought-provoking book that readers won't soon forget." A *Publishers Weekly* contributor similarly praises the work as "a searingly honest portrayal of adolescent society." Although not an autobiographical novel, Levitin adds a bit of a personal note to the plot when she briefly mentions that the teens are studying Walter Van Tilburg Clark's novel, *The Ox-Bow Incident,* in one of their classes.

Clark was instrumental in the development of Levitin's writing career as she met with him weekly for two years as part of San Francisco State College's Directed Writing Program in the late 1950s. Like Levitin's novel, which carries an echo of Clark's book even in its title, *The Ox-Bow Incident* explores the moral behavior of a group that acts outside the law.

Moral behavior is also a central issue in Levitin's *Adam's War*, a story written for readers aged nine to thirteen that was inspired by the 1992 Persian Gulf War. "Sometimes world events command a writer's attention," Levitin explained to *AAYA*, "because they force us to examine long held beliefs and the consequences of those beliefs. So it was for me during the Gulf War, when the U.S. battled Iraq for its aggression against tiny Kuwait. I do not believe in war; neither could I believe in subjugation. This presented a terrible quandary, forcing me to examine the whole concept of wars, how they begin, how they grow. And I concluded that wars, like peace, begin with *me*. Is there such a thing as a just war? Can a war, begun for a just cause, remain pure? Or do other things, like the desire for power, the need for unity, change the original ideal?

"Every war has its reasons, its instigators, and its victims. Today's children must decide, early on, how to deal with violence, not only the violence that is flung against them, but also the potential violence within. Thus Adam, a fine boy and a real leader, finds himself led down the road that all heroes (and all tyrants) travel on their way to war—a road filled with dreams of glory and justice, ending in tragedy. The story is played out in small spaces, a school yard and a park. But its meaning should reach far beyond that space to include every person who has ever asked himself, 'Will there always be wars? Must it be so?' No answers are provided here, only questions and the actions of people like you and me, leading to reactions, and finally to some understanding."

Heroic Journeys

The failure of people to understand one another remains a continuing concern of Levitin's. Besides her story of the flight of Jewish families from Nazi Germany, Levitin has written two other young adult novels about Jews forced to embark on treacherous journeys to avoid persecution: the award-winning *The Return* and her ambitious *Escape to Egypt*. *The Return* combines Levitin's interest in Jewish culture with her love of history.

The story is also a perfect vehicle for Levitin to express her keen interest in promoting interracial harmony and love between peoples of all nations. Just how important this novel is to her can be seen in her *SAAS* essay when she calls the story she retells in *The Return* "an event of ... heroic proportions" and says she "dropped everything to pursue it." Her novel is another tale of Jewish refugees, this time black Jews of Ethiopia who flee the oppression of their own country for the squalor and despair of the Sudanese refugee camps. Between November, 1984, and January, 1985, some eight thousand of them were secretly airlifted from Sudan to Israel in what was called "Operation Moses." "It was not hunger that sent us away," says fifteen-year-old Desta, the story's narrator. "We left for freedom, and because we were Jews,

In this 1988 thriller based on a real-life event, a group of teenagers decide to keep a terrible secret: the location of the body of a murdered classmate.

Beta Yisrael. The other tribes hated us, called us Falasha, stranger."

Called strangers in their own land, the small group—Desta, who is an orphan, and her two siblings, along with Dan, her betrothed, and his family—makes the dangerous journey from their remote villages through Ethiopia by foot and across the border to Sudan. Along the way they suffer near starvation and horrible thirst and have a series of encounters with other travelers, including a group of Ethiopian children who throw stones at them and a family of Muslims with whom they share their meager supplies. In the refugee camp, they encounter the same anti-Jewish prejudice as in Ethiopia, but after weeks of waiting they are told that they will be among those going on one of the secret humanitarian flights to Jerusalem. The novel

A group of Ethiopian Jewish refugees encounter terrible hardships on their journey to Sudan in this 1987 novel.

ends with Desta's poignant visit to the Western Wall, the religious center of the Jewish faith. Overcome with emotion, Desta observes: "All my life, just as I had heard about Jerusalem, the holy city, so had I heard about the wall, holiest place for a Jew in all the world. Still I was not prepared. How could anyone know the feelings that would gather here, at the wall?"

The novel has garnered more than a half dozen awards, including the Association of Jewish Libraries' Sydney Taylor Award and the National Jewish Book Award in children's literature. In her *New York Times Book Review* critique of the novel, Sheila Solomon Klass notes, "*The Return* is rich in ethnographic detail" and calls it "a memorable work." In the course of the story, the author introduces the reader to many Ethiopian customs and interjects Amharic—the national tongue of Ethiopia—words which are explained in a glossary in the back of the book. "The adventure of the exodus," *School Library Journal* contributor Amy Kellman observes, "is totally absorbing, and the emotional impact is strong." A *Publishers Weekly* reviewer also praises the moving retelling of the historical episode and writes that "Levitin's book is a glorious, heartrending account."

Levitin completed one of her most challenging endeavors yet when she wrote *Escape from Egypt*, a novelization of the biblical Exodus. Of this story, the author told *AAYA*, "The idea came to me one night, about four a.m., when I suddenly awakened to what seemed a clatter of voice in my head. 'Be still,' I told myself, 'and listen.' I lay quietly, receptive to the though that something important was taking place. Then, forcefully the idea emerged, that the biblical story of the Jews breaking their bonds of slavery, following Moses into the wilderness, where they encountered the living God and received His commandments, is surely the greatest story of all time. It is the paradigm of all enslavement, all liberation, all faith won by determination and risk. But could I tell it? Was I capable? And was it appropriate for me, a secular person and a spinner of tales, to 're-tell' the foremost story of my faith?

"Quickly I overcame my doubts as I discussed my idea first with my husband, then with my teacher and rabbi. Actually, for the past five years I had been preparing myself for just such a project. I had visited Israel five times, first to research *The Return*, and afterward, because of my new, intense devotion to that land, which I think of as my spiritual home. I had been studying Torah both on my own and with several teachers, and I had become, on a personal level, immersed in traditional Judaism. Judaism was now intellectually and personally fulfilling in new, exciting ways. I felt that everything I had done was leading in this direction.

"I resolved to clothe the ancient story in terms of conflicts that also face us today: our quest for prosperity, love, and recognition, while daily we battle countless enemies both external and within. People do not change; only the circumstances vary, and the scope differs. In Moses' time, what a grand scope! What a marvelous cast of characters! The background characters are Moses, Miriam, Aaron, and stubborn Pharoah. As primary characters, I created Jesse, an Israelite slave, caught between a mercenary and cruel father and an idealistic, God-fearing mother. Jesse falls in love with a half-Egyptian girl, and throughout the novel he wrestles with his several passions: the love of Jennat, the duty toward his people, the question as to whether the God who appeared at Sinai is the true One, and whether the 'promised land' is a geographical place or a territory within the human soul that each person must discover and nurture himself.

"Working on this book was one of the most exhilarating experiences of my career, for it brought together my love of research, the delight of rendering powerful and brilliant episodes described in the Bible, and exploring the questions that have engrossed mankind from the beginning of consciousness. The book is fast paced, filled with challenge, danger, strange sights, and ultimate triumph. One ultimate moment, the epiphany at Mt. Sinai, was drawn from my own visit to the Sinai in preparation for this novel. Thus the personal and the professional worlds merge, one augments the other. For me, this is true fulfillment."

■ **Works Cited**

Cooper, Ilene, review of *The Golem and the Dragon Girl*, *Booklist*, March 1, 1993, pp. 1222-1223.

Gleason, George, "Books Reviews: *The No-Return Trail*," *School Library Journal*, April, 1978, p. 94-95.

Graves, Elizabeth Minot, "A Selected List of Children's Books: *Journey to America*," *Commonweal*, May 22, 1970, p. 248.

Grover, Sharon, review of *The Golem and the Dragon Girl*, *School Library Journal*, March, 1993, p. 198.

Review of *Incident at Loring Groves, Publishers Weekly*, May 13, 1988, p. 278.

Kellman, Amy, review of *The Return, School Library Journal*, May, 1987, p. 115.

Klass, Perri, "Children's Books: *Annie's Promise*," *New York Times Book Review*, June 13, 1993, p. 26.

Klass, Sheila Solomon, "Waiting for Operation Moses," *New York Times Book Review*, May 17, 1978, p. 36.

Levitas, Gloria, "Stories of Adventure and Adversity," *New York Times Book Review*, May 24, 1970, pp. 26-27.

Levitin, Sonia, essay in *Something about the Author Autobiography Series*, Volume 2, Gale, 1986, pp. 111-126.

Levitin, Sonia, *The Return*, Atheneum, 1987.

Levitin, Sonia, *Silver Days*, Atheneum, 1989.

Levitin, Sonia, *The Golem and the Dragon Girl*, Dial, 1993.

Mellett, Elizabeth, review of *Incident at Loring Groves, School Library Journal*, June-July, 1988, p. 118.

Reid, Beryl, "Early Fall Booklist: *Roanoke: A Novel of the Lost Colony*," *Horn Book*, October, 1973, p. 466.

Review of *The Return, Publishers Weekly*, April 10, 1987, p. 96.

Siaulys, Tony, "Young People's Books: *The No-Return Trail*," *Best Sellers*, October, 1978, pp. 230-231.

Review of *Silver Days, Publishers Weekly*, February 24, 1989, p. 236.

Steinberg, Renee, review of *Annie's Promise, School Library Journal*, April, 1993, p. 122.

Sutherland, Zena, "New Titles for Children and Young People: *Journey to America*," *Bulletin of the Center for Children's Books*, February, 1971, p. 95.

Wilms, Denise M., "Children's Books: *The No-Return Trail*," *Booklist*, June 15, 1978, pp. 1618-1619.

Zeiger, Hanna B., review of *Silver Days, Horn Book*, May/June, 1989, p. 376.

■ **For More Information See**

PERIODICALS

Bulletin of the Center for Children's Books, July-August, 1976, p. 177.

Horn Book, July/August, 1986, pp. 455-456.

Publishers Weekly, June 27, 1986, pp. 92-93.

School Library Journal, April, 1976, p. 90; April, 1986, pp. 97-98; May, 1989, p. 126.
The Writer, August, 1972, pp. 18-20, 46.

—Sketch by Marian C. Gonsior

Jack London

■ Personal

Born John Griffith Chaney, January 12, 1876, in San Francisco, CA; assumed the name London after his adoptive father, September, 1876; died of gastro-intestinal uremia complicated by an over-dose of morphine, November 22, 1919, in Glen Ellen, CA; buried in Jack London State Park, Valley of the Moon, Sonoma County, CA; son of William Henry (an itinerant astrologer) Chaney and Flora (a spiritualist and music teacher) Well-man; married Bessie Mae ("Bess") Maddern (a tutor), April 7, 1900 (divorced, 1905); married Clara Charmian Kittredge, November 19, 1905; children: (first marriage) Joan, Bess; (second mar-riage) Joy (died, 1910). *Education:* Attended Uni-versity of California, Berkeley, c. 1897-1898. *Politics:* Member of Socialist Labor Party, 1896-1916.

■ Addresses

Home—Jack London Ranch (also known as Beauty Ranch), Glen Ellen, CA.

■ Career

Novelist, short story writer, and political essayist. Worked at a succession of odd jobs, including salmon canner, oyster pirate, patrol agent of Cali-fornia Fish Patrol, seal fisher, jute millworker, coal shoveler, and laundry worker, beginning c. 1890; joined Kelly's Army (a band of jobless men from California who marched to Washington, DC, to protest the plight of the unemployed), and tramped throughout the United States and Canada, beginning 1893; arrested for vagrancy and sen-tenced to thirty days in the Erie County Penitentia-ry, Buffalo, NY, 1894; gold miner in the Yukon Territory, 1897-1898; worked as a journalist and reported the Russo-Japanese War for Hearst News-papers, 1904; ran for mayor of Oakland, CA, on the Socialist ticket, 1905; lecturer throughout the United States, 1905-06; reported the Mexican Revolution for *Collier's*, 1914.

■ Writings

NOVELS

The Cruise of the Dazzler (first published serially in *St. Nicholas*, July, 1902), Century Co., 1902, with illustrations by Peter Thorpe, Star Rover, 1981.

A Daughter of the Snows, illustrations by Frederick C. Yohn, Lippincott, 1902.

(With Anna Strunsky) *The Kempton-Wace Letters* (first edition published anonymously,) Macmillan, 1903.

The Call of the Wild (first published serially in *Saturday Evening Post,* June 20-July 18, 1903), illustrations by Philip Goodwin and Charles Livingston Bull, Macmillan, 1903, introduction by E. L. Doctorow, Random House, 1990.

The Sea Wolf (first published serially in *Century,* January-November, 1904), illustrations by W. J. Aylward, Macmillan, 1904.

The Game (first published serially in *Metropolitan,* April 19-26, 1905), illustrations by Henry Hutt and T. C. Lawrence, Macmillan, 1905.

White Fang (first published serially in *Outing,* May-October, 1906, Macmillan, 1906, edited by Naunderle Farr, illustrations by Fred Carillo, Pendulum Press, 1977.

Before Adam (science fiction; first published serially in *Everybody's Magazine,* October, 1906-February, 1907), Macmillan, 1906.

The Iron Heel (science fiction), Macmillan, 1907, revised edition, Lawrence Hill, 1980.

Martin Eden (first published serially in *Pacific Monthly,* September, 1908-September, 1909), Macmillan, 1909, introduction by Andrew Sinclair, Penguin Books, 1984.

Burning Daylight (first published serially in the *New York Herald,* June 19-August 28, 1910), Macmillan, 1910.

Adventure (first published serially in *Popular Magazine,* November 1, 1910-January 15, 1911), Macmillan, 1911.

The Abysmal Brute (first published serially in *Popular Magazine,* September 1, 1911), Century Co., 1913.

John Barleycorn (first published serially in the *Saturday Evening Post,* March 15-May 3, 1913), illustrations by H. T. Dunn, Century Co., 1913, published in England as *John Barleycorn; or, Alcoholic Memoirs,* Mills & Boon, 1914, edited with introduction by John Sutherland, Oxford University Press, 1989.

The Valley of the Moon (first published serially in *Cosmopolitan,* April-December, 1913), Macmillan, 1913.

Mutiny of the Elsinore (first published serially in *Hearst's Magazine,* November, 1913-August, 1914), Macmillan, 1914, published as *Mutiny of the Elsinore: A Novel of Seagoing Gangsters,* Mutual Publishing, 1987.

The Scarlet Plague (science fiction; first published serially in *London Magazine,* June, 1912), illustrations by Gordon Grant, Macmillan, 1915.

The Star Rover (science fiction; first printed serially in *Los Angeles Examiner, American Sunday Monthly* magazine, February 14-October 10, 1914), Macmillan, 1915, published in England as *The Jacket,* Mills & Boon, 1915.

The Little Lady of the Big House (first published serially in *Cosmopolitan,* May-October, 1917), Macmillan, 1917.

Jerry of the Islands (first published serially in *Cosmopolitan,* January-April, 1917), Macmillan, 1917.

Michael, Brother of Jerry (first published serially in *Cosmopolitan,* May-October, 1917), Macmillan, 1917.

Hearts of Three (science fiction), Mills & Boon, 1918.

The Assassination Bureau, Ltd., (unfinished novel; completed by Robert L. Fish from notes by London), McGraw, 1963.

COLLECTIONS

The Son of the Wolf, Houghton, 1900, published in England as *An Odyssey of the North,* Mills & Boon, 1915, also published as *The Son of the Wolf: Tales of the Far North,* Houghton, 1930, and as *The Son of the Wolf: Stories of the Northland,* Star Rover, 1981.

The God of His Fathers, and Other Stories, McClure, Phillips, 1901, published in England as *The God of His Fathers: Tales of the Klondyke,* Isbister, 1902, also published as *The Man with the Gash, and Other Stories,* illustrations by P. Thorpe, Star Rover, 1981.

Children of the Frost, illustrations by Raphael M. Reay, Macmillan, 1902.

The Faith of Men, and Other Stories, Macmillan, 1904.

Tales of the Fish Patrol, illustrations by George Vairan, Macmillan, 1905.

Moon-Face, and Other Stories, Macmillan, 1906.

Love of Life, and Other Stories, Macmillan, 1906.

Lost Face, Macmillan, 1910.

When God Laughs, and Other Stories, Macmillan, 1911.

South Sea Tales, Macmillan, 1911, also published as *The Seed of McCoy, and Other Stories: South Sea Tales,* Pyramid Books, 1925.

The House of Pride and Other Tales of Hawaii, Macmillan, 1912.

A Son of the Sun, illustrations by A. O. Fischer and C. W. Ashley, Doubleday, Page, 1912, revised edition published as *The Adventures of Captain Grief,* World, 1954, published as *Captain David Grief,* Mutual Publishing, 1987.

Smoke Bellew, illustrations by P. J. Monahan, Century Co., 1912, revised edition, 1940, published in England as *Smoke and Shorty*, Mills & Boon, 1920.

The Night-Born, Century Co., 1913.

The Strength of the Strong (science fiction), Macmillan, 1914.

The Turtles of Tasman, Macmillan, 1916, published in England as *Turtles of Tasman, and Other Stories*, Mills & Boon, 1917.

The Human Drift (stories and essays), Macmillan, 1917.

The Red One (science fiction), Macmillan, 1918.

On the Makaloa Mat, Macmillan, 1919, published in England as *Island Tales*, Mills & Boon, 1923.

Dutch Courage, and Other Stories, Macmillan, 1922.

Contributor of numerous short stories to newspapers and periodicals, including *The Independent, Century, Smart Set, Woman's Home Companion, Pittsburgh Leader, Los Angeles Tribune, Youth's Companion, Cosmopolitan, Saturday Evening Post, Windsor Magazine*, and *International Socialist Review*. "The Apostate" (also printed as "The Apostate: A Parable of Child Labor"), "The Strength of the Strong," and "The Dream of the Debs" appeared widely as pamphlets and tracts. Many of the short stories have been printed individually in the "Perfection Micro-Classic" series, Perfection Form Co., and by Star Rover House at Jack London Heritage House.

PLAYS

The Great Interrogation, first produced in San Francisco, CA, 1905.

Scorn of Women: In Three Acts, Macmillan, 1906.

Theft: A Play in Four Acts, Macmillan, 1910.

The Acorn-Planter: A California Forest Play, Macmillan, 1916.

Daughters of the Rich, edited by James E. Sisson, Holmes Book Co., 1971.

(With Herbert Heron) *Gold: A Play*, edited by J. E. Sisson, Holmes Book Co., 1972.

NONFICTION

The People of the Abyss, Macmillan, 1903.

War of the Classes, Macmillan, 1905.

The Road, Macmillan, 1907.

Goliah, A Utopian Essay (first published in 1908), Thorp Springs Press, 1973.

Revolution, and Other Essays, Macmillan, 1910.

The Cruise of the Snark, Macmillan, 1911, published as *The Cruise of the Snark: A Pacific Voyage*, Odyssey Press, 1965.

Letters from Jack London: Containing an Unpublished Correspondence Between London and Sinclair Lewis, edited by K. Hendricks and Irving Shepard, Odyssey, 1965.

(With Will Irwin) *Reportage, the San Francisco Quake: Two Accounts*, Perfection Form Co., 1968.

Contributor of articles and social commentary to numerous newspapers and periodicals, including *Wilshire's Magazine, Saturday Evening Post, International Socialist Review, Century, Los Angeles Tribune, Everybody's Magazine, Collier's San Francisco Examiner, New York Herald*, and *Oakland Herald*. Many of London's essays were reprinted as pamphlets and tracts.

OMNIBUS VOLUMES

The Chinago, and Other Stories, Leslie-Judge Co., 1911.

Brown Wolf and Other Jack London Stories, edited by Franklin I. Mathiews, Macmillan, 1920.

The Call of the Wild, and Other Stories, edited by F. L. Mott, Macmillan, 1926.

London's Essays of Revolt, edited and introduced by Leonard D. Abbott, Vanguard Press, 1926.

Jack London's Stories for Boys, illustrations by C. Richard Schaare, Cupples & Leon, 1936.

Best Short Stories of Jack London, Sun Dial Press, 1945.

Love of Life, and Other Stories, introduction by George Orwell, P. Elek, 1946.

The Scarlet Plague [and] *Love of Life* [and] *The Unexpected: Three Stories*, Staples Press, 1946.

Jack London, American Rebel: A Collection of His Social Writings, Together With an Extensive Study of the Man and His Times, edited by Philip S. Foner, Citadel Press, 1947.

Best Short Stories of Jack London, Perma Books, 1949.

The Sun-Dog Trail, and Other Stories, World, 1951.

The Call of the Wild [and] *White Fang* [and] *The Scarlet Plague*, introduction by Bernard Fergusson, Collins, 1952.

Short Stories, edited and introduced by Maxwell Geismar, Hill & Wang, 1960.

The Call of the Wild, The Cruise of the Dazzler, and Other Stories of Adventure, with the Author's Special Report: Gold Hunters of the North, Platt & Munk, 1960.

The Call of the Wild, and Selected Stories, foreword by Franklin Walker, New American Library, 1960.

The Call of the Wild, and Other Stories, introduction, illustrations, and captions by Louis B. Salomon, Dodd, 1960.

The Best Short Stories of Jack London, introduction by Eugene Burdick, Fawcett, 1962.

The Call of the Wild [and] *White Fang,* introduction by F. L. Mott, Washington Square Press, 1962, afterword by Jack Sullivan, Reader's Digest Association, 1985.

The Bodley Head Jack London, edited and introduced by Arthur Calder-Marshall, Bodley Head, Volume 1: *Short Stories and The Call of the Wild,* 1963, published as *The Call of the Wild, and Other Stories,* illustrations by Robert Bates, Heron, 1969, Volume 2: *John Barleycorn, The Cruise of the Dazzler, The Road,* 1964, published as *The Pan Jack London,* 1968, Volume 3: *Martin Eden,* 1965, Volume 4: *The Klondike Dream,* 1966.

White Fang, and Other Stories, introduction and illustrations by A. K. Adams, Dodd, 1963.

The Sea-Wolf and Selected Stories, afterword by F. Walker, 1964.

The Selected Works, Parents' Magazine's Cultural Institute, 1964.

Great Short Works of Jack London, edited and introduced by Earle Labor, Harper, 1965.

Stories of Hawaii, edited by A. Grove Day, Appleton-Century, 1965.

The Great Adventure Stories of Jack London, edited and introduced by Abraham Rothberg, Bantam, 1967.

Short Stories, Funk, 1968.

The Scarlet Plague and Before Adam, edited and introduced by I. O. Evans, Arco, 1968.

The Call of the Wild [and] *The Cruise of the Dazzler,* illustrations by Ron King and Don Irwin, Childrens Press, 1968.

Twelve Short Stories, illustrations by David Barlow, Edward Arnold, 1969.

Selected Short Stories, introduction by Clarence A. Andrews, Airmont Publishing, 1969.

Jack London Reports: War Correspondence, Sports Articles, and Miscellaneous Writings, edited by K. Hendricks and I. Shepard, Doubleday, 1970.

Jack London's Articles and Short Stories in The (Oakland) High School Aegis, edited by J. E. Sisson, illustrations by Holly Janes, Wolf House, 1971.

Curious Fragments: Jack London's Tales of Fantasy Fiction, edited by Dale L. Walker, preface by Philip Jose Farmer, Kennikat Press, 1975.

The Science Fiction of Jack London: An Anthology, edited and introduced by Richard Gid Powers, Gregg Press, 1975.

Thirteen Tales of Terror, edited by Les Daniels and Diane Thompson, Scribner, 1977.

Revolution: Stories and Essays, selected and introduced by Robert Barltrop, Journeyman Press, 1979.

No Mentor But Myself: A Collection of Articles, Essays, Reviews, and Letters on Writings and Writers, edited by D. L. Walker, foreword by Howard Lachtman, Kennikat Press, 1979.

Jack London on the Road: The Tramp Diary, and Other Hobo Writings, edited by Richard W. Etulain, Utah University Press, 1979.

The Works of Jack London, edited by Paul J. Horowitz, Avenal Books, 1980, published as *Jack London: The Call of the Wild, White Fang, The Sea-Wolf, Forty Short Stories,* Chatham River Press, 1983.

The Call of the Wild: A Casebook with Text, Background Sources, Reviews, Critical Essays, and Bibliography, compiled and introduced by Earl J. Wilcox, Nelson-Hall, 1980.

The Call of the Wild, White Fang, and Other Stories, edited by Andrew Sinclair, introduction by James Dickey, Penguin Books, 1981.

The Unabridged Jack London, edited by Lawrence Teacher and Richard E. Nicholls, Running Press, 1981.

Nam-Bok, and Other Stories, illustrations by P. Thorpe, Star Rover, 1981.

Sporting Blood: Selections from Jack London's Greatest Sports Writing, edited by H. Lachtman, Presidio Press, 1981.

The Call of the Wild, and Other Stories, study guide by John Carey, Silver Burdett, 1981.

Novels and Social Writings (contains *The People of the Abyss, The Road, The Iron Heel, Martin Eden, John Barleycorn,* and essays), edited by Donald Pizer, Library of America, 1982.

Novels and Stories (contains *The Call of the Wild, White Fang, The Sea-Wolf,* and short stories), edited by D. Pizer, Library of America, 1982.

Jack London, Series II, edited by Claire Booss and Paul J. Horowitz, Avenal Books, 1982.

Tales of the Klondike, Penguin, 1982.

Tales of the Northland, illustrations by Brad Holland, Franklin Library, 1983.

A Klondike Trilogy: Three Uncollected Stories (contains "The Devil's Dice Box," "The Test: A Klondike Wooing," and "A Klondike Christmas"), illustrations by Jack Freas, Neville, 1983.

The Call of the Wild; "The Men of Forty-Mile"; "In a Far Country"; "The Marriage of Lit-Lit"; "Batard," Chatham River Press, 1983.

Jack London's Tales of Hawaii, introduction by Miriam Pappolt, Press Pacifica, 1984.

Young Wolf: The Early Adventure Stories of Jack London, edited and introduced by H. Lachtman, Capra, 1984.

To Build a Fire, and Other Stories, Bantam, 1986.

Jack London Novels, Simon & Schuster, 1987.

In a Far Country: Jack London's Tales of the West, edited and introduced by D. L. Walker, Jameson Books, 1987.

To Build a Fire [and] *The Mexican*, illustrations by Micah Schwaberow, Engdahl, 1989.

Jack London Stories of Adventure, Book Sales, 1989.

The Call of the Wild, White Fang, and Other Dog Stories, edited by E. Labor and Robert C. Leitz, III, Oxford University Press, 1990.

The Short Stories of Jack London: The Authorized Edition with Definitive Texts Selected by Earle Labor, Robert C. Leitz, III, and I. Milo Shepard, Macmillan, 1990.

The Collected Jack London: Thirty-six Stories, Four Complete Novels, a Memoir, edited by Steven J. Kasdin, Dorset, 1991.

The Complete Short Stories of Jack London, edited by E. Labor, R. C. Leitz, III, and I. M. Shepard, Stanford University Press, 1993.

London's writings have also been collected in eighteen volumes known collectively as *The Fitzroy Editions of the Works of Jack London*, edited and introduced by I. O. Evans, published by Arco, Archer House, and Horizon Press, beginning in 1962.

OTHER

Daddy Boy: A Series of Dedications to His First Wife by Jack London, Holt-Atherton Pacifica Center for Western Studies, 1976.

Five Poems, commentary by J. E. Sisson, Quintessence, 1984.

With a Heart Full of Love: Jack London's Presentation Inscriptions to the Women in His Life, edited and introduced by Sal Noto, Twowindows Press, 1986.

Jack London's California: The Golden Poppy and Other Writings, edited by S. Noto, Beaufort Books, 1986.

(With Dave Finkelstein) *Greater Nowheres: A Journey through the Australian Bush*, Harper & Row, 1988.

Also author of introduction for H. D. Umbstaetter's *The Red Hot Dollar and Other Stories from "The Black Cat,"* Page, 1911, and *The Cry for Justice: An Anthology of the Literature of Social Protest*, edited by Upton Sinclair, John C. Winston, 1915; author of foreword for Francis A. Cox's *What Do You Know about a Horse?*, G. Bell & Sons, 1915; author of preface for Osias L. Schwarz's *General Types of Superior Men: A Philosophical-Psychological Study of Genius, Talent, and Philistinism in Their Bearings upon Human Society and Its Struggle for a Better Social Order*, R. G. Badger, 1916. Short works also reprinted by Wolf House ("Wolf House Classic" series), Jamestown Publishers ("Jamestown Classic" series), and Shorey, including *Economics of the Klondyke* and *Gold Hunters of the North*, 1976. The largest portion of London's manuscript collection is held at the Huntington Library, San Marino, CA, and at the Merrill Library at Utah State University, Logan, UT, with smaller collections at numerous other libraries in the United States.

■ Adaptations

FILMS

The Abysmal Brute, Universal, 1923, later version released as *Conflict*, Universal, 1936.

Adventure, Paramount, 1925.

The Call of the Wild, United Artists, 1935.

White Fang, Twentieth Century-Fox, 1936, Buena Vista, 1991.

The Sea-Wolf, Warner Brothers, 1941.

The Adventures of Martin Eden (based on *Martin Eden*), Columbia, 1942.

Dozens of London's novels and short stories have been released on film, some of them numerous times, including: "A Piece of Steak" and "To Kill a Man," both Balboa Amusement Co., both 1913; *John Barleycorn*, Bosworth, Inc., 1914; *The Mutiny of the Elsinore*, released under the title *The Mutiny*, Shurtleff, Inc., 1920; *The Star Rover*, Shurtleff, Inc., 1920; *Burning Daylight*, Rowland Distributors, 1928; *Smoke Bellew*, First Division, 1929; *Alaska* (based on "Flush of Gold"), Monogram, 1944; *The Fighter* (based on "The Mexican"), United Artists/Gottlieb, 1952; and *The Assassination Bureau Ltd.*, Paramount, 1969.

RECORDINGS

Jack London: The Sea-Wolf, read by Anthony Quayle, Caedmon, 1981; "To Build a Fire," read by Robert Donly, Miller-Brody; *Jack London Cassette Library*, including *The Call of the Wild*, *Martin Eden*, and *The Sea Wolf*, read by Jack Dahlby, Listening Library; *The Call of the Wild*, read by Arnold Moss, Miller-Brody.

PLAYS

"The Iron Heel" was adapted for the stage by W. G. Henry and produced by the Karl Marx players in Oakland, CA, in 1911.

OTHER

London's writings have been adapted and published as comic books.

■ Sidelights

"I wanted to be where the winds of adventure blew," Jack London once wrote of his decision to take to the seas as an oyster pirate at the age of fifteen. "There was vastly more romance in being an oyster pirate or a convict than in being a machine slave." London's venturesome spirit brought him more adventure before he was twenty-three years old than most people experience in a lifetime. London was a coal shoveler, a sailor, a hobo and a convict all before he entered high school, and when he finally got to high school he found it so boring he packed his bags and headed for the Yukon in search of gold. London spent his first twenty-three years as an adventurer and a vagabond, but in 1899, after years of fitful trying, he finally began to achieve success as a writer. Before his death in 1916, London wrote nearly two-dozen novels—some of which have become classics of American literature—as well as hundreds of short stories. Today London is remembered as both one of America's greatest writers *and* one of the greatest adventure writers of all time.

The man readers as Jack London was born John Griffith Chaney in the strangest of circumstances. His mother, Flora Wellman, was raised in a wealthy Ohio family. Suffering from mental instability caused by a childhood case of typhoid fever, Wellman ran away from home at age seventeen and gave piano lessons in the growing western town of San Francisco, California. By 1894, she was living with a strange man named William Chaney, who advertised himself as a professor of astrology. Chaney was in fact a professional wanderer, according to London biographer Alan Schroeder: "Distrustful of people and prone to arguments, [Chaney] abandoned one wife after another, one occupation after another." In the summer of 1875, Wellman told Chaney that she was expecting a child. Chaney panicked, demanded that she terminate the pregnancy, and fled, never to see his son.

Wellman took Chaney's departure hard, consuming an overdose of opium and trying to shoot herself in the head with a pistol. When both attempts at suicide failed, Wellman reconciled herself to having a child, and gave birth to a son on January 12, 1876. Too weak to care for the child, Wellman turned him over to a black woman named Virginia Prentiss who had just lost her baby.

London grew to be very close to "Aunt Jennie," who raised him with all the love and affection of a real mother. Within a year, Wellman was living with a Civil War veteran named John London, who adopted the young boy, giving him an instant family that included two sisters, Eliza and Ida.

Living on the Edge

For most of London's childhood his family lived on the edge of poverty. John London was a hard worker, but he never struck upon the opportunities that made people view San Francisco as a boom town. The elder London worked as a Singer Sewing Machine salesman, a potato farmer, and a night watchman, but Flora London was perpetually dissatisfied with the family's situation. When London was eight, however, the family moved to a farm in Livermore, California, where they lived as comfortably as they ever had. The London's happiness was short-lived. An epidemic struck the family's flock of chickens, which had produced much of their income, and the Londons were unable to pay the bank for the house they had recently bought. Broke again, they packed up their potato wagon and made the joyless trek back to a life of poverty in Oakland. Flora had moved west to find opportunity, writes Schroeder, but "found only poverty and despair. She became a bitter, scheming woman, and almost always, Jack felt uneasy in her presence."

While living on the farm, young Jack London encountered two things that were to have great influence on his life: books and alcohol. Living on the isolated farm in Livermore, "I read everything that came my way," London remembered in *John Barleycorn*. When the family moved back to Oakland, London began to read like he had never read before: "I read mornings, afternoons, and nights. I read in bed, I read at table, I read as I walked to and from school, and I read at recess while the other boys were playing. I began to get the 'jerks.' To everybody I replied: 'Go away you make me nervous.'" No matter what else changed in London's life, he was constantly to be found with a pile of books by his bedside.

If books were the great benefit in London's life, alcohol was the great burden. His first experience with the "poison" came when he was just seven years old. Carrying a pail of beer to his stepfather working in the fields, Jack decided to taste the cool liquor. Though he felt pleasantly dizzy when he reached the field, it was not long before he was quite sick to his stomach. "I was aware of a deadly nausea," he wrote later. "My condition was like that of one who had gone through a battle with poison. In truth, I had been poisoned.... There was no escaping [John Barleycorn]." London later wrote a book-length description of his battle with alcohol titled *John Barleycorn*, the name he gave to the drink that was his nemesis. The book was later used by the Women's Christian Temperance Union in their efforts to encourage the prohibition of alcohol.

At the age of ten, Jack London began to seek out work so that he could contribute money to his struggling family. Delivering newspapers before and after school during the week, toting ice and setting up bowling pins on the weekend, London seemed always to be working. But he spent every spare minute reading in the Oakland Public Library, hanging around on the busy wharfs that lined the waterfront, or sitting in saloons soaking up the stories of seafaring men. Once London spent a rowdy afternoon with a band of opium smugglers aboard their ship, the *Idler*. "It was a glorious ... afternoon," wrote Schroeder, "with singing and laughter and sloppy vows of eternal friendship." Yet London's memories of this time are bittersweet: the adventure and romance of the time were always clouded by the constant pinch of poverty.

London graduated from grammar school when he was fourteen, and was soon exposed to hard labor in a pickle cannery. Working at least ten hours a day for a dime an hour, London was forced to choose sleep over his beloved books, while his mother demanded that he give all his earnings to her. London began to dream of owning a small boat of his own, and soon was working even longer hours to save the eight dollars he needed. "It was not uncommon to work a 15-or 18-hour day," wrote Schroeder, "and, on one occasion, Jack worked for 36 hours straight, cramming a sandwich into his mouth to keep up his strength." Finally, London bought a sloop named the *Razzle Dazzle* from an experienced oyster pirate named French Frank. Now London could follow "the winds of adventure [that] blew the oyster pirate sloops up and down San Francisco Bay, from raided oyster-beds and fights at night on shoal and flat, to markets in the morning against city wharves, where peddlers and saloonkeepers came down to buy." At age fifteen, London was the captain of his own ship.

Many of London's novels celebrate the author's love of the great outdoors.

Prince of the Oyster Pirates

An oyster pirate's work was dirty and dangerous, and if he was caught he faced the prospect of prison. But it was also tremendously exciting, and provided London with the first real sense of belonging he had ever felt. The youngest of the pirates, London soon became one of the best. Sailing stealthily under cover of darkness, he anchored his boat atop the richest of the private oyster grounds that dotted San Francisco Bay and poached all he could carry. Then, avoiding the snares of the California Fish Patrol, London brought his catch to market and celebrated with his mates. London's bravery and his generosity with his money earned him the cherished title "Prince of the Oyster Pirates." London would recount some of his adventures in *John Barleycorn*, *The Cruise of the Dazzler*, and the collection *Tales of the Fish Patrol*.

Though the Fish Patrol threatened London with prison, it was John Barleycorn that brought London face to face with death. Oyster pirates fueled their courage with whiskey, and London found himself caught up in the romance of the alcoholic binge. "I abandoned myself to the life," he wrote in *John Barleycorn*, "and developed the misconception that the secret of John Barleycorn lay in going on mad drunks, rising through the successive stages that only an iron constitution could endure to final stupefaction and swinish unconsciousness." After one drinking binge, London fell off the wharf and into the icy water, where a tidal current quickly pulled him out into the bay. London was an excellent swimmer, but he began to toy with the idea of letting himself drown. "This was the trick of John Barleycorn," he wrote later, "laying me by the heels of my imagination and in a drug-dream dragging me to death." Soon London found himself far out in the water, where death was a real possibility. Yet just when death seemed closest, he "discovered scores of reasons for living" and was picked up by a passing fishing boat.

London's brush with death convinced him he had to get away from John Barleycorn and the life of an oyster pirate, but his avenue of escape was no less dangerous. In the month that he turned seventeen,

An illustration from *The Son of the Wolf*, one of three pieces found in *Jack London: Three Novels*.

London signed on as crew for a seven-month stint aboard the *Sophie Sutherland*, a seal-hunting schooner headed for the Coast of Japan. London was literally forced to fight for his dignity amongst the seasoned sailors, finally winning their respect when he piloted the ship through a vicious storm. "For forty minutes I stood there alone at the wheel, in my grasp the wildly careening schooner and the lives of twenty-two men. But I had done it! With my own hands I had done my trick at the wheel and guided a hundred tons of wood and iron through a few million tons of wind and waves," London later recalled in *The Cruise of the Snark*. Though the voyage made a man of London, he was so disgusted with the carnage of the seal hunt that he declined to sign on for another voyage.

On the Road

Back in California, London began working in a series of jobs that would eventually turn him into a political radical. Laboring in a jute mill and shoveling coal, London received no more pay than he had working as a child in the cannery. Meanwhile, his mother pushed him to submit a sailing story to a writing contest sponsored by a local newspaper. Working for three nights by the light of an oil lamp, London penned "Story of a Typhoon Off the Coast of Japan" and won the $25 prize. Thrilled, he quickly submitted other stories to the same paper, only to be told that sea stories were out of vogue. Soon he was back to working twelve- and thirteen-hour days shoveling coal. When London found out his boss had assigned him the work of two men, he vowed that he would never be a work beast again. Within weeks, he took to the road.

"Perhaps the greatest charm of tramp-life is the absence of monotony," London wrote in *The Road*, a chronicle of his experiences as a hobo. "In Hobo Land the face of life is protean—an ever changing phantasmagoria, where the impossible happens and the unexpected jumps out of the bushes at every turn of the road." In 1894, London joined up with Kelly's army, one of many armies of unemployed men from all over the United States who marched to Washington, D.C. to protest the unemployment that accompanied the economic depression of 1893. Though London enjoyed the camaraderie of the caravan of men, the trek began to turn sour as his shoes turned to tatters, food grew scarce, and the inhabitants of the cities the men passed through grew increasingly inhospitable. "Eventually," wrote Schroeder, "starvation got the better of London. He could march no farther, and, hoping to have greater success on his own, he deserted the army in mid-May."

Becoming a Socialist

Tramping east, London soon found himself wandering the streets of Niagara Falls, New York, where the police stopped him for vagrancy. With the speediest of trials, he was sentenced to the thirty days in the Erie County Penitentiary, where he was surrounded by "degenerates, wrecks, lunatics, addled intelligences, epileptics, monsters . . . a very nightmare of humanity." How had he fallen so far, London wondered? Was there no justice for a man who only wanted a decent wage? As London looked around him he saw what he called the "Social Pit," a hole of despair into which all working men must eventually fall. In his essay "Why I Became a Socialist," London remembers vowing "I shall climb out of the Pit, but not by the muscles of my body shall I climb out. I shall do no more hard work, and may God strike me dead if I do another day's hard work with my body more than I absolutely have to do."

It was London's experience in the "Social Pit" that turned him into a socialist. "Since that day I have opened many books, but no economic argument, no lucid demonstration of the logic and inevitableness of Socialism affects me as profoundly and convincingly as I was affected on the day when I first saw the walls of the Social Pit rise around me and felt myself slipping down, down, into the shambles at the bottom." London was hardly alone in looking to Socialism for solutions to his problems. Like many Americans, London saw that capitalism was unable to provide for the common good. During the depression of 1893-1897, millions of Americans experienced poverty and many of them blamed it on the capitalists who controlled politics and the economy. Thus for the last decade of the nineteenth century and the first few decades of the twentieth century, the Socialist Party offered an alternative for those who thought that a capitalist economy guaranteed misery for working men and women.

Returning to his mother's house in Oakland, California in 1896, the 21-year-old London entered Oakland High School and began what he called "a frantic pursuit of knowledge." Working relentlessly, London crammed three years of reading into two months. Not surprisingly, London's classmates found him rather peculiar. Dressed in baggy clothes, smoking hand-rolled cigarettes, and spouting radical political ideas, London hardly fit in with his middle-class peers. A member of the Socialist Labor party, London took time away from his studies to deliver soapbox lectures on socialism. Local newspapers called him "the boy Socialist." London finally tired of the slow pace of high school, and decided to study for the entrance exams to the University of California, Berkeley on his own.

Redoubling his efforts, London studied nineteen hours a day for three months. "My body grew weary, my mind grew weary, but I stayed with it," he recalled. In the fall of 1896, London entered the university; weeks later, he realized that his pace was too furious even for college. London dropped out and decided to become a writer. "Heavens, how I wrote!," he recounted in *John Barleycorn.* "Never was there a creative fever such

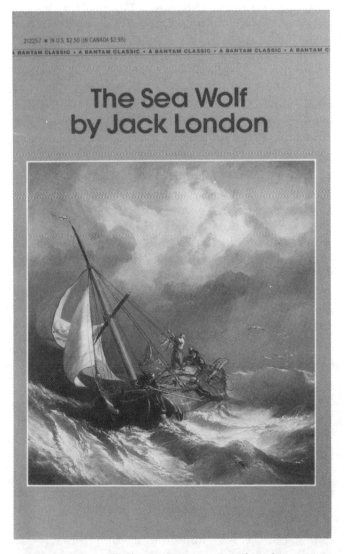

Based on the author's experiences as a sailor, this 1904 work further explores the theme of civilization versus nature.

as mine from which the patient escaped fatal results. The way I worked was enough to soften my brain and send me to a mad-house." His typewriter, he insisted, "was informed with an evil spirit.... The keys of that machine had to be hit so hard that to one outside the house it sounded like distant thunder or someone breaking up the furniture." All of London's feverish work brought few results, however, as his stories were rejected again and again. With his writing career stalled, the call of adventure beckoned again.

To the Klondike

Sometime during the summer of 1897, word reached San Francisco that gold had been discovered in the Klondike, a region in northwest Canada's Yukon Territory. According to Schroeder, newspapers hailed this new gold rush as the last great adventure of the nineteenth century. London was soon caught in the gold rush frenzy. On July 25, 1897, he sailed for the Klondike aboard the *SS Umatilla.* On board the ship, London found three other miners who agreed to form a team. The four men could hardly have known of the perils that would soon confront them as they spied the imposing Coast Range which separated them from gold.

Crossing the steep, snowy Chilkoot Pass was the first challenge facing the miners, made even more difficult because London, like many newcomers to the north country, had packed nearly 1,500 pounds of supplies. The miners decided to build a raft to float their belongings down the Fifty Mile River to Dawson, the center of the territory's mining activity. The next few weeks saw the miners racing the coming snows, shooting treacherous rapids to avoid having to make long portages, the overland trips that many miners used. As the men travelled in the increasing cold they began to hear rumors that Dawson was over-crowded, its inhabitants threatened with starvation, so they set up camp on Split-Up Island, about eighty miles from Dawson, and waited for winter. It was October, 1897.

At about the same time, London received a letter notifying him that his stepfather had died. Not long before that, London had received a response to his query to William Chaney, his natural father. He could not possibly be London's father, Chaney explained: "I was impotent at that time, [as a] result of hardship, privation & too much brainwork." Though London's mother could have cleared up this mystery, she never did. London's

depression over his lost fathers was compounded by the stifling arctic winter. The sun didn't rise above the horizon for months and the men huddled in their dark cabin, venturing forth only in search of firewood. Soon London was struck by scurvy, a disease resulting from the lack of fresh vegetables in the diet. As spring arrived, London was advised to return to civilization if he wished to be cured.

Though London left the Klondike with little more money than when he had begun, he carried home with him an immense treasure trove of stories, enough to last him a lifetime. Arriving back in San Francisco, London resolved to return to writing, but this time he was not out to write the great American novel. London wanted only to get paid. Within three months of returning home, London's first story was accepted by the prestigious Western literary magazine, *Overland Monthly,* which soon accepted a second story as well. Though London was happy to finally be published, the *Overland Monthly* paid very little for stories and London was sorely tempted to take a job as a postman. Luckily, a Boston magazine named *The Black Cat* offered him $40 for a story. "I was saved by the *Black Cat* story," London later recalled.

These first two stories London published—"To the Man on Trail" and "The White Silence"—are acknowledged to be among his best: they combine realistic description of the hardships of life in the far north with high drama. In "The White Silence," two trappers and an Indian woman travel across the stillness of an arctic landscape. London ponders the futility of man's fight against the elements: "Sole speck of life journeying across the ghostly wastes of a dead world, [man] trembles at his audacity, realizes that his is a maggot's life, nothing more.... And the fear of death, of God, of the universe, comes over him—the hope of the Resurrection and the Life, the yearning for immortality, the vain striving of the imprisoned essence—it is then, if ever, man walks alone with God." As the trio stops to rest beside a copse of trees, a lone pine gives way beneath the weight of the snow, breaking the White Silence as it crushes the body of one of the trappers. The broken man begs his friend to shoot him. As the story ends, a single gunshot echoes across the snow.

London's style was "completely fresh in its time," wrote Maxwell Geismar in *Rebels and Ancestors,* "offering a contrast to the sweetness and goodness of popular fiction of the 1900s." London was part of a new generation of literary talent that would change the face of American literature. Along with realists like Theodore Dreiser, Stephen Crane, and

Frank Norris, London introduced gritty, hard-hitting detail into his stories, and refused to provide readers the consolation of a happy ending. According to Schroeder, "London was a writer who believed that truth should be held up like a bloody, squirming beast; if it was upsetting to look at, so much the better. . . . Books had to reflect life itself, bluntly, without compromise." For Jack London, life was a struggle for survival in which only the fittest would survive; it was only fitting that his fiction should echo that belief.

Success!

By the fall of 1899, London was earning a respectable living as a writer. *Atlantic Monthly* had paid him $120 for a story, and he had settled all his debts and bought a new typewriter. In the spring of 1900, the publisher Houghton Mifflin bought nine of London's stories and published them as *The Son of the Wolf*. London's first book was well-received by the critics, who hailed London as the "Kipling of the North," referring to the great British writer of adventure tales, and suggested that he would "take his place among the few writers of really international reputation." Soon London received requests for stories from many of the magazines that had once rejected him. At the age of twenty-three, London had finally achieved his dream of being a writer.

London churned out stories in a blitz of activity between 1900 and 1903, a period in which he published two novels, the ill-received *A Daughter of the Snows* and *The Cruise of the Dazzler*, and two short story collections, *The God of His Fathers* and *Children of the Frost*. On April 7, 1900, London married Bessie Maddern, a longtime friend for whom he felt no real love. Bess, as she was called, bore London two daughters: Joan, born in 1901, and Becky, born in 1902. But Bess fit in poorly with the group of friends that London surrounded himself with. The London home soon became a center of Oakland's literary life, and Bess was a sullen outsider to their revels. In 1901, London attempted to parlay his newfound popularity into political success, running for mayor of Oakland on the Socialist Labor Party ticket. He received just 250 votes.

In 1903, London began work on a novel about a dog; thirty days later he completed the story of Buck, a huge spoiled farm dog who is kidnapped and sent to the Klondike to pull a sled. Buck slowly and painfully learns the ways of the savage North, which London called "the law of club and fang,"

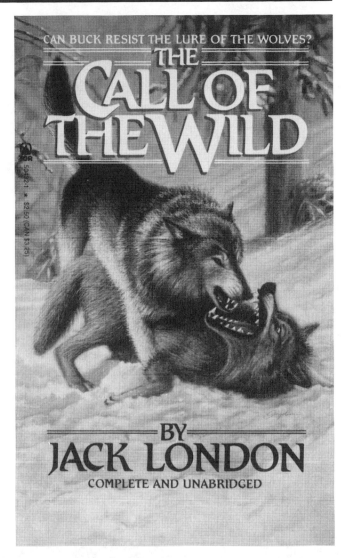

In London's most celebrated work—first published in 1903—a pampered farm dog learns the ways of the wilderness.

and becomes the leader of his sled-pulling team. When his master is killed, Buck escapes to the wild, fulfilling his biological destiny as the immortal Ghost Dog of Northland legend. Published as *The Call of the Wild*, this story is considered London's greatest work. *The Call of the Wild* is a story of action and of ideas. Filled with scenes of struggle and violence, it is also, according to Geismar, a "beautiful prose poem of the buried impulses," demonstrating the slow process by which Buck sheds the influence of civilization and returns to his instinctive and ancestral past. According to Schroeder, "the book sold out of its entire first edition within 24 hours and has never been out of print since."

In 1906, London published *White Fang*, a companion piece to *The Call of the Wild* which London said would "reverse the process. Instead of devolution or decivilization of a dog, I'm going to give the evolution, the civilization of a dog—the development of domesticity, faithfulness, love, morality, and all the amenities and virtues." Thus the wolf dog protagonist moves from a brutal struggle for survival in the frozen wastes of the North to a comfortable old age dozing in the California sun. Critics thought *White Fang* less successful than the earlier story, largely, wrote James Dickey in his introduction to a 1981 edition of *The Call of the Wild, White Fang, and Other Stories*, "because the events in *The Call of the Wild* are closer to what one wants to see happen: because we desire the basic, the 'natural,' the 'what is' to win [over] the world of streetcars and sentimentalism that we have made."

Critics lauded *The Call of the Wild* and *White Fang* for their allegorical portrait of man's struggle. London had managed to compress much of his philosophy and learning into his two dog stories, which reflect the tension between the powerful individual forging his own destiny and the civilizing influences of society, which will ultimately replace competition with cooperation and capitalism with socialism. London portrayed the basic, instinctual drives that lay within every man, yet he believed that men could live together only if they tamed those drives and looked out for the good of all. Thus London worked into his adventure stories the social Darwinism of Herbert Spencer, and the

socialism of Karl Marx. London explored these themes further in *The Sea Wolf* (1904), based on his stint as a sailor, and *Martin Eden* (1909), a loosely autobiographical account of a man's conversion to socialism. Gorman Beauchamp has suggested that America's greatest adventure writer might also have been one of its greatest intellectuals.

If London's works reflect the social concerns of his day, they also reflect its social prejudices. London's pages are filled with references to the inadequacy of women and of racial minorities, both of whom London considered inferior to the white Anglo-Saxon male. London's defenders have explained that these views were widespread at the turn of the century, and that London inherited his racism from his mother. "The majority of Caucasians in the United States would not have been offended by Jack's racial beliefs," writes Schroeder, though he acknowledges that such racism is "one of his most unattractive qualities." This racism provides one of the most difficult challenges for modern readers of London's work.

The Millionaire Author

In the years between *The Call of the Wild* and *Martin Eden*, London published most of his other major works. *The People of the Abyss* records the plight of London, England's East End poor; *War of the Classes* is an important collection of essays of

Ethan Hawke starred as Jack in Walt Disney's 1991 film adaptation of *White Fang*.

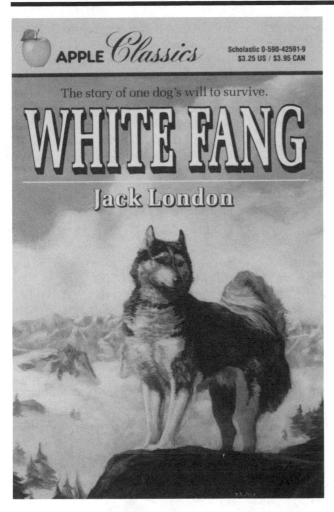

The story of one dog's will to survive.

WHITE FANG

Jack London

This 1906 companion to *The Call of the Wild* centers on a wild wolf dog that becomes tame.

social issues; *The Game*, one of the first examples of sports fiction in America, evokes both realistic and sentimental images of boxing; *The Road*, considered one of London's most engaging works, recounts London's adventures as a hobo riding the rails; and *The Iron Heel* provides a futuristic vision of the development of capitalism into fascism. In addition to these longer works, London continued to publish short stories, including the classics "To Build a Fire" and "Love of Life." London's productivity during this most creative period in his life was nothing short of amazing. By 1910, London was America's most famous and best-selling author, the first American writer ever to become a millionaire.

By 1905, London's marriage to Bess had ended, not least because he had fallen in love with another woman. Clara Charmian Kittredge was everything that Bess was not—high-spirited, outspoken, and willing to try anything. The lovers married within twenty-four hours of London's divorce from Bess,

which prompted many newspapers to condemn the now highly-visible author for his indecency and immorality. But the Londons could not be bothered with bad publicity, for they had an adventure planned. London had always wanted to sail his own boat around the world, and his financial success now made that dream possible. London declared that the boat he would build, the *Snark*, would be the finest yacht ever constructed in San Francisco.

From the beginning, the *Snark* was a disaster. Construction was halted by the San Francisco earthquake of 1906, the cost of materials skyrocketed, and the boat was rammed by two lumber scows as it sat at its moorings. In April, 1907, the Londons and their crew set sail for Hawaii, but things only got worse. The boat leaked terribly, the bathroom didn't work, and the navigator admitted that he didn't know how to navigate. Though they patched up some of the troubles in Hawaii, their voyage never became the carefree adventure they had desired. "By September, 1908," wrote Schroeder, "the *Snark* had become a floating hospital," as London and the crew suffered from all variety of tropical diseases. London received little consolation from recording their adventures in *The Cruise of the Snark*: even the book flopped.

Beauty Ranch

After 1909, London gave less attention to his writing and more attention to the sprawling tract of land in California's Sonoma Valley that he called the "Beauty Ranch." London was fascinated by farming and was eager to use the most advanced agricultural methods to turn his 1,100-acre ranch into a self-supporting paradise. And at the center of his kingdom he began construction on the mansion he called Wolf House. Built out of local stone and redwood, the enormous and sprawling multi-level house was designed to "stand for a thousand years." Though his income was great by the standards of the day, his expenses were greater, and London's oft-repeated claim that he worked only for money became ever truer. According to Andrew Sinclair, author of *Jack: A Biography of Jack London*, London mortgaged his future as an author to pay for his ambitious plans, "condemning himself to write the commercial at the expense of the good." London himself said "I write for no other purpose ... than to add three or four hundred acres to my magnificent estate.... To me, my cattle are far more interesting than my profession." The most successful book from this period was *John Barleycorn*, a highly personal account of

London's battle with alcohol that is still endorsed by Alcoholics Anonymous.

On August 22, 1913, fire consumed Wolf House, leaving only the stark skeleton of the house's chimneys standing. London was devastated, and his devastation was made the more complete by his failing health. By 1914, his kidneys were deteriorating and he began to suffer from acute rheumatism as well as an assortment of other ills, some complications of diseases he had incurred aboard the *Snark*. Moreover, the Londons had been unable to conceive the son Jack had so badly wanted (a daughter born in 1910 had died shortly after birth), and his first wife made contact with his daughters difficult. London's misery is evident in the now-famous letter he wrote to his twelve-year-old daughter, Joan, shortly after the fire at Wolf House: "What have you done for me in all the days of your life? What do you *feel* for me? Am I merely your meal-ticket? . . . Joan, my daughter, please know that the world belongs to the honest ones, to the true ones, to the right ones, to the ones who talk right out; and that the world does not belong to the ones who remain silent, who, by their very silence lie and cheat and make a mock of love and a meal ticket of their father."

Jack and Charmian London spent most of 1915 and 1916 in Hawaii, where London sought to recuperate from his illnesses. London continued to write during this time, earning money but writing little of merit. Of his last stories, only "The Red One," a science-fictional account of an indecipherable message sent to Earth from space, has merited critical attention. London sought relief from the pain he suffered by injecting himself with morphine, which provided hours of sleep. In July, 1916, the Londons returned to California, but Jack's condition grew steadily worse. On the morning of November 22, 1916, a servant sent to awaken London found him lying unconscious, his face blue and his breathing labored. Beside him was a nearly-empty vial of morphine. Despite the attempts of several doctors to rouse him, Jack London died that night on the porch of his house. A press bulletin cited his cause of death as "a gastro-intestinal type of uremia." On November 26, London's ashes were buried under a great stone at the Beauty Ranch.

Fans of Jack London can still visit the remains of his ranch at the Jack London State Historical Park in Glen Ellen, California. But one can best get a sense of London's life by reading the hundreds of stories he wrote, stories that bristle with the vitality and exuberance of a man who never turned down an adventure, who refused to give up on life even when he found himself clinging to the walls of the "Social Pit," and who tried to fuse his politics, his life, and his art. London climbed from the depths of poverty to the heights of literary stardom, and is now acknowledged as a master of realism and one of the finest short story writers of the century. But "the greatest story Jack London ever wrote," observed Alfred Kazin in *On Native Ground*, "was the story he lived."

■ Works Cited

Beauchamp, Gorman, *Jack London*, Starmount House, 1984.

Geismar, Maxwell, *Rebels and Ancestors: The American Novel*, Houghton, 1953.

Kazin, Alfred, *On Native Ground*, Harcourt, 1942.

Labor, Earle, *Jack London*, Twayne, 1974.

Labor, E., Robert C. Leitz, III, and I. Milo Shepard, editors, *The Letters of Jack London*, Stanford University Press, 1988.

London, Jack, *The Call of the Wild, White Fang, and Other Stories*, edited by Andrew Sinclair, introduction by James Dickey, Penguin, 1981.

London, Jack, *Novels and Social Writings* (contains *The People of the Abyss, The Road, The Iron Heel, Martin Eden, John Barleycorn*, and essays), edited by Donald Pizer, Library of America, 1982.

Schroeder, Alan, *Jack London*, Chelsea House, 1991.

Sinclair, Andrew, *Jack: A Biography of Jack London*, Harper, 1977.

■ For More Information See

BOOKS

Baltrop, Robert, *Jack London: The Man, the Writer, the Rebel*, Pluto, 1976.

Dictionary of Literary Biography, Gale, Volume 8: *Twentieth-Century American Science Fiction Writers*, 1981, Volume 12: *American Realists and Naturalists*, 1982, Volume 78: *American Short-Story Writers, 1880-1910*, 1989.

Feied, Frederick, *No Pie in the Sky: The Hobo as American Cultural Hero in the Works of Jack London, John Dos Passos, and Jack Kerouac*, Citadel, 1964.

Foner, Philip, editor, *Jack London: American Rebel*, Citadel, revised edition, 1974.

Franchere, Ruth, *Jack London: The Pursuit of a Dream*, Crowell, 1962.

Garst, Shannon, *Jack London: Magnet for Adventure*, Wolf House, 1972.

Hedrick, Joan D., *Solitary Comrade: Jack London and His Work*, University of North Carolina Press, 1982.

Hendricks, King, and I. Shepard, editors, *Letters from Jack London: Containing an Unpublished Correspondence between London and Sinclair Lewis*, Odyssey Press, 1965.

Johnston, Carolyn, *Jack London—An American Rebel?*, Greenwood Press, 1984.

Kingman, Russ, *A Pictorial Biography of Jack London*, Crown, 1979.

London, Charmian Kittredge, *The Book of Jack London*, two volumes, Century, 1921.

London, Joan, *Jack London and His Times: An Unconventional Biography*, Doubleday, Doran, 1939.

Lynn, Kenneth S., *Dream of Success*, Little, Brown, 1955.

Martin, Jay, *Harvests of Change: American Literature, 1865-1914*, Prentice-Hall, 1967.

McClintock, James I., *White Logic: Jack London's Short Stories*, Wolf House, 1976.

Mumford, Lewis, *The Golden Day: A Study in American Literature and Culture*, Boni & Liveright, 1926.

O'Connor, Richard, *Jack London: A Biography*, Little, Brown, 1964.

Ownby, Ray Wilson, editor, *Jack London: Essays in Criticism*, Peregrine Smith, 1978.

Sherman, Joan R., *Jack London: A Reference Guide*, G. K. Hall, 1983.

Stone, Irving, *Sailor on Horseback: The Biography of Jack London*, Houghton, 1938.

Walcutt, Charles C., *Jack London*, University of Minnesota Press, 1966.

Walker, Dale L., editor, *The Fiction of Jack London: A Chronological Bibliography*, Texas Western Press, 1972.

Walker, Franklin, *Jack London and the Klondike: The Genesis of an American Writer*, Huntington Library, 1966.

Watson, Charles N., Jr., *The Novels of Jack London: A Reappraisal*, University of Nebraska Press, 1983.

Woodbridge, Hensley C., John London, and George H. Tweney, *Jack London: A Bibliography*, Talisman Press, 1966, revised and enlarged edition, Kraus, 1973.°

—Sketch by Tom Pendergast

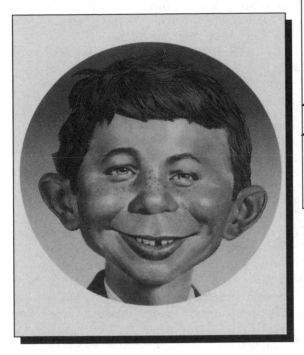

MAD Magazine

■ Personal

Full name, William Maxwell (Bill) Gaines; born March 1, 1922; died June 3, 1992; son of Max C. (a comic book publisher) and Jessie K. (Postlethwaite) Gaines; married Hazel Grieb, October 21, 1944 (divorced February 9, 1948); married Nancy Siegel, November 17, 1955 (divorced March 1, 1971); married Anne Griffiths, February 21, 1987; children: Cathy, Wendy, Chris. *Education:* Attended Policy Institute of Brooklyn, 1939-1942; New York University, B.S., 1948. *Hobbies and other interests:* Collector of models of dirigibles and models of the Statue of Liberty.

■ Addresses

Office—Mad Magazine, 485 Madison Ave., New York, NY 10022.

■ Career

Publisher. EC Publications, Inc., New York City, president, 1948—1992. Served with AUS, 1942-1946. *Member:* Wine and Food Society, In Search of Name Society (charter member), Phi Alpha.

■ Writings

"MAD" COLLECTIONS

The Mad Reader, introduction by Roger Price, Ballantine Books, 1954.
Mad Strikes Back, introduction by Bob and Ray, Ballantine Books, 1955.
Inside Mad, Ballantine Books, 1955.
Utterly Mad, Ballantine Books, 1956.
Mad for Keeps, introduction by Ernie Kovaks, Crown Publishers, 1958.
The Brothers Mad, Ballantine Books, 1958.
The Bedside Mad, New American Library, 1959.
Mad Forever, introduction by Steve Allen, Crown Publishers, 1959.
Son of Mad, New American Library, 1959.
A Golden Trashery of Mad, introduction by Sid Caesar, Crown Publishers, 1960.
The Organization Mad, New American Library, 1960.
Like Mad, New American Library, 1960.
The Ides of Mad, New American Library, 1961.
Fighting Mad, New American Library, 1961.
Mad Frontier, New American Library, 1962.
Mad in Orbit, New American Library, 1962.
The Voodoo Mad, New American Library, 1963.
Greasy Mad Stuff, New American Library, 1963.
Three Ring Mad, New American Library, 1964.
The Self Made Mad, New American Library, 1964.
The Mad Sampler, New American Library, 1965.
It's a World, World, World, World Mad, New American Library, 1965.
Raving Mad, New American Library, 1966.
Boiling Mad, New American Library, 1966.

The Questionable Mad, New American Library, 1967.

Howling Mad, New American Library, 1967.

Indigestible Mad, New American Library, 1968.

Burning Mad, New American Library, 1968.

The Ridiculously Expensive Mad, World Publishing Co., 1969.

Good'n'Mad, New American Library, 1969.

Hopping Mad, New American Library, 1969.

The Portable Mad, New American Library, 1970.

Mad Power, New American Library, 1970.

The Dirty Old Mad, Warner Books, 1971.

Polyunsaturated Mad, Warner Books, 1971.

The Recycled Mad, Warner Books, 1972.

The Non-Violent Mad, Warner Books, 1972.

The Rip-off Mad, Warner Books, 1973.

The Token Mad, Warner Books, 1973.

The Pocket Mad, Warner Books, 1974.

The Invisible Mad, Warner Books, 1974.

Dr. Jekyll and Mr. Mad, Warner Books, 1975.

Steaming Mad, Warner Books, 1975.

Mad at You!, Warner Books, 1975.

The Vintage Mad, Warner Books, 1976.

Hooked on Mad, New American Library, 1976.

The Cuckoo Mad, Warner Books, 1976.

The Medicine Mad, Warner Books, 1977.

A Mad Scramble, Warner Books, 1977.

Incurably Mad, Warner Books, 1977.

Swinging Mad, Warner Books, 1977.

Mad Overboard, Warner Books, 1978.

Mad Clowns Around, Warner Books, 1978.

A Mad Treasure Chest, Warner Books, 1978.

Mad Sucks, Warner Books, 1979.

Super-Mad, Warner Books, 1979.

The Abominable Snow Mad, Warner Books, 1979.

Mad about the Buoy Book, Warner Books, 1980.

Mad For Kicks, Warner Books, 1980.

The Uncensored Mad, Warner Books, 1980.

Pumping Mad, Warner Books, 1981.

Mad Horses Around, Warner Books, 1981.

Eggs-Rated Mad, Warner Books, 1981.

A Mad Carnival, Warner Books, 1982.

The Explosive Mad, Warner Books, 1982.

Mad Barfs, Warner Books, 1982.

Eternally Mad, Warner Books, 1983.

Mad about Town, Warner Books, 1983.

Big Mad on Campus, Warner Books, 1983.

The Endangered Mad, Warner Books, 1984.

Stamp Out Mad, Warner Books, 1984.

The Forbidden Mad, Warner Books, 1984.

Monster Mad, Warner Books, 1985.

The Plaid Mad, Warner Books, 1985.

Son of Mad Sucks, Warner Books, 1985.

Qwerty Mad, Warner Books, 1986.

Monu-Mentally Mad, Warner Books, 1986.

Big Hairy Mad, Warner Books, 1986.

The Wet and Wisdom of Mad, Warner Books, 1987.

Mad Duds, Warner Books, 1987.

'Til Mad Do Us Part, Warner Books, 1987.

Mad Blasts, Warner Books, 1988.

The Mad Cooler, Warner Books, 1988.

The Spare Mad, Warner Books, 1988.

Mad in a Box, Warner Books, 1989.

Mad Jackpot, Warner Books, 1989.

Soaring Mad, Warner Books, 1989.

Weather Mad, Warner Books, 1990.

BOOKS BY SELECTED "MAD" CONTRIBUTORS; SERGIO ARAGONES

Viva Mad, New American Library, 1968.

Mad-ly Yours, Warner Books, 1972.

In Mad We Trust, Warner Books, 1974.

Mad as the Devil, Warner Books, 1975.

Mad about Mad, foreword by Albert B. Feldstein, Warner Books, 1977.

Shooting Mad, Warner Books, 1979.

Mad Marginals, Warner Books, 1980.

Mad as a Hatter, Warner Books, 1981.

Mad's Sergio Aragonés on Parade, Warner Books, 1982.

Mad Menagerie, Warner Books, 1983.

More Mad Marginals, Warner Books, 1985.

Mad Pantomimes, Warner Books, 1987.

More Mad Pantomimes, Warner Books, 1988.

BOOKS BY SELECTED "MAD" CONTRIBUTORS; DAVE BERG

Mad's Dave Berg Looks at People, New American Library, 1966.

Mad's Dave Berg Looks at Modern Thinking, foreword by Jerry De Fuccio, New American Library, 1969.

Mad's Dave Berg Looks at Our Sick World, New American Library, 1971.

Dave Berg Looks at Living, Warner Books, 1973.

Mad's Dave Berg Looks at Things, Warner Books, 1974.

Dave Berg Looks Around, Warner Books, 1975.

Dave Berg's Mad Trash, Warner Books, 1977.

Mad's Dave Berg Takes a Loving Look, Warner Books, 1977.

Mad's Dave Berg Looks, Listens and Laughs, Warner Books, 1979.

Mad's Dave Berg Looks at You, Warner Books, 1982.

Mad's Dave Berg Looks at the Neighborhood, Warner Books, 1984.

Mad's Dave Berg Looks at Our Planet, Warner Books, 1986.

Mad's Dave Berg Looks at Today, Warner Books, 1987.

BOOKS BY SELECTED "MAD" CONTRIBUTORS; DON EDWING

Don Edwing's Mad Bizarre Bazaar, Warner Books, 1980.
Mad Book of Almost Superheroes, Warner Books, 1982.
Mad Variations, Warner Books, 1984.
Mad's Sheer Torture, Warner Books, 1988.
Mad Fantasy, Fables and other Foolishness, Warner Books, 1989.

BOOKS BY SELECTED "MAD" CONTRIBUTORS; STAN HART AND PAUL COKER, JR.

The Mad Book of Revenge, Warner Books, 1976.
The Mad Guide to Careers, Warner Books, 1978.
Mad's Fast Look at Fast Living, Warner Books, 1982.
The Mad Survival Handbook, Warner Books, 1983.

BOOKS BY SELECTED "MAD" CONTRIBUTORS; FRANK JACOBS

(With Bob Clarke) Mad Goes Wild, New American Library, 1974.
(With B. Clarke) The Mad Jumble Book, Warner Books, 1975.
(With B. Clarke) More about Mad Sports, Warner Books, 1977.
(With B. Clarke) Get Stuffed with Mad, Warner Books, 1981.
Mad's Talking Stamps, Warner Books, 1984.
Mad Goes to Pieces, foreword by Nick Meglin, Warner Books, 1984.
Mad Zaps the Human Race, Warner Books, 1984.
(With B. Clarke) Mad's Believe It or Nuts, Warner Books, 1986.

BOOKS BY SELECTED "MAD" CONTRIBUTORS; AL JAFFEE

The Mad Book of Magic and Other Dirty Tricks, New American Library, 1970.
Al Jaffee's Mad Monstrosities, Warner Books, 1974.
(Editor) Clods' Letters to Mad, foreword by Jerry De Fuccio, Warner Books, 1974.
Mad's Al Jaffee Spews Out Snappy Answers to Stupid Questions, Warner Books, 1975.
Mad's Al Jaffee Spews Out Still More Snappy Answers to Stupid Questions, Warner Books, 1976.
Al Jaffee's Mad Inventions, Warner Books, 1978.
Mad's Al Jaffee Spews Out More Snappy Answers to Stupid Questions, foreword by Nick Meglin, Warner Books, 1979.
Good Lord! Not Another Book of Snappy Answers to Stupid Questions, Warner Books, 1980.
Mad's Al Jaffee Freaks Out, Warner Books, 1982.

Mad's Vastly Overrated Al Jaffee, Warner Books, 1983.
Snappy Answers to Stupid Questions #5, Warner Books, 1984.
Mad Brain Ticklers, Puzzles and Lousy Jokes, Warner Books, 1986.
Mad's Very Best Snappy Answers to Stupid Questions, Warner Books, 1986.
Once Again Al Jaffee Spews Out Snappy Answers to Stupid Questions, Warner Books, 1987.
Al Jaffee Sweats Out Another Book, Warner Books, 1988.
Mad's All New Snappy Answers to Stupid Questions, Warner Books, 1989.

BOOKS BY SELECTED "MAD" CONTRIBUTORS; DON MARTIN

Mad's Maddest Artist Don Martin Steps Out, foreword by Albert B. Feldstein, New American Library, 1962.
(With E. Rosenblum) Mad's Maddest Artist Don Martin Bounces Back, New American Library, 1963.
Mad's Don Martin Cooks up More Tales, New American Library, 1969.
(With Dick de Bartolo) Mad's Don Martin Comes on Strong, New American Library, 1971.
Don Martin Drops Thirteen Stories, Warner Books, 1973.
Mad's Don Martin Carries On, Warner Books, 1973.
The Completely Mad Don Martin, Warner Books, 1974.
Mad's Don Martin Steps Further Out, Warner Books, 1975.
Don Martin Forges Ahead, Warner Books, 1977.
Mad's Don Martin Digs Deeper, Warner Books, 1979.
Mad's Don Martin Grinds Ahead, Warner Books, 1981.
The Adventures of Captain Klutz II, Warner Books, 1983.
Mad's Don Martin Sails Ahead, Warner Books, 1986.

BOOKS BY SELECTED "MAD" CONTRIBUTORS; NICK MEGLIN AND GEORGE WOODBRIDGE

The Sound of Mad, Warner Books, 1980.
A Mad Look at the 50s, Warner Books, 1985.
A Mad Look at the 60s, Warner Books, 1989.

BOOKS BY SELECTED "MAD" CONTRIBUTORS; PAUL PETER PORGES

The Mad How Not to Do It Book, foreword by John Putnam, Warner Books, 1981.
A Mad Book of Cheap Shots, Warner Books, 1984.

Mad Lobsters and Other Abominable Housebroken Creatures, Warner Books, 1986.

BOOKS BY SELECTED "MAD" CONTRIBUTORS; ANTONIO PROHIAS

Mad's Spy vs. Spy Follow up File, New American Library, 1968.
The Third Mad Dossier of Spy vs. Spy, Warner Books, 1972.
The All New Mad Secret File on Spy vs. Spy, Warner Books, 1973.
The 4th Mad Declassified Papers on Spy vs. Spy, Warner Books, 1974.
The 5th Mad Report on Spy vs. Spy, Warner Books, 1978.
Mad's Spy vs. Spy, Warner Books, 1978.
The 6th Mad Report on Spy vs. Spy, Warner Books, 1982.
Mad's Big Book of Spy vs. Spy Capers and other Surprises, Warner Books, 1982.

BOOKS BY SELECTED "MAD" CONTRIBUTORS; LARRY SIEGEL AND ANGELO TORRES

The Mad Make Out Book, Warner Books, 1979.
Mad Clobbers the Classics, Warner Books, 1981.
Mad's How to Be a Successful Dog, Warner Books, 1984.

BOOKS BY SELECTED "MAD" CONTRIBUTORS; LOU SILVERSTONE AND JACK RICKARD

Politically Mad, Warner Books, 1976.
A Mad Look at the Future, Warner Books, 1978.
The Mad Book of Mysteries, Warner Books, 1980.

OTHER

Mad magazine appears in numerous foreign languages, including German, Dutch, Chinese, Italian, and Spanish.

■ Adaptations

The Mad Show was a theatrical revue first produced in New York City, 1966; the *Mad* board game was introduced by Parker Brothers, Inc., 1980; motion pictures are currently in development based on the "Alfred E. Neuman" character and on Antonio Prohías's "Spy vs. Spy" series of cartoons.

■ Sidelights

In April of 1954, a United States Senate judiciary committee began to look at comic books, and they did not like what they saw: witchcraft, cannibalism, the walking dead, bug-eyed monsters from outer space—not to mention tales of crime and war in which sometimes the good guy died or the criminal

went unpunished. The senators were looking for the cause of juvenile delinquency, and they began to think that they'd found it at the corner newsstand.

Bill Gaines's Entertainment Comics (EC) Publications was not the most outrageous publisher of horror and crime comics, but it may have invented the style. Every other month, EC brought its fans titles like *Tales from the Crypt, The Vault of Horror, The Haunt of Fear* and *Weird Science*, lovingly wrought tales of gore, violence and macabre terror—the work of artists who could enjoy a good bloody story just as much as kids did. The people at EC didn't take themselves or their ghost stories too seriously: most of the stories had bad puns in their titles (for example, a man chews off his leg in a story entitled "Stumped!"). They even published a comic book that made fun of the other comic books, one whose cover promised "Tales Calculated to Drive You *MAD:* Humor in a Jugular Vein."

But other people were taking these comics *very* seriously. Condemnations of comics—in books such as psychologist Frederic Wertham's *Seduction of the Innocent*, and magazine articles in *Reader's Digest, Ladies' Home Journal* and elsewhere—usually mentioned EC prominently. When members of the Senate Judiciary Committee's Subcommittee to Investigate Juvenile Delinquency put comic books on trial, they allowed Bill Gaines to take the stand in their defense. Gaines tried to make the case that the enjoyment of suspense is harmless, and that parents, police officers and members of Congress should not be afraid of comic books or the children who read them. He presented his conviction that "delinquency is the product of the real environment in which the child lives and not of the fiction he reads."

Gaines faced an uphill battle. The panel he appeared before had just heard a respected psychiatrist testify to the damage done to children by comic books and the crimes that children had committed after reading them. It was Gaines's job then to try to explain to that group of concerned adults exactly what about comics was so pleasurable, to convince them of how that pleasure is actually harmless. As it happened, some of the horror, suspense, war and science fiction comics that Gaines published were submitted to the committee as evidence against comic books in general, and Gaines was questioned about both the stories and the pictures in them. On national television, one senator asked him about an illustration of a man with a bloody axe in one hand and a woman's severed head in the other. Gaines defended the illustration, saying that if it had been a little bit more gory it might then be considered to be in bad taste. Gaines did not win any important allies to his cause that day.

The "New Trend" Comics

Gaines had been studying education at New York University when his father, comic book pioneer Max Gaines, died in a boating accident. At his mother's persuading, the younger Gaines stepped in to take over his father's languishing company, Educational Comics Publications. Max Gaines had invented comic books as reprints of the Sunday funnies, and he always believed passionately in the power of comics to teach. The books he published, such as *Picture Stories from Science* and *Animal Fables*, tended to be more popular with parents than with kids. When Bill Gaines took the company over at age twenty-five, EC Publications was not financially successful.

While he finished school, Gaines let his father's staff continue to run the day-to-day operations of EC, but began to push the company in directions he hoped would be more profitable. After he finished school, Gaines became more involved in editing the books and working with the artists and writers. He found that he had a real enthusiasm for comics. After spending a few years trying to match the successes of other publishers by following them from trend to trend, from super hero stories to teen-age stories to westerns to romances, Gaines and editor Al Feldstein began to develop categories of stories that they themselves enjoyed. Inspired by the radio horror programs they both used to listen to as children, the duo began writing horror stories, and created two new comic books to feature them: *The Crypt of Terror* (later renamed *Tales from the Crypt*) and *The Vault of Horror*. To mark the change in direction, Gaines changed the company's name: "EC" now stood for "Entertaining Comics." EC's new motto announced "A New Trend in Comic Books." Other "New Trend" comics followed, all featuring the same combination of heightened suspense, preposterous plots, shocking endings, carefully drawn but gruesome illustrations and terrible joke titles.

Tales Calculated to Drive You *Mad*

Congress and the public seemed to be reaching a consensus that laws were needed to either prohibit horror and crime comics or at least to clean them up. Gaines still believed that the public could be won over to the side of those who loved the fun and artistic freedom of comic books that censorship would have ended. He sent letters to subscribers urging them to let their representatives know how they felt about horror in comics. He tried to bring the other publishers—fierce and often bitter competitors—together to present a united front in opposition to censorship. Instead, the other publishers voted to form a committee and set of guidelines to censor themselves.

These self-censors, who came to be known as the "Comics Code Authority," prohibited not only the graphic depiction of violence, but also stories in which criminals or other villains were shown to be happy or successful, or police or other authority figures were depicted as corrupt or unworthy of respect. Comics which did not have the Comics Code Authority's stamp of approval could not be carried by the distributors, which in effect meant that they could not be sold publicly and would be forced out of business. Before the Comics Code Authority was set up on September 16, 1954, EC published *Tales from the Crypt*, *The Vault of Horror*, *The Haunt of Fear*, *Shock SuspenStories*, *Crime SuspenStories*, *Two-Fisted Tales*, *Frontline Combat*, *Weird Fantasy*, *Weird Science*, *Panic* and *Mad*. Soon after the code went into effect, only *Mad* remained.

Mad founder Bill Gaines used his father's company, **Educational Comic Publications**, to launch his own satirical publication.

Mad is infamous for its satires,

such as this 1994 spoof of t.v.'s *Baywatch*.

Humor in a Jugular Vein

Mad escaped the fate of EC's other books because it was different. *Mad* was a satire of the world of comic books, and the people who were trying to eliminate bad influences on children were not yet looking at satire. *Mad* reflected the vision of its creator, Harvey Kurtzman. Kurtzman wrote and edited EC's war comics, *Two-Fisted Tales* and *Frontline Combat,* giving them a realism, an attention to detail and a distinct anti-war message that set them apart from the other action comics of the day. He assembled the *Mad* creative team from artists he had already collaborated with on the war comics. The first issues of *Mad* spoofed EC's other comics; issue number one, from the summer of 1952, featured parodies of crime, horror, science fiction and western stories. By issue number four, *Mad* had broadened its scope, and parodies of other publishers' comics appeared for the first time.

Behold the *Mad*

Once the Comics Code Authority was put in place, *Mad* became EC Publications's only remaining success. Two clouds hovered on the horizon, endangering *Mad*'s (and therefore EC's) survival: 1. Harvey Kurtzman was ready to go on to bigger and better things—and already had an attractive job offer from a respectable magazine, and 2. censorship seemed to be prevailing in the world of comics, and Gaines began to wonder how much

Don Martin's memorable style has become a hallmark of the magazine.

longer he would be able to get *Mad* past the Code. To keep Kurtzman at EC, Gaines allowed him to transform *Mad* into a magazine. Since *Mad* was no longer a comic book, it would no longer be subject to the restrictions imposed by the Comics Code Authority.

Kurtzman, thrilled with his total artistic control over every aspect of the magazine, recreated *Mad* from the printing press to the choice of paper to the typesetting. "It was a great moment for me, Bill gave me *carte blanche*," he recalled to Maria Reidelbach for her book, *Completely Mad*. "There were no guidelines. Make up the guidelines: now that was a great creative moment for me."

While it often broke new ground visually, the *Mad* comic book had a look that naturally borrowed heavily from the comics it lampooned. For the new *Mad* magazine, Kurtzman wanted a fresh look, something even he had never seen before. He came up with a format somewhere in between comics and magazines: a black-and-white book printed on a better grade of newsprint than the comic book had used, with typeset text, contributions from humorists outside the world of comics (while Kurtzman had written all the material in the *Mad* comic books himself), and innovative layouts that had not been seen before in either comics or magazines. The printing process allowed for more detailed drawings, giving *Mad's* artists the ability to mimic the styles of a variety of publications, as well as to create their own styles beyond what the comic book format had permitted.

About the same time that *Mad* switched from a comic book to a magazine format, a new mascot named Alfred E. Neuman appeared. His dopey, widely grinning face was first seen in the anthology *Mad Reader* in 1954 (though the character didn't officially have a name yet). Neuman began appearing in issues of the magazine in 1955; by 1956, the caricature was accompanied by his now-famous slogan, "What—me worry?" By issue twenty-nine of the magazine, after names like Melvin Coznowski and Mel Haney had been tried, the "What—me worry?" kid had received the name he's been known by ever since.

As *Mad's* mascot for almost forty years, Alfred E. Neuman assumed many guises and appeared on more than 300 magazine covers. Usually he is transformed, cast as the star of that month's movie or television parody. Sometimes he is a contemporary social icon, like a hippie or a happy face button. And sometimes he's just *there*, grinning—and that's enough. Alfred E. Neuman also has a life

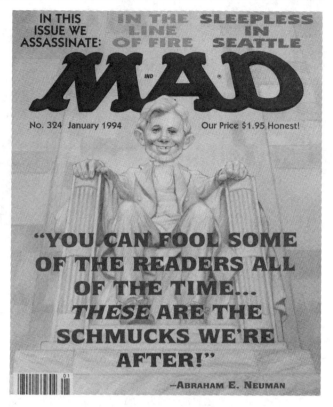

Alfred E. Neuman's dopey grin has graced the covers of more than 300 issues of *Mad* over the course of nearly forty years.

outside the pages of *Mad* magazine. Because he is so recognizable, adaptable and commonly understood to represent idiocy, he has become a favorite of political cartoonists. In the 1992 United States presidential election, newspapers and magazines bigger and smaller than *Mad* borrowed Neuman for caricatures of Bill Clinton, George Bush *and* Ross Perot.

In *Mad's* early days as a comic book, it focused its humor on other comic books, featuring such spoofs as "Superduperman," "Mickey Rat" and "Starchie." But even then its satire was not limited to the Supermans, Mickey Mouses and Archies of the world of comics. On any page, in any panel, a careful reader might find famous people standing where they probably don't belong, advertisements placed where they clearly don't belong, and off-handed comments in various ancient, modern or even fictitious languages. By the time *Mad* became a magazine, its humor targeted a range of topics, but it had found a few themes that would carry it through the next forty years. The creators of *Mad* had all been affected by the censorship of the 1950s, both as a force of repression and as a cause of blandness and shallowness in the world, and took issue against any institution that sought to control people's—and especially kids'—minds. In *Completely Mad*, Gaines summed up his philosophy: "Editorially, we're trying to teach [our readers] 'Don't believe in ads. Don't believe in government. Watch yourself—*everybody* is trying to screw you!'"

The Critical *Mad*

Each issue of *Mad* usually features an extended parody of a current movie and a current television show. Where the characters in *Mad*'s cartoons might look more or less cartoonish, depending on the artist's style, the characters in these parodies, whether drawn by Mort Drucker, Angelo Torres, Jack Davis or another illustrator, are usually more realistic, carefully-drawn and recognizable caricatures of the screen actors. The characters generally introduce themselves on the first page or two, then recreate key scenes from the movie or a typical storyline from the television series. The edges of the illustrations are often crowded with characters from similarly-themed movies or series, commenting on the action or simply being there to remind the readers that much of what appears on screen has been seen before in one form or another.

If it was natural for *Mad* to begin by spoofing other comic books, then the advertisements which filled three to five pages of almost every comic book were an obvious next step. In issue number twenty-one from March of 1955, bogus ads for air rifles, postage stamp collections and bubble gum appeared in an issue with a bogus mail-order catalog cover. The following issue featured the first (but not the last) *Mad* story to mock advertising itself, mimicking a number of popular ad campaigns in the course of describing a fictional career in the ad business. Magazine publishers usually make more of their money selling ads than they make selling the magazines themselves, so the decision to spoof advertising—and risk offending their paying advertisers—could not have been taken lightly. Gaines decided that in order to enjoy the freedom to satirize whatever they wanted, *Mad* would no longer take advertising. To this day, the only advertising in *Mad* is for its own subscriptions, paperbacks and special issues.

No longer caring whether or not those in the advertising business like it, *Mad* has been relentless in its ridicule. The writers are quick to spot emerging trends in advertising and lampoon them, carrying a concept—like celebrity endorsements, or "product placement" in movies—well beyond their logical conclusion.

The Changing *Mad*

Mad magazine was a success from the start, quickly growing to a monthly circulation of some 325,000. Many times before in EC's history, the profits from more successful titles were used to sustain less successful ones that the company wanted to keep alive. Early on, the horror comics had kept *Mad* going before it found its audience. By 1956, *Mad* was EC's only title, and *it* kept the entire company alive. Kurtzman eventually wanted a larger budget, both to be able to develop the magazine the way he envisioned it, and to offer more money to his contributing artists and writers. (At the time, he was working on a straight salary from Gaines, who kept sole control over the company's often uncertain finances.) Kurtzman wanted to share some of that control, and told Gaines that he would quit if Gaines didn't give him a fifty-one percent stake in the magazine.

Kurtzman ended up leaving *Mad*—and taking most of the magazine's artists with him—to create a full-color magazine of his own with the backing of *Playboy* publisher Hugh Hefner. Gaines then hired Al Feldstein, who had edited most of EC's "New Trend" comics (including *Panic*, an early imitation of *Mad*), to replace Kurtzman as editor. Without Kurtzman or the other artists who had created *Mad* and given it its style, Feldstein had to recreate the magazine along new lines. Where Kurtzman's *Mad* had been a very personal creation, filled with inside jokes that he could sustain over months because he wrote much of the material himself, Feldstein opened the magazine up to a variety of writers with quite different perspectives and types of humor. His approach expanded *Mad*'s audience, and the circulation rose to one million by 1960. Many of the writers and artists Feldstein brought to *Mad* between his first issue as editor in 1956 and his retirement in 1984 still contribute to the magazine on a frequent basis.

The Usual Gang of Idiots

Although nearly all of the writing and artwork in *Mad* is freelance, bought directly from artists who are not on the permanent staff, the magazine has been a home for many of its contributors, issue after issue, for years. Identified on the contents page only as "the usual gang of idiots," but always credited by name alongside their work, these artists have developed highly personal styles that are also closely identified with the magazine.

Antonio Prohías's "Spy vs. Spy," in which his two beak-headed, dark-eyed and fedoraed spies have futilely pursued each other through *Mad*'s pages for almost thirty years, while uniquely his own, is also one of *Mad*'s more recognizable features. Similarly, in the pages of *Mad* in the sixties and seventies, Don Martin created an unmistakable graphic style, featuring cartoonish people who always seem to be lurching and whirling and staggering across the page, their feet flapping and many-chinned heads bobbing. The reader knows that his characters make squishing, springing or flapping noises when they move, because it says so on the page: words like "Squitch," "Sproing" and "Phwap-phwap-phwap" surround them. Martin's characters still remind people of *Mad*, even when they appear in a music video or on a pinball machine (and even though Martin no longer contributes to the magazine).

Today, *Mad* is co-edited by Nick Meglin, who began at the magazine more than thirty years ago as a contributing writer and associate editor, and John Ficarra, who grew up reading the magazine. Gaines eventually sold *Mad* magazine to a holding

Mad staff members reunited on the occasion of Bill Gaines's 1987 marriage to Anne Griffiths.

company, but continued as its publisher for the next thirty years, watching while a dizzying series of corporate mergers and acquisitions ultimately left *Mad* under the ownership of Time-Warner, a media conglomerate so vast as to be beyond the scope of satire.

Gaines was publisher of *Mad* until his death in 1992. "My staff and contributors create the magazine," he once told *Newsweek* magazine. "What I create is the atmosphere." He set and maintained that atmosphere of determined chaos as much through his personality and presence as through his policies. He demanded an informal environment in the *Mad* office: as editor Nick Meglin recalled to *Time* magazine, "He became uncomfortable if people started to wear shirts and ties and pinstripe suits, because he figured they were looking to become corporate creeps, as he would call them." He kept production costs low, but paid artists and writers generously. His respect for the artists and their work was evident from the freedom he allowed them in EC's and *Mad*'s pages, yet he never let them retain the copyrights to their work (a condition many artists find intolerable). A publishing revolutionary, he often resisted change. He confessed to Reidelbach "The philosophy of the outfit was to do what we liked, as long as it fit certain compulsive frameworks which I had."

Mad began as a sort of anti-comic-book comic book, driven to break the rules of a medium almost too new to have any rules. Where comics had already become locked in conventions that hardly anyone thought about anymore, Kurtzman's early *Mad* comics called attention, pointed and laughed out loud. As Kurt Anderson pointed out in *Time* magazine, "Where else [but in *Mad*] could you see Donald Duck baffled by his three fingers and white gloves?"

When it was no longer safe to be a comic book, *Mad* became an anti-magazine magazine, mocking not only the style and content of magazines, but their business traditions as well. There are certain "rules" in magazine publishing, which do not guarantee success but are nevertheless considered essential: know who your readers are; advertise like crazy to reach your readers; offer discounts and promotions to encourage subscriptions (subscribers only save twenty-five cents off the newsstand price); and *always* put something "hot" on the cover. *Mad* does not advertise in other media, and nobody else advertises in *Mad*. *Mad* has never conducted a readership survey. As Gaines explained to the business magazine *Forbes*, "We've always taken the position that we don't care who reads *Mad*. We publish *Mad* to please ourselves. It isn't very businesslike, but it's the way I do it."

■ Works Cited

Andersen, Kurt, "A Perfect *Mad* Man," *Time,* June 15, 1992, p. 63.

Leerhsen, Charles, "Humor in a Jugular Vein," *Newsweek,* June 15, 1992, p. 70.

Reidelbach, Maria, *Completely Mad: A History of the Comic Book and Magazine,* Little, Brown, 1991.

Slutsker, Gary, "The Secret Is in the Repackaging," *Forbes,* June 15, 1987, pp. 230-32.°

—Sketch by Todd Ableser

Meredith Ann Pierce

■ Personal

Born July 5, 1958, in Seattle, WA; daughter of Frank N. (a professor of advertising) and Jo Ann (an editor and professor of agriculture; maiden name, Bell) Pierce. *Education:* University of Florida, B.A., 1978, M.A., 1980. *Hobbies and other interests:* Music (composition, harp, and voice), picturebook collecting, film and theater, anthropology, archaeology, languages, folklore and mythology, cats, science fiction, fantasy, and children's literature.

■ Addresses

Home—424-H Northeast 6th St., Gainesville, FL 32601.

■ Career

Writer. Bookland, Gainesville, FL, clerk, 1981; Waldenbooks, Gainesville, clerk, 1981-87; Aluchua County (FL) Library District, library assistant, 1987—. Treasurer, Children's Literature Association Conference, Gainesville, 1982; University of Florida, instructor in creative writing, 1978-80. *Member:* Phi Beta Kappa.

■ Awards, Honors

First prize, Scholastic/Hallmark Cards creative writing contest, 1973; Best Books for Young Adults citation, and Best of the Best Books,1970-1982 citation both from the American Library Association (ALA), *New York Times* Notable Children's Book citation, and Parents' Choice Award Superbook citation, all 1982, Children's Book Award from the International Reading Association, 1983, California Young Reader Medal, 1986, and *Booklist* Best Books of the Decade (1980-89) list, all for *The Darkangel;* Jane Tinkham Broughton Fellow in writing for children, Bread Loaf Writers' Conference, 1984; Best Books for Young Adults semifinalist, ALA, 1985, for *A Gathering of Gargoyles;* Parents' Choice Award for Literature citation, 1985, and New York Public Library Books for the Teen Age exhibit citation, 1986, both for *The Woman Who Loved Reindeer;* Individual Artist Fellowship Special Award for Children's Literature, Florida Department of State, Division of Cultural Affairs, 1987; Best Books for Young Adults citation, ALA, 1991, for *The Pearl of the Soul of the World.*

■ Writings

YOUNG ADULT FANTASY NOVELS

The Darkangel (first novel in the "Darkangel" trilogy; also see below), Little, Brown, 1982.
A Gathering of Gargoyles (second novel in the "Darkangel" trilogy; also see below), Little, Brown, 1984.

Birth of the Firebringer (first novel of the "Firebringer" trilogy), Macmillan, 1985.

The Woman Who Loved Reindeer, Little Brown, 1985.

The Pearl of the Soul of the World (third novel in the "Darkangel" trilogy; also see below), Little, Brown, 1990.

The Darkangel Trilogy (contains *The Darkangel, A Gathering of Gargoyles*, and *The Pearl of the Soul of the World*), Doubleday, 1990.

Dark Moon (second novel in the "Firebringer" trilogy), Little, Brown, 1992.

OTHER

Where the Wild Geese Go (picturebook), illustrated by Jamichael Henterly, Dutton, 1988.

(Contributor) *Four from the Witch World* (contains novella "Rampion"), edited by Andre Norton, Tor Books, 1989.

Contributor to anthologies and to periodicals, including *Mythlore, Horn Book, ALAN Review, Voice of Youth Advocates*, and *New Advocate*.

■ **Work in Progress**

The third installment of the "Firebringer" trilogy.

■ **Sidelights**

"Like good baklava, a work of fiction should be multilayered. If it doesn't have its components properly situated in correct proportion, the taste and texture will be off. Plot is like the pastry: The body and support. Theme is the nut: The kernel and the heart. Style is the savor, blending honey and spice. Nothing is more delicious either to fashion or to devour," Meredith Ann Pierce once commented. Certainly, from her first novel, *The Darkangel*, to the more recent *Dark Moon*, Pierce has presented her readers with fantasies that have as many levels as a delicate pastry. She has established herself as "one of the foremost young authors of fantasy today. Her work combines a mythic inventiveness with such elemental themes as love, conflict and quest," according to Joan Nist in the *ALAN Review. Fantasy Review* contributor Walter Albert thinks Pierce's "Darkangel" trilogy "will surely be ranked with the small number of enduring fantasy classics." Such words of praise have been heaped on Pierce since the publication of *The Darkangel* and have continued with each succeeding novel.

Describing fantasy worlds full of strange beings, creatures, and places, Pierce works hard on creating the details behind the history, structure, and motivation for her characters. Sometimes the explanations and discussions the author has provided have led critics to call her prose style awkward. For example, in her review of *Birth of the Firebringer*, Hazel Rochman notes in *Booklist* that the "language is poetic, with a wonderful rhythm and sweeping images of sky and plain, but it is sometimes overheightened and awkwardly archaic." Pierce answers her critics by refusing to simplify her complex language. In a *Something about the Author* interview conducted by Diane Telgen, the author defends her writing: "I can't change the way I think and I can't change my vocabulary and pretend that I don't know words that I know.... There are lots of word games in my stories, coined words and made up words, compound words, because I like doing that, it's very enjoyable."

Born in Seattle, Washington, Pierce says that as a child she would spend hours talking and playing with imaginary companions. She also joined her brothers and sister in their own make-believe games. A precocious child who began to read at the age of three, Pierce started to read so young that she did not have to depend on her parents or any other adults for information. The advantage of this, she says, was that "that I could feed myself information." One book that had a decided influence on Pierce was Lewis Carroll's *Alice in Wonderland*; the movie *The Wizard of Oz*—based on the Frank L. Baum book—also had a strong effect on her. "*Alice in Wonderland* is like my religion," she tells Telgen. "It was introduced into my system before my immune system was complete, so it's wired into my psyche. I can't distinguish between my own mythology and early influences like *Alice in Wonderland* or the movie *The Wizard of Oz*. Some of the stuff that I saw really impressed me when I was very little and just went straight into my neurons—it's inseparable from my way of thinking."

Pierce was reading adult material from the library by the time she was in the sixth grade. She had a fairly easy time at school, but did not settle into any of the usual cliques. As she tells Telgen, "I didn't have this need to belong to a group ... that's not my scene." Although she did write stories, she was never sure any of them were worth publishing. Her parents thought writing was "another one of those obsessive little hobbles," Pierce recalls. Their argument was: "'Why would you rather be writing than doing something else normal?'"

The Darkangel Begins a Trilogy

Pierce first realized writing could be a serious career when she took a class taught by children's author Joy Anderson at the University of Florida. "Through her I got a much better idea of what writing is all about," says Pierce. Anderson gave constructive criticism and encouragement as Pierce wrote her first novel, *The Darkangel*, a fantasy that takes place on the moon. The basic idea for the book, according to Nancy Willard in her review for the *New York Times Book Review*, "came to the writer 'all of a piece' during a long bus ride." Pierce was inspired by a real-life case she read about in the autobiography by famous psychiatrist Carl Jung. A woman who was one of Jung's patients told him how she had once lived on the moon, where she met a handsome vampire who took her captive. "Jung's account of his patient and her fascinating delusion," Pierce relates in a *Horn Book* article, "served as the germinal model for [the main character] Aeriel and the first two chapters of *Darkangel*." Later parts of the tale borrow from the fairy tale "Beauty and the Beast" and the Greek myth "Psyche and Eros." Critics have also noticed how Pierce has—either consciously or unconsciously—borrowed from other stories. For example, in a *New York Times Book Review* review of the sequel to *The Darkangel*, *A Gathering of Gargoyles*, Eleanor Cameron sees echoes of other fantasies, from "Le Guin's Orm Embar and Pendor come Miss Pierce's Orm and Pendar; from the cycles of Susan Cooper and Jane Louise Curry come the precognitive riddling rhyme that structures Aeriel's searches as she carries out her task."

In *The Darkangel*, readers are introduced to the young servant girl Aeriel, who must struggle to destroy the vampire who has kidnapped her mistress and thus helped to prevent evil from taking over her world. Aeriel marries the vampire Irrylath and makes him human by exchanging her heart for his. In the second volume of the trilogy, *A Gathering of Gargoyles*, Irrylath is still bound to the evil White Witch and cannot love anyone else. To help him, Aeriel searches the moon to find their world's Ions, ancient animal guardians who will help lead the battle against the Witch's forces. (The Ions are the gargoyles of the title that Irrylath and his vampire brothers will use to ride against the White Witch.) In the last novel of the series, *The Pearl of the Soul of the World*, Aeriel sets out to defeat the White Witch once and for all. But after a silver pin is driven into her skull, Aeriel wanders through underground caves, unaware of who she is and

THE DARKANGEL TRILOGY
by **Meredith Ann Pierce**

The courageous servant girl Aeriel marshals the forces of good against the evil White Witch in this award-winning fantasy trilogy.

unable to speak. She is finally rescued by Ravenna, the last of the ancient wise ones who created the world. Removing the pin and placing all her knowledge and powers into the luminous pearl Aeriel wears around her neck, Ravenna tells her to use the pearl in her final confrontation with the witch.

Showdowns between good and evil have fascinated Pierce ever since she discovered the "Prince Valiant" comic series. "I just love the whole medieval ethos," the author reveals to Telgen. "I know they were all starving to death and had all these diseases and their teeth were falling out and all that. But in a lot of the medieval legends, people were intensely religious and everything was important, everything was a struggle between heaven and hell. Good and evil has influenced my writing even though I'm not a Christian and don't belong to an organized religion. This sort of spirituality pervades the books whether I want it to or not."

The strength and courage that Aeriel shows in confronting evil has been noted by several reviewers. *Signal Review* contributor Elizabeth Hammill, for one, sees Aeriel as "a brave and resourceful heroine—fascinating because she possesses that fairy-tale compassion for apparently base creatures which enables her to recognize their true nature and, hence, to redeem them." Hammill goes on to say that the book effectively shows an adolescent developing a meaningful adult identity, in terms of her relationships with and effect upon others. Aeriel's courage and persistence, her determination to stand her ground in the face of danger, are a reflection of Pierce's own childhood experiences, as the author writes in her *Horn Book* article. Pierce once had to cope with an alcoholic and abusive relative who one day "had made up his mind to do me violence." But the author refused to be bullied by the relative who, faced with such determination, backed off. It was "a little bit of a revelation—that a lot of human relationships are

The third novel in the "Darkangel" trilogy, this 1990 work details Aeriel's dangerous showdown with the White Witch.

bluff, and that's an important thing to know," she concludes.

A feature of the "Darkangel" books that critics have particularly noticed is Pierce's use of language. Cameron describes the author's style as "intensely visual, even poetic, in her descriptions and imaginative in her surprising plot turns." Walter Albert also comments in *Fantasy Review* on Pierce's poetic language in *A Gathering of Gargoyles*. "As in the earlier book," Albert attests, "one of her great strengths is her ability to capture the colors and textures of the physical world and the voyage of Aeriel across the perilous Sea-of-Dust is a splendid achievement that confirms Pierce's stylistic growth." Albert also admires her secure handling of characters and says "the airborne conclusion is exhilarating and moving." Ann A. Flowers notes in her *Horn Book* review of *The Pearl of the Soul of the World*, "The great strength of the story, besides the wraithlike, haunting heroine, is the style, with shimmering, fragile textures and delicate, shadowy descriptions." Some critics have pointed out that Pierce's writing helps make her imaginary world more believable. "Pierce's thoughtful characterization and well-constructed plot lead to a poignant and believable conclusion," a *Publishers Weekly* reviewer notes about *The Pearl*. "The meticulous, creative use of language gives form and substance to a fascinating mythic world." In *School Library Journal*, Ruth Vose similarly comments on Pierce's creativity: "Pierce continues to have the power to capture the imagination of her readers. Her creativity never falters."

The Husk-Myth

"As with *Darkangel*," Pierce reveals in her *Horn Book* article, "the inception of [*The Woman Who Loved Reindeer*] was sudden, taking place on the last day of either my first or second year of high school. As I stood looking out over the flat, barren, empty playing field, a vivid image came to mind of a woman dressed in doeskin standing stock still, her mouth open, her hands reaching out after a great stag that is carrying away her child. . . . The woman is speechless, but the child is screaming . . . with delight." Pierce later developed this vision into a story by building on the Native American husk-myth in which an animal can cast off its skin to take human form; then she set her tale on an imaginary world. "The two-mooned planet on which this magical fantasy is set is a cross between Yellowstone and Lapland," as Ruth M. McConnell describes it in *School Library Journal*.

The Woman Who Loved Reindeer begins by telling how young Caribou, who lives alone after her father's death, is given her sister-in-law's baby. Caribou cares for the newborn—whom she calls Reindeer—taking herbs to cause her milk to flow, even though she feels he is not quite human. She finally realizes he is a trangl—one who can take on the form of an animal or a human. When he grows old enough, Reindeer runs off to join his people—the other reindeer—but occasionally returns as a golden young man and becomes Caribou's lover. He changes from man to deer several times as he helps Caribou lead her people from their homes, which have been rent by earthquakes and eruptions, to a place on the other side of the world beyond the Land of the Broken Snow. Pregnant with Reindeer's child, Caribou now must decide whether or not to follow Reindeer by becoming a trangl herself.

"The author," McConnell concludes in her *School Library Journal* review of *The Woman Who Loved Reindeer,* "convincingly and poetically portrays [the characters'] lives and adventures.... Her dealings with troll hedgewives and her visit to the Fireking's underground world are wonderfully realized." A reviewer in the *Bulletin of the Center for Children's Books* sees the love story as "convincing, the dangers of the long trek suspenseful, but the style is overdramatic, with much blanching, trembling, and throat-closing in addition to unnecessary exposition." In another *Horn Book* article, however, Flowers sees the romance as "believable and satisfying." The "author's imaginary world is an intriguing combination of realistic, folkloric, and fantastic elements; her style is smooth, clear, and elegant, with never a word in the wrong place. A remarkably fine fantasy by an emerging master of the genre."

A Unicorn Trilogy

With *The Birth of the Firebringer* Pierce began a second trilogy that paints an elaborate picture of a world inhabited by unicorns. Jan, a young unicorn, proves his worth to his father, Prince of the Unicorns, and is allowed to accompany the initiates on their pilgrimage to the ancient homeland now inhabited by evil wyverns. Jan sees no vision as the others do in the sacred well and runs away, but as he flees he runs into a wyvern who tries to get him to betray his people. When Jan kills the wyvern, his noble deed results in his being able to see visions concerning his destiny as firebringer of the unicorns.

Caribou's love for Reindeer, a trangl who can take human or animal form, forces her to make a difficult decision in this 1985 fantasy.

Pierce's use of language is again praised in reviews of *The Birth of the Firebringer.* For example, one *Kirkus Reviews* contributor writes, "The language here is as elegant as the unicorn people it chronicles. Unicorn rituals and mythology are woven skillfully into the story, strengthening characterization and making the fantasy believable." *School Library Journal* contributor Holly Sanhuber also comments on Pierce's use of language in her review: "The untangling of the satisfying plot and Pierce's ability to foster belief in her unicorns ... are enhanced by her stately use of language and the sense of their history and culture which she creates and sustains." Rochman, however, qualifies her enthusiasm for Pierce's prose in a *Booklist* review: "The language is poetic, with wonderful rhythm and sweeping images of sky and plain, but

In this 1985 novel—the first book in the "Firebringer" series—the young unicorn Jan travels to his homeland, which is occupied by the treacherous Wyverns.

it is sometimes overheightened and awkwardly archaic."

Dark Moon, the second work in the trilogy, finds Jan falling in love and taking a mate named Tek. However, Jan's happiness is cut short when he and the other unicorns are attacked by harpies and Jan is swept out to sea. It seems to the other unicorns that Jan has perished, and his father goes berserk with grief, almost bringing disaster upon the entire herd. Escaping the fury of Jan's father, Tek escapes to the home of her mother—a healer—in time to give birth to two foals. Meanwhile, Jan is saved by some human unicorn worshippers who put him on a boat and take him to their city, where he is penned up with a harem of mares. Although she is not a unicorn, a mare befriends Jan and accompanies him back to his own land when they escape their human captors. He and the mare are taken home across the sea on the backs of narwhals, or

sea unicorns. Realizing that the only way to rid his land of the wyverns is for the unicorns to unite with all the other creatures with whom the unicorns have fought, Jan decides in the end that they must make peace with the harpies.

Pierce is currently working on the third novel that will conclude the "Firebringer" trilogy. In addition to her writing, she works full-time at her local county library. As she tells Telgen, she has "a reasonably good time telling little children to quit running on the stairs and helping them look for the shark books." But although she enjoys working in the library, she prefers writing, comparing it to "going to sleep and dreaming a wonderful dream." "To write a novel," she concludes in *Horn Book*, "is to be in love."

■ Works Cited

Albert, Walter, "One of a Small Number of Fantasy Classics," *Fantasy Review*, May, 1985, p. 20.

Review of *Birth of the Firebringer*, *Kirkus Reviews*, October 1, 1985, p. 1090.

Cameron, Eleanor, review of *A Gathering of Gargoyles*, *New York Times Book Review*, December 30, 1984, p. 19.

Flowers, Ann A., review of *The Woman Who Loved Reindeer*, *Horn Book*, March/April, 1986, p. 208-209.

Flowers, Ann A., review of *The Pearl of the Soul of the World*, *Horn Book*, May/June, 1990, p. 340.

Hammill, Elizabeth, review of *The Darkangel*, *The Signal Review: A Selective Guide to Children's Books*, edited by Nancy Chambers, Thimble Press, 1984, pp. 49-50.

McConnell, Ruth, review of *The Woman Who Loved Reindeer*, *School Library Journal*, December, 1985, p. 104.

Nist, Joan, review of *The Woman Who Loved Reindeer*, *ALAN Review*, winter, 1985, p. 31.

Review of *The Pearl of the Soul of the World*, *Publishers Weekly*, February 9, 1990, p. 63.

Pierce, Meredith Ann, "A Lion in the Room," *Horn Book*, January/February, 1988, pp. 35-41.

Pierce, Meredith Ann, in an interview with Diane Telgen for *Something about the Author*, June 4, 1991.

Rochman, Hazel, review of *Birth of the Firebringer*, *Booklist*, February 15, 1986, p. 870.

Sanhuber, Holly, review of *Birth of the Firebringer*, *School Library Journal*, January, 1986, p. 70.

Vose, Ruth S., review of *The Pearl of the Soul of the World*, *School Library Journal*, April, 1990, p. 145.

Willard, Nancy, review of *The Darkangel*, *New York Times Book Review*, April 25, 1982, pp. 35, 47.

Review of *The Woman Who Loved Reindeer*, *Bulletin of the Center for Children's Books*, December, 1985, p. 75.

■ For More Information See

BOOKS

Children's Literature Review, Volume 20, Gale, 1990.

PERIODICALS

Booklist, October 15, 1985, p. 330; November 1, 1985, p. 396; January 1, 1990; January 15, 1990, p. 991; March 1, 1990, p. 1356; March 15, 1991, p. 1478; May 15, 1992, p. 1674.

Book Report, May, 1986, p. 32; May, 1990, p. 49.

Bulletin of the Center for Children's Books, July/August, 1982; February, 1985, p. 114; January, 1986, p. 94.

English Journal, April, 1985, p. 84; January, 1991, p. 80.

Fantasy Review, April, 1986, p. 31.

Horn Book, August, 1982, p. 416; September, 1983, p. 245; October, 1984, p. 765; May/June, 1988, p. 349.

Horn Book Guide, January, 1990, p. 254.

Journal of Reading, November, 1990, p. 234.

Kirkus Reviews, January, 1985, p. 1090; September 15, 1985, p. 992; February 1, 1988, p. 205; January 1, 1990, p. 49; May 15, 1992, p. 674.

Locus, January, 1990, p. 52; July, 1990, p. 15; October, 1990, p.53; October, 1991, p. 52; June 1992, p. 56.

Magazine of Fantasy and Science Fiction, November, 1984, p. 38.

New York Times Book Review, November 30, 1982; February 16, 1986, p. 22.

Publishers Weekly, November 30, 1984, p. 92; June 7, 1985, p. 80; December 20, 1985, p. 65; February 12, 1988, p. 82.

School Library Journal, December, 1984; June/July, 1988, p. 94; July, 1990, p. 27; June, 1992, pp. 139-40.

Voice of Youth Advocates, April, 1986, p. 41; June, 1990, p. 138; August, 1992, p. 178.

Wilson Library Bulletin, March, 1986, pp. 50-51.°

—Sketch by Hazel K. Davis

Christopher Pike

■ Personal

Education: College dropout. *Hobbies:* Astronomy, meditating, long walks, reading.

■ Addresses

Agent—c/o Archway Paperbacks, 1230 6th Ave., New York, NY 10020.

■ Writings

Slumber Party, Scholastic Inc., 1985.
Chain Letter, Avon, 1986.
Weekend, Scholastic, Inc., 1986.
Last Act, Archway, 1989.
Remember Me, Archway, 1989.
Scavenger Hunt, Archway, 1989.
Spellbound, Archway, 1989.
Gimme a Kiss, Archway, 1989.
Witch, Archway, 1990.
Fall Into Darkness, Archway, 1990.
See You Later, Simon & Schuster, 1990; Archway, 1991.
Whisper of Death, Archway, 1991.
Last Act, Archway, 1991.
Die Softly, Archway, 1991.

Bury Me Deep, Archway, 1991.
Chain Letter 2: The Ancient Evil, Archway, 1992.
Monster, Archway, 1992.
Master of Murder, Archway, 1992.
The Ancient Evil, Archway, 1992.
Road to Nowhere, Archway, 1993.
The Eternal Enemy, Archway, 1993.
The Wicked Heart, Archway, 1993.
The Midnight Club, Archway, 1994.
The Last Vampire, Archway, 1994.

"FINAL FRIENDS" SERIES

The Party, Archway, 1991.
The Dance, Archway, 1991.
The Graduation, Archway, 1991

OTHER

Thrills, Chills and Nightmares (short stories), Scholastic, 1987.
The Tachyon Web (young adult science fiction), Bantam, 1987.
Sati (adult), St. Martin's, 1990.
The Season of Passage (adult science fiction), Tor Books, 1993.

■ Work in Progress

The Cold One (adult fiction), Tor Books.

■ Sidelights

"I'm often called the young Stephen King," says Christopher Pike. "But I prefer to call King the old Christopher Pike." Pike is kidding, of course, but critics do often compare his books to King's, and the comparison is apt. Both authors write well-crafted, taut suspense novels that fans (and even critics) find nearly impossible to put down; both writers also regularly make the bestseller lists. But, while King writes for and about adults, Pike's characters and his audience are mainly comprised of teenagers.

Surprisingly, Pike never aspired to be "the master of YA macabre fiction," as reviewer Drue Wagner-Mees describes him in a review of *Gimme A Kiss*. Pike originally had his sights set on a career writing science fiction, which he had loved as a child growing up in southern California. A college dropout, Pike worked briefly as a computer programmer, then turned to painting houses to support himself while he wrote adult novels that were ultimately rejected by publishers. When Pike's agent suggested he take a stab at writing for teens, Pike figured he had nothing to lose. The result was *Slumber Party*, which did very well for a "first" novel. Pike subsequently sold two more young adult novels, *Chain Letter* and *Weekend*, to Avon and Scholastic respectively, before settling into a long relationship with Archway Paperbacks, the publisher of his remaining twenty-six young adult novels.

In an interview with *AAYA*, Pike comments that "I did sort of fall into writing for teens, but I think I've stayed with it, not just because of the money, but because I have a very romantic idea of high school. I guess I'm very nostalgic." While nostalgia may draw Pike to his teenage characters, he certainly does not present a rosy, romantic view of the teen years. The characters in his books have serious problems. Dusty Shame (*The Wicked Heart*) lives with his mother, who has been ravaged by Alzheimer's, a disease that has destroyed her mind. Marvin Summer (*Master of Murder*) supports his alcoholic mother and his little sister, sometimes having to defend them against his abusive father. Shari Cooper (*Remember Me*), looking on from beyond the grave, knows she was murdered even though her death is treated as a suicide. Other Pike characters have more commonplace problems—like a jealous boyfriend or an unrequited love—that they take very much to heart.

Teens on Their Own

When it comes to the problems faced by Pike's characters, the adults in their lives aren't much help. If parents—or other "responsible" adults—aren't actually the cause of the kids' problems, they offer very little in the way of support or aid.

Most of Pike's characters come from single-parent families, and that one parent is often somehow incapacitated. Some of his teens, like Julia Florence of *Witch* and Carl Timmons of *Scavenger Hunt*, are more or less on their own, even if they are still minors. (Julia's mother has recently died, and Carl's father is a long-distance trucker who is rarely home.) When Pike's characters have parents who truly serve as authority figures, they manage to be out of touch at climactic moments.

Left to their own devices and buffeted by the intense emotions of adolescence, Pike's characters frequently resort to extreme actions in an attempt to solve a problem, or to at least find some kind of escape. Herb Trasker (*Die Softly*), tired of lusting after girls who won't give him a second look, sets up a hidden camera in the girls' locker room to take pictures of the cheerleaders as they shower. Jane Retton (*Gimme a Kiss*) wants revenge too, as does Martin Summer. Publicly humiliated when a page of her diary is circulated around school, Jane fakes her own death so that it appears her tormentors have killed her. Marvin devises an ingenious murder plot to eliminate the guy he thinks has stolen the girl he loves.

Not too surprisingly, their outrageous acts tend to land these teens in deep trouble. Herb photographs a murder with his hidden camera and then finds himself out of his league with an enigmatic girl who might just be the killer. Jane unwittingly sets the scene for her boyfriend's murder, then finds herself hunted as well. Marvin ultimately finds himself unwilling to carry out his plan, but his intended victim has no such qualms about attempting to take Marvin's life.

A Hotline to the Teenage Psyche

In spite of the complexity of the situations they find themselves in and the unusual extremes to which they sometimes are driven, Pike's teens are convincingly drawn. Critics have repeatedly praised the author's skill at creating believable and interesting characters. Perhaps it is here that Pike's nostalgia comes into play, enabling him to develop what Amy Gammerman of the *Wall Street Journal* describes as his "apparent hot-line to the teenage psyche." Pike examines his characters' motivations, good and bad, in sufficient detail to allow his readers to feel they really know the kids who inhabit his books. As Sue Tait and Christy Tyson state in a review of *Last Act* in *Emergency Librarian*, "It is the relationship between the characters that makes (the book) work.... These are people who are really involved with each other, and when they are in danger the reader can't help but feel it too. Again, Pike's clear portraits provide the hook that is missing in many mysteries written for young adults." In a review of *Die Softly* in the *Wilson Library Bulletin*, Cathi Dunn MacRae also praises Pike's ability to create realistic characters: "This tightly plotted mystery places baser human instincts under a penetrating microscope.... [Pike's] knack for portraying characters' personal quirks paints them vividly."

Pike earns raves for his skill at creating suspense as well. In a review of *Scavenger Hunt*, Joyce Hamilton of *Voice of Youth Advocates* (*VOYA*) comments that "readers looking for a horror book will love it ... [*Scavenger Hunt*] will be impossible to put down." JoEllen Broome, in a review of *Spellbound* in *VOYA*, writes that "This well-told tale of horror

Like many of Pike's publications, this 1989 tale blends horror, adventure, and romance.

sparkles ...with high adventure, daring and romance.... A fun, frightening frolic indeed." And in a review of *Gimme A Kiss*, a *Booklist* critic notes that "Pike pulls out all the stops ... a fast, suspenseful tale."

Too Violent for Teens?

While critics often applaud Pike's characters and the pace of his novels, they are sometimes less than enthralled with his willingness to use graphic violence when the story line calls for it. In books such as *The Wicked Heart* and *Monster*, which have violent themes, Pike does not shy away from gore—and even his less inherently violent books have their bloody moments. In *Harper's*, Tom Engelhardt calls Pike's books "novelizations of horror films that haven't yet been made," and claims that in them, "junior psychos reign supreme," and "no mutilation is too terrible for the human face." Reporting on violence in young adult books, *Time* magazine's Paul Gray worries that "these hair-raising books are being tailored and energetically hawked to children.... Maybe the youngsters will move upward in their tastes." Gray adds, "Or maybe they will boil the cat in the spaghetti."

Pike believes that the criticism of the violence in his books is unjustified. "I feel that in order to have a great hero, you have to have a great villain," Pike tells *AAYA*. "Much of the classic literature that has been written is very violent. Look at *The Lord of The Rings*, which may be the classic work of our time—it's a very violent book. Yet the heroes in that book are very noble, and it's only because the villains are so atrocious that the heroes can be so great. I feel that the moral center of my books is very good. The 'point of view' character usually is a good person, someone who is trying to do what is right. Even in a book like *Die Softly*, which is a dark story, drugs and violence are seen as a terrible way to go. I don't feel like I ever glorify violence."

As Pike attests, most of his protagonists are depicted as truly ethical people at heart, even when they engage in extreme behavior. One exception is Dusty Shame of *The Wicked Heart*. Dusty, one of the two point-of-view characters, is a high school student who is also a serial killer. But even Dusty has his good side; he doesn't want to kill, but is driven by an evil force greater than himself. Pike describes the book as one he wrote "almost against my will. I never wanted to write a serial killer book because (the subject) is just too real." (Pike adds that the book *Silence of the Lambs* terrified him.)

"There are really people out there like that," the author concedes, "but I felt sort of haunted by Dusty's character, like I had to get it out of my mind. I tried to portray Dusty not as a sympathetic character, but as someone who was very screwed up, who wasn't having much fun. I didn't want to portray a serial killer that was enjoying the process of killing. I could not do that."

Pike has considerable respect for his readers, which may be another reason he doesn't feel it is necessary to keep a tight rein on the violence to make them "appropriate" for teens. "I have a very high opinion of teenager's intelligence," says Pike for *AAYA*, a fact that is reflected in his main characters, who tend to be quick-witted and so-phisticated. He adds: "I think teens are very, very smart. Some of the mail I receive is startling in its maturity and clarity, in terms of the abstract thoughts they have on some of the books and their own lives." Pat MacDonald, Pike's editor at Arch-way, has noted that part of the author's appeal is his refusal to water down his visions. "Pike doesn't talk down to kids," MacDonald once noted. "He treats them as individuals." In addition, Pike feels that his readers know what they're getting into when they choose to read one of his books. "They want to be scared or they would not pick up the book and read it. The kids have fair warning, and know it's all in good fun," he tells Gray.

Another complaint critics have frequently voiced concerns the lack of a "moral" in some of his books. Pike admits he is more interested in telling a good story than preaching to teens. "I don't try to write a book with a moral," he remarks. "If one naturally comes out of it, that's fine. *Road to Nowhere*, which dealt with suicide, was one book that had a very nice moral, and that I got a lot of mail on. I have about thirty letters from kids who said they were contemplating suicide, and that the book really helped them. But I don't often try to do that. Generally I just write a story because it has occurred to me. I do not try to get a moral in. I just write it as it comes, because it's fun."

A Novel for a Special Fan

The Midnight Club is an exception to the rule, in that Pike wrote it with a "message" in mind. The story—which takes place in a hospice—is about five teens, all of whom are dying. Pike wrote the book partly because one of his readers, a young woman named Shari, requested that he deal with the subject of teens facing death. Pike contacted Shari after receiving a letter from her, along with a

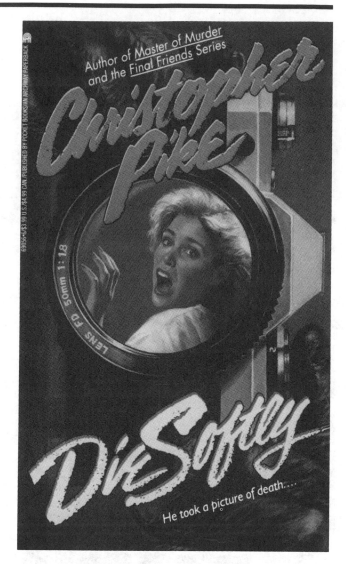

In this 1991 thriller, Herb Trasker plots revenge on the cheerleaders who reject him.

note from her mother informing Pike that Shari was dying of cancer. "Her letter was very beauti-ful," Pike recalls, "so I decided to call her." He spoke to her twice, one time two weeks prior to her death, and a second time the night she died. Shari asked him what he thought would happen to her after she died. Pike shared his beliefs on life after death with her, and felt she derived some comfort from them even though his ideas—like anyone else's—could only be conjecture. "It was an intense conversation," the author remembers. When Shari asked him to write a novel about how teenagers face death, an idea he had been thinking about for some time began to crystalize. "The story sounds depressing," MacDonald tells *AAYA*, "but it isn't. Only Christopher Pike could do a book like this."

Shari's letter and his response to it were unusual, but Pike does hear from his fans often, and they are insatiably curious about him. Pike guards his privacy closely, refusing to give out his real name ("Christopher Pike" is a pseudonym taken from a character on an early episode of *Star Trek*) or much personal information. Fans who have read *Master of Murder* sometimes assume that the character of Marvin Summer—who is a seventeen-year-old author of bestselling mysteries for teens—is really Pike himself. Although Pike admits to some similarities, he is quick to point out that he is not really a high school student. "For that to be true, I'd have to have written my first book when I was about seven," Pike comments wryly.

Like Marvin, though, Pike sometimes writes his books very quickly (but only after having thought about them for a long time); he also has a younger sister named Ann who once accused him of writing "dead sister" books because so many of his doomed characters have "Ann" as a middle name. Like Marvin, Pike got very little encouragement about his writing from his high school teachers. The character of Mrs. Jackson, Marvin's English teacher, is based on a teacher Pike once had. "She gave me terrible grades," Pike says. In *Master of Murder*, Marvin receives a "B" for a funny short story entitled "The Becoming of Seymour the Frog." "I actually wrote that story when I was in high school," Pike recalls, "but the teacher didn't give me a 'B' on it—it was more like an 'F.'" Like Marvin's Mrs. Jackson, Pike feels his English teacher had no understanding of how he wrote best. In spite of Mrs. Jackson's suggestion that Marvin learn to "control himself" in his writing, Marvin felt that "it was when he was out of control that he wrote his best—when the power flowed"—an accurate description of the way Pike himself works.

A Dark Story for Dark Nights

Unlike Marvin, Pike doesn't often base a character's feelings or experiences on his own. Again, *The Wicked Heart* was an exception to that rule. The physical pain Dusty feels and the emotional pain Sheila feels both grew out of real-life ordeals for Pike. "My girlfriend had just left me, and I'd had an injury to my side which ran into complications with my liver, so I was in tremendous pain. I remember writing that book in incredible pain, sometimes just sweating to death. It was a very hard book to write. I wrote it mainly at night, because I couldn't sleep at all. And when Sheila is pining away for her boyfriend—I just took that out of my own life," Pike says. The circumstances

under which the book was written explain the unusual dedication in the book, which reads: "For myself. This dark story for those dark nights."

These days, Pike is doing just fine. He recently revisited his own teen years by going out with the first girl he dated. He went out with her one time only, five days after graduating from high school. "I never dated in high school," Pike admits to *AAYA*. "I was too shy. I was going to go out with her a second time, but she stood me up. She went out with another guy, and then she married him." Pike ran into her again and discovered she was getting a divorce. As a teenager he had planned to take her to a Jethro Tull concert on their second date. By chance, the band happened to be in town when he met up with her again. So, as it turned out, they finally had their second date, many years later. "She's a real nice girl," Pike comments. "I've

Author of *The Immortal* and *The Eternal Enemy*

Christopher Pike

The Wicked Heart

An innocent turned evil....

Dusty Shame is a serial killer whose mother suffers from Alzheimer's in Pike's 1993 novel.

put her in my new book. But she might have to die—I'm not sure."

Pike is currently at work on two books: a young adult novel and another adult novel (his third). A sequel to *Remember Me*, which Pike considers to be his best young adult novel, is also being planned. In addition, he's getting a taste of Hollywood—five of Pike's books are on the verge of being made into movies (including *Sati*, which has been optioned by actress Meg Ryan).

Clearly, Pike will continue to make his mark on the world of young adult fiction and his books will undoubtedly continue to make the bestseller lists. Nevertheless, the author's success doesn't seem to be going to his head. "I know I'm famous," Pike divulges, "but I'm not really out there. I lead a very solitary life. I've got the ocean in front of me and the woods behind me . . . it's like my own little world." Pike doesn't sound at all unhappy about that. "I just love writing books," he tells *AAYA*, adding "I don't think I could do anything else."

■ Works Cited

Broome, JoEllen, review of *Spellbound, Voice of Youth Advocates*, August 1988, p. 135.

Engelhardt, Tom, "Reading May Be Harmful To Your Kids," *Harper's*, June 1991, pp. 55-62.

Gamerman, Amy, "Gnarlatious Novels: Lurid Thrillers for the Teen Set," *Wall Street Journal*, May 28, 1991, p. A20.

Review of *Gimme a Kiss, Booklist*, October 15, 1988, p. 400.

Gray, Paul, "Carnage: An Open Book," *Time*, Aug. 2, 1992.

Hamilton, Joyce, review of *Scavenger Hunt, Voice of Youth Advocates*, February 1990, p. 346.

MacRae, Cathi Dunn, review of *Die Softly, Wilson Library Bulletin*, October, 1991. p. 101.

Pike Christopher, in an interview with Sarah Verney for *Authors and Artists for Young Adults*, November, 1993.

Pike, Christopher, *The Wicked Heart*, Archway, 1993.

Pike, Christopher, *Master of Murder*, Archway, 1992.

Tait, Sue and Christy Tyson, "Paperbacks for Young Adults," *Emergency Librarian*, January-February, 1989, pp. 53-54.

Wagner-Mees, Drue, review of *Gimme A Kiss, Voice of Youth Advocates*, April, 1989, p. 31.

—Sketch by Sarah Verney

Sylvia Plath

English instructor, 1957-58. Guest editor for *Mademoiselle* magazine, summer, 1953. *Member:* Phi Beta Kappa.

■ Awards, Honors

Mademoiselle College Board contest winner in fiction, 1953; Irene Glascock Poetry Prize, Mount Holyoke College, 1955; Bess Hokin Award, *Poetry* magazine, 1957; first prize, Cheltenham Festival, 1961; Eugene F. Saxton fellowship, 1961; Pulitzer Prize in poetry, 1982, for *Collected Poems*.

■ Writings

POETRY

The Colossus, Heinemann, 1960, published with alternate selection of poems as *The Colossus, and Other Poems,* Knopf, 1962.

(Editor) *American Poetry Now* (supplement number two to *Critical Quarterly*), Oxford University Press, 1961.

Uncollected Poems (booklet), Turret Books (London), 1965.

Ariel, edited by Ted Hughes and Alwyn Hughes, Faber, 1965, published with alternate selection of poems, Harper, 1966.

Wreath for a Bridal, limited edition, Sceptre Press, 1970.

Million Dollar Month, Sceptre Press, 1971.

Child, Rougemont Press, 1971.

Crossing the Water: Transitional Poems, edited by T. Hughes, Faber, 1971, published with alternate selection of poems, Harper, 1971.

■ Personal

Has also written under the pseudonym Victoria Lucas; born October 27, 1932, in Jamaica Plain (now part of Boston), MA; committed suicide, February 11, 1963, in London, England; buried in Heptonstall, Yorkshire, England; daughter of Otto Emil (a professor) and Aurelia (a teacher; maiden name, Schober) Plath; married Ted Hughes (a poet), June 16, 1956 (separated, 1962); children: Frieda Rebecca, Nicholas Farrar. *Education:* Attended Harvard University, summer, 1954; Smith College, B.A. (summa cum laude), 1955; Newnham College, Cambridge, M.A., 1957. *Religion:* Unitarian Universalist. *Hobbies and other interests:* Beekeeping, horseback riding.

■ Addresses

Home—Court Green, North Tawton, Devonshire, England.

■ Career

Poet and novelist. While in college, worked as a volunteer art teacher at the People's Institute, Northampton, MA; Smith College, Northampton,

Crystal Gazer and Other Poems, limited edition, Rainbow Press (London), 1971.

Lyonnesse, limited edition, Rainbow Press, 1971.

Winter Trees, edited by T. Hughes, Faber, 1971, published with alternate selection of poems, Harper, 1972.

Pursuit with an Etching and Drawing by Leonard Baskin, Rainbow Press, 1973.

Two Poems, Sceptre Press, 1980.

The Collected Poems, edited by T. Hughes, Harper, 1981.

Dialogue over a Ouija Board: A Verse Dialogue, Rainbow Press, 1981.

The Green Rock, Embers Handpress, 1982.

Stings: Original Drafts of the Poem in Facsimile, Reproduced from the Sylvia Plath Collection at Smith College, essay by Susan R. Van Dyne, Smith College, 1982.

Sylvia Plath's Selected Poems, edited by T. Hughes, Faber, 1985.

Has had poetry published in anthologies, including *The New Yorker Book of Poems*, Viking, 1969. *Early Poems*, a collection of Plath's work, was published as the May, 1967, issue of *Harvard Advocate;* fifty of her early unpublished poems appeared in the *Times Literary Supplement*, July 31, 1969.

NOVELS

(Under pseudonym Victoria Lucas; and illustrator) *The Bell Jar*, Heinemann, 1963, published under Plath's real name, Faber, 1965, Harper, 1971.

OTHER

Three Women: A Monologue for Three Voices (radio play; broadcast on British Broadcasting Corp. in 1962), limited edition, Turret Books, 1968.

Letters Home: Correspondence, 1950-1963, selected and edited with a commentary by mother, Aurelia Schober Plath, Harper, 1975.

The Bed Book (for children), illustrated by Emily Arnold McCully, Harper, 1976.

Johnny Panic and the Bible of Dreams: And Other Prose Writings, edited by T. Hughes, Faber, 1977, published as *Johnny Panic and the Bible of Dreams: Short Stories, Prose, and Diary Excerpts*, Harper, 1979.

A Day in June: An Uncollected Short Story, Embers Handpress, 1981.

The Journals of Sylvia Plath, edited by Frances McCullough and T. Hughes, Dial, 1982.

Above the Oxbow: Selected Writings, Catawba Press (Northampton, MA), 1985.

Contributor to *Seventeen, Christian Science Monitor, Mademoiselle, Harper's, Nation, Atlantic, Poetry, London Magazine*, and other publications. Significant collections of Plath's manuscripts, journals, and other papers are kept at Indiana University and Smith College.

■ Adaptations

The Bell Jar was adapted into a film directed by Larry Peerce, Avco Embassy Pictures, 1978; *Letters Home* was adapted into a play by Rose Leiman Goldemberg and staged in 1979; a recording of Plath reading poems collected in *The Colossus, Ariel, Crossing the Water, Collected Poems*, and *Letters Home* is available from Caedmon.

■ Sidelights

"I was supposed to be having the time of my life. I was supposed to be the envy of thousands of other college girls just like me all over America who wanted nothing more than to be tripping about in those same size-seven patent leather shoes I'd bought in Bloomingdale's one lunch hour with a black patent leather belt and black patent leather pocketbook to match." So complains Esther Greenwood, the protagonist of poet Sylvia Plath's only novel, *The Bell Jar*. Set in the 1950s, Esther's story is a study of one woman's struggle to assert her identity in a society that did not as yet recognize women as equals. Critics generally agree that the events and inner turmoils discussed in the novel are based on Plath's own experience, and that *The Bell Jar* therefore allows the reader to better understand the poet's personal conflicts, which inspired her famous confessional poetry and ultimately led to her death.

Plath was born in 1932 in Jamaica Plain, Massachusetts, at a time when women had limited options as to what they were allowed to do with their lives. But instead of accepting a preordained role of housewife and mother, Plath desired a career in a male-dominated field. The resistance she met in pursuing this goal and her battles with more private demons caused the poet to suffer recurring depression and several breakdowns. In an article in *Contemporary Literature*, Marjorie G. Perloff wrote that it's "beautifully ironic that Sylvia Plath, who never heard of Women's Liberation . . . has written one of the most acute analyses [*The Bell Jar*] of the feminist problem that we have in contemporary fiction." In a discussion of Plath's verses, Joyce Carol Oates also commented in an article that appeared in *Southern Review:* "All of this appears to be contemporary, but Sylvia Plath's poems are in fact the clearest, most precise (be-

This photograph from Anne Stevenson's *Bitter Fame: A Life of Sylvia Plath* shows the London home in which Plath committed suicide in 1963.

cause most private) expression of an old moral predicament that has become unbearable now in the mid-twentieth century." The author summarized her desires more poetically in *The Bell Jar:* "the last thing I wanted," she wrote, "was . . . to be the place an arrow shoots off from. I wanted . . . to shoot off in all directions myself."

Plath was the first child born to Aurelia Schober and Otto Emil Plath. Days after her eighth birthday, her father died as a result of complications due to a long-undiagnosed case of diabetes mellitus. It was a loss that would profoundly influence the future poet. "The death of her father when Sylvia was only 8 sadly altered [the stability of her family life]," wrote Elaine Kendall in a *Los Angeles Times Book Review* article, "and despite the best efforts of her extended family, that early loss would remain the central trauma of an otherwise happy girlhood." After her husband's death, Plath's mother took her daughter and son Warren with her to Wellesley, Massachusetts, where they lived with Plath's grandparents. Once there, Plath's mother took on teaching jobs to support the family.

Although her new life in Wellesley was not a bad one, Plath would forever maintain idyllic memories of those first years spent near the sea while her father was still alive. Kendall observed that, contrary to what one might expect, "the immediate result [of Plath's father's suicide] was not despair but achievement. No adolescence is entirely tran-

quil, but there is little in Sylvia Plath's history to presage her mental breakdown and early suicide." In fact, it was at the age of eight—around the same time as her father's death—that Plath's first published poem appeared in the *Boston Traveller.* She wrote steadily throughout her childhood and once described her early work, as A. Alvarez recalled in a radio obituary published in *TriQuarterly,* as being mostly about "birds, bees, spring, fall—all those subjects which are absolute gifts to the person who doesn't have any interior experience to write about." Plath published her first "mature" work while still a teenager. In 1950 the *Christian Science Monitor* accepted an essay she co-wrote with a classmate. That same day, she received an acceptance letter from *Seventeen,* to which she had submitted the story "And Summer Will Not Come Again."

After graduating summa cum laude from Smith College in Northampton, Massachusetts, Plath accepted a Fulbright scholarship to Cambridge University, where she earned a master's degree and met and married poet Ted Hughes. Her relationship with Hughes had a profound effect on Plath, and their courtship and marriage brought new happiness into her life. "Hughes . . . seemed to her a kind of ideal man, something she had never expected to find," Ellen Rosenberg reported in the *Concise Dictionary of American Literary Biography: 1941-1968.* "Her wonder and joy were ecstatically expressed in letters to her mother: 'I shall tell you now about something most miraculous and thundering and terrifying. . . . It is this man, this poet, this Ted Hughes. I have never known anything like it.'"

Although during this time she continued to get her poems published, Plath had other ambitions. Upon the release of some of her journal writings during the late 1970s, critics were surprised to learn that the famous poet had really aspired to be a travel journalist and a popular magazine fiction writer. Author Margaret Atwood's reaction to this news, published in a *New York Times Book Review* article, was typical: "It was a shock akin to seeing the Queen in a bikini to learn that Sylvia Plath, an incandescent poet of drastic seriousness" had such ambitions.

Plath's Poetry

Poetry remained a staple of her writing efforts, however, but although she had had individual poems published in various periodicals for years, Plath's first collection was not accepted by a publisher until 1960. That collection, *The Colossus*, is often critically measured against her later work posthumously published in *Ariel, Crossing the Water*, and *Winter Trees*. The earlier poems are generally considered to be more painstakingly written, controlled, emotionally restrained, and written with a concern for technique. Plath was influenced by such poets as Robert Lowell—whose seminar at Boston University Plath audited in 1959—Marianne Moore, Elizabeth Bishop, William Butler Years, Theodore Roethke, and Ted Hughes, and she diligently strove to learn from their work. According to an essay by J. D. McClatchy published in Harold Bloom's *Sylvia Plath: Modern Critical Edition*, the young Plath was "an assiduous apprentice," who "put herself resolutely through the traditionalist paces." McClatchy quoted from an early interview Plath gave to Lee Anderson: "Technically," said the poet, "I like [poetry] to be extremely musical and lyrical, with a singing sound.... At first I started in strict forms [such as the sonnet and villanelle]—it's the easiest way for a beginner to get music ready-made.... I lean very strongly toward forms that are, I suppose, quite rigid in comparison certainly to free verse. I'm much happier when I know that all my sounds are echoing in different ways throughout the poem." Most of the poems included in *The Colossus* were written between 1956 and 1959, the first three years of her marriage to Hughes.

After *The Colossus*, Plath began to find her own voice in her poetry. "[But] it is generally thought to be the poems in the posthumous *Ariel* [Plath's second collection] that are her most significant," according to Betty Abel in *Contemporary Review*. In a *Nation* review of *The Collected Poems*, which contains the verses from both of Plath's first two collections, Katha Pollitt observed that the poems from *Ariel* show "just how hard Plath worked to transform herself from a subdued, well-mannered student of [W. H.] Auden, [T. S.] Eliot, [John Crowe] Ransom, and Lowell" and became "a superb craftsman" who "was always becoming more distinctly herself." Alicia Ostriker wrote in *Language and Style* that "the difference between *The Colossus* and *Ariel* lies in the poet's advancing will and ability to do it, so it feels real, without veils." Plath's work represents "the startling phenomenon," she continued, "of a poet finding her own voice in the space of a very few years." But in a more disturbing interpretation of Plath's growth, Paul West pointed out that the more intense and personal her poems became, the closer Plath crept toward depression and suicide. The verses she

wrote toward the end of her life, West observed in *Book World*, "tell us how close you can go before you fall in."

Plath's most common themes include the tension between order and chaos, male-female relationships—especially as they relate to her father—pain, birth, rebirth, and death. Violence becomes an overriding element as her work progresses, but the issue of control is paramount throughout her writings from *The Bell Jar* to *Ariel*. In a 1962 interview quoted in *The Poet Speaks: Interviews with Contemporary Poets*, Plath herself said that she believed "one should be able to control and manipulate experiences, even the most terrifying, like madness, being tortured, this kind of experience, and one should be able to manipulate these experiences with an informed and an intelligent mind. I think that personal experience is very important, but certainly it shouldn't be a kind of shut-box and mirror-looking, narcissistic experience.... [It] should be *relevant*, and relevant to the larger things ... such as Hiroshima and Dachau and so on."

Controversy

Plath has been severely criticized for her use of images of the Holocaust in her poetry. In "Lady Lazarus," for example, a poem about her suicide attempts, the speaker describes her skin as "Bright as a Nazi lampshade." Later she lists remnants commonly found in the crematoriums in concentration camps as if they were parts of her own remains. About "Lady Lazarus," Alvarez quoted Plath as saying, "She is the Phoenix, the libertarian spirit, what you will. She is also just a good plain, very resourceful woman." In "Daddy," the speaker describes her father as a Nazi soldier; and this is how she describes herself: "I began to talk like a Jew. / I think I may well be a Jew." George Steiner asserted in *The Art of Sylvia Plath: A Symposium* that because of "the vehemence and intimacy of the verse," the poems are "difficult to judge." But he defended the poet's choice of metaphors by stating that "committing the whole of her poetic and formal authority to the metaphor, to the mask of language, Sylvia Plath *became* a woman being transported to Auschwitz on the death trains." Yet he questioned whether "these final poems [are] entirely legitimate," and wondered if Plath committed a "subtle larceny" by invoking the horrors experienced by six million people and applying them to herself. Irving Howe, in a *Harper's* essay, took a less ambiguous stand, proclaiming that there "is something monstrous when tangled emotions about one's father are deliberately compared with the historical fate of the European Jews." Charles Newman, meanwhile, refuted this argument in *The Art of Sylvia Plath* by asserting that "it is essential to both biographical fact and the measure of her poetry to see these shifts in role as a poet's search for the most authoritative voice possible. She is not relating herself to history ... any more than she related herself to nature in her early work. She is using history, like nature, to explain herself."

The controversy relates to a broader issue that some critics consider an even deeper element in her work; it is an issue which may shed light on not only her writing, but also on her emotional suffering as well: that Plath lacked empathy, a concern for others as individuals in their own right. As John Romano put it in an essay that appeared in *Commentary*, "Where Sylvia Plath's failure as an artist is not rooted in a failure to apprehend herself, it is rooted in a failure to apprehend the self in others." *Encounter* contributor Anthony Thwaite was "struck by the way in which these poems are indeed quarrels with herself, dramatic debates between action and stillness, fulfillment and blankness, hope and despair, anger and love." In an article in the *Atlantic Monthly*, Katha Pollitt also tackled this disturbing issue. She commented after reading *The Journals of Sylvia Plath* that while "other people did not seem real to [Plath] except as they served as yardsticks for comparison ... Plath did not seem real to herself, either. She wrote that she was loathsome, not human, full of 'rot'; or else she felt nothing at all."

The Bell Jar

Though it is for her poetry that Plath is most often admired and written about, her sole novel has generated much critical attention as well, not to mention a large audience that includes many teenage readers. Critics generally believe that *The Bell Jar* echoes the significant events and personal encounters in Plath's life during the summer of her junior year at Smith College. It was at that time that she won a one-month guest editorship at *Mademoiselle* magazine in New York City, along with eleven other winners from colleges and universities all over the United States. The brief editorship was extremely stressful on Plath, who found herself doubting her abilities because she was unable to satisfy her "capricious and demanding" senior editor, as Kendall described Plath's supervisor. Her feelings of inadequacy were further exacerbated after she returned home to Massachusetts and learned that she had been denied

Published just one month before Plath's death, this fictionalized autobiographical account of the author's life as an undergraduate at Smith College was lauded by many critics for its brutal honesty.

admission to a summer fiction writing program at Harvard. Plath became severely depressed and underwent electro-shock treatments that did little or nothing to relieve her condition. Her subsequent attempt to commit suicide by swallowing sleeping pills failed, however, and she was sent to a therapist until she was well enough to return to college.

In the novel, Plath becomes Esther Greenwood, a college student who has just arrived in New York with several other young women to work at *Ladies Day* magazine "for a month, expenses paid, and piles and piles of free bonuses, like ballet tickets and passes to fashion shows and hair stylings at a famous expensive salon and chances to meet successful people in the field of our desire and advice about what to do with our particular complexions.'' Indeed, Plath received similar perks while working at *Mademoiselle*, including the chance to interview novelist and short story writer Elizabeth Bowen and poet Marianne Moore. But to Plath the whole experience was an overwhelming whirlwind of new activities, including a frantic night life, a bout of ptomaine poisoning—suffered by all who consumed the crabmeat salad at an ad agency's luncheon—and the drudge work of a guest managing editor, all of which is described in the novel, though some parts are more fictionalized than others.

The Bell Jar can be divided into three major parts: Esther's trip to New York to work at the magazine; her return home, where she can't eat, can't write, becomes depressed—the final blow being her rejection from the Harvard summer writing program—and her attempted suicide following her first visit to her father's grave; and her hospitalization, electroshock therapy, and finally her release back into the world. The novel concludes with Esther leaving the hospital, "patched, retreaded and approved for the road." But she still does not feel confident she will not become depressed again. The last mention of the bell jar in the story has not gone unnoticed by critics, as it hints at Plath's own suicide less than two years later: "How did I know that someday—at college, in Europe, somewhere, anywhere—the bell jar, with its stifling distortions, wouldn't descend again?" The recurring symbol of the bell jar "represents the condition of mental breakdown," according to *Dictionary of Literary Biography* contributor Nancy Duvall Hargrove. "Esther imagines her illness as a gigantic bell jar that descends upon her, imprisoning her, suffocating her, isolating her from others, and distorting her view of the world."

Throughout the novel, Esther worries about her looks and ability to attract men and constantly compares herself to other women around her. She feels ambivalent about her intellectual and creative ambitions and entertains doubts about whether they will get in the way of her finding a husband, which is what the society she lives in ultimately expects a nice, intelligent young woman to do. Critics point to this conflict as a major theme in all of Plath's writing. And the conflict between living and creating art—a popular theme among artists in general—is even more intense because she is a woman. As Pamela J. Annas wrote in *A Disturbance in Mirrors: The Poetry of Sylvia Plath*, "to identify oneself as a woman poet . . . was to admit that you did not expect to be taken seriously. Even the most

cursory survey of American literary criticism yields examples of negative and patronizing pronouncements based on [gender]. Yet the themes of Plath's strongest poetry are clearly based on her experience as a woman poet trying to do creative work . . . in a world which did not take women's creativity seriously."

The novel that fictionalizes these occurrences wasn't written by Plath until 1961, about seven years after the events it recounts. There were a number of factors that kept her from writing her novel. After marrying Ted Hughes and earning her master's degree at Cambridge, she and her new husband returned to the United States, where Plath taught freshman English at Smith College. They then moved to Boston before returning to England at the end of 1959. In addition to her frequent moves, Plath's life was filled with the duties of being a new mother, and she also suffered from poor health. In the course of only a couple of years, the poet suffered from a miscarriage, an appendectomy, and constant bouts with sinusitis. Still, she managed to continue publishing her poetry, all the while delaying work on her novel.

But Hargrove recounted another important reason why Plath put off her novel. In a letter to a friend the poet explained that "she had 'been waiting to do this for ten years but had a terrible block about Writing A Novel. Then suddenly . . . the dykes broke. . . .' She had become interested in novel writing because, as she said in an interview with Peter Orr, 'you can get in toothbrushes and all the paraphernalia than one finds in daily life, and I find this more difficult in poetry.'" When *The Bell Jar* was finally published in England in 1963, one month before Plath's death, the poet used the pseudonym Victoria Lucas to protect the feelings of her family and friends, particularly her mother. Paul Alexander, in his biography *Rough Magic*, reported that the American edition was delayed until 1971 because Plath's mother pressured Hughes—who owned the rights to all of Plath's writings—not to publish it. Aurelia Plath finally relented when Hughes offered her the rights to publish letters from her daughter in exchange.

Early reviews of *The Bell Jar* reflected a variety of reactions. One of the most common was to compare it to J. D. Salinger's novel of a young man's attempt to reconcile himself with the world, *The Catcher in the Rye*. Saul Maloff, in a 1971 *New Republic* review, saw the novel as incomplete without considering her poetry, suggesting that together they compose a sort of autobiography: "She laid out the elements of her life, one after the other, and left to the late poems the necessary work of imagining and creating it." But some reviewers felt the novel was a weak effort. For example, *Prairie Schooner* critic Linda Ray Pratt preferred the later poems, calling *The Bell Jar* an "early and unsatisfactory novel which never gets below the surface of its real materials." On the other hand, Howard Moss wrote in a *New Yorker* article: "Its material, after all, is what has been transcended. It is a frightening book, and if it ends on too optimistic a note as both fiction and postdated fact, its real terror lies elsewhere. Though we share every shade of feeling that leads to Esther's attempts at suicide, there is not the slightest insight . . . into suicide itself. That may be why it bears the stamp of authority. Reading it, we are up against the raw experience of nightmare, not the analysis or understanding of it."

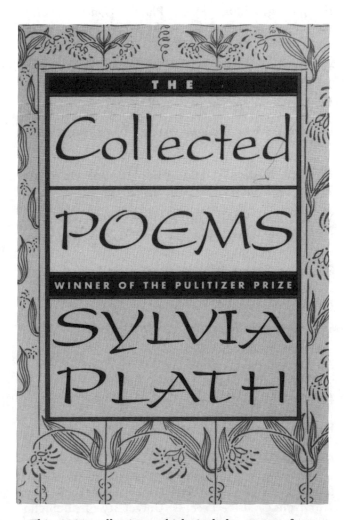

This 1981 collection, which includes poems from Plath's major works *The Colossus* and *Ariel*, won the Pulitzer Prize.

The Blue Hour

Plath suffered a major emotional blow when Hughes, the poet she once thought would make the ideal spouse, left her for another woman. Separated from her husband and living with her two young children in a London flat in which William Butler Yeats once resided, Plath spent the final two months of her life completing *The Bell Jar*, beginning a second novel, and writing most of the poems later included in *Ariel* and *Winter Trees*. Abandoning her careful and technically precise style for spur-of-the-moment writing, the poet poured her soul into her final poems. Alvarez quoted Plath's note to the BBC in 1962: "These new poems of mine have one thing in common. They were all written at about four in the morning—that still blue, almost eternal hour before the baby's cry, before the glassy music of the milkman, settling his bottles." The *Winter Trees* poems are particularly full of Plath's pain, as they allude to the circumstances of how her marriage failed. This event, according to Rosenberg, left Plath "bitter and devastated." "Although her health was poor, her responsibilities for the children demanding, and her emotional state depressed," Rosenberg later wrote, "[Plath] continued to write and to struggle for a stable and meaningful life. Yet she seemed unable to throw off the effects of the past months." Too depressed to continue living, Plath turned on the gas in her kitchen and asphyxiated herself on February 11, 1963.

In *Seduction and Betrayal*, Elizabeth Hardwick pondered: "If anything could have saved Sylvia Plath it would have been that she, in life, might have had the good fortune to know her own fulfillment, her hard, glittering achievement." Today, critics can only speculate about what Plath might ultimately have achieved had she lived past the age of thirty. As to how Plath will be assessed in the future for her contributions, Howe suggested that after "the noise abates and judgment returns, Sylvia Plath will be regarded as an interesting minor poet whose personal story was deeply poignant. A few of her poems will find a place in anthologies—and when you consider the common fate of talent, that, after all, will not be a small acknowledgment." Romano similarly insists that the facts of Plath's life should be kept separate from analyses of her writings when he said: "Her death . . . begs all questions of sincerity in her poems. . . . It is impossible to read her poetry without being convinced of the pain in which it had its origin. It is impossible not to be moved. But in the end we must make judgments based upon our allegiance to life."

■ Works Cited

Abel, Betty, "The Troubled Life and Verse of Sylvia Plath," *Contemporary Review*, March, 1988, pp. 166-167.

Alexander, Paul, *Rough Magic: A Biography of Sylvia Plath*, Viking, 1991, pp. 106-15, 347-348.

Allen, Mary, "Sylvia Plath's Defiance: 'The Bell Jar,'" *The Necessary Blankness: Women in Major American Fiction of the Sixties*, University of Illinois Press, 1976, pp. 160-165.

Alvarez, A. "Sylvia Plath," *TriQuarterly*, fall, 1966, p. 66.

Annas, Pamela J., *A Disturbance in Mirrors: The Poetry of Sylvia Plath*, Greenwood Press, 1988, pp. 158-61.

Atwood, Margaret, "Poet's Prose," *New York Times Book Review*, January 28, 1979, p. 10.

Bloom, Harold, editor, *Sylvia Plath: Modern Critical Edition*, Chelsea House, 1989, pp. 80-81.

Hardwick, Elizabeth, "Sylvia Plath," *Seduction and Betrayal: Women and Literature*, Random House, 1974, pp. 120-121.

Hargrove, Nancy Duvall, "Sylvia Plath," *Dictionary of Literary Biography*, Volume 6: *American Novelists since World War II, Second Series*, Gale, 1980, pp. 259-261.

Howe, Irving, "Sylvia Plath: A Partial Disagreement," *Harper's*, January, 1972, pp. 89-91.

Kendall, Elaine, "The Foiled Biography of a Fallen Poet," *Los Angeles Times Book Review*, January 31, 1988, p. 12.

Maloff, Saul, "Waiting for the Voice to Crack," *New Republic*, May 8, 1971, pp. 33-35.

Moss, Howard, "Dying: An Introduction," *New Yorker*, July 10, 1971, p. 75.

Newman, Charles, editor, *The Art of Sylvia Plath: A Symposium*, Indiana University Press, 1970, pp. 50-51.

Oates, Joyce Carol, "The Death Throes of Romanticism: The Poems of Sylvia Plath," *Southern Review*, Volume 9, 1973, p. 509.

Orr, Peter, editor, *The Poet Speaks: Interviews with Contemporary Poets*, Routledge & Kegan Paul, 1966.

Ostriker, Alicia, "'Fact' as Style: The Americanization of Sylvia," *Language and Style*, winter, 1968, p. 202.

Perloff, Marjorie G., "'A Ritual for Being Born Twice': Sylvia Plath's 'The Bell Jar,'" *Contemporary Literature*, autumn, 1972, p. 512.

Plath, Sylvia, *The Bell Jar*, Harper, 1971.

Pollitt, Katha, "A Note of Triumph," *Nation*, January 16, 1982, pp. 52-53.

Pollitt, Katha, "Poet in Training," *Atlantic Monthly*, May, 1982, pp. 104-105.

Pratt, Linda Ray, "The Spirit of Blackness Is in Us," *Prairie Schooner*, spring, 1973, pp. 87-90.

Romano, John, "Sylvia Plath Reconsidered," *Commentary*, April, 1974, pp. 47-52.

Rosenberg, Ellen, "Sylvia Plath," *Concise Dictionary of American Literary Biography: 1941-1968*, Gale, 1987, pp. 408-421.

Sexton, Anne, "The Barfly Ought to Sing," *Ariel Ascending: Writings about Sylvia Plath*, edited by Paul Alexander, Harper, 1985, p. 183.

Steiner, George, *Language and Silence*, Atheneum, 1967.

Thwaite, Anthony, "Out of the Quarrel: On Sylvia Plath," *Encounter*, August, 1979, p. 42.

West, Paul, "Fido Littlesoul, the Bowel's Familiar," *Book World*, January 9, 1972, p. 8.

■ For More Information See

BOOKS

Aird, Eileen, *Sylvia Plath: Her Life and Work*, Oliver & Boyd, 1973.

Alexander, Paul, editor, *Ariel Ascending: Writings about Sylvia Plath*, Harper, 1985.

Alvarez, A., *The Savage God: A Study of Suicide*, Weidenfeld & Nicolson, 1971.

Barnard, Caroline King, *Sylvia Plath*, Twayne, 1978.

Broe, Mary Lynn, *Protean Poetic: The Poetry of Sylvia Plath*, University of Missouri Press, 1980.

Bundtzen, Lynda K., *Plath's Incarnations: Woman and the Creative Process*, University of Michigan Press, 1983.

Butscher, Edward, *Sylvia Plath: Method and Madness*, Seabury Press, 1976.

Contemporary Literary Criticism, Gale, Volume 1, 1973; Volume 2, 1974; Volume 3, 1975; Volume 5, 1976; Volume 9, 1978; Volume 11, 1979; Volume 14, 1980; Volume 17, 1981; Volume 50, 1988; Volume 51, 1989; Volume 62, 1991.

Dictionary of Literary Biography, Volume 5: *American Poets since World War II, Part 2: L-Z*, Gale, 1980.

Holbrook, David, *Sylvia Plath: Poetry and Existence*, Athlone, 1976.

Kroll, Judith, *Chapters in a Mythology: The Poetry of Sylvia Plath*, Harper, 1976.

Lane, Gary, *Sylvia Plath: New Views on the Poetry*, Johns Hopkins University Press, 1979.

Melander, Ingrid, *The Poetry of Sylvia Plath: A Study of Themes*, Almqvist & Wiksell, 1972.

Poetry Criticism, Volume 1, Gale, 1990.

Steiner, Nancy Hunter, *A Closer Look at Ariel: A Memory of Sylvia Plath*, Harper's Magazine Press, 1973.

Stevenson, Anne, *Bitter Fame: A Life of Sylvia Plath*, Houghton, 1989.

Uroff, Margaret D., *Sylvia Plath and Ted Hughes*, University of Illinois Press, 1979.

Wagner, Linda, editor, *Critical Essays on Sylvia Plath*, G.K. Hall, 1984.

Walsh, Thomas P., and Cameron Northouse, *Sylvia Plath and Anne Sexton: A Reference Guide*, G.K. Hall, 1974.

World Literature Criticism, Volume 4, Gale, 1992.

PERIODICALS

American Spectator, January, 1992.
Nation, March 23, 1992, p. 385.
People, December 4, 1989, p. 99.
Studies in American Fiction, autumn, 1984, p. 161.°

—Sketch by Helene Henderson

Rob Reiner

■ Personal

Full name, Robert Reiner; born March 6, 1945, in New York, NY; son of Carl (an actor, writer, director and producer) and Estelle (Lebost) Reiner; married Penny Marshall (an actress and director), 1971 (divorced, 1981); married Michele Singer (a photographer), May 19, 1989; children: (first marriage) Tracy Reiner (stepdaughter), (second marriage) Jake. *Education:* Attended University of California, Los Angeles, 1965-68. *Hobbies and other interests:* Attending professional baseball games.

■ Addresses

Office—Castle Rock Entertainment, 335 North Maple Dr., Suite 135, Beverly Hills, CA 90210. *Agent*—Creative Artists Agency, 9830 Wilshire Blvd., Beverly Hills, CA 90212.

■ Career

Actor, director and writer. Actor in regional theatre companies and improvisational troupes, including "The Session" and "The Committee," 1965-68; television and film actor, 1967—; film writer/director, 1967—; Castle Rock Entertainment, Beverly Hills, CA, partner, 1987—. Appeared on stage as Danny in Broadway production of *The Roast,* Winter Garden Theatre, New York City, 1980. Actor in television series, including Snake, *The Partridge Family,* American Broadcasting Companies, Inc. (ABC-TV), 1970; Michael "Meathead" Stivic, *All in the Family,* Columbia Broadcasting System, Inc. (CBS-TV), 1971-78; producer, creator, and played role of host of *Morton & Hayes,* CBS-TV, 1991; also appeared in *That Girl* and *Gomer Pyle.* Appeared in roles in television movies, including Joel Forrest, *Thursday's Game,* ABC-TV, 1974. Other television appearances include *The Beverly Hillbillies,* CBS-TV; *The Mickie Finns Finally Present How the West Was Lost,* syndicated, 1975; *Battle of the Network Stars,* ABC-TV, 1977; *Celebrity Challenge of the Sexes 1,* CBS-TV, 1977; *People,* CBS-TV, 1978; *The Billy Crystal Comedy Hour,* National Broadcasting Company, Inc. (NBC-TV), 1982; and *The Billy Crystal Comedy Special,* Home Box Office (HBO), 1986. Actor in films, including *Throw Momma from the Train,* Orion, 1987; *Postcards from the Edge,* Columbia, 1990; and *Sleepless in Seattle,* Columbia, 1993. Director of films, including *The Sure Thing,* Embassy, 1985; *Stand By Me,* Columbia, 1986; *The Princess Bride,* Twentieth Century-Fox, 1987; *Misery,* Columbia, 1990; and *A Few Good Men,* Columbia, 1992. *Member:* American Federation of Television and Radio Artists, Actors' Equity Association, Screen Actors Guild, Directors Guild.

■ Awards, Honors

Emmy awards, best supporting actor in a comedy, 1974, and outstanding continuing performance by a supporting actor in a comedy series, 1978, both for *All in the Family;* Directors Guild nomination, best director, 1986, for *Stand By Me.*

■ Writings

SCREENPLAYS

(Coauthor; and played Clark Baxter) *Enter Laughing,* Columbia, 1967.

(And played Leaky Couloris) *Halls of Anger,* United Artists, 1970.

(And played Roger) *Where's Poppa?* (also known as *Going Ape*), United Artists, 1970.

(And played Don) *Summertree,* Columbia, 1971.

(And played Miguelito) *How Come Nobody's on Our Side?,* American Films, 1975.

(And played Russel Fikus) *Fire Sale,* Twentieth Century-Fox, 1977.

(With Christopher Guest, Michael McKean, and Harry Shearer; and played Marti DiBergi; and director) *This Is Spinal Tap,* Embassy, 1984.

(With Nora Ephron and Andy Scheinman; and producer with others; and director) *When Harry Met Sally ...,* Columbia, 1989.

TELEVISION SERIES

(Coauthor and creator with Phil Mishkin) *The Super,* ABC-TV, 1972.

(With Mishkin, Sy Rosen, and Earl Pomerantz; executive producer with Mishkin; and played Joseph Brenner) *Free Country,* ABC-TV, 1978.

Contributor of script material to *The Smothers Brothers Comedy Hour,* CBS-TV, beginning 1968; *The Glen Campbell Show,* CBS-TV, 1968; *Headmaster,* CBS-TV, beginning 1970; and television specials.

TELEVISION MOVIES

(With Mishkin; executive producer with Mishkin; and played Alan Corkus) *More Than Friends,* ABC-TV, 1978.

(With others; executive producer with Mishkin; and actor) *The TV Show* (pilot), ABC-TV, 1979.

(With Mishkin and Dick Wimmer; producer with Peter Katz; and played Monte Miller) *Million Dollar Infield,* CBS-TV, 1982.

OTHER

Author, with Mishkin, of stage works.

DIRECTOR

The Sure Thing, Embassy, 1985.

Stand By Me (based on the "The Body," by Stephen King), Columbia, 1986.

(And producer with Arnold Scheinman) *The Princess Bride,* (based on the novel by William Goldman), Twentieth-Century-Fox, 1987.

(And producer with others) *Misery* (based on the novel by Stephen King), Columbia, 1990.

(And producer with others) *A Few Good Men* (based on the stage play by Aaron Sorkin), Columbia, 1992.

(And producer with others) *Sleepless in Seattle,* Columbia, 1993.

■ Work in Progress

Plans are being made to produce a movie musical with songs by Stephen Sondheim.

■ Sidelights

"[When] people say 'Have a nice day' to me, I feel a lot of pressure; I don't know how ... to *do* it," director and actor Rob Reiner once revealed to David Rosenthal in a *Playboy* interview. "I have moments when I seem joyful, but they always catch me by surprise.... To be honest, I think I've been happy 18 seconds in my whole life, and they've been spread out. Where there's hope, though, is that I feel there's a happy person trying to creep out of this depression."

Despite his renown as the director of such popular films as *Stand by Me, When Harry Met Sally, Misery,* and *A Few Good Men,* Reiner has lived so long under the shadow of his famous father, comedian Carl Reiner, that he has never been completely satisfied with his own accomplishments. In a *Film Comment* interview conducted by Harlan Jacobson, the director modestly commented, "I'm not great at anything, but I'm real good at a lot of things. I'm a pretty good actor, a pretty good writer. I have pretty good music abilities, pretty good visual and color and costume sense. I'm not great at any of these things, but as a director I have the opportunity to utilize all these things in one job. Which is why I like doing it."

Life among the Comedians

Reiner actually started his career by writing for and acting in television comedies, which isn't surprising considering the household in which he grew up. The oldest of three children, Reiner was born in 1947 in the Bronx, where his family lived in a modest apartment while his father worked first on the stage and then on the memorable comedy variety program, *Your Show of Shows*. The young Reiner was constantly surrounded by his father's friends, brilliant comedians and comediennes like Mel Brooks, Sid Caesar, Norman Lear, Imogene Coca, Howard Morris, Neil Simon, Larry Gelbart, and Buddy Hackett, some of whom even spent time babysitting Carl's son. Yet even though young Reiner was surrounded by laughter, to his father he seemed to be a sullen child whose most creative efforts involved writing depressing poetry. "[My father] never thought I was funny," Reiner told Rosenthal. "When I was eight or nine and we were spending the summer on Fire Island, Norman Lear was there. Norman remembers me playing jacks with him one day and making up jokes and doing shtick. I made him laugh. But when he went and told my father, 'You know, Rob is really a funny kid,' my father answered, 'Get out of here! That kid? That sullen, brooding kid is *not* funny. No way.'"

While his father was a much more outgoing person who, as an actor, craved his audience's attention, Reiner attributes his more artistic and reflective nature to his mother. Reiner described her to Jacobson as "a great musical person; she's an artist. She's very smart and very sensitive, a talented person. I've got a lot of her in me." But the young Reiner still wanted his father's attention and approval. He wished so much to be like his father that once, as he related to *Interview* contributor Betsy Barns, "I came to him when I was a kid and said, 'Dad, I want to change my name.' He figured, 'Oh ... he can't deal with the pressure of the Reiner name.' He asked me what I wanted to change it to, and I said, 'Carl.' Instead of being Rob Reiner, I wanted to be Carl Reiner."

The main reason Reiner didn't try to be a comic when his father's friends visited was that he was so intimidated by the obvious talent of these professionals. When he was about sixteen, however, Reiner dared to add his two-cents' worth to one of Carl's comedy bits. One of the continuing skits that Carl Reiner and Mel Brooks are famous for is "The Two-Thousand-Year-Old Man," a routine in which Brooks played an ancient man who is asked questions by Carl about how various customs and inventions evolved over time. Rob suggested a joke about how people invented applause. "The first applause," Reiner explained the gag to April Bernard in *Interview*, "was, when somebody would see something that they liked, they would go, 'Oh boy, that's good!' [*slaps hands on sides of face*] If

they really liked something, they'd really hurt themselves. So one day, a guy pulled his head out when nobody was looking and just slapped his hands together." Reiner was elated when his father actually decided to use his material.

Getting the Acting Bug

Reiner's father discouraged his son from following his footsteps, but Reiner—who in high school had spent many a summer vacation day watching his father make the popular 1960s comedy, *The Dick Van Dyke Show*—had caught the theater bug. As a high school senior, he acted in his first play and, for the first time in his life, began to come out of his shell and become popular with his peers. He enrolled as a theater arts major at the University of California, Los Angeles, and spent his first two summers as a college student acting in small theater productions on the East Coast. Reiner's parents watched some of these early performances, which, according to Carl in a New York *Daily News Magazine* article, were not too promising: "Rob was so awful that my wife . . . and I almost died. We didn't know how to tell him to get out of the business." In a glimpse of things to come, it was his son's directing that first caught Carl's attention. When Rob was nineteen, he told Rosenthal, "[I] directed a production of [Jean Paul] Sartre's *No Exit* at a little playhouse in Beverly Hills, the Roxbury. . . . I'll never forget it, because my father came backstage, looked me straight in the eye and said, 'That was *good.* No bullshit.' It was the first time I'd gotten that sort of validation from him."

While at college, Reiner was also involved in the formation of a comedy troupe called "The Session," which performed in clubs in both New York City and Los Angeles. The group included such luminaries as future movie star Richard Dreyfuss and Larry Bishop, whose father was the famous comic Joey Bishop. The troupe only stayed together for a year before disbanding, and at about that same time Reiner was kicked out of school for missing too many classes. The Vietnam War was at its height at the time, and as a college drop-out Reiner was in danger of being drafted. He was rescued from this fate when his psychiatrist—Reiner underwent therapy from the age of eighteen to twenty-two—called the draft board and convinced the Army that his patient wasn't fit for combat. Reiner was strongly against the United States' policies in Vietnam, and to this day he remains angry that he and other protestors are considered unpatriotic because of their beliefs. As he told Rosenthal, "You were told you weren't patriotic because you didn't want to go and kill people whose country we had no business being in the first place. That, to me, was the biggest crime of all.''

Occasionally acting with another comedy troupe, "The Committee," Reiner spent a lot of time in the San Francisco area where the group often performed and where he had a girlfriend. In the late 1960s, San Francisco, especially the Haight-Ashbury district, symbolized a generation struggling to obtain peace and find love at a time when nuclear war between the super powers was a constant threat. Drugs such as marijuana and LSD—or "acid"—were an inseparable part of the hippie culture Reiner found himself in. But although he admitted to Rosenthal that he was a "moderate user," Reiner also insisted that he didn't use drugs as heavily as many of his friends did.

About this time, Reiner began to land some small parts in various movies and television shows. Because of his long hair, bell-bottom jeans, and tie-dyed shirts, he was typecast in rolls in which he played a hippie. He appeared in such shows as *The Beverly Hillbillies* and *Gomer Pyle* and the movies *Halls of Anger, Summertree,* and *Where's Poppa?,* which was directed by his father. He also wrote for the short-lived television series *The Glen Campbell Show, The Headmaster,* and *The Super.* His biggest break, however, came when he was hired on as part of the writing staff for *The Smothers Brothers Comedy Hour,* a popular but controversial show that was eventually canceled because of its liberal political viewpoint. One of Reiner's fellow writers on the show was Steve Martin, with whom he formed a friendship. Later, in the 1980s, Martin's movie career took off with films directed by Carl Reiner, which gave cause for some jealousy on Rob's part. "[It] was a little weird," Reiner told Rosenthal, "because here was Steve, a contemporary of mine, and my father—Steve was like another son, the son my father would have liked to have, the funny son, not the brooding, introverted child that was me. I think I was a little bit jealous, a little bit threatened. But by the same token, I knew that I could never do the kinds of things that Steve did and does." Reiner did get some small roles in shows his father directed, but he never starred in any of them.

All in the Family

Reiner met with the same kind of resistance from his father's friend, Norman Lear, when Lear was auditioning actors to star in his television show, *All in the Family.* Reiner had to go through three auditions before he was finally accepted for the part of Mike "Meathead" Stivic. The character of Stivic, not surprisingly, was a radical hippie whose opinions served as a contrast to the chauvinistic, racist, and ignorant comments made by Meathead's father-in-law, Archie Bunker, played by Carroll O'Connor. *All in the Family* broke new ground because of the willingness of its writers to address controversial issues such as prejudice and women's rights. The show became a hit and aired on CBS from 1971 to 1979, and Reiner earned best supporting actor Emmy awards in 1974 and 1978 for his work. More importantly for Reiner, however, was that after the third season on the series he began to take an active role in the actual writing and editing for the show. "I was involved in helping structure the stories, in rewriting, in editing—all the things that made the program," he told Rosenthal. "If I had just had to do my part as an actor, go in every week and play the part, I think I would have been unhappy. It was an egoless show, though, and it taught me that actors, writers, directors must serve the piece. *All in the Family* was a pure example of that."

During the 1970s, Reiner was riding high on a wave of success. *All in the Family* afforded him a steady income, as well as an ongoing education on how to write and direct a show. In 1971, he also married Penny Marshall, who at the time was a struggling actress. Ironically, Marshall had lived across the street from Reiner's apartment in Brooklyn when they were both children, and when Reiner was auditioning for *All in the Family,* Marshall had tried out for the role of Mike Stivic's wife, Gloria—the part that eventually went to Sally Struthers. Reiner and Marshall first met at a Los Angeles bar called Barney's Beanery. They dated for a while and then lived together for over a year before finally getting married in an informal ceremony in Reiner's parents' back yard. For some time, the marriage went well. Reiner and Marshall were friends as well as husband and wife, and the actor formed a close bond with his new stepdaughter, Tracy.

The seeds of future problems were planted, however, when Marshall's career took off with her role as Laverne in the popular comedy series, *Laverne & Shirley,* which ran on ABC from 1976 to 1983. But even though his wife's series was a success, Reiner didn't think the show was very good and wasn't shy about telling Marshall what he honestly felt. He did point out that he liked the way Marshall played Laverne, but she nevertheless took his criticism of the show itself as an attack on her work. The marriage became more shaky when Reiner left *All in the Family* in 1978 and signed a contract with ABC to write, produce, and act in new television programs. None of the shows he worked on, including a short-lived comedy-drama called *Free Country* and the TV movies *More Than Friends* and *The Million Dollar Infield,* were well received. Reiner's career was at a low ebb, and Marshall, who when they had first gotten married was barely getting by as an actress, was making much more money. The stress Reiner was feeling further strained the marriage until it finally broke apart. In a tongue-in-cheek moment, Reiner told Rosenthal how he and Marshall finally decided to get a divorce in 1981. They saw a television "ad for the *National Enquirer* and it said, 'National Enquirer predicts Penny and Rob will split.' ... [That's] the reason we got divorced—we didn't want to make the *National Enquirer* look bad. We wanted to preserve the integrity of the publication."

Single again and without a steady income, Reiner understandably suffered from depression. When his stint on *All in the Family* had ended, the actor was offered a two-million-dollar contract to co-star with Sally Struthers in an *All in the Family* spin-off to be called *Mike and Gloria,* but he turned it down because he didn't want to be "Meathead" forever.

He tried, instead, to explore new areas as a film director and producer. Reiner's first idea for a movie was inspired by a rock 'n' roll parody skit that aired on *The Midnight Special,* a late-night television program. The problem was to get the financial backing needed to produce the movie. Although he was willing to invest his own money in the project, Reiner still needed several million dollars more than he had. He went to Embassy Pictures, which was partially owned by Norman Lear, and, after heatedly arguing for the film, convinced Embassy to produce his project despite the fact that he had never directed a film before. It took Reiner five years to raise all the money he needed—about two million dollars of which came from Lear—but in 1984 *This Is Spinal Tap* finally debuted in movie theaters.

Sitting in the Director's Chair

This Is Spinal Tap is a parody both of heavy metal bands and pretentious documentary films. In the movie, Reiner plays director Marty DiBergi, who is filming a documentary about a British rock 'n' roll trio whose main claim to fame is that their music is very loud. Singer David St. Hubbins, guitarist Nigel Tufnel, and bass player Derek Smalls are played respectively by Michael McKean, Christo-

The 1984 mock documentary *This Is Spinal Tap* presents the exploits of a fictional heavy metal band.

pher Guest, and Harry Shearer. Along with Reiner, the three comedians created the characters and wrote the music and lyrics to their songs, including such inspired tunes as "Gimme Some Money," "Silent But Deadly," and "The Sun Never Sweats." In the mock rockumentary, DiBergi records the group's travels on the road as the pathetic ensemble suffers embarrassment after embarrassment. Yet the three rockers survive because of their strong friendship and mutual love of music. The satire grossed about seven million dollars at the box office, earning a modest but respectable profit of five million dollars.

Though praised by many critics for its playful jabs at the music industry, the humor of the film escaped many people who thought Spinal Tap was an actual group. The confusion is understandable considering the way the movie was promoted: MTV aired a video of the group's song "Hell Hole," and commercials were broadcast advertising an album of Spinal Tap's greatest hits. Even after the film's release, Spinal Tap lived on. Shearer, Guest, and McKean enjoyed playing the band members so much that after the film they continued to don their wigs and costumes to perform in night clubs; and in 1992 MCA Records released Spinal Tap's second album *Break Like the Wind,* their first album being the soundtrack to the movie. Of the confusion between fact and fantasy, *Newsweek* contributor David Ansen noted, "It is the highest compliment to *This Is Spinal Tap*... that a number of people are going to take their time getting the joke." Later Ansen concluded, "This is surely the funniest movie ever made about rock and roll, and one of the funniest things about it is that it may also be one of the most accurate."

For Reiner, *This Is Spinal Tap* was more than just a satirical film for the new director: it also reflected some of his own personal concerns. As Reiner told the *New York Times,* reported *American Film* contributor Robert Lloyd, "[Spinal Tap is] about people who are frightened of leaving the nest and cling to each other ... which was basically the four of us [the actors and Reiner] who were making the film." Reiner's next film, *The Sure Thing,* also had some personal importance to him. Lloyd continued to quote Reiner: "*The Sure Thing,* while conforming generally to the outlines of a teen movie, 'is about discovering that love and sex can be one and the same thing, which, although I was 37 then, I was just figuring out.'" *The Sure Thing* is a romantic comedy about a college freshman who wants to travel cross-country to meet a girl who, according to his friend, will go to bed with him. To

make his date, he has to bum a ride off a girl that he doesn't like. During the course of the long trip, however, the two gradually put aside their differences and fall in love. Reiner made the film because he wanted to create a movie for teenagers that was more thoughtful than other popular films like *Porky's.* Most teenager movies, he told Barns, "are about the first sexual experience—[having sex] for the first time, guys looking through peepholes.... Ridiculous. This was about a boy who discovers that you can have a sexual experience that is connected with feelings of love."

The Sure Thing was also a modest success, earning about fifteen million dollars in profits. But this came nowhere close to Reiner's next film, *Stand by Me,* which he has also called one of his most personal works. *Stand by Me,* starring Wil Wheaton, Jerry O'Connell, Corey Feldman, and River Phoenix, is based on the Stephen King short story, "The Body." Superficially, the story is about four young friends who go on a camping trip to find the body of a dead boy. The real thrust of the film, though, is the personal problems each of the boys must endure and how their friendship helps them to grow. As Jacobson remarked, referring to Reiner's relationship with his father, "The subject here is parents causing their children pain, either through misdeeds, misspent lives, or misplaced priorities.... It does not take a shrink to see what Rob saw in the project." Reiner reflected in *Playboy* after the film was released that it's "the story of a twelve-year-old boy, misunderstood by his father, who starts to like himself and think he's valid. That's what's beginning to happen to me now." "[Making] this last film ... really has helped me gain confidence," Reiner further revealed to Gene Siskel in the *Chicago Tribune.*

Reiner changed gears from realistic films to fantasy with his next directing effort, *The Princess Bride.* He had read the original William Goldman story on which the movie is based when he was twenty-six and "fell in love with it," as he told Jacobson. "I read it again a dozen years later," he later added, "and I wondered if that would be a good film." Like *Stand by Me,* for which Reiner had a very difficult time finding a studio to provide the money, *The Princess Bride* was bounced from studio to studio for about ten years before Twentieth Century-Fox finally agreed to do it. The problem was that no one really knew how to handle the purely escapist, good versus evil fantasy. To solve this problem, Reiner thought audiences could relate more to the story if it was framed within a realistic setting. "The film," he explained to Jacobson, "is about a little boy who is sick in bed and his grandfather comes over to read him a book [*The Princess Bride*]. And the little boy is resistant to seeing his grandfather and to hearing the book read to him. And by the end of the film he's brought closer to his grandfather and he is now interested in books."

The Beginning of Castle Rock

With a seventeen-million-dollar budget, Reiner was able to hire some big-name stars like Billy Crystal and Mandy Patinkin, and he was able to make a much more elaborately produced film—though he refrained from letting special effects overwhelm the story. Still, he was growing tired of always having to fight to get financial backing for his projects. So, after the release of *The Princess Bride*, the director began to brainstorm ideas with four of his close friends—Alan Horn, Andrew Scheinman, Glenn Padnick, and Martin Shafer—to see how they could resolve this problem. It was Horn who invested one million dollars of his own money and made the rounds of the Hollywood studios to propose an intriguing deal: for an initial

investment of thirty million dollars, the five partners would promise to make four quality movies a year for the studio. A lot of studios were interested in the offer, except they wanted creative control over what kinds of movies the partners would make. In the end, a contract was signed with Columbia Pictures—through Coca-Cola Television—and Castle Rock Entertainment was born.

The fundamental philosophy held by the Castle Rock partners was that no matter how hard a studio tried to cater to the tastes of the public or how much it invested, there were no guarantees that a film would succeed. A film could have a huge budget and popular actors and actresses and still be a flop at the box office. Therefore, the partners agreed to try to make quality movies and television programs without worrying about what audiences might want. At first, this plan didn't go over well with Columbia's executives, who tried to gain more control Castle Rock's business decisions. But the partners stubbornly resisted the larger company's attacks and began filming their first movies and television pilots. *Winter People,* Castle Rock's first film, was a complete flop, causing the young

Reiner received a Directors Guild nomination for his 1986 film, *Stand by Me,* in which four friends on a camping trip learn about each other as they search for the body of a dead boy.

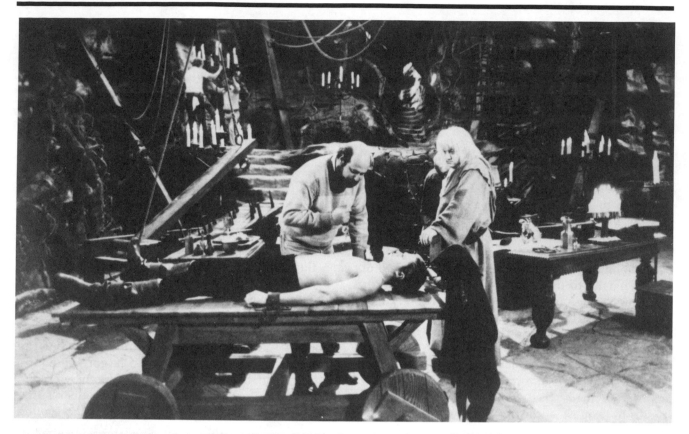

Reiner directs Cary Elwes and Mel Smith in the 1987 comedic fantasy *The Princess Bride.*

company to lose five million dollars. Their first television pilots were also unsuccessful, except for *Seinfeld,* which ran for two mediocre seasons before finding a large audience.

By 1989 Castle Rock was in desperate straits, having lost about twenty million dollars in failed investments. With only nine million dollars in assets left, Reiner and his friends resolved to make a last ditch effort that would either make or break the company. Reiner had an idea for a movie that he hoped would make a profit for the company, and he hired acclaimed screenplay writer Nora Ephron to write the script. "When Ephron met Reiner to discuss the script," reported Richard Corliss in *Time,* "the director said, 'I want to do a movie about two people who become friends and are really happy they become friends because they realize that if they had sex it would have ruined everything. And they have sex and it ruins everything.'" The film idea, which was entitled *When Harry Met Sally . . .,* is partly based on Reiner's "life after being divorced from actress Penny Marshall," according to Corliss. Basically, as the director explained to Corliss, the film shows how men "and women desperately want to be with each other, but at the same time they can't stand each other and don't understand each other."

When Harry Met Sally . . . starred Billy Crystal and Meg Ryan and was a box-office smash. Reiner was hoping that the film would make about forty million dollars and put Castle Rock comfortably in the black. To everyone's surprise, however, the movie grossed over twice that: ninety-two million dollars. The film also received positive reviews from a number of critics. In an issue of *Rolling Stone,* for example, one reviewer called *When Harry Met Sally . . .* "a ravishing, romantic lark brimming over with style, intelligence and flashing wit." On the other hand, *New Yorker* critic Terrence Rafferty complained that Reiner was losing his touch as a director: "Rob Reiner was a better director when he wasn't trying to dispense rueful wisdom," Rafferty declared. The critic later added that scoring a hit with the nostalgic *Stand by Me* "may have ruined him: he seems determined now to *touch* the audience rather than merely tickle it. In *When Harry Met Sally . . .* he runs after us with outstretched arms, but he's losing his touch with actors, which was his best quality as a director."

The observation that Reiner was "losing his touch with actors" in his films is especially ironic in the case of *When Harry Met Sally . . .,* considering that star Billy Crystal is one of Reiner's best friends. Crystal and Reiner have known each other since

1976, when Crystal made a guest appearance on *All in the Family*. Since then, the two friends have appeared in and worked on several films together, and Crystal has become a familiar face in Castle Rock features.

Irregardless of whether or not he was starting to lose his edge as a director, after making *When Harry Met Sally . . .* Reiner sensed that he needed to explore new directions. He did so by filming a movie based on the Stephen King novel, *Misery*. Yet the horror film, which is about an author held hostage by a psychopathic woman, is also consistent with Reiner's characteristic personal involvement in much of his work. In *Misery*, an author is trying to break free of his career as a romance novelist famous for the creation of his heroine, Misery. But the woman who imprisons him after he is injured in a car accident forces him to write a new installment of the series. "The genre is new for Reiner," Lloyd observed, "but the approach— 'The allegory is that he's battling with his own demons to force himself to grow . . . and this psychotic fan represents the demons inside him'— strikes the familiar note of the psycho-personal. 'Just by doing *Misery*,'" Lloyd quoted the director as saying, "'I'm in a sense mirroring the character in the film.'"

An Uncertain Future

Misery did well in movie theaters, but in the meantime Castle Rock was again suffering from a lack of successful films. Although the producers scored hits with *City Slickers*, starring Billy Crystal, and the Clint Eastwood film *In the Line of Fire*, they had several movies that either lost money or barely broke even, including *Year of the Comet*, *Mr. Saturday Night*, and *Honeymoon in Vegas*. The television division of Castle Rock also suffered when the market for syndicated series declined and the company only had one hit sitcom: *Seinfeld*. In 1992, Reiner and company vested their hopes in *A Few Good Men*, the military trial drama based on

When Harry Met Sally . . ., the 1989 box-office hit which Reiner cowrote, coproduced, and directed, explores contemporary male-female relationships.

Tom Cruise starred in Reiner's successful 1992 military drama, *A Few Good Men.*

the play by Aaron Sorkin. Using big-name stars like Tom Cruise, Demi Moore, Jack Nicholson, Kevin Bacon, and Kiefer Sutherland, the film was, indeed, a big success and received positive reviews. *New York Times* writer Vincent Canby called it "a big commercial entertainment of unusually satisfying order," and in a *Time* article Richard Schickel deemed it "hugely entertaining."

Yet, despite this more recent success, Peter Biskind predicted in a *Premiere* article that "*A Few Good Men* will not dramatically change [Castle Rock's fortunes], even if it does return money to the company—and one knowledgeable source estimates that with Columbia footing the bill and with all the big bites out of the back end, the film probably has to gross $175 million to $200 million before Castle Rock sees a penny." With all its financial troubles, there has been some concern within the company that Reiner—now a well-respected director—will leave for greener pastures. "'If Rob left tomorrow,'" Biskind quoted an anonymous source at the studio, "'we'd be out of

business.'" While Biskind doesn't believe Reiner would abandon the company he helped found, he maintained that "it does raise some interesting questions, at once aesthetic, commercial, and personal."

Since the late 1980s, Reiner's personal life has greatly improved. In 1989 he married photographer Michele Singer, whom he had met on the set of *When Harry Met Sally....* The couple now has a son named Jake. Biskind hinted that having a more fulfilling private life might make directing a secondary concern for Reiner. "'Part of the reason Rob got involved in Castle Rock,'" Biskind quoted director Barry Sonnenfeld, "'was that his life was his work.... If Castle Rock didn't exist and someone came to Rob today and said, "Do you want to start this company with us?" I don't know that he would.'" Steve Nicolaides, a producer who has worked for Castle Rock, told Biskind, "A lot of us who are Rob's friends and who have worked with him through the years think he's coming to a crossroads."

Despite having a new family and his growing success as a film director, Reiner still derives very little pleasure out of his life. "Reiner," according to Lloyd, said he "likes making films because, among other reasons, 'I'm a little less depressed when I'm working than when I'm not, because it keeps me focused on something.'" The director's view on life, as he revealed to Jacobson, is that "life is pain—mostly pain, with a lot of moments of joy and happiness here and there." One of those moments of joy came when a fan walked up to Reiner and thanked him for all the pleasure that he and his father had given him. "And, for the first time," Reiner recalled, "I let it in. Something has happened to this guy; because of my existence on this planet this guy feels a little bit better. You have x amount of days on this planet, and if you've given someone more pleasure than he would have gotten, wow, what a thing to be able to do!"

■ Works Cited

Ansen, David, "Rocky Road," *Newsweek*, March 5, 1984, pp. 81-82.

Barns, Betsy, "True Confessions: *Stand by Me*," *Interview*, October, 1986, pp. 90, 92.

Bernard, April, "Reiner's Reasons," *Interview*, July, 1989, pp. 70-71, 96.

Biskind, Peter, "A Few Good Menshes," *Premiere*, January, 1993, pp. 50-60.

Canby, Vincent, "Two Marines and Their Code on Trial," *New York Times*, December 11, 1992, p. C20.

Corliss, Richard, "When Humor Meets Heartbreak," *Time*, July 31, 1989, pp. 65-66.

Jacobson, Harlan, "Prince Rob," *Film Comment*, October 1987, pp. 58, 60-62, 64-65.

Lloyd, Robert, *American Film*, August, 1989, p. 28-33, 48.

Rafferty, Terrence, "The Current Cinema: Lies, Lies, and More Lies," *New Yorker*, August 7, 1989.

Reiner, Carl, interviewed in *Daily News Magazine* (New York), June 10, 1973.

Rosenthal, David, "Playboy Interview: Rob Reiner," *Playboy*, July, 1985, pp. 61-76, 158.

Schickel, Richard, "Close-Order Moral Drill," *Time*, December 14, 1992, p. 70.

Siskel, Gene, "'Meathead' Rob Reiner Meets and Defeats His Longtime Demons," *Chicago Tribune*, August 17, 1986, Section 13, pp. 6-7.

■ For More Information See

PERIODICALS

American Film, January/February, 1987, pp. 57-58.

Detroit Free Press, August 22, 1986.

Detroit News, August 29, 1986.

High Fidelity, November, 1985, pp. 69-70.

Los Angeles Times, March 8, 1984.

Macleans, October 5, 1987, p. 58; December 3, 1990, p. 88.

New Leader, March 25, 1985, pp. 20-21.

New Republic, April 8, 1985, pp. 24-25; August 21, 1989, pp. 26-27.

Newsweek, March 5, 1984, pp. 81-82; May 14, 1984, p. 69; August 25, 1986, p. 63; October 5, 1987, p. 85.

New York, August 18, 1986.

New Yorker, September 8, 1986, pp. 108-113; October 19, 1987; August 7, 1989.

New York Times, July 9, 1989.

People, September 1, 1986, p. 12; July 24, 1989, p. 13; December 10, 1990, pp. 14-15; December 17, 1990, p. 91; August 5, 1991, p. 13.

Rolling Stone, May 24, 1984, pp. 37-39; August 10, 1989, p. 32.

Time, March 5, 1984, p. 86; August 25, 1986; September 21, 1987, p. 74; July 31, 1989, pp. 65-66; December 10, 1990, p. 87; July 22, 1991, p. 55.

Washington Post, April 13, 1984; April 15, 1984; August 22, 1986.°

—*Sketch by Janet L. Hile*

Willo Davis Roberts

■ Personal

Born May 28, 1928, in Grand Rapids, MI; daughter of Clayton R. and Lealah (Gleason) Davis; married David W. Roberts (a building supply company manager, photographer, and writer), May 20, 1949; children: Kathleen, David M., Larrilyn (Lindquist), Christopher. *Education:* Graduated from high school in Pontiac, MI. *Religion:* Christian. *Hobbies and other interests:* Travel, playing the organ.

■ Addresses

Home—12020 West Engebretsen Rd., Granite Falls, WA 98252. *Agent*—Curtis Brown, 10 Astor Place, New York, NY 10019.

■ Career

Writer. Has worked in hospitals and doctors' offices; past co-owner of dairy farm. Lecturer and workshop leader at writers' conferences and schools; consultant, executive board of Pacific Northwest Writers' Conference. *Member:* Mystery Writers of America, Society of Children's Book Writers, Authors Guild, Authors League of America, Seattle Freelancers, Eastside Writers.

■ Awards, Honors

Notable Children's Trade Book citation, National Council for the Social Studies/Children's Book Council, 1977, Young Hoosier Book Award, Association for Indiana Media Educators, 1980, West Australian Young Readers Award, 1981, and Georgia Children's Book Award, University of Georgia, 1982, all for *Don't Hurt Laurie!*; Mark Twain Award, Missouri Library Association/Missouri Association of School Librarians, 1983, and California Young Readers Medal, California Reading Association, 1986, both for *The Girl with the Silver Eyes*; *Eddie and the Fairy Godpuppy* was named a West Virginia Children's Book Award honor book, 1987; Pacific Northwest Writers Conference Achievement Award, 1986, for body of work; Edgar Allen Poe Award, Mystery Writers of America, 1989, for *Megan's Island*; Washington State Governor's Award for contribution to the field of children's literature, 1990, for body of work; Mark Twain Award, Young Hoosier Book Award, South Carolina Children's Book Award, and Nevada Young Reader's Award, all for *Baby-Sitting is a Dangerous Job*; Outstanding Science Trade Book for Children citation, National Science Teachers Association/Children's Book Council, for *Sugar Isn't Everything*.

■ Writings

THE "BLACK PEARL" SERIES; ALL PUBLISHED BY POPULAR LIBRARY

The Dark Dowry, 1978.
The Stuart Strain, 1978.
The Cade Curse, 1978.
The Devil's Double, 1979.
The Radkin Revenge, 1979.
The Hellfire Heritage, 1979.
The Macomber Menace, 1980.
The Gresham Ghost, 1980.

JUVENILE FICTION

The View from the Cherry Tree, Atheneum, 1975.
Don't Hurt Laurie!, illustrated by Ruth Sanderson, Atheneum, 1977.
The Minden Curse, illustrated by Sherry Streeter, Atheneum, 1978.
More Minden Curses, illustrated by Streeter, Atheneum, 1980.
The Girl With the Silver Eyes (Junior Literary Guild selection), Atheneum, 1980.
House of Fear, Scholastic, 1983.
The Pet-Sitting Peril (Junior Guild selection), Atheneum, 1983.
No Monsters in the Closet, Atheneum, 1983.
Eddie and the Fairy Godpuppy, illustrated by Leslie Morrill, Atheneum, 1984.
Elizabeth, Scholastic, 1984.
Caroline, Scholastic, 1984.
Baby-Sitting is a Dangerous Job (Junior Literary Guild selection), Atheneum, 1985.
Victoria, Scholastic, 1985.
The Magic Book, Atheneum, 1986.
Sugar Isn't Everything Atheneum, 1987.
Megan's Island, Atheneum, 1988.
What Could Go Wrong? Atheneum, 1989.
Nightmare, Atheneum, 1989.
To Grandmother's House We Go, Atheneum, 1990.
Scared Stiff, Atheneum, 1991.
Dark Secrets, Fawcett/Juniper, 1991.
Jo and the Bandit, Atheneum, 1992.
What Are We Going to Do About David?, Atheneum, 1993.

ADULT FICTION

Murder at Grand Bay, Arcadia House, 1955.
The Girl Who Wasn't There, Arcadia House, 1957.
Murder is So Easy, Vega Books, 1961.
The Suspected Four, Vega Books, 1962.
Nurse Kay's Conquest, Ace Books, 1966.
Once a Nurse, Ace Books, 1966.
Nurse at Mystery Villa, Ace Books, 1967.
Return to Darkness, Lancer Books, 1969.

Devil Boy, New American Library, 1970.
Shroud of Fog, Ace Books, 1970.
The Waiting Darkness, Lancer Books, 1970.
Shadow of a Past Love, Lancer Books, 1970.
The Tarot Spell, Lancer Books, 1970.
The House at Fern Canyon, Lancer Books, 1970.
Invitation to Evil, Lancer Books, 1970.
The Terror Trap, Lancer Books, 1971.
King's Pawn, Lancer Books, 1971.
The Gates of Montrain, Lancer Books, 1971.
The Watchers, Lancer Books, 1971.
The Ghosts of Harrel, Lancer Books, 1971.
The Secret Lives of the Nurses, Pan, 1971, published in the United States as *The Nurses,* Ace Books, 1972.
Inherit the Darkness Lancer Books, 1972.
Nurse in Danger, Ace Books, 1972.
Becca's Child, Lancer Books, 1972.
Sing a Dark Song, Lancer Books, 1972.
The Face of Danger, Lancer Books, 1972.
Dangerous Legacy, Lancer Books, 1972.
Sinister Gardens, Lancer Books, 1972.
The M.D., Lancer Books, 1972.
Evil Children, Lancer Books, 1973.
The Gods in Green, Lancer Books, 1973.
Nurse Robin, Lennox Hill, 1973.
Didn't Anyone Know My Wife?, Putnam, 1974.
White Jade, Doubleday, 1975.
Key Witness, Putnam, 1975.
Expendable, Doubleday, 1976.
The Jaubert Ring, Doubleday, 1976.
Act of Fear, Doubleday, 1977.
Cape of Black Sands, Popular Library, 1977.
The House of Imposters, Popular Library, 1977.
Destiny's Women, Popular Library, 1980.
The Search for Willie, Popular Library, 1980.
The Face at the Window, Raven Press, 1981.
A Long Time to Hate, Avon, 1982.
The Gallant Spirit, Popular Library, 1982.
Days of Valor, Warner, 1983.
The Sniper, Doubleday, 1984.
Keating's Landing, Warner Books, 1984.
The Annalise Experiment, Doubleday, 1985.
Different Dream, Different Lands, Worldwide, 1985.
My Rebel, My Love, Pocket Books, 1986.
To Share a Dream, Worldwide, 1986.
Madawaska, Worldwide, 1988.

■ Sidelights

"Seconds before the windshield shattered into a crazed, opaque spider web pattern, Nick saw the terrified face that would remain forever imprinted on his mind: eyes wide and unseeing, mouth

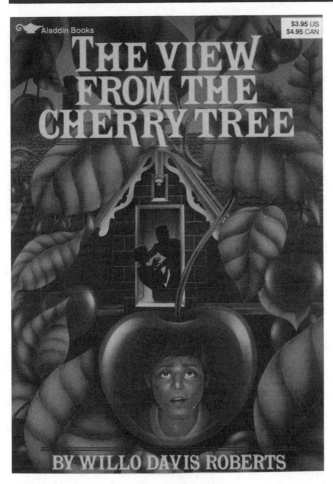

$3.95 US
$4.95 CAN

Aladdin Books

THE VIEW FROM THE CHERRY TREE

BY WILLO DAVIS ROBERTS

Rob must convince his family that he has witnessed a murder in Roberts's 1975 novel.

stretched in a grimace of horror. Nick didn't hear the scream, but he knew there had to be one.... Not that it mattered. The man who had fallen from the overpass onto the hood of Nick's old, blue Pinto was already dead, his neck broken when he struck the car."

In this, the opening to *Nightmare,* Willo Davis Roberts delivers immediate horror and surprise of the kind that few would like to feel in real life, but which many may love to experience vicariously through fiction. Who could imagine the horror of such a thing happening to them? And how can one put down the book until there is an explanation for why it did happen? How will things turn out? As a writer of suspense thrillers and mysteries for both young readers and adults, Roberts wastes no words in getting right at the action, a device, she suggests, that is imperative to the genre. "The opening is the most important part of the novel. This applies to almost every work of fiction, but particularly suspense novels," she writes in *The Writer* magazine. Roberts continues, "The opening has to

have that narrative hook, that grabber that makes a reader turn the page and become immediately absorbed in the story."

As readers become absorbed in *Nightmare,* they find Nick's suspicions of foul play confirmed when he takes off on an interstate trip in the family motorhome to visit his brother and finds that he and his stowaway passenger, Daisy, are being followed by two menacing bad guys who must be daringly eluded until the teen-aged pair can unravel the mystery of the "accident" at the overpass. Roberts explains in *The Writer* that she usually doesn't know in advance exactly how things will turn out in her mysteries: "It's more fun for me to write if the action develops out of the characters, when I say 'What would I do if I were confronted by this problem?' What I would actually do would be to get hysterical and call the cops, but one's protagonist must have more fortitude than that. What I want is for the characters to develop to the stage where they are 'real' people, and then act as sensibly or courageously as they can." Though *Nightmare*'s ending was deemed "a bit farfetched" by reviewer Ethel R. Twichell in *Horn Book,* the novel carries the kind of building suspense that is common to most of Roberts's work for young people.

Writing for Kids: Serendipitous Success

A productive author with a total of eighty-seven books to her credit, Roberts began her writing career with adult mystery novels, the first of which was published in 1955 (a time when she was working to raise and help support, with her husband David, her four children). From there—though mystery writing is the core of her work—she followed a genre writing path that led to "nurse novels," Gothics, and historical fiction and, beginning with *The View from the Cherry Tree,* to writing for kids.

The latter is something Roberts says she never intended to do. In various accounts, Roberts explains that though *Cherry Tree* was written as an adult suspense novel, her editor and agent felt it would fare better as a children's book. After about a year, Roberts relented and reworked it for a prospective audience of younger readers. Now, many critics consider the book a classic of its kind. "I hadn't anticipated the non-monetary rewards of writing for kids, such as the volume of fan mail," Roberts comments in an essay for the *Something About the Author Autobiography Series* (SAAS). "Adults write to an author primarily to tell her what she [or he] did wrong. Kids write to you for that, too, but more often they tell you what they love about your books. Their letters are warm and funny and poignant and wonderful." She continues, "I never had any trouble switching from adult to kids' books; I think in essence I've remained about eleven myself."

Roberts's books for young people now number twenty-five; more than half of them are mysteries. Others Roberts tomes deal with the problems that many children face, things like divorce, abuse, isolation, physical problems, or moving to a new town. As Roberts further explains in *SAAS*: "Children are still vulnerable; they have little control over their lives and the adults around them are not always aware of nor responsive to their fears and problems. They feel inadequate, awkward, shy, frightened, and they still respond to encouragement and love. I know about those things."

Difficulties of a Here-and-There Childhood

Roberts was born and raised in Michigan, spending winters in various towns in the lower part of the state, and most summers further north along Lake Michigan, where she developed a love for the woods and water. She demonstrated her storytelling ability at an early age: "I began to write as soon as I could put the stories on paper; before that I just made them up and told them to my younger sisters," she remarks in an essay for the *Fifth Book of Junior Authors and Illustrators*. Her father, whom she describes in *SAAS* as a man with "a quick mind and a quick tongue" and quite a storyteller in his own right, supported the family by doing various kinds of jobs, including truck driving and running trolling boats. "We always ate, but we never had anything in a material sense. It didn't bother him if his family lived in a shack as long as we were warm and had food in the house," Roberts recalls in *SAAS*.

The family never stayed in one town for long and the frequent moves—Roberts attended as many as six schools during her fourth grade year—resulted in a number of difficulties for the author. Not only were there gaps in her education—such as never fully learning the multiplication tables—but it was also hard to make and maintain friendships with other kids her age.

For the young Roberts, reading and writing were both a joy and a refuge. In *SAAS*, she cites *Black Beauty, Heidi, Anderson's* and *Grimm's Fairy Tales*, and *Hans Brinker, or the Silver Skates* as early favorites; later on she enjoyed the "Nancy Drew"

and "Hardy Boys" series, as well as murder mysteries that her parents had on hand. Libraries were a treasure trove for her. Roberts writes in *SAAS* that by age ten, she had read every juvenile book in the libraries of two towns: "When adults assured me that these school days were the best ones of my life, I nearly despaired. It's possible, though, that if school hadn't been so miserable, and moving around so traumatic as it was, I wouldn't have spent nearly as much time writing. . . . I was writing my own stories for two basic reasons at that point. They entertained me when I couldn't find enough books to read, and they took me out of the real world when other people around me made me feel inadequate and without worth."

At age seventeen, Roberts conceived of and began writing a historical novel, and even though she eventually decided that she wasn't yet up to the task, she didn't give up on that early, original idea. Some thirty-five years later, she sold a proposal based on it to a publisher, and, because of the story's length, it was eventually published as two books: *The Gallant Spirit* and *Days of Valor*.

Writing a Living

Once she graduated from high school, Roberts began to seriously consider writing as a way to eventually earn a living. It was at this time that she met David Roberts, who had just spent three years in the Navy and was on his way to the West Coast. The couple's courtship was unusual in that they did not go out on as much as one single date; but after five months of letter writing, Roberts joined her husband-to-be in Oregon where he had found a job, and the two were married. Roberts writes in *SAAS* that though "we would never recommend our methods to anyone else (especially not our kids!) we are still happily married . . . and we're still best friends."

The Robertses would have to draw on that friendship for strength during some of the hard times ahead of them. With a family of four children—Kathleen, David, Larrilyn, and Christopher—to raise, Roberts found little time for her writing. For twelve years, the family operated a dairy farm in California's San Joaquin Valley. Despite long days spent in hard work, the farm fell into debt, largely because of factors the Robertses could not control, like destructive weather conditions and livestock illnesses. In the midst of the family's struggles, however, Roberts's had her first publishing success: she sold a mystery for adults, *Murder at Grand Bay*, for $150. Soon after, however, Roberts made the realization—a devastating one at the time—that she couldn't yet earn enough money with her writing to help support the family.

Roberts got a job at a small local hospital where, as she tells C. Herb Williams in *Writer's Digest,* "I did everything from dispatching the ambulance to processing paper work in the emergency room." She also managed to sell several more mysteries to publishers. In a "side" benefit, while working at the hospital, Roberts became familiar with "nurse novels," which were essentially Gothic-like suspense stories that featured young aides as their heroines. Using some of her newly gained knowledge about the workings of hospitals, Roberts wrote and sold several tales for $1,000 advances before the demand for the genre dried up and publishers stopped buying them.

After the Robertses left the dairy farm, both worked at full-time jobs, he as a manager of a building supply company and she in doctors' offices. Undaunted by circumstances that left her with little creative time, Roberts continued to produce saleable novels by writing at night. "I used to come home from work exhausted, feed the kids, and lie down for an hour, setting the timer so I wouldn't pass out for the night. I got up around 8:30 or 9 and worked until 11 every night. It got to the place where I told my family, 'Don't bother me unless you're bleeding,'" she tells Williams.

Educated by Life

Roberts's long list of published books indicates that her hard work paid off: in the 1970s alone, she had more than forty books published. "I was lucky that my husband, David, was always supportive. Without that, everything would have been so much harder," she admits in *SAAS.* Once the children were grown and on their own and Roberts had enough book contracts to support them for a time, her husband retired from his job and the two of them began travelling. When not on the road, they spent time at home on their country place in Washington. Looking back, Roberts says in *SAAS,* she has few regrets about her life. In fact, she indicates her struggles were opportunities to learn and grow and that she doesn't feel shortchanged that she never got a college education. "I urge young people to get as much education as they can manage. But I would also say to those for whom college is not an option that they needn't despair over that," she advises in *SAAS.* "Learning can be done anywhere, through reading and through life's experiences. It's possible to have multiple degrees,

for instance, and have no understanding of what other people go through, how they struggle just to survive and to cope with the mishaps life dishes out."

In fact, some of Roberts's life experiences, particularly those from family life, have made their way into her books. Sometimes it's in the small details, like the Robertses' Airedales Susie and Rudy, who show up as book characters' pets. Sometimes those experiences become the basis for plots themselves. A good example is Roberts's first book for young people, *The View from the Cherry Tree,* which is about Rob, eleven-year-old boy who climbs to his favorite hiding place high up in the crook of a cherry tree limb in order to get away from the household brouhaha created by preparations for his sister's wedding. While in the tree, he witnesses the mysterious murder of the cranky old woman next door, with whom his past encounters have nearly always gotten him into trouble. When Rob tries to tell various family members and friends that the old woman's death was no accident, no one believes him—except for the actual murderer, who is among them. Rob must then summon up all the courage he can in order to outwit and expose the murderer on his own. Roberts writes in *SAAS* that she got the idea for *Cherry Tree* while her own daughter, Larrilyn, was preparing for her wedding: "The book was based largely on things that really happened (exaggerated, naturally) and my kids said I should be ashamed to take money for the book because they provided all the material."

It took Roberts only two weeks to write *The View from the Cherry Tree.* She says the only other book that came to her as easily was *Nightmare,* and, again, in this book one can detect the connection to the author's own experiences: Roberts and her husband—who now does freelance photography and writing on outdoors and wildlife subjects—do their extensive travelling in a motorhome like the one described in careful detail in *Nightmare* (theirs, however, is equipped with an office and computer so that they can write while on the road). And while they have had some adventures during their travels (like the grizzly bear that attacked the trailer in Alaska), the couple have not experienced any adventures like the dark one that Nick has while driving his interstate nightmare. As in all fiction, the author's imagination picks up where real life experiences leave off.

Roberts's books for young readers bear a great many similarities to each other. They feature young characters (many of them red-headed) in unfamiliar surroundings. Either the young protagonists have just moved to a new town or have come to stay with grandparents or other relatives whom they don't know well. They soon find themselves thrust, quite unexpectedly, into difficult—and in the mysteries, usually dangerous—circumstances. Adults either can't be relied upon for action or can only be helpful to a point, so the kids use their own gumption and ingenuity to find a way out of their predicaments. Many of the stories feature big, old houses, the kind that are likely to be haunted, ones with towers or turrets that figure prominently in the youngsters' attempts to thwart crooks.

Keeping Readers in Suspense

But the most common and more general element of all Roberts's books is the suspense they create, that mixed feeling of anxiety and uncertainty that a reader gets, which grows steadily in anticipation of a story's resolution. When one picks up a mystery, one expects suspense, and reviewers recommend Roberts's mysteries most often because they are

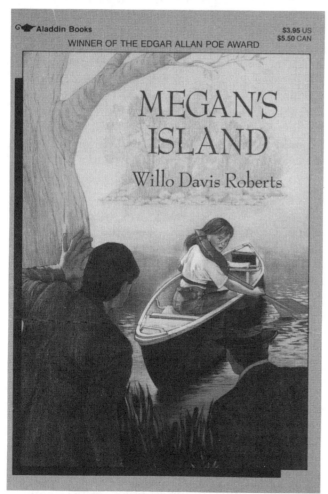

Megan attempts to uncover the secrets behind her family's frequent moves in this 1988 novel.

solidly constructed and sustain a high level of suspense (regardless of how believable the plots may or may not be). Along the way, Roberts provides clues and motives that both create question marks and make it possible for alert readers to try to figure out the mystery. In *Nightmare*, for instance, what might a chain of soda can tabs Nick absently picks up off the ground at the scene of the accident have to do with his being followed later on? Why, in *More Minden Curses*, would two old ladies with few resources see to it that their many cats be decked out in glittery collars? How does picking up a discarded newspaper in an airport make three children kidnapping victims in *What Could Go Wrong?*

"These days many so-called mysteries are not mysteries at all, in the sense that you have a puzzle to solve," Roberts explains in her *The Writer* article. Her mysteries, in which she provides puzzles aplenty, range in their intensity levels. On the "high" end are books like *Cherry Tree* and *Nightmare*, in which kids' accidental involvement in a mystery or crime actually puts them in peril. In *Baby-Sitting is a Dangerous Job*, thirteen-year-old Darcy takes a baby-sitting job for the children in a wealthy family. She soon finds there is more to the job than she bargained for. Not only are the three kids a handful, but they are also being watched by two suspicious men who turn out to be kidnappers. Darcy and her charges are kept prisoners-for-ransom in a remote old house until they can come up with a scheme to both alert the police to their location and foil their captors. A reviewer for *School Library Journal* deemed the novel "a solid suspense story" in which Roberts gives "a very resourceful young girl plenty of chances to show her mettle."

Megan's Island also features resourceful young characters, but ones who are in a different kind of pinch. Megan and her younger brother Sandy begin their summer vacation before school is even out when they are abruptly packed up one night by their single-parent mother and taken on an all-night drive to their grandfather's lake cottage in Minnesota. The children's mother, who gives no reason for the family's sudden departure and seems afraid, makes arrangements for their household things to be put in storage, and goes away to look for a job and a place for them to live in a new town. Though the family's past moves from town to town did not make Megan suspicious, it becomes clear to her now that the trio have been—and still are—on the run. A mysterious situation becomes more so when one by one, Megan begins discovering clues that indicate there are secrets about her family's past. Then strange men come poking around the place, with one even asking questions about red-haired kids like Megan and Sandy. With the help of a newly made friend, Ben, the children claim one of the lake's many islands, where they build a tree house for fun and end up using it as a hiding place when their pursuers threaten their safety.

In a *Junior Literary Guild* article, Roberts explains that she got the idea for *Megan's Island* while she and her husband were on a 1986 research trip to Canada that took them through the area of the St. Lawrence River's Thousand Islands. It reminded her of childhood days in northern Michigan. "I was so enchanted by these islands," she writes, "some of them barely large enough for a person to stand on, many the size to hold a house, that I asked my husband to take pictures of them." (The photos were later used by illustrator Leslie Morrill to create the book's cover.) According to a review of *Megan's Island* by Zena Sutherland in the *Bulletin of the Center for Children's Books*, "fluid writing style, the excitement of the action," and "solidity of the characterization" make up for an "occasionally turgid" plot.

Lightening it Up

In some of her mysteries, Roberts uses a lighter touch, incorporating humor and creating mysteries that unfold within the ordinary routines of daily life, rather than ones that interrupt or occur outside those normal circumstances. In *The Minden Curse*, young Danny Minden comes to stay with his grandfather and aunt in a small lake town while his father is overseas. He and Gramps seem to be cursed with the "ability" to always be on the scene when accidents or strange things happen, and in this case, it's a bank robbery and dog-napping. The follow-up book, *More Minden Curses*, is described by a critic in *Booklist* as the "more cohesive tale" of the two, in which Danny starts school, after having been tutored for years while on the road with his photographer father. In the book, Danny becomes involved with the town's elderly Caspitorian sisters (the "Cat Ladies"), whom someone is trying to force out of their home because the family treasure is supposedly hidden there; he also has to try to kidnap the sisters' nasty cat "Killer" as a rite of initiation into his new friends' secret club. In addition to the mystery action it provides, the book delves into the difficulties of making friends and settling into a new place.

Roberts uses a similar formula—children who must prove themselves after being uprooted and sent to stay with relatives—in *Jo and the Bandit,* but puts a twist on it by giving it a historical setting. The story takes place in 1860s Texas, when the grandmother who is raising Josephine and her little brother Andrew dies, and the children are sent to stay with their rough-edged bachelor Uncle Matthew until they can be taken in by an aunt. On their way, their stagecoach is ambushed by bandits, including a young red-headed one who mysteriously returns Josephine's stolen locket once she and her brother are settled in at Uncle Matthew's. Jo uses her artistic abilities to draw wanted posters of the bandits and becomes involved in a potentially dangerous scheme to trick and catch the outlaws; she must also find a way to keep the kind young bandit from being convicted along with them. Reviewer Jeanette Larson, writing in *School Library Journal,* suggested that though the story's pace may be slow in spots, "it is refreshing to find a strong-minded, independent female protagonist in

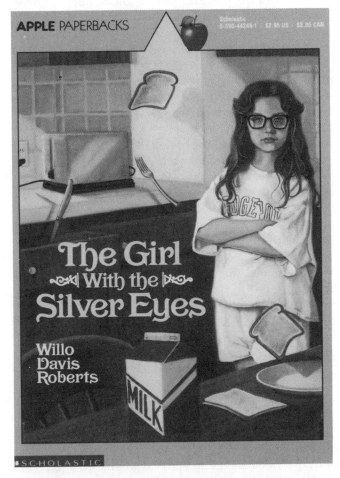

In this award-winning 1980 work, Katie struggles with her friends' reactions to her telepathic and telekinetic powers.

a genre [Westerns] usually overwhelmed by bonnets and gingham.''

Other "lighter" mysteries by Roberts have supernatural elements to them. Most notable is *The Girl with the Silver Eyes*, winner of the Mark Twain Award and the California Young Reader Medal. Roberts says in a *Junior Literary Guild* article that, like *Cherry Tree*, *The Girl with the Silver Eyes* was also first imagined as an adult suspense novel: "At first, editors (of adult books) felt that my young characters were too precocious, their vocabularies too advanced, etc. for their ages. I finally convinced them that these were the only kinds of children I knew, and that there were such kids, like my own, and eventually these were accepted.''

Katie, the girl with the silver eyes, is a good example of an advanced child who is not readily accepted by her peers. Aside from her strange eyes, she is set apart from other children her age by her above-average intelligence, her ability to communicate in a telepathic way with animals, and her telekinetic powers, which allow her to move objects without touching them. Almost everyone finds her unsettling, including her own divorced mother, with whom she's just been reunited after living for a time with a stern grandmother. She makes friends with Mrs. Michaelmas, an eccentric older woman in the apartment building, who lends her books and has no trouble believing in Katie's special powers. She consoles Katie: "Seems to me you're better than most folks. And maybe that's it; they don't want anyone to be better, or smarter, or more powerful in any way. They're afraid of people who are different, so they make fun of them. Attack them. It's foolish, but it's the way people are." Another new friend—the paper boy Jackson Jones—later comes to Katie's aid when a new neighbor, Mr. Cooper, starts asking too many questions and the young heroine begins to think that she might be in danger. Katie later learns of a drug that her mother and other women took while they were pregnant; she also finds there are other kids like her. When all of these kids come together to help Katie, they discover, for the first time, how it feels not to be the only one.

Dreaming the Dreams of an Underdog

Like her character Mrs. Michaelmas, Roberts expresses an empathy for those who are different, perhaps because as a youngster she too felt set apart from her peers. In *SAAS*, she writes about "underdogs": "Such people are everywhere, though they don't wear labels on their foreheads so

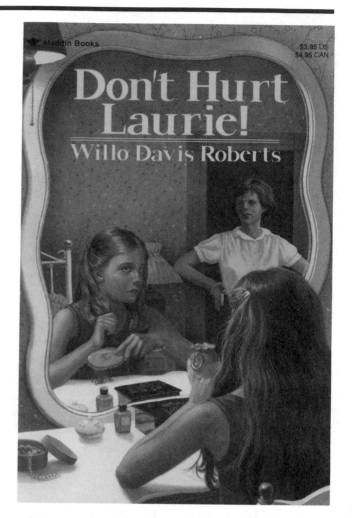

Roberts received the Young Hoosiers Book Award and the West Australian Young Readers Award for her 1977 book about child abuse.

you would notice them. They tend not to push themselves forward, not to create a fuss to win you over to their side. But oh! how lovely it is for them when anyone expresses understanding or sympathy. I often write from the viewpoint of the underdog because it comes so naturally. I've been there. Plain. Poor. Bright, but too timid to claim any honors or recognition for that. Dreaming so many dreams, and all of them, it seemed, unattainable.''

In her second book for young people, *Don't Hurt Laurie!*, Roberts takes on the difficult subject of child abuse by writing about a bright girl with a few simple dreams that are, quite literally, beaten down by her mother, Annabelle. Laurie's father walked out when she was very young. Because Laurie reminds Annabelle of him, whenever her mother gets angry or has one of her migraines, she takes it out on her daughter by beating, burning or cutting her. When hospital or school personnel get suspicious about Laurie's frequent injuries or Annabelle's explanations about how clumsy her daughter is, Annabelle and Laurie move to a new place.

The abuse continues even after Annabelle remarries. And although she is able to keep the secret from her travelling salesman husband, it's not long before Laurie's new stepbrother Tim and her next-door friend George figure out what is going on. In the past, Laurie has been afraid that no adult would believe her story. But when things get so out of hand that Annabelle beats Laurie in Tim's presence, the children flee to the safety of Tim's grandmother's home, where the truth finally comes out. Annabelle is confronted and is taken away for psychiatric help. The ending implies that they will someday be able to be rejoined as a family. "I was not an abused child, but my father was, and I had several friends who were, also," Roberts writes in *SAAS*. "*Don't Hurt Laurie!* came out of their experiences."

The book elicited varying responses from critics. Judith Viorst, writing in *The New York Times Book Review*, says that "its subject matter is inevitably lurid, sadistic, and violent" and deemed it ultimately not "necessary" for young readers. A reviewer for *Horn Book*, however, claims that "the book's strength lies in the realistic and believable portrayal of the young girl's frustration and helplessness." And a reviewer for the *Bulletin of the Center for Children's Books* cites the novel for its "excellent characterization" and an approach that "is both realistic about the problem and realistically encouraging about its alleviation." According to Roberts, the book is still popular with kids. "Librarians have told me it is among the most stolen books in their libraries, presumably by battered kids who can't afford to own it but want to read and re-read it," she explains.

Roberts's most recent book for kids is *What Are We Going to Do About David?*. Marilyn Long Graham, writing in *School Library Journal*, calls it the "fine story" of "an introspective, keenly sensitive child" with a plot that "unfolds at a brisk pace, with the concerns of a preadolescent boy convincingly portrayed." When David's parents decide to separate, he gets sent to stay with his grandmother, Ruthie, who lives in a small town along the Washington coast. There, with Ruthie's nurture and the companionship of her energetic dog and a new friend—who is disfigured and has problems of his own to confront—David begins to overcome his feelings of loneliness, homesickness, and worry about his family situation. He is even able to stand up for himself before his parents when the time comes for him to make a decision about his future.

"One way to hold your readers is to make them care what happens to the protagonist," Roberts explains in *The Writer*. "Make them fear for her, laugh with her, cry for her. Make the reader identify with your characters, feel the sorrow, the pain, the fear, the thumping heart and the labored breathing." She continues, "A character not only can, but should, have flaws that make him human."

The young characters in Roberts's novels ultimately find their own ways of overcoming their personal limitations and obstacles. For several of them—David included—books and writing provide a good way to cope. For Roberts, who has persevered through many obstacles throughout her life using her natural love of those very things for both pleasure and profit, the writing life has proved to be a good one. Her advice to would-be writers is also about practice and perseverance. In *SAAS*, she writes, "I do think it's very important to write regularly and to set priorities that allow this, if you ever want to be published. It's also essential to develop such a strong belief in what you want to do that you get thick-skinned about criticism of your dreams." With her own children also writing and having work published and her grandchildren showing promise, it seems that it is possible to pass on the love of a writing life. As the author tells Williams, "If you reach a point where you can make a living doing something you really enjoy, you're ahead of 99 percent of the rest of the world."

■ Works Cited

Review of *Baby-Sitting is a Dangerous Job*, *School Library Journal*, May, 1985.

Review of *Don't Hurt Laurie!*, *Bulletin of the Center for Children's Books*, June, 1977.

Review of *Don't Hurt Laurie!*, *Horn Book*, August, 1977.

Graham, Marilyn Long, review of *What Are We Going to Do About David?*, *School Library Journal*, April, 1993.

Larson, Jeanette, review of *Jo and the Bandit*, *School Library Journal*, July, 1992.

Review of *More Minden Curses*, *Booklist*, June 15, 1980.

Roberts, Willo Davis, *The Girl with the Silver Eyes*, Atheneum, 1980.

Roberts, Willo Davis, essay in *Junior Literary Guild*, September, 1980.

Roberts, Willo Davis, essay in *Fifth Book of Junior Authors and Illustrators*, edited by Sally Holmes Holtze, Wilson, 1983.

Roberts, Willo Davis, essay in *Junior Literary Guild*, April-September, 1988.

Roberts, Willo Davis, *Nightmare*, Atheneum, 1989.

Roberts, Willo Davis, essay in *Something About the Author Autobiography Series*, Volume 8, Gale, 1989.

Roberts, Willo Davis, "Writing a Successful Suspense Thriller," *The Writer*, February, 1990.

Sutherland, Zena, review of *Megan's Island*, *Bulletin of the Center for Children's Books*, April, 1988.

Twichell, Ethel R., review of *Nightmare, Horn Book*, November, 1989.

Viorst, Judith, review of *Don't Hurt Laurie!*, *New York Times Book Review*, April 17, 1977.

Williams, C. Herb, "The Writing Life: This Willo Isn't Weeping," *Writer's Digest*, August, 1981.

—Sketch by Tracy J. Sukraw

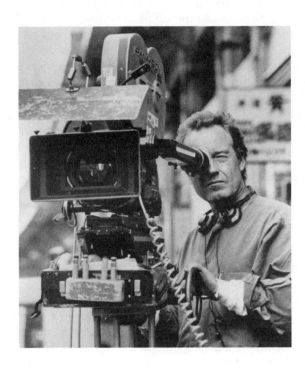

Ridley Scott

■ Personal

Born November 30, 1937, in South Shields, Northumberland, County Durham, Britain; brother of film director Tony; married with three children. *Education:* Studied at West Hartlepool College of Art, and at the Royal College of Art, London.

■ Addresses

Agent—c/o International Creative Management (ICM), 8899 Beverly Boulevard, Los Angeles, CA 90048.

■ Career

Film and commercial director. Set designer for the British Broadcasting Corporation (BBC); director for BBC-TV, including episodes of *Z-Cars*, 1966, and *The Informer*, 1966-67; founder, Ridley Scott Associates Production Company (commercial production company), 1967—. *Member:* Directors Guild of America.

■ Awards, Honors

Special Jury Prize, Cannes Film Festival, 1977, for *The Duellists;* numerous awards for commercials, including the Golden Lion, Venice Film Festival, 1984.

■ Films

The Duellists, Paramount, 1977.
Alien, Brandywine-Shusett/Twentieth Century-Fox, 1979.
Blade Runner, Warner Bros., 1982, re-released as *Blade Runner: The Director's Cut* (including some new material and deleting voiceover narration), 1992.
Legend, Twentieth Century-Fox/Universal,1985.
(And executive producer) *Someone to Watch Over Me*, Columbia, 1987.
Black Rain, Paramount Pictures, 1989.
(Coproducer with Mimi Polk) *Thelma & Louise*, MGM-Pathe Entertainment, 1991.
1492: Conquest of Paradise, Paramount Pictures, 1992.

Also director of *Boy on a Bicycle* (film short), 1965.

■ Sidelights

Some film directors shun the commercial aspect of their product, preferring to stress the artistic side of their work; Ridley Scott, however, revels in it. Lush visuals and a fast-moving camera make Scott's films immediately betray his direction, whether it's the arresting Orwellian *1984*-influenced advertisement for Apple Computers, or the all-out, heart-stopping space horror feature *Alien.* Even with his successful career as a director of feature films, Scott continues to make occasional commercials, or "pocket versions of feature films," as he likes to describe advertisements. His consistently elaborate and astonishing sets, the meticulous attention to detail, and his heavy stylization have made him one of the most influential filmmakers in the United States; paradoxically, critics have taken his work to task for these very qualities.

Scott grew up in the northeastern, industrial section of Britain. He was drawn to movies early. Recollecting his first cinematic experience at age five, Scott told Michael Buckley of *Films in Review* that "it was a swashbuckler, *The Black Swan* [a 1942 Tyrone Power epic]. I had to be torn out of my seat, my fingers pried loose—and that was after sitting through it twice."

Scott was attracted to the visual arts, and studied painting at the West Hartlepool School of Art for several years before electing to pursue the advertising-illustration program rather than the fine arts program. He then moved on to the Royal College of Art in London, where he studied advertising and graphic design. Scott also learned filmmaking during his three years there, and in his last year—1965—he directed his first film, a short entitled *Boy on a Bicycle.* This thirty-minute movie featured the director's younger brother, Tony and their father and was shot in South Shields and West Hartlepool. Writing in the London *Sunday Times Magazine,* Gordon Burn noted that this film was "directly autobiographical in a way that none of his subsequent films have been." According to *Film and Filming,* the film is no longer available; a spokeswoman for the British Film Institute, which helped to finance the movie, said that Scott came and took all the prints away. In the meantime, Tony Scott has gone from acting in his brother's film to his own successful directoral career, a career which includes such popular hits as *Beverly Hills Cop* and *Top Gun.*

Following the completion of his studies, Scott won a travel scholarship in design that took him to New York; once there, he worked for documentary filmmakers. When he returned to London, Scott spent three years laboring as a set designer for the BBC. Speaking with Martin Kasindorf in *New York Newsday,* Scott remembered that: "They gave me a production course to give me insight into production problems. They meant me to go back as a senior designer, but once I'd done that side of it, of course, I wanted to direct."

Scott got started in television commercials after an advertising agency saw his BBC sets and requested that he direct a spot. Scott quickly showed himself to be an extremely gifted visual persuader. In 1984, *Films and Filming* praised him as the British director who "raised the level of the advertising film to an art form." Scott has made some 3,000 commercials since he founded his production company, Ridley Scott Associates, in 1967. Writing in *American Film* in 1979, Harlan Kennedy and Nigel Andrews claimed that "Scott is one of the few television-commercial directors who has an instantly recognizable style. Light pours across the screen in a kind of phosphorescent mist; heavy backlighting and the use of incense smoke as a filter to create a nostalgic-romantic ambiance.

One of Scott's best-known commercials—for a brand of British brown bread—is set in an antique bakery almost literally shrouded in the mists of time. That was the same year that his *Share the Fantasy* advertisement for Chanel No.5 alerted viewers to his deft use of fantastic and suggestive imagery. In the Chanel ad, a woman lies perched on the edge of a pool dressed in a revealing swimsuit. A man appears at the far end of the pool and swims toward her as a woman's voice intones: "I am made of blue sky and golden light, and I will feel this way forever." In 1986, Christine Dugas ventured the opinion in *Business Week* that "this spot probably paved the way for today's creative revolution." Scott later caused a sensation in America with his attention-grabbing spot to introduce the Macintosh line of Apple computers, a commercial that *Business Week* termed a "mini-epic." In an interview with that magazine's Barbara Rosen, Scott remarked that it can take between one and ten days to film a commercial, compared with several weeks or months on a feature film. As he told Rosen: "The advantage with advertising is you don't have to live with something for months on end."

Making the Jump from Commercials to Features

Scott's first foray into full-length filmmaking was in 1977, when British producer David Puttnam enlisted him to direct *The Duellists.* This lavish period piece, which was based on a short story by Joseph Conrad entitled *The Duel,* details a series of duels between two French officers during the Napoleonic era. Scott chose Harvey Keitel to play Feraud, a commoner who challenges nobleman D'Hubert (Keith Carradine) to a match following a trifling incident about which Feraud takes offense. Up-

Scott used his fine arts training to create a frightening and claustrophobic setting for the 1979 science fiction/horror film, *Alien*.

holding the aristocratic code of honor, D'Hubert accepts and during the course of Napoleon's rise to power, the men carry out their feud.

The film was praised for its stunning tableaux and won the illustrious award for best first feature at the Cannes Film Festival in 1977. The critics had more mixed feelings. Molly Haskell noted in *New York* magazine that Scott had created "what amounts to an impersonal catalog of late-eighteenth century and early nineteenth century French painting," and she blamed him for overkill, claiming that the director "ODs [overdoses] on the cinematic luxuries of landscapes and period details." Taking a very different tack, Vincent Canby wrote in the *New York Times* that the film was "marvelous" in every way. The critic went out of his way to laud Keitel and Carradine as "splendid," claiming that "what one carries away from the film is a memory of almost indescribable beauty, of landscapes at dawn, of overcrowded, murky interiors, of underlit hallways and brilliantly sunlit

gardens. It's not a frivolous prettiness, but an evocation of time and place through images that are virtually tactile, and which give real urgency to this curious tale."

Alien, Scott's next project, blended the science fiction and horror genres to produce one of the biggest hits of the 1979 summer season. Speaking with Mary Blume of the *Los Angeles Times*, Scott noted that the project appealed to him because it didn't have the usual hallmarks of the genre: "The script is so simple, clean, and powerful. There's none of the silly, intellectual speculations you get in sci-fi." *Alien*, which stars Sigourney Weaver and Tom Skerrit as part of a seven-person crew of a commercial intergalactic ship named the *Nostromo*, details the events that follow the ship's response to a distress signal from an uncharted planet. When the crew lands, they find an alien spacecraft that unleashes a Pandora's box of appalling, slimy and relentless creatures bent on using available humans as hosts for further breeding.

Scott incorporated his art early training into his pre-production work on the movie, largely by planning certain aspects of the working schedule in advance. As he told Buckley, "I started painting quite seriously when I was twelve years old. The seven years in art school was time well-spent. On *Alien,* we nearly doubled the budget because I drew storyboards that enabled the producers to see other elements which would make the film very interesting and, therefore, worth the investment." Along with his storyboard planning, Scott commissioned elaborate sets from surrealist painter H.R.Giger (sets which, in retrospect, have come to be regarded as works of art themselves). The studio balked at the director's original *film noir* ending, according to *Films in Review*'s Buckley: "In the unfilmed version, the creature jams in the door of the shuttle and boomerangs. It tears Ripley's (Weaver's) head off, ejects her body, assumes her seat, presses some buttons and—perfectly mimicking her voice—gives her last speech. It then settles back and *waits* for the landing." Speaking to Andrews and Kennedy, Scott described the film as "unpretentious," adding that it was "very violent, yet a lot of character came through, and I just felt

it was an amazing piece of entertainment. Also, to me it is more than a horror film, it is a film about terror."

Following his success with a large budget and special-effects-heavy film, Warner Brothers and the Ladd Company chose Scott to take charge of *Blade Runner,* an ambitious $30 million project. Based on Philip K. Dick's 1968 science-fiction novel *Do Androids Dream of Electric Sheep?,* the story takes place in a United States of the near future in which nearly everyone has escaped to "Offworld," as the outer planets are known. The Earth these settlers have left behind is plagued by worker robots who have fled there rather than serve as drones elsewhere and who must now be destroyed. Bounty hunters, among them Rick Deckard (Harrison Ford), do this unpleasant and dangerous job for hefty fees.

Capitalizing on his screen design background, Scott commissioned sets that treated viewers to an amalgam of *film noir,* cartoons, expressionism, sci-fi, and even punk styles, creating what Kennedy termed "a densely figured kinetic tapestry" and "Scrap-Heap Futurism." In an interview with

Blade Runner, a 1982 thriller starring Harrison Ford, borrows from a variety of styles, including expressionism and cartoons.

Kennedy, Scott admitted that "my initial reaction on reading the script was that it seemed on the surface another futuristic script, and I figured I'd just done that and I ought to change gear. But when I thought about it more, I thought it's not *really* futuristic. It's set 40-years on, but it could take place in any time slot." He added that "the film isn't 'predictive,' if that's the word; it's a kind of comic strip. I still relate very strongly to that kind of material, to comic strips and comic-strip characters."

The critics had mixed reactions to *Blade Runner*, with the *New Yorker*'s Pauline Kael claiming that "Scott doesn't seem to have a grasp of how to use words as part of the way a movie moves. *Blade Runner* is a suspenseless thriller; it appears to be a victim of its own imaginative use of hardware and miniatures and mattes." On the other hand, *Time*'s Richard Corliss said "the movie delivers" and noted that "the pleasures of texture have rarely been so savory." Writing in the *New Republic*, Stanley Kauffmann praised *Blade Runner* for being "splendid, a strong argument for the 'Style Is All' thesis."

A Fairy Tale & Two Modern-Day Thrillers

Scott delved deep into mythic fantasy for his next project, a fairy-tale epic called *Legend*. At the center of this allegory of good and evil is Jack o'the Green, a young swain (Tom Cruise) and his princess love, Lili (Mia Sara). Lili and Jack are separated when she catches the eye of the Prince of Darkness (Tim Curry) who tries to take her for his bride. Aided by assorted elves and pixies, Jack eventually manages to rescue her. The approximately $30 million picture was shot in the Pinewood Sound Studios in Britain and included Scott's trademark elaborate sets, special effects, and ornate costumes. Reviewers were not impressed, however, and the ticket-buying public stayed away also. In the *Nation*, Terrence Rafferty found *Legend* stylized "in a way that emphasized, rather than disguised, the naïveté of Scott's imagination; he went all the way with the dumb, self-consciously 'mythic' ideas in William Hjortsberg's script, and the intensity of his conviction made the movie a true folly, more embarrassing than if it had been directed by someone less gifted or committed."

After moving back and forth between the future and the past, Scott chose to make a film about contemporary society. *Someone to Watch Over Me* is an urban thriller with a love triangle at its core. Mike Keegan (Tom Berenger), a Queens detective,

In 1985, Mia Sara starred with Tom Cruise and Tim Curry in the mythic fantasy, *Legend*.

is assigned to protect beautiful, wealthy Claire Gregory (Mimi Rogers) who has witnessed a murder. Complicating matters is Keegan's wife and son—and the yet-to-be-apprehended killer. In *Time*, Corliss found that Scott successfully created a "Deluxe color version of an Old Hollywood vision: Manhattan in the '40s, with its twin thrills of glamour and romance." Corliss noted, however, that: "For all its tech-noir gloss, this is still a traditional thriller, eager to deliver moral lessons with its frissons." In the *New Yorker*, Kael described *Someone to Watch Over Me* as "all moods.... Prodigious planning and editing have gone into them, along with a lot of smoke, Gothic lighting, and interior decoration. They give the picture a high-class hauntedness. You drift into it. You can even trance out on it, because Scott works like a visual hypnotist: he seduces you by the repetitive monotony of the stimuli." In *New York* magazine, David Denby accused Scott of losing himself "in décor and visual clutter—the steam hissing onto Manhattan's streets, the Disneyland of crystal, mirrors, and windows in Rogers's apartment."

Scott's next film *Black Rain*, was also set in the present and again featured a New York police officer as its protagonist—this time, however, in Japan. Michael Douglas played detective Nick Conklin, who, along with his partner, is assigned to escort Sato (Yusaku Matsuda), a Japanese gang leader, back to Osaka. There, they are hoodwinked into handing him over to his henchmen, who con the cops into believing that they are police officers. Conklin and his partner manage to alienate both the Japanese and the American authorities as they attempt to recapture Sato. For the first time, Scott took on overtly politically charged subjects; the black rain was the combination of ash and rain that fell on Hiroshima and Nagasaki in the aftermath of the nuclear bombs that were dropped on Japan in 1945. Despite its popular success in Japan, American critics were dour about *Black Rain*. Kauffmann described it as "the sort of film in which no trouble is spared to get every physical detail realistically right but in which there is small realism in action or character ... Ridley Scott is ... justly known as a pictorialist, but here some of his striking shots are counterproductive." In *MacLean's*, Brian D.Johnson declared *Black Rain* "a thriller with few thrills, just some moments of grisly violence.... And after a while, *Black Rain* begins to resemble an overblown travelogue, a nasty foreign escapade unredeemed by humor or sex."

Two Strong Women & A Famous Explorer

Sex and humor—and two strong women characters—were in ample supply in Scott's next effort, *Thelma & Louise*. The road movie details the story of Thelma (Geena Davis), married to a loutish carpet salesman who treats her like something the cat dragged in, and Louise (Susan Sarandon), a

Geena Davis and Susan Sarandon starred as two strong women who have a series of adventures in the 1991 motion picture, *Thelma and Louise*.

jaded waitress whose decent boyfriend refuses to make a commitment. The two pals decide to escape from their humdrum lives for the weekend at a friend's cabin. The duo's relatively tame adventure becomes wild when they stop at a roadhouse for a drink and Thelma's innocent flirting leads her to near rape in the parking lot. She is saved when Louise rescues her at gunpoint—then, when he abuses her verbally, Louise kills the attacker in cold blood. On the lam, the women encounter various other characters along the way and make several discoveries about themselves and each other, staving off their inevitable capture until they wind up getting chased by the FBI into the Grand Canyon, only to throw themselves over the edge in a double suicide.

Writing in *Rolling Stone*, Peter Travers remarked on the conflicting feelings that might haunt viewers: "Are they feminist martyrs or bitches from hell? Neither is the case. They're flesh-and-blood women out to expose the blight of sexism.... Director Scott, whose films ... are noted for their slick surface, cuts to the marrow this time. This wincingly funny, pertinent and heartbreaking road movie means to get under your skin, and it does." *Newsweek*'s Jack Kroll praised the film for its fusion of writing and direction into "a genuine pop myth about two women who discover themselves through the good old American ways of cars and criminality." In *Commonweal*, Richard Alleva said that "the joy that pervades so much of *Thelma and Louise* is the joy that comes from knowing that everything is going to end in a smash." He felt that "Khouri's juicy script gives director Ridley Scott the opportunity to do his best work since his first feature film, *The Duellists*. Scott makes the shot that kills the rapist echo on the soundtrack like the roar of doom ... Not the least of Scott's achievements is to give the landscape ... such an aura of masculinity (oil pumps vertically thrusting, weight lifters working out at filling stations, deserts that seem haunted by the ghost of John Ford) that their very passage through land so phallocentric becomes an act of defiance itself." Alleva concluded that "*Thelma and Louise* is a cultural milestone."

Although he credited Scott with "a strong visual sense," Denby reviewed the film for the *National Review* with far less enthusiasm: "This overlong, underrealized, and overmanicured movie reflects the deludedness of its makers. They think that by exultantly sacrificing their lives, Thelma and Louise somehow justify their anti-social anabasis." And the film sparked a wide-ranging debate on its message. As Schickel reported in *Time*, "It remains the most intriguing movie now in release. No other cheers one's argumentative spirit, stirs one's critical imagination, and awakens one's protective affection in quite the way *Thelma & Louise* does."

After three modern-day pictures, Scott returned to the past again, this time to film the story of Christopher Columbus in *1492: Conquest of Paradise*. With Gérard Depardieu cast in the title role, this version of the Italian adventurer's exploits showed him to be aware that, as Travers said, "exploration and exploitation go hand in hand." Travers praised Scott for achieving "visual wonders" but said the film was "trivialized by a goosed-up Vangelis score and a script that manages to be both ponderous and thunderously silly." Travers concluded that "you keep waiting for *1492* to bust through to the crazed lyricism of Werner Herzog's *Aguirre: The Wrath of God* or even Scott's expressionist *Alien*. It never does." In *New York*, Denby pronounced the film "exhausting and about half satisfying," while in *Newsweek*, Kroll noted the film's "stunning images," but concluded that "this $50 million spectacle must be one of the least entertaining epic films ever made." And Alleva found Scott's direction "confused" and that "*1492* betrays lack of nerve, lack of imagination, and lack of faith in a difficult but fascinating undertaking."

In 1992, Warner Brothers released *Blade Runner: The Director's Cut*, which omitted much of Deckard's voiceover narration and included a dream sequence and the film's original ending, both of which had been deleted from the first release. This new version is, however, eight minutes shorter than the earlier one. Travers was led to remark that Scott is a "master stylist, as evidenced by the recently released director's cut of his stunning 1982 *Blade Runner* minus the narration and the sappy ending." In *Film Comment*, Mike Wilmington deemed the reconstructed *Blade Runner* "a film of dread, tension, angst and grief: a darkness that back in 1982—the Spielberg Era—must have seemed offkey and excessive to exputives gung ho for Indiana Jones." He concluded that "Scott's preferred version has more: more mystery, more tenderness, more sense of threat, more deadly lyricism, and more of a sense of life trembling at the abyss." *Video* magazine's Kenneth Korman noted that the new version brought "the movie's many strengths . . . to the fore. Its unique rhythm and feel can be savored without distraction, and the still-unsurpassed special effects, set designs and cinematography appear more spellbinding than ever." In *The New York Times*, Donald Albrecht

noted that: "Some people see [*Blade Runner*] as a contemporary carrier of ancient myths. Gregory Nagy, a professor of Classical Greek literature at Harvard, screens the film for his students to get them talking about the concept of the hero in ancient Greek culture."

His early influences included Tony Richardson and Francois Truffaut, as well as Joseph Mankiewicz and Preston Sturges; he has gone on to influence a whole generation of filmmakers. Unapologetically commercial, Scott relies on breathtaking visuals and stunning details of light, mood and design, to convey his message and to mirror his own fascination with the cinematic medium. For this director, film is film, whether it's a full-length production or a 30-second spot. As he told Rosen, "If you're a filmmaker and you're not filming, that's a fallow period. It's like being an athlete. If you're not running around the track, you're losing your edge."

■ Works Cited

Albrecht, Donald, review of *Blade Runner: The Director's Cut*, *New York Times*, September 20, 1992.

Alleva, Richard, "Over the Edge?" *Commonweal*, September 13, 1991.

Alleva, Richard, "Goodby, Columbus," *Commonweal*, November 20, 1992.

Buckley, Michael, "Take Five," *Films in Review*, January, 1987.

Burn, Gordon, review of *Boy on a Bicycle*, *Sunday Times Magazine* (London), December 2, 1985.

Canby, Vincent, review of *The Duellists*, *New York Times*, January 14, 1978.

Corliss, Richard, review of *Blade Runner*, *Time*, July 12, 1982.

Denby, David, "True to Formula," *New York*, November 2, 1987.

Denby, David, "Movie of the Moment," *National Review*, July 8, 1991.

Denby, David, "Columbus Daze," *New York*, October 19, 1992.

Dugas, Christine, "And Now, a Wittier Word from Our Sponsors," *Business Week*, March 24, 1986.

Films and Filming, June, 1984.

Haskell, Molly, review of *The Duellists*, *New York*, January 30, 1978.

Johnson, Brian D., "Clichés in Conflict," *MacLean's*, October 2, 1989.

Kael, Pauline, review of *Blade Runner*, *New Yorker*, July 12, 1982.

Kael, Pauline, review of *Someone to Watch Over Me*, *New Yorker*, November 2, 1987.

Kasindorf, Martin, interview with Ridley Scott, *Newsday*, October 13, 1987.

Kauffmann, Stanley, review of *Blade Runner, New Republic*, August 9, 1982.

Kauffman, Stanley, review of *Black Rain, New Republic*, October 16, 1989.

Kennedy, Harlan, "21st Century Nervous Breakdown," *Film Comment*, July/August, 1982.

Kennedy, Harlan and Nigel Andrews, career overview of Ridley Scott, *American Film*, March, 1979.

Korman, Kenneth, review of *Blade Runner: The Director's Cut, Video*, June, 1993.

Kroll, Jack, "Back on the Road Again," *Newsweek*, May 27, 1991.

Rafferty, Terrence, review of *Legend, The Nation*, October 24, 1987.

Rosen, Barbara, "How the Man Who Made Alien Invaded Madison Avenue,"
Business Week, March 24, 1986.

Schickel, Richard, "Gender Bender," *Time*, June 24, 1991.

Scott, Ridley, interview with Mary Blume, *Los Angeles Times*, July 29, 1979.

Sheehan, Henry, *Hollywood Reporter*, May 6, 1991.

Travers, Peter, "Women on the Verge," *Rolling Stone*, April 18, 1991.

Travers, Peter, "Hard Times for Heroes," *Rolling Stone*, October 29, 1992.

Wilmington, Mike, "The Rain People," *Film Comment*, January/February, 1992.

■ For More Information See

PERIODICALS

American Film, August, 1991.
Positif, September, 1985.
New Yorker, October 19, 1992.
Time, February 10, 1986.°

—*Sketch by Megan Ratner*

Zoa Sherburne

■ Personal

Full name, Zoa Morin Sherburne; born September 30, 1912, in Seattle, WA; daughter of Thomas Joseph and Zoa (Webber) Morin; married Herbert Newton Sherburne, June 5, 1935 (deceased, 1966); children: Marie (Brumble), Norene (Purdue), Zoey (Brott), Herbert Jr., Thomas, Philip, Anne (Sandberg), Robert. *Education:* Attended parochial schools in Seattle, WA. *Avocational interests:* Bowling, dancing, civic activities, and public speaking about writing.

■ Addresses

Home—3711 164th Street SW, No. E19, Lynnwood, WA 98037. *Agent*—Ann Elmo Agency Inc., 52 Vanderbilt Avenue, New York, NY 10019.

■ Career

Writer and lecturer. Cornish School of Allied Arts, Seattle, WA, teacher of short story writing, 1957. *Member:* National League of American Penwomen (second vice-president, Seattle national branch), Seattle Freelance Writers (president, 1954), Phi Delta Nu (president, 1950).

■ Awards, Honors

Woman of Achievement award, Theta Sigma Phi Matrix, 1950; Woman of the Year, Phi Delta Nu, 1951; Best Book for Young People award, Child Study Association, 1959, for *Jennifer*; Henry Broderick Award, 1960; Governor's Writers' Day Award, 1967.

■ Writings

YOUNG ADULT FICTION

Almost April, Morrow, 1956.
The High White Wall, Morrow, 1957.
Princess in Denim, Morrow, 1958.
Jennifer, Morrow, 1959.
Evening Star, Morrow, 1960.
Ballerina On Skates, Morrow, 1961.
Girl in the Shadows, Morrow, 1963.
Stranger in the House, Morrow, 1963.
River At Her Feet, Morrow, 1965.
Girl in the Mirror, Morrow, 1966.
Too Bad about the Haines Girl, Morrow, 1967.
The Girl Who Knew Tomorrow, Morrow, 1970.
Leslie, Morrow, 1972.
Why Have The Birds Stopped Singing?, Morrow, 1974.

OTHER

Shadow of a Star, Hurst & Blacklett, 1959.
Journey out of Darkness, Hurst & Blacklett, 1961.

Also contributor of over three hundred short stories, articles, and numerous verses to periodicals.

■ Adaptations

Stranger in The House was adapted for television as *Memories Never Die*, starring Lindsay Wagner, first broadcast by Columbia Broadcast System, Inc. (CBS-TV) in December, 1982.

■ Sidelights

For years—ever since she was a young schoolgirl, in fact—Zoa Sherburne wrote every chance she got, largely because she loved words more than anything. At the age of ten, she "had a notebook of original poems, handwritten, often with misspelled words," she writes in the *Something about The Author Autobiography Series* (SAAS). "I gave it to my mother for her birthday, or perhaps it was Mother's Day. Mother really treasured that book."

But Sherburne's real writing career, she feels, began long after she was married and had three children ("and a half," she says, because she was pregnant with the fourth). It was on the day her mother burst into her house with a large bag of donuts—and a bright idea. "I gathered up a whole batch of your poetry," Sherburne's mother told her, "and sent it to Mike Mitchell. He wants to publish it in his newspaper."

From that small encouragement, Sherburne went on to become a writer of novels for young adults— but not just any novels. Sherburne's books realistically look at the problems of modern teens. Her novels first became very popular because of their teenage characters, who struggled with personal problems such as unrequited first love, unpopularity, unwanted pregnancy, and drug use, as well as family problems such as divorce, remarriage, death, and parents with mental illness or physical disabilities. Perhaps Sherburne's best-known work is *Too Bad about the Haines Girl*, one of the first young adult books to confront the problem of teenage pregnancy. Between 1956 and 1974, Zoa Sherburne wrote fourteen books (sometimes one per year), all published by William Morrow.

Beginnings of A Career

Thanks to her mother's idea, Sherburne's poems *were* published in Mike Mitchell's paper, the *Ballard Tribune*. The poems were about the author's family—often from her children's point of view—and they quickly became very popular. Sherburne wrote two or three poems every week, enough to have a weekly column. Although she had to take care of four small children, a large house, a husband, and get the newspaper column out every

week, Sherburne always found time to write. Her typewriter, named Maud, lived on the dining room table, where the author would sit tapping out stories and poems every chance she got—while the children took naps, while she ate lunch, when her husband was bowling, "while dinner was cooking, and sometimes while dinner was burning," she remarks in *SAAS*.

Sherburne also began to enter some of her writing in contests, winning quite a few. One particular prize was $200, which her husband told her to spend on something for herself. Sherburne chose to use the money to register for a writing class, which met evenings for four months. At the end of the session, the teacher told the class that it would probably take them two years to sell two stories (and *that* would only happen if they wrote ten stories a year). "It was very impressive and I was sure he knew exactly what he was talking about," Sherburne comments in her essay, "but I had no intention of waiting for the second year. I went

Following her older sister's marriage, a middle child seeks a love of her own in Sherburne's 1965 tale.

home and wrote twenty stories." (After all, she planned to get her money back since she had invested it in the class!) Fortunately, it was easy for Sherburne to get ideas for stories, and she used them all.

Only four months after she began writing her short stories, Sherburne sold one. Soon, she began getting invitations to speak at writer's clubs, all the while continuing to send her stories and articles to magazines. Sherburne's stories began to be published on a regular basis.

Magazine editors started to call and an agent offered to represent her, soon selling her stories not only in the United States, but in Canada and overseas as well. Although some of her stories were for adults, Sherburne realized that "the market that really fit me like a thumb in a mitten was the young adult short story. I was at home with these young people, I sympathized with them, laughed with them and even cried with them."

At that time—the 1950s—television was a new oddity, just becoming a popular form of entertainment for American families. As a result, magazines were not buying as many short stories. Agents and editors advised Sherburne to try to write a book, but the author felt she wasn't able to. She continued to write stories—until one of her editors told her about a novel-writing contest, suggesting the frustrated writer enter a sample of her work. Sherburne's entry, which she finished two hours before the deadline, was called *Almost April*, about a difficult year in a the life of a young girl. Unfortunately, the contest had to be canceled, but Sherburne's agent called to tell her that a publisher was interested in the book.

Earning A New Audience

Almost April was published in 1956. As Alberta Eiseman explains the story in the *New York Times Book Review:* "When Karen [Hale] went to live with her father and his new wife Jan, she was set to dislike them both. She had not seen her father for years, and her mother's recent death had left her bitter and unhappy. The Hales' love and understanding, and Jan's obvious desire to make her happy, won Karen over. Then her friendship with Nels Carlson reopened the rift with her father." Louise S. Bechtel notes in the *New York Herald Tribune Book Review* that the tale "is well written and expert at describing teen-age emotions."

Sherburne's editors sent her letters of praise, encouraging her to get right to work on another

book. But the author was way ahead of them: she was already working on a second piece, *The High White Wall*. "The publication of *Almost April* showed me a new world," Sherburne comments in *SAAS*. "People who had never heard of me (and really didn't care) suddenly recognized my name, or at least the title of my book. I was invited to things. Conferences, book fairs, autograph parties. My circle of friends and acquaintances widened."

The *High White Wall*, published in 1957, is about the experiences of Leeann Storm, an eighteen-year old who works for a rich family in their beautiful house behind a high wall in the most exclusive section of town. Over time, Leeann falls in love with the older son of her employer. Sherburne's next book, *Princess in Denim*, tells how young Eden learns a lot about herself and life during the experience of becoming a beauty contest winner.

No Glamorous Topics Here

By this time, it was clear that Sherburne was not writing simple, ordinary stories about young romance. Her novels for readers between eleven and thirteen years old were exploring the traumatic family situations and personal problems often faced by real young adults. "People started asking why I chose such controversial subjects for my young adult books," Sherburne recalls in her essay. "What I was really trying to say to these sometimes bewildered, often impatient and always searching young people was 'YOU ARE NOT ALONE.' I had already started to receive fan mail from the first two books so I knew that some of those girls who were my readers identified closely with the girl whose parents were divorced; the girl who didn't really love her grandmother; the girl who couldn't wait to leave her home and family; the girl who knew the heartbreak of losing a beloved sister, or watching her mother die. These were the problems they lived with, the real nitty gritty problems in their real world. NOT . . . will I get a date to the prom? Will I be able to afford a new dress? Will the boy-next-door-come-back-to-me-when-the-new-girl-goes-back-home?"

Sherburne's next book was *Jennifer*, a story about the effects of a mother's alcoholism on a sixteen-year-old girl. "Someone pointed out that it didn't sound very light and cheerful," Sherburne recalls. "I said it wasn't supposed to be light and cheerful, it was supposed to be true because, I reasoned, even if the girl reading my story couldn't identify with the situation *herself* it was almost certain that one or two of her acquaintances could." Despite its

GIRL IN THE MIRROR

BY ZOA SHERBURNE

In this 1966 work, Ruth Ann's father is killed in a car crash, leaving the young girl and her new stepmother to start over together.

sometimes grim subject matter, the book won the Best Book for Young People award from the Child Study Association.

Sherburne's next two books were *Evening Star,* which has a racial theme, and *Ballerina On Skates,* about the problems of a "too-tall" girl. In the former work, Nancy fears that she will not find social acceptance because of the way she looks. A summer guest and a new love help show the teen that it is her exotic background that makes her so very special. *River At Her Feet* was the first book turned down by Sherburne's publisher (who did, however, agree to publish it a couple of years later). "After her older sister's marriage, sixteen-year-old Elizabeth, the middle Stacy girl, hopes to gain a different status and to make a social life of her own," writes Sally C. Estes of the novel in *Booklist.* "When she meets Eric Killian, a twenty-four-year-old New York concert violinist who is recuperating from an illness at the home of his

aunt, Elizabeth understandably mistakes his friendship for romantic interest. Despite a rather hackneyed theme, the believable characterizations and perceptive treatment of first love make this an above-average story for younger teen-age girls." Grace M. Zahn, writing in *Library Journal,* disagrees with this assessment: "Following her sister's wedding, sixteen-year-old Elizabeth expected a dramatic change in her own life. When a twenty-three-year-old celebrity visited a neighbor, Elizabeth interpreted his casual friendship as love. The familiar plot, contrived setting, and breezy style make Elizabeth's ensuing anguish unconvincing."

In the meantime, one of Sherburne's grandchildren was stillborn and the next book she began to work on—*Girl in the Mirror*—reflects the author's sadness. "Perhaps because of the sorrows and loss of the past year this was a more somber story," she muses in *SAAS.* "I had never tried to avoid the subject of death in my books because I reasoned that this was something my young readers would have to experience. So I started work on *Girl in the Mirror* even though I was uncertain of the reception it would get from my publisher."

At a writer's conference that summer, Sherburne met a Catholic nun named Sister Dominic who introduced herself as one of the writer's "over-age" fans. During their conversation, Sister Dominic suggested that Sherburne write a book about teen-age pregnancy, largely because the young girls who were reading her books might be interested in the topic. So Sherburne went home, put *Girl In the Mirror* in a drawer, and started work on the new story—*Too Bad about the Haines Girl.* Unfortunately, the *Haines* novel was rejected; Sherburne put it aside and returned to *Girl In the Mirror.*

Deidre Wulf writes in *World Journal Tribune* that *Girl in the Mirror* "is the account of how awkward, overweight Ruth Ann copes with the remarriage of her widowed father. It goes almost without saying that the new stepmother, Tracy, is tall, slim, elegant, gracious, as well as a very paragon of patience in her handling of the nasty child. When Ruth Ann's father is killed in a car crash, the two women are thrown together to make a new life for themselves." Ruth Ann's feelings of inadequacy are compounded by her horrible feelings of loss. It is only in food that she finds relief—and acceptance. Eventually, however, Ruth Ann discovers that food can't help all the time, and that there is much more to life than feeling sorry for oneself. In her assessment of the novel, Joan Lear Sher comments in the *New York Times Book Review:* "Zoa Sherburne's poignant picture of a girl who has retreated from reality is well drawn, although Ruth Ann sometimes tends to be a parlor analyst, and at other times is incredibly naive.''

Poor Little Haines Girl

Sherburne was still trying to figure out why *Girl in the Mirror* had been accepted so readily ''and my poor little Haines girl rejected.'' Even though publishers weren't willing to print the book, Sherburne couldn't get the ''Haines'' character out of her mind. She rewrote the story and mailed it to her agent, with instructions to take it to other publishers if Morrow didn't want it. But Morrow decided to reconsider the story—in fact, the company sent copies of the manuscript to librarians around the country with a set of questions, asking if they would buy the book if it was published, what changes they thought were needed, how old the readers would be. When the results came in, the publishers were very happy: ''*No one* turned the book down because of the subject matter,'' Sherburne remembers. ''This is going to be your most popular book to date!' was the somewhat surprising verdict of my publishers,'' Sherburne adds—a prediction that happily came true.

''Mrs. Sherburne's junior romances have often dealt with complex problems—alcoholism in the family, mental illness, a death in the family, etc.,'' writes Phyllis Cohen in *Young Readers Review*. In *Too Bad about the Haines Girl*, ''she tackles the increasingly common problem of the teen-age unwed mother, and it is by far her best book. Of all that I've read ... *Too Bad about the Haines Girl* comes closest to an honest discussion of the whole problem. This book is not a sermon. The author does not discuss the moral aspects at all. She has presented a common situation and one normal, healthy girl's reactions.'' In the novel, Melinda and Jeff have a relationship that ends in Lindy's pregnancy. When the news gets out, reaction to the couple and their predicament is mixed. Over time, Lindy begins to resent her situation; she lashes out at those who want to help her, while at the same time, she desperately needs someone to lean on.

Zena Sutherland describes Sherburne's success with a touchy subject in *Saturday Review:* ''Although not the first book for teen-age girls that focuses on the problem of the young unwed mother, this is one of the best to date. When an author has tackled such serious problems as alcoholism, mental illness, and prejudice with candor and dignity, it is expectable that the subject of premarital pregnancy will be handled the same way.'' Nancy E. Paige, in a slightly negative vein, opines in *Library Journal* that ''this book about a popular, intelligent, 'nice' high school girl who becomes pregnant is well written, peopled by believable, appropriate characters, but it goes no farther than to tell us that an unmarried, pregnant high school girl is a miserable person whose future is in very serious jeopardy.... Whether she and her boyfriend will forsake their educational plans to marry and raise an unwanted child, or whether Melinda will, instead, bear the illegitimate child and give it up for adoption, and how both young people will deal with the social, emotional, and other pressures attendant on either decision are matters beyond the scope of the book.'' And Irene Hunt, commenting on both the novel and its subject matter for the *New York Times Book Review*, offers: ''These books deal with a problem of serious and tragic concern among today's adolescents and adults: the problem of girls who find

Sherburne's well-received 1967 novel was among the first young adult works to confront the issue of teenage pregnancy.

themselves pregnant—and unwed. *Too Bad about the Haines Girl* handles the theme for readers twelve and up in an expert and credible manner.... Sherburne hews to the line with the integrity of a skilled writer; she diverts us with no bright subplots and leaves the reader with little promise of anything but heartache for Melinda."

Later Years, Other Topics

In addition to her realistic novels, Sherburne has also written science fiction and Gothic novels. *The Girl Who Knew Tomorrow*, for example, is the story of Angie, a girl with extrasensory perception who must learn to use her gift without abusing it. "When the girl's special gift becomes known, her lonely mother is influenced by the attentions of a man who persuades the family to exploit her," explains Marianne Hough in *Library Journal*. "TV publicity gradually forces Angie into the lonely world of the celebrity; her own sister, envious, turns against her. Finally, her beloved Grandmother dies, but not before Angie has been transferred mentally for a deathbed conversation in the old woman's room thousands of miles away. The final message to Angie is, of course, to give it all up until her gift can be used only for helping others."

Sherburne took on another heavy topic—teenage drug use—in the book *Leslie*, but her reviews were generally not favorable. In the novel, Leslie is convinced by the local high school pusher to try pot. Unfortunately, her experience takes on deadly ramifications when she—still high—gets involved in a hit-and-run accident. As a result, Leslie must struggle with both her guilt over taking drugs and her horror at being involved in a terrible crime. Jeanne M. Chase, in a review for *Library Journal*, is blunt about her reaction to Sherburne's presentation of Leslie's plight: "Although this may appeal to junior high readers who dote on problem situations, *Go Ask Alice* is a more hard-hitting, realistic depiction of teenage drug use."

When her beloved husband died in 1966, Sherburne stopped writing for a while. But she resumed work in 1974 with her last book, *Why Have The Birds Stopped Singing?* "It started out to be a story of survival," she recalls in her essay, "but somehow, mid-stream, it became a 'back-in-time story.' The girl was a victim of epilepsy. The story wrote itself." *Why Have The Birds Stopped Singing?* is an unusual tale in which Sherburne combines romance and time travel. The main character, Katie, is epileptic. She travels back in time, assuming the identity of one of her ancestors, who was also epileptic. For many critics, Sherburne's sympathetic discussion of this affliction is the strongest asset of the book. Sarah Law Kennerly remarks in a *Library Journal* review, "Sixteen-year old Katie, an epileptic, sees a portrait of her great-great-great grandmother on which is written 'Kathryn, May 1873. A loving heart but a clouded mind.' Excited and puzzled over the implications of the inscription, she neglects to take her medication and has a seizure.... The chief value of this Gothic fantasy lies in its sympathetic, matter-of-fact treatment of epilepsy."

In 1978—having largely retired from full-time writing—Sherburne moved away from Seattle to Bellingham to attend school and work toward a degree at Fairhaven College. She still lives in Washington, her home state, and maintains an active interest in the problems facing young people.

■ Works Cited

Bechtel, Louise S., review of *Almost April*, *New York Herald Tribune Book Review*, March 11, 1956.

Chase, Jeanne M., review of *Leslie*, *Library Journal*, January 15, 1973.

Cohen, Phyllis, review of *Too Bad about the Haines Girl*, *Young Readers Review*, May 1967.

Eiseman, Alberta, "A Crucial Year," *The New York Times Book Review*, February 5, 1956.

Eiseman, Alberta, "Escape," *The New York Times Book Review*, February 3, 1957.

Estes, Sally C., review of *River At Her Feet*, *Booklist*, November 15, 1965.

Hough, Marianne, review of *The Girl Who Knew Tomorrow*, *Library Journal*, December 15, 1970.

Hunt, Irene, "Girls In Trouble," *New York Times Book Review*, March 5, 1967.

Kennerly, Sarah Law, review of *Why Have the Birds Stopped Singing?*, *Library Journal*, May 15, 1974.

Paige, Nancy E., review of *Too Bad about the Haines Girl*, *Library Journal*, April 15, 1967.

Sher, Joan Lear, review of *Girl in the Mirror*, *New York Times Book Review*, November 6, 1966.

Sherburne, Zoa, essay in *Something about The Author Autobiography Series*, Volume 18, 1994.

Sutherland, Zena, review of *Too Bad about the Haines Girl*, *Saturday Review*, March 18, 1967.

Wulf, Deirdre, "Young Ladies In Distress," *World Journal Tribune*, October 23, 1966.

Zahn, Grace M., review of *River At Her Feet*, *Library Journal*, April 15, 1965.

■ **For More Information See**

BOOKS

Contemporary Literary Criticism, Volume 30, Gale, 1984.

—Sketch by Diane Patrick

R. L. Stine

York City, 1968-71; editor, *Search* magazine, Scholastic, Inc., New York City, 1972-75; editor/creator, *Bananas* magazine, Scholastic, Inc., New York City, 1975-84; editor/creator, *Maniac* magazine, Scholastic, Inc., New York City, 1984-85; freelance writer of books for children and young adults; 1982—. Head writer for *Eureeka's Castle*, Nickelodeon cable television network. *Member:* Mystery Writers of America.

■ Awards, Honors

Childrens' Choice Award, American Library Association, for several novels.

■ Writings

JUVENILE

The Time Raider, illustrations by David Febland, Scholastic, 1982.

The Golden Sword of Dragonwalk, illustrations by Febland, Scholastic, 1983.

Horrors of the Haunted Museum, Scholastic, 1984.

Instant Millionaire, illustrations by Jowill Woodman, Scholastic, 1984.

Through the Forest of Twisted Dreams, Avon, 1984.

Indiana Jones and the Curse of Horror Island, Ballantine, 1984.

Indiana Jones and the Giants of the Silver Tower, Ballantine, 1984.

Indiana Jones and the Cult of the Mummy's Crypt, Ballantine, 1985.

The Badlands of Hark, illustrations by Bob Roper, Scholastic., 1985.

The Invaders of Hark, Scholastic., 1985.

■ Personal

Full name, Robert Lawrence Stine; has also written under the name Jovial Bob Stine, and pseudonyms Eric Affabee and Zachary Blue; born October 8, 1943 in Columbus, OH; son of Lewis (a retired shipping manager) and Anne (Feinstein) Stine; married Jane Waldhorn (owner/managing director of Parachute Press), June 22, 1969; children: Matthew Daniel. Education: Ohio State University, B.A. 1965; graduate study at New York University, 1966-67. *Religion:* Jewish. *Hobbies and other interests:* Swimming, watching old movie classics from the 1930s and 1940s, reading (especially P.G. Wodehouse novels).

■ Addresses

Office—c/o Parachute Press 156 5th Avenue, New York, NY 10010.

■ Career

Social studies teacher at a junior high school in Columbus, OH, 1965-66; writer for several magazines in New York City, 1966-68; assistant editor, *Junior Scholastic* magazine, Scholastic, Inc., New

Demons of the Deep, illustrations by Fred Carrillo, Golden Books, 1985.

Challenge of the Wolf Knight ("Wizards, Warriors and You" Series), Avon, 1985.

James Bond in Win, Place, or Die, Ballantine, 1985.

Cavern of the Phantoms, Avon, 1986.

Operation: Deadly Decoy, Ballantine, 1986.

Jungle Raid ("G.I. Joe" Series), Ballantine, 1988.

JUVENILE; UNDER NAME JOVIAL BOB STINE

The Absurdly Silly Encyclopedia and Flyswatter, illustrations by Bob Taylor, Scholastic, 1978.

How to Be Funny: An Extremely Silly Guidebook, illustrations by Carol Nicklaus, Dutton, 1978.

The Complete Book of Nerds, illustrations by Sam Viviano, Scholastic, 1979.

The Dynamite Do-It-Yourself Pen Pal Kit, illustrations by Jared Lee, Scholastic, 1980.

Dynamite's Funny Book of the Sad Facts of Life, illustrations by Lee, Scholastic, 1980.

Going Out! Going Steady! Going Bananas!, photographs by Dan Nelken, Scholastic, 1980.

The Pig's Book of World Records, illustrations by Peter Lippman, Random House, 1980.

(With wife, Jane Stine) *The Sick of Being Sick Book*, edited by Ann Durrell, illustrations by Nicklaus, Dutton, 1980.

Bananas Looks at TV, Scholastic, 1981.

The Beast Handbook, illustrations by Taylor, Scholastic, 1981.

(With J. Stine) *The Cool Kids' Guide to Summer Camp*, illustrations by Jerry Zimmerman, Scholastic, 1981.

Gnasty Gnomes, illustrations by Lippman, Random House, 1981.

Don't Stand in the Soup, illustrations by Nicklaus, Bantam, 1982.

(With J. Stine) *Bored with Being Bored!: How to Beat the Boredom Blahs*, illustrations by Zimmerman, Four Winds, 1982.

Blips!: The First Book of Video Game Funnies, illustrations by Bryan Hendrix, Scholastic, 1983.

(With J. Stine) *Everything You Need to Survive: Brothers and Sisters*, illustrated by Sal Murdocca, Random House, 1983.

(With J. Stine) *Everything You Need to Survive: First Dates*, illustrated by Murdocca, Random House, 1983.

(With J. Stine) *Everything You Need to Survive: Homework*, illustrated by Murdocca, Random House, 1983.

(With J. Stine) *Everything You Need to Survive: Money Problems*, illustrated by Murdocca, Random House, 1983.

Jovial Bob's Computer Joke Book, Scholastic, 1985.

Miami Mice, illustrations by Eric Gurney, Scholastic, 1986.

One Hundred and One Silly Monster Jokes, Scholastic, 1986.

The Doggone Dog Joke Book, Parachute Press, 1986.

Pork & Beans: Play Date, illustrations by Jose Aruego and Ariane Dewey, Scholastic, 1989.

Ghostbusters II Storybook, Scholastic, 1989.

One Hundred and One Vacation Jokes, illustrated by Rick Majica, Scholastic, 1990.

The Amazing Adventures of Me, Myself and I, Bantam, 1991.

JUVENILE; UNDER PSEUDONYM ERIC AFFABEE

The Siege of the Dragonriders, ("Wizards, Warriors and You" Series), Avon, 1984.

G.I. Joe and the Everglades Swamp Terror ("G. I. Joe" Series) Ballantine, 1986.

Attack on the King, Avon, 1986.

G.I. Joe-Operation: Star Raider ("G. I. Joe" Series), Ballantine, 1986.

The Dragon Queen's Revenge, ("Wizards, Warriors and You" Series), Avon, 1986.

JUVENILE; UNDER PSEUDONYM ZACHARY BLUE

The Protectors: The Petrova Twist, Scholastic, 1987.

The Jet Fighter Trap, Scholastic, 1987.

YOUNG ADULT NOVELS

Blind Date, Scholastic, 1986.

Twisted, Scholastic, 1987.

Broken Date ("Crosswinds" Series), Simon & Schuster, 1988.

The Baby-Sitter, Scholastic, 1989.

Phone Calls, Archway, 1990.

How I Broke Up with Ernie, Archway, 1990.

Curtains, Archway, 1990.

The Boyfriend, Scholastic, 1990.

Beach Party, Scholastic, 1990.

Snowman, Scholastic, 1991.

The Girlfriend, Scholastic, 1991.

Baby-Sitter II, Scholastic, 1991.

Beach House, Scholastic, 1992.

Hit and Run, Scholastic, 1992.

Hitchhiker, Scholastic, 1993.

Baby-sitter III, Scholastic, 1993.

The Dead Girl Friend, Scholastic, 1993.

Halloween Night, Scholastic, 1993.

"FEAR STREET" SERIES

The New Girl, Archway, 1989.

The Surprise Party, Archway, 1990.

The Stepsister, Archway, 1990.

Missing, Archway, 1990.

Halloween Party, Archway, 1990.
The Wrong Number, Archway, 1990.
The Sleepwalker, Archway 1991.
Ski Weekend, Archway, 1991.
Silent Night, Archway, 1991.
The Secret Bedroom, Archway, 1991.
The Overnight, Archway, 1991.
Lights Out, Archway, 1991.
Haunted, Archway, 1991.
The Fire Game, Archway, 1991.
The Knife, Archway, 1992.
Prom Queen, Archway, 1992.
First Date, Archway, 1992.
The Best Friend, Archway, 1992.
Sunburn, Archway, 1993.
The Cheater, Archway, 1993.

"FEAR STREET: SUPER CHILLER" SERIES

Party Summer, Archway, 1991.
Goodnight Kiss, Archway, 1992.
Silent Night, Archway, 1992.
Broken Hearts, Archway, 1993.
Silent Night II, Archway, 1993.

"FEAR STREET: CHEERLEADERS" SERIES

The First Evil, Archway, 1992.
The Second Evil, Archway, 1992.
The Third Evil, Archway, 1992.

"FEAR STREET SAGA" SERIES

The Betrayal, Archway, 1993.
The Secret, Archway, 1993.
The Burning, Archway, 1993.

"GOOSEBUMPS" SERIES

Welcome to Dead House, Scholastic, 1992.
Stay Out of the Basement, Scholastic, 1992.
Monster Blood, Scholastic, 1992.
Say Cheese and Die, Scholastic, 1992.
The Curse of the Mummy's Tomb, Scholastic, 1993.
Let's Get Invisible, Scholastic, 1993.
Night of the Living Dummy, Scholastic, 1993.
The Girl Who Cried Monster, Scholastic, 1993.
Welcome to Camp Nightmare, Scholastic, 1993.
The Ghost Next Door, Scholastic, 1993.
The Haunted Mask, Scholastic, 1993.
Be Careful What You Wish For, Scholastic, 1993.
Piano Lessons Can Be Murder, Scholastic, 1993.
The Werewolf of Fever Swamp, Scholastic, 1993.
You Can't Scare Me, Scholastic, 1993.

■ Sidelights

"As she gazed at the plate, the eggs shimmered, then transformed themselves. Corky's mouth dropped open as she now stared at two enormous wet eyeballs. 'No!' The eyeballs stared back at her. Their color darkened to gray. Then the gray became a sickening green, the green of decay, and a foul odor rose up from the plate." Where does R. L. Stine, the author of more than 100 books for children and teenagers, get ideas for scenes like this one? "That's the question people ask me most often, but to this date I don't really have a good answer," Stine tells *AAYA*. "I get ideas from all kinds of places. People know how desperate I am for ideas, because I'm doing so many books, so they try to help me. Just recently I was on vacation, lying on the beach, talking to a guy I'd just met. I told him I wrote horror books, and he said, 'You should do one on earwigs. Earwigs are really scary.' Everybody has an idea . . . sometimes people send me things like newspaper clippings of stories they found. I actually did a "Fear Street" based on a true story, about a girl who planned to murder her teacher. I've never dreamed an idea—kids always ask me if I have—and I've never woken up in the morning with one. It's a shame . . . I'm still waiting for that. Mostly, I spend a lot of time just thinking about it. My son always asks me, 'Dad, how do you get an idea?' And I have to say, 'You sit down and think until you have one.' He hates that answer, but I have no choice—I have to have the ideas."

With two best-selling series going full speed, Stine *really* doesn't have a choice. For his popular "Fear Street" series and his newer "Goosebumps" series, Stine writes twenty-four horror novels a year. As if that weren't enough to keep him almost perpetually chained to his computer, Stine also does the occasional "special" title (i.e., not part of a series) for either Scholastic or Archway. "It's a lot of books," Stine concedes. "I never really planned to work this hard."

From Laughs to Frights

For that matter, Stine never planned to write horror novels in the first place. For many years, R.L. Stine was known as "Jovial Bob Stine," and his specialty was making younger kids laugh, not giving teens the shivers. He began his career in children's publishing at Scholastic, where he spent sixteen years working on four different magazines, two of which he created. These two periodicals, *Bananas* and *Maniac*, focused on humor, and eventually led Stine to his career as an author of children's books. Ellen Rudin, an editor at Dutton, was impressed with *Bananas*, and asked Stine to consider writing a humorous book for younger readers. Since starting his magazine career, Stine hadn't thought seriously about writing a book, but he readily agreed to work up an idea anyway. The result was *How to Be Funny by Jovial Bob Stine*, published in 1978. Many more funny books followed during the late seventies and well into the eighties. Most of these titles were published by several different publishing houses, and some were co-authored by Stine's wife, Jane (who at that time was the editor of *Dynamite*, another children's magazine published by Scholastic).

During the eighties, Stine also began writing "Twistaplot" books for Scholastic, as well as other "You Choose the Storyline" books for Ballantine and Avon, some under the pseudonyms Eric Affabee and Zachary Blue. These books, which featured as many as thirty endings and many plot twists, proved to be great training for future novel writing.

When Scholastic began having financial trouble in the mid-1980s, Stine was let go in a reorganization. Far from a personal disaster, however, being fired provided Stine with the opportunity to devote more time to writing books. It was around this time that Jean Feiwel, editorial director of Scholastic Books, suggested that the author try his hand at a horror novel. The result was *Blind Date*, which features a teenage boy with a memory lapse, the mysterious teenage girl who wants to date him, and plenty of twists and turns in the plot.

Like several of Stine's horror novels that have been written in the interim, *Blind Date* had a title long before it had characters or a storyline. Feiwel suggested the title, and Stine went home to build a novel around it. Since then, titles often come to him before the stories themselves. "If I can get a title first, then I start getting ideas for it. Like *The Baby-sitter*. You start to think, what's scary about being a baby-sitter? Or *The Stepsister* . . . what would be scary about getting a new stepsister? Usually the title will lead me to ideas about what the book should be," Stine tells *AAYA*.

Welcome to Fear Street

This same process worked for Stine's "Fear Street" series. With the success of *Blind Date* and two Scholastic novels that followed, *Twisted* and *The Baby-sitter*, it occurred to the author and his wife that a series of novels that came out on a regular basis might sell well. By this time, Jane had also left Scholastic to open her own book packaging company, Parachute Press. Jane suggested that Stine come up with a concept for a series that she could sell through Parachute Press. "So I sat down and

thought," Stine once remarked. "When the words "Fear Street" sort of magically appeared, I wrote them down, and then came up with the concept."

The "Fear Street" series, which now has thirty titles and millions of copies in print, is a collection of novels connected primarily by their setting. The main characters usually reside on Fear Street, a place "where your worst nightmares live," according to the cover copy on early titles. All the series' characters attend Shadyside High, a school where the death rate must be horrific, since nearly every book features at least one murder.

As Paul Gray noted in *Time* magazine, "Fear Street" stories, like other "teen tinglers" subscribe to "a fairly consistent set of formulas." The teenage heroes or heroines are normal (although not always nice) kids who suddenly find their lives

Typical high school students find themselves terrorized by supernatural forces in Stine's "Cheerleaders" series.

fraught with danger. Sometimes the menace comes from supernatural forces, as in the "Cheerleaders" trilogy. The first book of this series introduces Bobbi and Corky Corcoran, sisters who join the cheerleading squad at their new school, Shadyside High. After Bobbi dies in a bizarre "accident," Corky realizes there may have been some truth to her sister's ravings about the strange things she had seen and experienced recently. Investigating her sister's death, Corky discovers the "evil," a century-old force that has risen from the grave. Although she seemingly outwits the evil by the end of the book, it returns to terrorize the cheerleading squad through two more books, until Corky is finally able to permanently destroy it.

Sometimes the villains in the "Fear Street novels" are mere mortals with murderous tendencies, as in *Silent Night* and *Broken Hearts*. *Silent Night* is the story of Reva Dalby, a beautiful but cold rich girl who finds herself on the receiving end of some cruel practical jokes. When two people are murdered, it appears that Reva may be the killer's next target. *Broken Hearts* features another entirely human killer. This murderer announces his intentions by sending future victims valentines with nasty messages inside ("Who's sending these cards?/ Don't bother to wonder/ On Valentine's Day/ You'll be six feet under.")

Whatever the source of the menace, these kids don't turn to adults for salvation. They consult friends and do their best to find their own way out of their predicaments. Or sometimes, like Bobbi in *The First Evil* and Josie in *Broken Hearts*, they never find a way out, but simply die trying.

Other important components of the "Fear Street" formula are an emphasis on plot over characterization, and a hair-raising pace. One way Stine keeps his stories moving is to end every chapter with a cliff-hanger, a feature the author says his readers find particularly appealing. It doesn't seem to matter that the suspense sometimes dissolves instantly when the reader turns the page, such as when the "hideous, bloated head of a corpse" in Corky's bed turns out to be Halloween mask, or when the man who tries to accost Reva in a dimly lit department store turns out to be a mannequin she's brushed against. As Stine once commented, his fans "like the fact that there is some kind of jolt at the end of every chapter. They know that if they read to the end of the chapter they're going to have some kind of funny surprise, something scary, something that's going to happen . . . and force them to keep reading."

While Stine's fans don't seem to mind the formulaic nature of his books, the critics are sometimes less generous. In a review of *Twisted*, a *Publishers Weekly* reviewer says that "For shock value, this book adds up to a lot of cheap tricks." A Publisher's Weekly review of *Ski Weekend* is similarly disparaging, noting that "the contrived plot barely manages to hold together a series of bland cliffhangers." In a review of *The Second Evil* for *Voice of Youth Advocates* (VOYA), Caroline S. McKinney declares that "these formula stories are very predictable and require very little thought on the part of the reader." Nevertheless, many reviewers have recognized—sometimes begrudgingly—Stine's talent for hooking his readers and keeping them entertained. Alice Cronin, in a review of *The Sleepwalker* for *School Library Journal*, states that "Stine writes a good story. Teens will love the action." In a review of *Curtains,* a Publishers

In this 1993 work, a murderer sends threatening Valentine's Day greetings to his intended victims.

Weekly columnist says that although "the book . . . will never be mistaken for serious literature, it is sure to engross Stine's considerable following." And in a review of *Silent Night* in *VOYA*, Sylvia C. Mitchell declares that "If all series books were this good, I'd begin to drop my . . . prejudices against them."

Safe Scares

Stine agrees that the merit of his work lies in the books' entertainment value, not their literary significance, but he sees nothing wrong with that. "I believe that kids as well as adults are entitled to books of no socially redeeming value," he once noted. And although his books may be frightening, the scares are "safe scares," as he tells Gray. "You're home in your room and reading. The books are not half as scary as the real world."

In fact, Stine makes a point of ensuring that the horror in his books retains an element of the unreal. "I don't put in anything that would be too close to their lives," he assures *AAYA*, when asked what would be going too far for his readers. "I wouldn't do child abuse, or AIDS, or suicide, or anything that could really touch someone's life like that. The books are supposed to be just entertainment, that's all they are."

To work, though, the teens in his books must seem real, even if the horror elements stay in the realm of the fantastic. Stine works hard at making his characters talk like real kids, dress like real kids, and have the concerns of real kids. Though they may be worried about some unseen evil or a mysterious killer, they still care about whether or not they have a date for Saturday night. When it comes to the way his characters look, sound and behave, "I don't want to sound like some middle-aged guy who doesn't know what he's doing," Stine comments.

Luckily, Stine has a thirteen-year-old son, Matt, who provides him with plenty of first-hand experience with teens. "He's got lots of older friends," Stine said in his interview, "and I listen to them." Stine does his homework, too, by reading magazines such as *Sassy* and watching MTV. "It's very important in these books," he says, "that the kids sound and look like real kids, suddenly trapped in something horrible."

One thing Stine does not do, however, is try to keep up with the latest in teen slang. "I don't have them saying things like 'gnarly,' and other stuff people accuse me of putting in," Stine says. "I'd

Published in 1991, this horror story is played out against a yuletide setting.

like these books to be read five years from now, and that kind of slang really dates them fast. Besides," he adds, "most kids talk normal."

The Exhilaration of Success

Whether or not the books will be widely read five years from now remains to be seen, but clearly, Stine is making a hit with teens right now. His "Fear Street" books regularly appear on young adult bestseller lists, with separate titles sometimes occupying all three of the top positions. This level of success is still relatively new to the author, and he is enjoying popularity. "It's very exhilarating, being a hit," he admits to *AAYA*. "I've never been a hit before. That part is really fun."

Another indication of the degree of admiration Stine engenders in his readers is the amount of fan mail he receives, which now averages about 400 letters each week. Stine says the letters are the "best part" of his success, and he reads every one. Most of the kids who write tell Stine how much they enjoy his books, and some say that his novels are the only ones they read. Stine gets letters from teachers and librarians too, sometimes telling about students who would never read a book before, but now can't wait for the next Stine thriller.

On one occasion, though, the mail brought a strange letter that baffled and disturbed Stine. A girl from Florida wrote, "I loved your book *The Baby-sitter*. You made it all seem so real. The same thing happened to me, only it was my uncle who tried to kill me. Keep up the good work. Thanks a lot." Stine didn't quite know what to make of it. "I didn't know if she was putting me on, or if it was a plea for help, or what," he says. Fortunately, the letter came in a group from a class, and Stine had the teacher's name and address: "I wrote to her and said, 'Maybe you should look into this.'" Stine never got a response from the teacher, though, and he still wonders what the real story behind that letter was.

At times, teen writer-wannabes ask Stine for his advice on becoming successful. He tells them not to do what he did, which was spend a good portion of his teen years sending his work to publishers, hoping to make a sale. All he accomplished, Stine says, was to waste people's time and collect a lot of rejection letters, which was "horrible." Instead, Stine tells them to read, read—and read some more. That way "you pick up all these different styles, almost by osmosis," he says, "and you'll be a better writer for it."

Aspiring writers might also want to take a tip from Stine's method of crafting his horror stories. These days he always begins with a chapter-by-chapter outline that details the action. This wasn't the case with his first novels. "I started doing it this way kicking and screaming," Stine recalls. "I didn't want any part of these outlines, because sometimes you end up revising the outline, and revising it again until (the editor) approves it, and it's an arduous process. But that's the whole work. An outline helps me see whether or not the books make sense. I always start with the ending—that's the first thing I know. Then I can go back and figure out how to fool the reader, how to keep them from guessing the ending. By the time I sit down to write the book, I really know everything that's going to happen. I can just have fun and write it."

Although he claims he's had "the most boring life you can imagine" because he's "only done one thing my whole life," Stine really does seem to be having a great time with his horror novels. Perhaps that's the main reason he won't consider hiring someone else to do the actual writing after he puts together the outlines. (Some of the other popular series books are done this way.) "I'm too vain and too greedy for that," Stine jokes. Or maybe he's just having too much fun.

■ Works Cited

Cronin, Alice, review of *The Sleepwalker*, *School Library Journal*, September, 1990.

Review of *Curtains*, *Publishers Weekly*, September 28, 1990, p. 104.

Review of *Fear Street: Ski Weekend*, *Publishers Weekly*, December 7, 1990, p. 830.

Gray, Paul, "Carnage: An Open Book," *Time*, August 2, 1992, p. 54.

McKinney, Caroline S., review of *Cheerleaders: The Second Evil*, *Voice of Youth Advocates*, February, 1993, p. 360.

Mitchell, Sylvia C., review of *Silent Night*, *Voice of Youth Advocates*, April 1992, pp. 36-37.

Stine, R. L., *The Third Evil*, Archway, 1992.

Stine, R. L., *Broken Hearts*, Archway, 1993.

Review of *Twisted*, *Publishers Weekly*, July 10, 1987, p. 87.

■ For More Information See

BOOKS

Roginski, Jim, *Behind the Covers*, Libraries Unlimited, 1985, pp. 206-213.

PERIODICALS

School Library Journal, December, 1989.
Publishers Weekly, July 5, 1993.

—*Sketch by Sarah Verney*

Boris Vallejo

■ Personal

Born January 8, 1941, in Lima, Peru; emigrated to the United States, 1964; son of a lawyer; married Doris Maier (a writer), 1967; children: Dorian, Maya. *Education:* Escuela Nacional de Bellas Artes, graduate, 1959; also studied pre-med for two years. *Hobbies and other interests:* Playing the violin.

■ Addresses

Agent—c/o Alaska Momma, Inc., 303 5th Ave., New York, NY 10016.

■ Career

Freelance artist. During the mid-1960s, worked in the advertising department for a store chain in Hartford, CT, then New York City; worked as a freelance artist of fashion art, Christmas cards, and comic books. Work has been licensed for merchandising on many products, including calendars, posters, jigsaw puzzles, greeting cards, figurines, t-shirts, board games, beer steins, skateboards, belt buckles, jewelry, metal buttons, bookmarkers, bookplates, trading cards, plastic beverageware, masks, mirrors, bedding, and computer programs. *Exhibitions:* Has had major exhibits at Museo Nacional de Arte, Lima, Peru; Harvard Club, New York City; Society of Illustrators, New York City; Delaware Art Museum, Wilmington, DE; Brandywine Fantasy Gallery, Kenilworth, IL; Pendragon Gallery, Anapolis, MD; Robin Hutchins Gallery, Maplewood, NJ; Leo Burnett Agency, Chicago, IL; and Feria Internacional, Barcelona, Spain.

■ Awards, Honors

Gold Medal, Escuela Nacional de Bellas Artes, 1959; first prize, Feria Internacional del Pacifico, 1960; first prize, Campaign of Social Awareness (Lima, Peru), 1962; first prize, Bienal del Pacifico, 1963; first prize, Festival de las Artes, 1963; Best Fantasy Artist of the Year, San Diego Fantasy and Science Fiction Convention, 1978; Best Mystery Cover of the Year, 1979; Hugo Award nomination, 1980, for best science fiction artist of the year; Best Cover Artist of the Year, Toutain Publishing (Barcelona, Spain), 1984 and 1986.

■ Illustrator

Doris Vallejo, *The Boy Who Saved the Stars* (juvenile), O'Quinn Studios, 1978.
D. Vallejo, *Enchantment* (short stories), Ballantine, 1984.
Larry Niven, *Achilles' Choice*, Tor, 1991.
D. Vallejo, *Ladies: Retold Stories of Goddesses and Heroines*, ROC, 1992.

COLLECTIONS

The Fantastic Art of Boris Vallejo, introduction by Lester del Rey, Ballantine, 1978.
(And author of text) *Fantasy Art Techniques,* Arco Publishing, 1985.
Mirage, text by D. Vallejo, Ballantine, 1986.

Work also collected in *Boris I,* Anaconda; *Boris II,* Anaconda; *A Guide to Fantasy,* Dragon's World; *Diva,* Zoom Press (France); *Fantasy,* Volksverlag (Germany); and *Boris Vallejo Fantasztikus Vilaga,* Konyvtar (Hungary).

■ Sidelights

"The elements of a fantasy illustration need make no pretence of imitating life such as they must in, say, an illustration for a gothic, a mystery, or a novel," asserted fantasy artist Boris Vallejo in *Fantasy Art Techniques.* "Fantasy engages the imagination to a much larger extent; the creatures portrayed may come partly or entirely from your head. And yet, to be successful, the scenes from your imagination must be convincing enough for a viewer to be willing to go along with you: to willingly suspend his disbelief and say, '*Yes, this could work'.*"

Although his paintings won't be found hanging in New York's Metropolitan Museum of Art or the hallowed rooms of the Louvre in Paris, Vallejo has made a name for himself in the art world. Reproductions of his fantastic paintings of well-muscled barbarians, sexy heroines, and bizarre beasts are especially hard to avoid if one reads many fantasy or science fiction novels, though his work can also be found on the covers of mysteries, gothic romances, mainstream novels, and even on boxes for fantasy computer games, all with the tell-tale signature "Boris" in the corner. Enthusiasts of Vallejo's imaginative visions can purchase Boris Vallejo calendars and art book collections, as well as hundreds of merchandising items. Because of the commercialism surrounding Vallejo's art, many critics refuse to take the artist's work seriously. As Lester del Rey pointed out in his introduction to *The Fantastic Art of Boris Vallejo,* however, "the self-styled cognoscenti . . . forget that much of the greatest art of all time was produced on commercial assignment."

An Art Prodigy

The son of a lawyer, Vallejo was born into an affluent home in Lima, Peru, on January 8, 1941. From an early age, Vallejo had a keen interest in

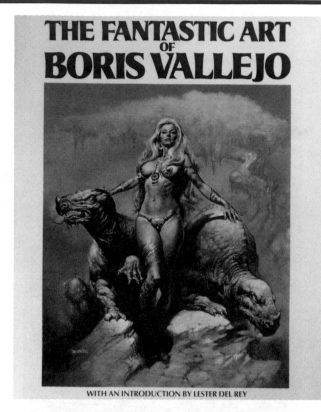

The paintings in this 1978 collection reflect both the artist's classical training and love for comic book art.

art that was encouraged by his father. "When I was about 10," the artist remembered in *The Guide to Fantasy Art Techniques,* "my father bought me a set of about fifty 8 x 10 inch prints of famous paintings, beautifully reproduced in full colour on fine-grain canvas-like paper. . . . I treasured those prints. They were all Old Masters such as Vermeer, Rembrandt, Van Gogh, Da Vinci and so on. I spent several years copying these paintings. My basic training in art was as a fine artist—I liked classical painters best. My favourites were two Spanish painters—Murillo and Velasquez. I considered their work to be the highest standard of painting."

But painting was not Vallejo's only interest. For seven years he studied to become a concert violinist, but he decided that a career as a doctor might be a more practical pursuit than either music or art. However, at the age of fourteen—and still assuming that he would eventually become a physician—Vallejo began to study art formally at the Escuela Nacional de Bellas Artes on a full scholarship he received after winning a national competition. The youngest student ever to be admitted to that institution, young Vallejo was placed even further ahead of his peers when he began his studies of figure drawing at the second year level. Two years later, in 1957, he enrolled in a pre-med program while continuing to hone his art technique.

Medical school did not last long, though, and in 1959 Vallejo gave it up to pursue art full time. That same year, he became the youngest student to win the Gold Medal for best student of the year at his art school. One reason Vallejo decided to abandon medicine was that he was offered a job drawing instruction sheet diagrams—suddenly, it actually seemed possible to earn a living as an artist. Another opportunity came the artist's way in 1963, when Vallejo was offered a scholarship sponsored by the Italian embassy for art study in Florence. For many young artists, such a chance was a once-in-a-lifetime break, but Vallejo chose to pass up the scholarship so he could emigrate to the United States.

Moving to America

In 1964, Vallejo—who didn't as yet speak English—arrived in New York City to become a professional artist. With eighty dollars in his pocket and no friends, family, or business connections, the young artist had to find a job quickly before he ended up on the streets. Fortunately, he met some of his fellow countrymen in a restaurant one day, and they provided him with a room in the Bronx for only ten dollars a week. It was also one of these new friends who located an employer willing to hire Vallejo as an advertising artist. Moving to Hartford, Connecticut, Vallejo worked for the company—a large chain store—for half a year before returning to New York City. It was here that he first met his future wife, Doris Maier.

Vallejo didn't want to stay in advertising forever, and the desire to do something more creative caused him to leave a steady paycheck behind for the uncertain life of a freelance artist. Accepting assignments from wherever they came, Vallejo worked under tight deadlines, drawing everything from Christmas cards to fashion designs. "I had already been working professionally for several years when I began to direct my efforts toward fantasy art," Vallejo recalled in *Fantasy Art Techniques*. "I had tried children's book illustration, mystery, men's magazines, and so on. But something jelled when I became aware of fantasy illustration." There was one major influence behind Vallejo's attraction to fantasy art. Ever since his first sessions drawing nude models at art school, Vallejo had been fascinated with the physical form of living creatures, whether they be human or animal. As a body builder, Vallejo was particularly interested in creating images of perfect human shapes. "I am interested in what I can do with a figure, and how well I can do it, how close to perfection I can come," the artist said. "And, by 'perfection' I don't mean how true to life but, rather, how true to a personal mental image or vision. I strive not only to copy life but also in a sense, to enhance it." The fantasy genre, where humans are often heroic and larger-than-life and monsters pose challenging anatomy problems, fit Vallejo's passions perfectly.

Vallejo was first exposed to the possibilities of fantasy art by reading comic books. His interest piqued by the illustrations he saw in these magazines, Vallejo copied the comic-book style as well as he could and, in 1971, submitted the results to Marvel Comics. To his amazement, the publisher accepted his paintings immediately, and it was not long before his illustrations were in great demand. When Vallejo decided to take the next step by taking his painting to book publishers, however, he was rejected several times. Chris Evans explained in *The Guide to Fantasy Art Techniques* that Vallejo later realized these rejections were the result of his "not being objective enough about his work. He believes that the artist has to cultivate an awareness of his shortcomings before he can begin to improve and produce professional work."

In *Fantasy Art Techniques*, Vallejo related how, after completing a few assignments for comic books, his confidence had grown—only to be knocked back down again when he attended his first Society of Illustrators show in New York City: "Since the annual show is supposed to contain the best that has been done in illustration for the given year, I was eager to see how my opinion of my work stacked up against the facts. The show was truly an eye opener—it made me realize how far I still had to go. I was disturbed for about a week, but after that I was simply determined to improve. As such, the show was not just a humbling experience for me but an inspiration and an impetus toward growth."

Resolving to break into the paperback market, Vallejo fine-tuned his technique during the mid-1970s and then took some of his comic illustrations to Ballantine Books. As del Rey recalled, "I remember the session we held at Ballantine Books when Boris first left his portfolio. I hardly had time to arrive at the office of my wife Judy-Lynn, who edits all the science fiction, before she urged me toward the art department. There Ian Summers, who was then Art Director, spread out half a dozen paintings to fill the room. 'Will you look at those

Vallejo—who received a 1980 Hugo Award nomination for best science fiction artist—strives to create images that are both inventive and believable.

backgrounds!' he called over his shoulder. 'Look at the detail—the depth.' Such enthusiasm in a busy art department is unusual, to say the least.'' Ballantine quickly agreed to pay Vallejo for several cover illustrations. In a matter of months, the artist's skills were in great demand, and in 1978 he won the best fantasy artist of the year award at the San Diego Fantasy and Science Fiction Convention.

Selling a Fantasy

It was through Ballantine that Vallejo created the book covers that would gain him a large circle of fantasy art fans. Already known for his depictions of Conan the Barbarian for Marvel Comics, he was selected to do the covers for Ballantine's reissue of seven of the *Gor* novels by John Norman and all of Edgar Rice Burroughs's Tarzan books; Vallejo also received attention for his work on the "Doc Savage" series. Of the artist's renditions for the Burroughs stories, del Rey judged that the "result was the finest series of paintings of the exploits of Edgar Rice Burroughs' ape-man ever to appear.

The artist's interest in the human form is evident in these fantasy sketches from his 1985 compilation, *Boris Vallejo: Fantasy Art Techniques.*

The series won such instant acclaim that Ballantine Books then issued the first fully-illustrated Tarzan calendar, with many of the cover illustrations from the books and a splendid centerfold showing La of Opar, especially drawn for the calendar. Fans of Tarzan had long requested such a calendar, but the proper material for it simply wasn't in existence. Now it exists, through the artistry of Boris Vallejo.''

Vallejo's paintings not only helped sell fantasy and science fiction novels to readers who had never picked up such books before; fans who already owned Tarzan, Conan, and Gor books were buying reprints simply for their new jacket illustrations. "There is an old saying,'' Vallejo commented in *Fantasy Art Techniques,* "that one shouldn't judge a book by its cover. But often enough a book is bought precisely because of its cover.'' The artist's talents had finally found a niche.

Although Vallejo has also painted covers for gothics, romances, westerns, mysteries, and science fiction novels, his fame mostly rests on his fantasy work, and it is these paintings that have also caused him the most grief from his critics (a number of whom have discredited the artist for his tendency to portray his subjects with little or no clothing). Vallejo, as one *Washington Post Book World* critic reported, "gets a bit irascible when he hears [his paintings] called 'soft-porn.'" And it's not only art critics, but also Vallejo's publishers who have censored his creations. "He's . . . learned to live with the frustrations of having cover-art returned to him with brass brassieres or G-strings added to cover up the more delicate parts of his female anatomies,'' commented Evans. As a response to those who would prefer that Vallejo keep his art a little more tame, the artist produced a collection of uncensored paintings entitled *Mirage.*

Painting the Boris Way

To help him paint his heroes and damsels, Vallejo first used professional models, "but now I find I get a more spontaneous and natural feeling if I work with non-professional people,'' he said in *The Guide to Fantasy Art Techniques.* Among these non-professionals are his friends, his wife Doris, and himself. Professional models are expensive to employ, and having them pose for long periods of time—even if the model is a friend or spouse—can be a tiresome experience for both model and artist. As a result, Vallejo usually uses photographs. "Today, 99% of all illustrators work from photographs,'' he remarked in *Fantasy Art Techniques.*

"It saves time and money. Students have asked me if this isn't cheating. First of all, you have to define what cheating is in the context of any given project. It is not as though specific rules are set down for the production of an illustration, and if you don't follow them, you are cheating. You must do whatever facilitates the process of getting the painting finished. This is especially important when you have to deal with deadlines." Whenever his students persist in their arguments by saying the Old Masters never used photographs, Vallejo logically argues that "I'm quite sure that if cameras had been available to the Old Masters, many of them would have preferred working from photographs rather than having the model shifting and moving and falling asleep, or whatever."

This doesn't mean, however, that an artist should reproduce exactly what he sees in a photograph. When it comes to painting a monster, Vallejo obviously has to improvise. But even when portraying humans and more conventional animals such as horses, "I rarely attempt to do a portrait or achieve a faithful likeness of my model," he revealed, later adding that "I sacrifice authenticity to achieve effect." Referring to one painting he did of a mounted warrior woman, the artist confessed, "I exaggerated an action and altered anatomy to heighten the sense of drama and movement." At the same time, he strives not to have his characters look like comic book heroes, with their dramatic and over-exaggerated poses. "He is also," Evans further noted, "at pains to avoid the photographic strangeness of frozen action, aiming for a more graceful, classical movement."

Vallejo wrote in *Fantasy Art Techniques* that knowing when and when not to break the rules is a decision best left to a fully trained artist. There is more than one way to achieve this goal. "More or less 'self-taught' artists will often discount the value of formal study. On the one hand I agree that the experience of painting itself is the most effective teacher.... On the other hand, nothing can take the place of being part of a learning community of your peers," he said, asserting later, "I did go to art school. I did become well acquainted with established methods and rules. I did study and copy the paintings of the Old Masters." A combination of formal and informal study worked well for Vallejo, but it was the informal training that was the most valuable. "One of his friends was a talented artist himself," reported Evans, "and Vallejo believes that he learned more from being coached by him than from formal classes at art school."

Because of his respect for the older techniques he learned in art school, Vallejo prefers to use oils when he paints, rather than the acrylics most commercial artists prefer. Acrylics are usually used because they dry much faster than oils, but Vallejo is able to achieve what del Rey called "a much wider range of tones and a feeling of what I can only describe as transparency that makes the painting seem deeper and more alive." The artist does this by adding coats of gesso, acrylic, and oil paint before beginning the actual painting. The combination of this base and the oil paints results in the effect that del Rey and so many others admire.

When Vallejo completes a painting, the final touch is to apply "one or two coats of retouch varnish to even out the colours," as he related in *Fantasy Art Techniques*. This will not preserve a work of art as well as adding a heavy varnish coat, but Vallejo is somewhat ambivalent about saving his art for posterity. His works are meant for commercial reproduction, so he is not too concerned about their immortality (though in his contracts he requests that his original paintings be returned to him after copies have been made). "Maybe I should be more interested in posterity, but I'm not

Vallejo created this advertisement for the 1985 film, *National Lampoon's European Vacation*, starring Chevy Chase.

at this time," he said. On the other hand, Vallejo switched from using ordinary illustration board to a higher quality, acid-free board that will keep his works from deteriorating. In *The Guide to Fantasy Art Techniques* he said, "Formerly I used to feel that if a painting lasted as long as I did, that was fine. But now I feel that if I really put myself into a painting I would like it to last as long as possible." Whether or not his paintings endure for future generations, Vallejo remains unique among fantasy artists because, as del Rey attested, "the vision of Boris is one that can penetrate to our deepest wish-dreams and give them the full visualization that makes them seem real and alive."

■ Works Cited

Dean, Martyn, editor, *The Guide to Fantasy Art Techniques*, text by Chris Evans, Arco Publishing, 1984.

Vallejo, Boris, *The Fantastic Art of Boris Vallejo*, introduction by Lester del Rey, Ballantine, 1978.
Vallejo, Boris, *Fantasy Art Techniques*, Arco Publishing, 1985.
Washington Post Book World, October 24, 1982, p. 15.

■ For More Information See

BOOKS

Weinberg, Robert, *Biographical Dictionary of Science Fiction and Fantasy Artists*, Greenwood Press, 1988.

PERIODICALS

Booklist, February 15, 1986, p. 845.
School Library Journal, May, 1986, p. 117.°

—*Sketch by Janet L. Hile*

Rosemary Wells

■ Personal

Born January 29, 1943, in New York, NY; married Thomas Moore Wells (an architect), 1963; children: Victoria, Marguerite (Bezoo). *Education:* Studied at the Museum School, Boston, MA.

■ Addresses

Home—738 Sleepy Hollow Rd., Briarcliff Manor, NY 10510.

■ Career

Freelance author and illustrator, 1968—. Worked for Allyn and Bacon, Boston, MA, and Macmillan Publishing Co., New York City.

■ Awards, Honors

Honor Book citation in the twelve to sixteen-year-old category, *Book World* Spring Children's Book Festival, 1972, for *The Fog Comes on Little Pig Feet*; Children's Book Showcase Award, Children's Book Council, 1974, for *Noisy Nora*; Citation of Merit, Society of Illustrators, 1974, for *Benjamin and Tulip*; Art Book for Children citation, Brooklyn

Museum and Brooklyn Public Library, 1975, 1976, and 1977, all for *Benjamin and Tulip*; Irma Simonton Black Award, Bank Street College of Education, for *Morris's Disappearing Bag: A Christmas Story*; Edgar Allan Poe Special Award, Mystery Writers of America, 1981, for *When No One Was Looking*; *Hazel's Amazing Mother* was named one of the *New York Times* Best Illustrated Books, 1985; Washington Irving Children's Book Choice Award, Westchester Library Association, 1986, for *Peabody*, and 1988, for *Max's Christmas*; Boston Globe-Horn Book Award, 1989, for *Shy Charles*; Child Study Association Children's Books of the Year citations for *Morris's Disappearing Bag* and *Don't Spill It Again, James*; *Booklist* Children's Editor's Choice citations for *Max's Toys: A Counting Book, Timothy Goes to School*, and *Through the Hidden Door*; *Horn Book* Fanfare citation and West Australian Young Readers' Book Award, both for *When No One Was Looking*; International Reading Association/Children's Book Council Children's Choice citations for *Timothy Goes to School, A Lion for Lewis*, and *Peabody*; Virginia Young Readers Award, and New York Public Library Books for Teenagers citation, both for *The Man in the Woods*; Cooperative Children's Book Center citation for *Max's Bedtime*; runner-up for Edgar Allan Poe Award, Mystery Writers of America, and ALA Best Books for Young Adults citation for *Through the Hidden Door*; *Bulletin of the Center for Children's Books* Blue Ribbon for *The Little Lame Prince*; Parents' Choice Award, Parents' Choice Foundation, for *Shy Charles*; Golden Kite Award, Society of Children's Book Writers, and International Reading Association Teacher's Choices list, both for *Forest of Dreams;* International Reading Association Children's Choices citation for *Max's Chocolate Chicken;* many of Wells's books were named among the best books of the year by *School Library Journal* or received American Library Association (ALA) Notable Book citations or *American Bookseller* "Pick of the Lists" citations.

■ Writings

YOUNG ADULT FICTION

(And illustrator) *The Fog Comes in on Little Pig Feet,* Dial, 1972.
None of the Above, Dial, 1974.
Leave Well Enough Alone, Dial, 1977.
When No One Was Looking, Dial, 1980.
The Man in the Woods, Dial, 1984.
(And illustrator) *Through the Hidden Door,* Dial, 1987.

JUVENILE

Forest of Dreams, illustrated by Susan Jeffers, Dial, 1988.
Lucy's Come to Stay, illustrated by Patricia Cullen-Clark, Dial, 1992. *Waiting for the Evening Star,* illustrated by Jeffers, Dial, 1993.

JUVENILE; SELF-ILLUSTRATED

John and Rarey, Funk, 1969.
Michael and the Mitten Test, Bradbury, 1969.
The First Child, Hawthorn, 1970.
Martha's Birthday, Bradbury, 1970.
Miranda's Pilgrims, Bradbury, 1970.
Unfortunately Harriet, Dial, 1972.
Benjamin and Tulip, Dial, 1973.
Noisy Nora, Dial, 1973.
Abdul, Dial, 1975.
Morris's Disappearing Bag: A Christmas Story, Dial, 1975.
Don't Spill It Again, James, Dial, 1977.
Stanley and Rhoda, Dial, 1978.
Good Night, Fred, Dial, 1981.
Timothy Goes to School, Dial, 1981.
A Lion for Lewis, Dial, 1982.
Peabody, Dial, 1983.
Hazel's Amazing Mother, Dial, 1985.
Shy Charles, Dial, 1988.
The Little Lame Prince (based on a story by Dinah Mulock Craik), Dial, 1990.
Fritz and the Mess Fairy, Dial, 1991.

"MAX" SERIES; SELF-ILLUSTRATED

Max's First Word, Dial, 1979.
Max's New Suit, Dial, 1979.
Max's Ride, Dial, 1979.

Max's Toys: A Counting Book, Dial, 1979.
Max's Bath, Dial, 1985.
Max's Bedtime, Dial, 1985.
Max's Breakfast, Dial, 1985.
Max's Birthday, Dial, 1985.
Max's Christmas, Dial, 1986.
Max's Chocolate Chicken, Dial, 1989.
Max's Dragon Shirt, Dial, 1991.
Max and Ruby's First Greek Myth: Pandora's Box, Dial, 1993.

"VOYAGE TO THE BUNNY PLANET" SERIES; SELF-ILLUSTRATED

First Tomato: A Voyage to the Bunny Planet, Dial, 1992.
The Island Light: A Voyage to the Bunny Planet, Dial, 1992.
Moss Pillows: A Voyage to the Bunny Planet, Dial, 1992.

ILLUSTRATOR

William S. Gilbert and Arthur Sullivan, *A Song to Sing, O!* (from *The Yeoman of the Guard*), Macmillan, 1968.
Gilbert and Sullivan, *W. S. Gilbert's "The Duke of Plaza Toro"* (from *The Gondoliers*), Macmillan, 1969.
Paula Fox, *Hungry Fred,* Bradbury, 1969.
Robert W. Service, *The Shooting of Dan McGrew [and] The Cremation of Sam McGee,* Young Scott Books, 1969.
(With Susan Jeffers) Charlotte Pomerantz, *Why You Look Like You When I Tend to Look Like Me,* Young Scott Books, 1969.
Rudyard Kipling, *The Cat That Walked by Himself,* Hawthorn, 1970.
Winifred Rosen Casey, *Marvin's Manhole,* Dial, 1970.
Marjorie Weinman Sharmat, *A Hot Thirsty Day,* Macmillan, 1971.
Ellen Conford, *Impossible, Possum,* Little, Brown, 1971.
Beryl Williams and Dorrit Davis, *Two Sisters and Some Hornets,* Holiday House, 1972.
Virginia A. Tashjian, editor, *With a Deep-Sea Smile: Story Hour Stretches for Large or Small Groups,* Little, Brown, 1974.
Lore G. Segal, *Tell Me a Trudy,* Farrar, Straus, 1977.

OTHER

(With Johanna Hurley) *Cooking for Nitwits* (adult nonfiction), Dutton, 1989.

(Contributor) *Worlds of Childhood: The Art and Craft of Writing for Children* (adult nonfiction), edited by William Zinsser, Houghton Mifflin, 1990.

(Contributor) *So I Shall Tell You a Story: The Magic World of Beatrix Potter,* Warne, 1993.

■ Adaptations

Max's Christmas and *Morris's Disappearing Bag* have been adapted as short films by Weston Woods.

■ Sidelights

"I do not feel that I get ideas. Books come on the [word processing] screen from outer space," writes Rosemary Wells, author and illustrator of picture books for toddlers and novels for teens, in an autobiographical *Horn Book* essay. Seeming to diminish the theory that writing is hard work, Wells's words, offered as if in reply to the question always asked of writers, "Where do you get your ideas?," might shock aspiring writers looking for advice on how to perfect their own creative techniques. Elsewhere, however, Wells admits to more conventional sources of ideas including observing her own children for inspiration for many of her books for her youngest readers, or consulting memories from her own youth for her work for young adults. "I put into my books," she notes in her *Something About the Author Autobiography Series* (SAAS) sketch, "all of the things I remember.... Those remembrances are jumbled up and churned because fiction is always more palatable than truth. They become more true as they are honed and whittled into characters and stories."

Wells's earliest remembrances are of her parents, two creative people who bestowed their love of the arts on their daughter. Both parents left from home at fourteen and went on to live rather colorful lives. Wells's father was a playwright who had the satisfaction of seeing one of his plays produced on Broadway in 1939. Besides his writing career, he was among other things a rancher in Australia and a stunt rider during the silent screen era in Hollywood. Wells's mother was a dancer who performed in the Ballet Russe de Monte Carlo and with the great Russian ballet star Pavlova. As Wells's recalls in her *SAAS* entry, her mother "spent half her life dancing in England and France." Her parents not only introduced her to the world beyond that of rural New Jersey, but they also instilled in their daughter a life-long love of books. In a *Horn Book* article in which Wells promotes a campaign for reading with children, she observes: "My parents and their generation, more than any other single thing, were readers. They loved and honored the written word and how the written word filled their minds and conversation with history, poetry, and ideas."

Wells's early years were also influenced by the loving presence of her grandmother to whom she was close enough to consider a third parent. Her grandmother lived just five miles away from the Wells family farm in a large Spanish-style house with a private beach. As if the sand and the sea were not enough to entertain a young girl the home boasted ivy-covered walls, a flourishing greenhouse, a fishpond with huge goldfish, and two granite fountains and other amenities. "I spent so much time in her enormous stucco house," Wells writes in *SAAS*, "that most of my sentimental and favorite memories, good and bad, come from that place and time on the New Jersey shore." When Wells was thirteen, for reasons that still remain mysterious, her parents sent her to a boarding school with her grandmother footing the bill. Unfortunately, the younger Wells hated boarding-school life and made a traumatic homecoming after just three weeks. Her horrendous experience at the boarding school is described in Wells's first novel for young adults, *The Fog Comes on Little Pig Feet.*

A love of things artistic and love itself called Wells away from the New Jersey seascapes that form such a large part of her memories. Like most children, Wells began drawing at an early age, but her drawings were much better than those of her peers. By the time she was in first grade she had already decided she wanted to be an artist when she grew up. She attended school in Red Bank and graduated from high school there in 1961. After high school, Wells she decided to study oil painting at the Museum School in Boston. The trendy dominance of abstract expressionism that Wells encountered among the faculty and students of the school soon discouraged her from pursuing her studies. "I hated it," she said of the school in a *Publishers Weekly* interview with Jean F. Mercier. "I quit to get married at 19 and was delighted at the chance to say goodbye to my teacher, who said it was no loss, I was nothing but an illustrator, anyway."

A "Lucky Break"

In 1963, the author married Tom Wells, an aspiring architect student at nearby Dartmouth. Wells gained a foothold in publishing when she took what appeared to be a temporary position filling in for a vacationing art editor at Allyn and Bacon, textbook publishers. Wells was soon hired, however, to replace the absent employee on a permanent basis. In *SAAS* Wells calls this her "first lucky break and the only one I ever needed." Two years later, the couple moved to New York City so Tom could pursue his architectural studies at Columbia University. There, Wells found a job at the children's books division of Macmillan. She set her course for a career as an art director.

One day Wells happened to hear a song from the popular Gilbert and Sullivan opera, *The Yeoman of the Guard,* and quickly made some sketches using birds instead of people to illustrate the lyrics. She gave the sketches, placed together to resemble a finished book, to the editor in chief, Susan Hirshman, and waited to hear the reaction. In *Horn Book,* Wells recounts what happened next: "She looked at it. Then she put it down and sang the whole thing. Several other editors were invited into her office to join choruses from [two other Gilbert and Sullivan operas] *The Mikado* and *H.M.S. Pinafore.* Then, by the by, she said, 'Sit down, Rosemary, you're a Macmillan author now.'" Wells's first book, *A Song to Sing, O!,* was published in 1968. Encouraged by her success, Wells decided to illustrate another Gilbert and Sullivan song, this time "The Duke of Plaza Toro" from *The Gondoliers.* This book was published the following year.

Within a couple of years Wells had settled with Dial Books for Children as her publisher and Phyllis Fogelman as her editor. By 1974, she had enough of a reputation that *Christian Science Monitor* contributor Jennifer Farley Smith claimed that Wells was part of the elite group of the country's "most gifted picture-book illustrators." Wells's influence as an illustrator of books for children was secured when the book series for which she is most widely known—the books featuring Max and his sister Ruby—were born. After listening to the way her daughter Victoria bossed around her younger sister Marguerite (more commonly known as Beezoo), Wells seized upon the idea for what would become the first installment in the Max series, *Max's First Word,* in 1977. Working on pieces of illustration board that happened to be on her drawing table, Wells took only a few hours to produce a major innovation in children's literature. In "The Well-Tempered Children's Book," Wells's essay in *Worlds of Childhood: The Art and Craft of Writing for Children,* she recalls the experience: "I couldn't really

understand what had happened. I had created what was clearly a picture book, but it was only sixteen pages long and wasn't for the usual nursery school and kindergarten crew. Picture books were thirty-two pages long, some even forty." Wells had succeeded in producing a funny, enjoyable story in only sixteen pages. Her editor loved it and asked her for three more and so *Max's Ride, Max's New Suit* and *Max's Toys* followed. Continuing the story, Wells notes with pride: "Thus were born what came to be known in book circles as 'board books'—books that could survive a certain amount of infant vandalizing without coming apart and, even more important, could make mother and fathers and their babies laugh at themselves and each other and the world around them."

Interaction between siblings—especially in the form of sibling rivalry—is a theme that surfaces in several of Wells's young adult novels as well as in the "Max" books. But her novels for young people are so different from her picture books that some people—even librarians—are often startled to find they are written by the same person. Some readers might even question why such a successful illustrator would want to write lengthy books with, for the most part, no illustrations. Wells explains her motives in an essay she contributed to *Publishers Weekly* on whether story or pictures are the most important aspect of a children's book. "I am both an artist and a writer," claims the author. "But I am firmly convinced that the story comes first.... The child may be charmed, intrigued or even inspired by good illustration, but it is the sound of the words and the story that first holds the child's attention." Assessing her own talents in the same essay, Wells declares she is in fact "a better writer than ... an illustrator."

Not So Fond Memories

As if easing into the world of writing for young adults, Wells first novel in the genre, *The Fog Comes on Little Pig Feet,* includes about a half a dozen full-page line drawings to illustrate the story. It is her only young adult novel that she illustrated throughout, although her 1987 mystery novel, *Through the Hidden Door,* does contain a few small drawings by the author. For inspiration for *The Fog Comes on Little Pig Feet* Wells searched her own memories. The novel tells the similar story of Rachel Saseekian who at thirteen is sent unwillingly to a boarding school. The novel is told in diary form through entries covering a two-week time period.

Like Wells, Rachel cannot really understand her parents' reasons for sending her away from home and she feels like an outcast almost as soon as she gets there. Rachel's alienation grows as she discovers that most of the other girls at the school are from rich families while she is the daughter of an electrician from Brooklyn. She also learns that the daily schedule the students must follow is so tightly regimented that free time or just time alone is nearly nonexistent. When she tries to arrange to have more time to practice the piano, she is rebuffed by rigid school administrators. To make herself feel better, Rachel writes in her diary at night while sitting in a bathtub behind a partition in the lavatory or escapes from her room to enjoy the stillness of the deserted school grounds. "Some reassurance does come from these funny old-fashioned partitions," one diary entry reads, "behind which, as last resort, everyone can just be herself. The schedule we are asked to live by here affords so little free time, and when free time is allowed, it's almost always arranged to be spent in the presence of others, so I've decided that sitting in this cubicle is the only way to be alone."

Rachel also takes comfort in lying, which she does often and with humorous results. Within the first week at school she has claimed the following: she is Jewish (so she can get out of the nightly vespers service), she has a boyfriend named Pete, her father is French and her father's name is Norman Mailer. When she winds up in the school infirmary, she meets Carlisle Daggett, an older girl known as a mischief maker who encourages Rachel to sneak out of the infirmary window and take a streetcar to Boston with her. Rachel confides in the older girl that she really wants to do well for her parents' sake. "They want me to have better than they did—and I guess I really love them very much, and anyway I want to do what's right. I don't want to be a coward and let them down." In Boston, Carlisle catches a bus to Greenwich Village where she plans to live with some friends. When Carlisle leaves Rachel promises not to tell anyone where she has gone, and the conflict of the novel begins. Confronted by the school's Honor Court for disobeying many of the school's strict rules and for not revealing what she knows about Carlisle's disappearance, Rachel finally even pressures her parents into lying for her so she won't have to go back on her promise.

Wells's inclusion of many autobiographical details in the book helped the main character come alive in the story, a point noticed by many critics. In *Publishers Weekly* Mercier summarizes critical

Wells's first young adult work centering on male characters was published in 1987.

thought on the novel noting: "The book won raves, with most reviewers impressed by the real-life feel of the chief character." Some critics remarked on Wells's admirable transition from picture books to the novel genre. Mrs. John G. Gray claims in *Best Sellers* that *The Fog Comes On Little Pig Feet* proves that Wells's "writing abilities are an easy match for her already famous artistic talents." In her *School Library Journal* review of the novel Alice Miller Bregman declares, "Young teens will devour this fast-paced, adequately written entertainment."

Dealing with Consequences

In 1974, Wells produced another novel for young adults, *None of the Above*, this time much more serious in tone and dealing with older teens. Like Rachel, Marcia Mill, the novel's main character, has to discover how to deal with the consequences of the choices she makes in her life. The novel is divided into six chapters, one each for each year of Marcia's life from the time she is thirteen until she turns eighteen. As the novel begins Marcia's father has recently married a long-time family friend, "Sparky" Van Dam, after Marcia's mother and Mrs. Van Dam's husband both died. Marcia tries to get accustomed to living with her new stepmother—who seems to be intent on "improving" Marcia—and her brainy step-sister, Christina, and quiet step-brother, John. While Marcia struggles to cope with her stressful home environment she also has to deal with the normal concerns shared by most adolescents like wanting to be popular, enduring dull classes and deciding on a career choice. Like Rachel, Marcia often finds it easier to pretend than risk appearing different. For example, when she gets a job as a waitress she tells everyone her name is Kimberly. "She liked being called Kim," the narrator tells us. "She enjoyed being good and being liked." Marcia's boyfriend, Raymond, and the couple's sexual relationship also play an important part in the development of the novel.

In her interview with Wells, Mercier refers to "the generally favorable notices" the book received while admitting that some critics objected in particular to the sense of hopelessness the novel's ending seemed to display. In Mercier's own *Publishers Weekly* review of the novel she finds the characters in the book too "unsavory" to care about and calls Marcia "a dolt who is more irritating than sympathetic." Although in her *School Library Journal* review Joni Bodart seems equally unimpressed by Marcia, the critic praises Wells's handling of this "doltish" character. Bodart calls the book "timely, realistic and moving." Wells tells Mercier in their interview that the main point of the novel's end was not whether it was optimistic or not, but that Marcia had finally made a decision entirely on her own without anyone pushing her into it and for her this was "the beginning of independence."

It's a Mystery

With her next young adult novel, *Leave Well Enough Alone*, Wells begins a yet another successful transition in her career. This time she becomes a mystery writer, a role that she must enjoy, for her next two novels for young adults also follow the same format. Like Rachel and Marcia, the teenage protagonists of Wells's mysteries must also make important ethical choices. Their decisions seem even more important because in these novels often the wrong choice could lead to physical danger. As to be expected, Wells once again delves into her past for a framework on which to set her narrative. Invoking her own memories of being a fourteen-

year-old mother's helper in Pennsylvania, Wells weaves the story of Dorothy Coughlin, a fourteen-year-old girl from Newburgh, New York, who also spends one summer working as a mother's helper in Pennsylvania. As an added hint to the autobiographical nature of the novel, it is set in 1956, the year Wells herself became a teenager.

Among other remembrances of Wells's childhood in this novel one finds that the Hoade estate where Dorothy works had at one time a greenhouse and fishponds like the author's grandmother's house. Knowing of Wells's habit of using autobiographical details in her works, one critic wrongly assumed that because Dorothy is Catholic and phones a nun friend of hers that Wells also grew-up as a Catholic. As Mercier describes the situation in *Publishers Weekly*, the unnamed critic went as far as to write that Wells relied "on her Irish-Catholic background, her intimacy with nuns as teachers especially, in creating the heroine." Wells finds that particular review very complementary because she is not Catholic but apparently was able to create a realistic heroine of that faith. She actually derived background material for Dorothy from memories of her best childhood friend who was Catholic and who told Wells about her own experiences in parochial school. In fact, Wells would again write about the Catholic school experience and nuns in a later novel.

Dorothy comes to the lavish country estate of John and Maria Hoade to take care of the couple's daughters, eleven-year-old Jenny and nine-year-old Lisa. As it turns out, Mrs. Hoade does not have a job but wants to have extra time for her experiments with recipes for the cookbook she is writing. In an revelatory episode near the beginning of the novel, Dorothy explains that sometimes lying is justified to avoid "getting someone else into trouble," but notes that her own mother is "so scrupulously honest that she put dimes back in vending machines and telephones that gave more change than they ought." As the story continues, Dorothy herself often lies to cover up things that embarrass her; she tells Mrs. Hoade, for example, that her father is chief-of-police in her hometown when he's actually just a "beat cop." But Dorothy is not the only one with something to cover up because as Jenny notes, "Mom's a big liar.... She usually tells people things that will suit them, depending on who they are. For instance she tells Daddy's Jewish friends she's Jewish even though she isn't, and she told our Spanish nurse in South America that she was Catholic, which she isn't." Mrs. Hoade tells the girls that their newborn sister—whom they've never seen—has a cold, while confiding in Dorothy that the infant is really being kept separate from her siblings because she is has Down's Syndrome. Eventually the reader finds themselves doubting everything and everybody because, as *New York Times Book Review* contributor Susan Terris notes, the Hoade home is a "place [that] reeks of menace, mystery and lies."

Curious about the baby and several other things that just don't seem right to her, Dorothy begins snooping around the house looking for clues that would reveal the truth that the Hoades seem to be hiding. Her pushy older sister, Maureen, and several other people warn her "to leave well enough alone" and mind her own business, but Dorothy cannot stop until she discovers the whole story herself. Then, in a final moment of truth, she must decide what is the right thing to do with the information she has uncovered.

The reader is taken along for an exciting ride from clue to clue in this well-received mystery. Although several critics, like Zena Sutherland in *Bulletin of the Center for Children's Books,* find the plot a little "overcrowded," most reviewers admire Wells's sense of humor and moral questions developed in the narrative. Jane Abramson calls the book "Wells'[s] finest novel yet" and finds the plot "raises thorny ethical questions and discusses them compellingly and with great humor." In *Book World* Katherine Paterson writes, "I began this book laughing with delight at Rosemary Wells's marvelous re-creation of fourteenness." Terris claims that the book is "well-written" and also applauds the fact that after the reader finishes the novel he or she will continue to "wrestle with the question of whether 'leaving well enough alone' *is* the right solution to a complicated moral dilemma."

Tennis, Anyone?

In Wells's next young adult novel, *When No One Was Looking,* the author explores the world of tennis. This mystery features Kathy Bardy, a fourteen-year-old tennis star from Plymouth, Massachusetts who loves tennis but harbors a secret ambition—just as Wells did, according to her *SAAS* entry—to be a baseball player. Like Rachel's parents in *The Fog Comes on Little Pig Feet,* and Marcia's stepmother in *None of the Above,* Kathy's parents push their daughter to excel. As Kathy looks forward to the New England Championship competition where a win would guarantee her a spot in the Nationals, her father lays out his plan

for her success: "Well, you better crack the books tonight. After that you have nothing to do but run, work out all your kinks on the court, sleep and eat. You've got to get ready Saturday morning for the biggest match of your life." He also forbids her from playing baseball so she won't accidentally hurt her arm.

But Wells isn't interested in writing just about tennis or family communication, for as Paul Heins notes in *Horn Book,* while *When No One Was Looking* begins "as a story of athletic prowess, the novel gradually develops as a series of moral issues that take on tragic overtones." When Ruth Gumm, the one tennis player skilled enough to beat Kathy, is found dead in the swimming pool at the Plymouth Bath and Tennis Club where Kathy practices with her coach, Marty, Kathy and her supporters are immediately under suspicion. One by one the suspects are cleared, but Kathy feels compelled to continue her sleuthing even after the real detectives consider the case closed. Her moral compulsion to find out all the facts related to the crime

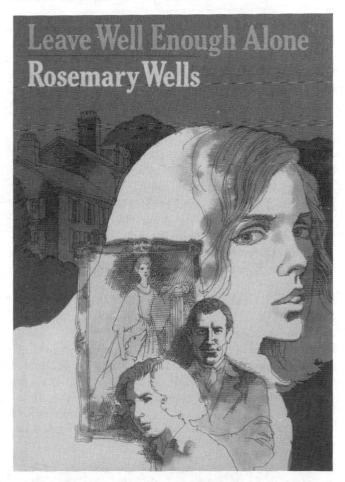

This 1977 book revolves around Dorothy, a teenager who discovers a web of lies surrounding her summertime employers.

leads her to an unexpected conclusion. Realizing what consequences the truth will bring, Kathy cries bitterly to herself: "If only I hadn't bothered to go down to the police station, then at least I wouldn't know. *I don't* want *to know. Why wasn't it enough for me to just know that I didn't do it?*"

When No One Was Looking was a runner-up for the prestigious Edgar Allan Poe Award, given annually by the Mystery Writers of America. It also won a *Horn Book* Fanfare citation, a West Australian Young Readers' Book Award and was on the American Library Association and the *School Library Journal* lists of best books of the year. Although some critics point to either one or another character in the novel as being ill-defined, Wells is generally praised for this offering for the mystery-lovers book shelf. *School Library Journal* contributor Robert Unsworth observes: "There is a lot to this novel and most of it is excellent." Similarly, in the *New York Times Book Review* Anne Tyler notes that the book "has energy and style, and it ought to rivet the most restless young reader."

Punk Rock Thrower Strikes Again

Wells continued her string of successful mysteries with publication of *The Man in the Woods* in 1984. Like other Wells novels, this one features a teenage heroine who must struggle with a moral dilemma. In this case, fourteen-year-old Helen Curragh tries to figure out the identity of the Punk Rock Thrower after she accidentally witnesses him causing yet another car to crash after breaking its windshield with a tossed rock. Helen and fifteen-year-old Pinky Levy meet on the second day of school at New Bedford Regional High School, discover they're both on the staff of the school paper, the *Whaler*, and soon become embroiled in a frantic search through New Bedford documents dating back to the time of the Civil War. Together they gather clues, narrowly escape death, and uncover a secret one of New Bedford's oldest families has been covering up for over a hundred years. As the story ends, Helen wrestles with the desire to write a story for the *Whaler* about their search and have a chance at being the first freshman ever to win the coveted gold medal for best story of the year or to keep what she knows to herself.

Critics praise the mystery-within-a-mystery plot developed in *The Man in the Woods*. They also applaud Wells finely drawn characters. Here, the author again draws on recollections of her child-

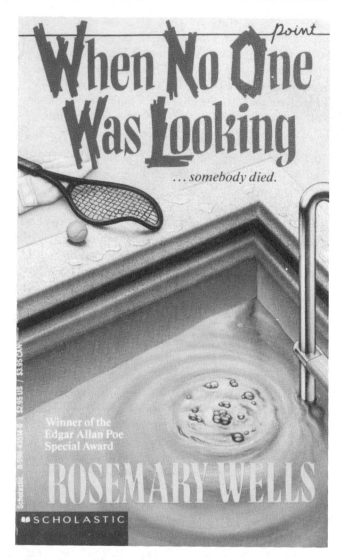

In this Edgar Award-winning 1980 novel, a young tennis player attempts to uncover the mystery behind her opponent's death.

hood Catholic friend to help in the characterization of Helen who mentions in the novel that she went to a Catholic elementary school. At one point Helen even contacts a former teacher, Sr. Ignatius Paul, just as Dorothy does in *Leave Well Enough Alone*. In *School Library Journal*, for example, Drew Stevenson finds the historical details in the novel "a fascinating subplot," and in an additional comment writes, "the book ... boasts an array of interesting characters, deftly brought to life." In *Horn Book*, Ethel L. Heins also calls attention to the novel's "wealth of vivid characters" and labels the work "a riveting contemporary tale of emotion, mystery, and suspense."

For the Boys

Although Pinky figured prominently in *The Man in the Woods, Through the Hidden Door*, Wells's 1987 mystery novel, is her first young adult offering which depends almost entirely on male characters. Barney Pennimen is from Landry, Colorado, but attending Winchester Boys' Academy out East because his mother is dead and his father's antiques business takes him traveling a lot. Like parents in other Wells novel, Barney's father has a ambitious goals for his son. "The Plan," according to Barney, includes the following: "Go to Winchester. Graduate with honors. Go on to Hotchkiss. Graduate with honors. Get into Harvard. Magma cum laude from there and on to Yale or Oxford (as he did)." Barney is an honor student who in order to fit in chooses to befriend a group of cruel but popular boys. As the friendships go sour and even

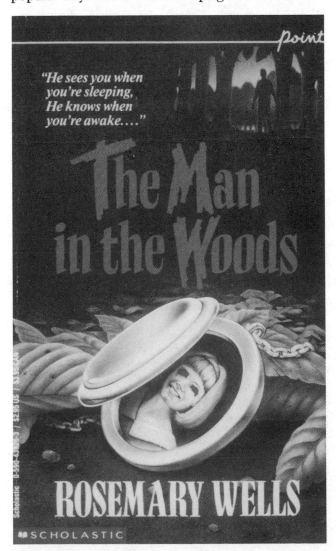

A high school journalist searches for the identity of the Punk Rock Thrower in Wells's 1984 mystery.

the school headmaster turns against him, Barney seeks the company of a bookish freshman loner named Snowy Cobb. The younger boy eventually leads Barney to a hidden cave where the two spend hours uncovering archaeological treasures. The cave becomes a safe-haven where Snowy and Barney can enjoy themselves and not be concerned about outside pressures of peers or parents.

Through the Hidden Door was a runner-up for the Edgar Allan Poe award of the Mystery Writers of America and received citations recognizing it as both one of the American Library Association's Best Books for Young Adults and one of *Booklist's* Children's Editor's Choices for the year. In her *Bulletin of the Center for Children's Books* review Zena Sutherland gives the novel her highest recommendation, calling it "one of the best stories Rosemary Wells has written." *Kliatt Young Adult Paperback Book Guide* contributor Mary I. Purucker finds the book "fast paced, [and] well written." Other reviewers such as David Gale and Ilene Cooper praise Wells for her ability to develop both plot and characters with superb results. According to Gale's *School Library Journal* review, Snowy and Barney "are both fully realized characters" and the novel as a whole as "an absorbing school story with a twist." In her *Booklist* review Cooper describes *Through a Hidden Door* as "a riveting psychological thriller" and lauds the author's development of "her story in ways sure to get readers thinking."

Wells has seen publishing from both sides—as a designer of books and as an author—and succeeded at both. As an author she has successfully written and illustrated children's books, illustrated other people's books, written mysteries, school stories and pursued moral issues with young adults. All the while she has delighted parents, critics and readers. Although her vivid memories of the past seem to be invaluable to her continued success, her wide audience of readers can only wait and wonder what she will tackle in the future. Given her view of the creative process Wells might just be waiting for that next idea to appear on her word processing screen. "I believe that all stories," she explained in *Worlds of Childhood,* "and plays and paintings and songs and dances come from a palpable but unseen space in the cosmos. Ballets and symphonies written during our lifetime were there before we were born. According to how gifted we are, we are all given a large or small key to this treasury of wonders. I have been blessed with a small key to the world of the young."

■ **Works Cited**

Abramson, Jane, review of "Leave Well Enough Alone," *School Library Journal*, May, 1977, p. 73.

Bodart, Joni, review of "None of the Above," *School Library Journal*, November, 1974, p. 69.

Bregman, Alice Miller, review of "The Fog Comes on Little Pig Feet," *School Library Journal*, May, 1972, p. 89.

Cooper, Ilene, review of "Through the Hidden Door," *Booklist*, April 15, 1987, p. 1296.

Gale, David, review of "Through the Hidden Door," *School Library Journal*, April, 1987, p. 114.

Gray, Mrs. John G., review of "The Fog Comes on Little Pig Feet," *Best Sellers*, July 15, 1972, p. 200.

Heins, Ethel L., review of "The Man in the Woods," *Horn Book*, September-October, 1984, pp. 601-02.

Heins, Paul, review of "When No One Was Looking," *Horn Book*, October, 1980, pp. 529-30.

Mercier, Jean F., review of "None of the Above," *Publishers Weekly*, August 5, 1974, p. 58.

Paterson, Katherine, "The Case of the Curious Babysitter," *Book World*, May 1, 1977, p. E4.

Purucker, Mary I., review of "Through the Hidden Door," *Kliatt Young Adult Paperback Book Guide*, April, 1989, p.20.

Smith, Jennifer Farley, "Animals Are Enduring Heroes," *Christian Science Monitor*, March 6, 1974, p. F2.

Stevenson, Drew, review of "The Man in the Woods," *School Library Journal*, May, 1984, p. 104.

Sutherland, Zena, review of "Leave Well Enough Alone," *Bulletin of the Center for Children's Books*, October, 1977, p. 40.

Sutherland, Zena, review of "Through the Hidden Door," *Bulletin of the Center for Children's Books*, July-August, 1987, p. 220.

Terris, Susan, review of "Leave Well Enough Alone," *New York Times Book Review*, July 10, 1977, pp. 20-21.

Tyler, Anne, review of "When No One Was Looking," *New York Times Book Review*, February 1, 1981, p. 28.

Unsworth, Robert, review of "When No One Was Looking," *School Library Journal*, October, 1980, p. 159.

Wells, Rosemary, *The Fog Comes on Little Pig Feet*, Dial, 1972.

Wells, Rosemary, *None of the Above*, Dial, 1974.

Wells, Rosemary, *Leave Well Enough Alone*, Dial, 1977.

Wells, Rosemary, *When No One Was Looking*, Dial, 1980.

Wells, Rosemary, interview with Jean F. Mercier, *Publishers Weekly*, February 29, 1980, pp. 72-73.

Wells, Rosemary, essay in *Something about the Author Autobiography Series*, Volume 1, Gale, 1986, pp. 279-291.

Wells, Rosemary, "The Artist at Work: The Writer at Work," *Horn Book*, March/April, 1987, pp. 163-170.

Wells, Rosemary, "Words & Pictures: The Right Order," *Publishers Weekly*, February 27, 1987, p. 146.

Wells, Rosemany, *Through the Hidden Door*, Dial, 1987.

Wells, Rosemary, "The Well-Tempered Children's Book," in *Worlds of Childhood: The Art and Craft of Writing for Children*, edited by William Zinsser, Houghton Mifflin, 1990, pp. 121-143.

Wells, Rosemary, "'The Most Important Twenty Minutes of Your Day!,'" *Horn Book*, May/June, 1993, pp. 307-310.

■ **For More Information See**

BOOKS

Sadker, Myra Pollack, and David Miller Sadker, *Now Upon a Time: A Contemporary View of Children's Literature*, Harper, 1977, pp. 66-67.

PERIODICALS

Best Sellers, February 15, 1975, p. 519-520.

Bulletin of the Center for Children's Books, April, 1975, p. 139.

Growing Point, May, 1976, pp. 2891-92.

Horn Book, May/June, 1987, pp. 368-71.

Times Literary Supplement, October 1, 1976, p. 1243.°

—Sketch by Marian C. Gonsior

Acknowledgments

Acknowledgments

Grateful acknowledgment is made to the following publishers,
authors, and artists for their kind permission to reproduce copyrighted material.

ISAAC ASIMOV. Cover of *I, Robot*, by Isaac Asimov. Ballantine Books, 1983. Copyright © 1950 by Isaac Asimov. Copyright renewed © 1977 by Isaac Asimov. Cover art by Don Dixon. Reprinted by permission of Ballantine Books, a division of Random House, Inc./ Cover of *Foundation's Edge*, by Isaac Asimov. Cover art copyright © 1991 by Stephen Youll. Reprinted by permission of Bantam Books, a division of Bantam Doubleday Dell Publishing Group, Inc./ Cover of *The Caves of Steel*, by Isaac Asimov. Bantam Books, 1991. Copyright © 1953, 1954 by Isaac Asimov. Cover art copyright © 1991 by Stephen Youll. Reprinted by permission of Bantam Books, a division of Bantam Doubleday Dell Publishing Group, Inc./ Cover of *Foundation*, by Isaac Asimov. Ballantine Books, 1983. Copyright © 1951 by Isaac Asimov. Reprinted by permission of Ballantine Books, a division of Random House, Inc./ Jacket of *Robots And Empire*, by Isaac Asimov. Doubleday, 1985. Copyright © 1985 by Nightfall, Inc. Jacket design by Barclay Shaw. Reprinted by Doubleday, a division of Bantam Doubleday Dell Publishing Group, Inc./ Cover of *Isaac Asimov's Science Fiction*, Vol. 13 No. 5. Davis Publications, Inc., 1989. Cover art by Christos Achilleos copyright © 1985. Reprinted by permission of Christos Achilleos./ Photograph from *In Memory Yet Green: The Autobiography of Isaac Asimov, 1920-1954*, by Isaac Asimov. Copyright © 1979 by Isaac Asimov. Reprinted by permission of Doubleday, a division of Bantam Doubleday Dell Publishing Group, Inc./ Cover of the Isaac Asimov issue of the *Magazine of Fantasy & Science Fiction*, October 1966. Copyright © 1966 by Mercury Press, Inc. Reprinted by permission of the *Magazine of Fantasy & Science Fiction.* / Photograph © Estate of Alex Gotfryd.

FRANCESCA LIA BLOCK. Cover of *Weetzie Bat*, by Francesca Lia Block. Copyright © 1989 by Francesca Lia Block. Cover art copyright © 1992 by Wendy Braun. Copyright © 1992 by HarperCollins Publishers. Reprinted by permission of HarperCollins Publishers, Inc./ Jacket of *Missing Angel Juan*, by Francesca Lia Block. Photo copyright © 1993 by Chris Michaels, FPG International Corp. Jacket design by Steven M. Scott. Jacket copyright © 1993 by HarperCollins Publishers. Jacket design reprinted by permission of HarperCollins Publishers. Jacket photo reprinted by permission of Chris Michaels, FPG International./ Cover of *Witch Baby*, by Francesca Lia Block. Copyright © 1991 by Francesca Lia Block. Cover art copyright © 1992 by Wendy Braun. Cover copyright © 1992 by HarperCollins Publishers. Reprinted by permission of HarperCollins Publishers, Inc./ Photograph courtesy of HarperCollins Publishers, Inc.

MEL BROOKS. Movie still from *Blazing Saddles*, courtesy of Warner Brothers./ TV still from *Your Show of Shows*, courtesy of NBC-TV./ Movie still from *The Nude Bomb*, courtesy of Universal City Studios, Inc./ Movie still from *Young Frankenstein*, courtesy of Twentieth Century-Fox./ Movie still from *The Producers*, courtesy of Embassy Home Entertainment./ Movie still from *Robin Hood: Men in Tights*, courtesy of Twentieth Century-Fox.

CHRISTOPHER and JAMES LINCOLN COLLIER. Cover of *War Comes to Willy Freeman*, by James Lincoln Collier and Christopher Collier. Copyright © 1983 by James Lincoln Collier and Christopher Collier. Cover painting by Gordon Crabb. Reprinted by Dell Books, a division of Bantam Doubleday Dell Publishing Group./ Cover of *My Brother Sam Is Dead*, by James Lincoln Collier and Christopher Collier. Copyright © 1974 by James Lincoln Collier and Christopher Collier. Cover art by Di Cesare. Reprinted by permission of Scholastic Inc./ Photograph of brothers at home, courtesy of Christopher Collier./ Photographs courtesy of Scholastic Inc.

SUSAN COOPER. Cover of *Dawn of Fear*, by Susan Cooper. Cover illustration copyright © 1989 by Samson Pollen. Cover design by Lynn Braswell. Reprinted by permission of Samson Pollen./ Cover of *Silver on the Tree*, by Susan Cooper. Cover illustration copyright © 1986 by David Wiesner. Reprinted by permission of Collier Books, an imprint of Macmillan Publishing Company./ Cover of *The Grey King*, by Susan Cooper. Cover illustration copyright © 1986 by David Wiesner. Reprinted by permission of Collier Books, an imprint of Macmillan Publishing Company./ Cover of *The Dark Is Rising*, by Susan Cooper. Cover illustration copyright © 1986 by David Wiesner. Reprinted by permission of Collier Books, an imprint of Macmillan Publishing Company./ Cover of *Over Sea, under Stone*, by Susan Cooper. Cover illustration copyright © 1989 by Jeffrey Lindberg. Reprinted by permission of Jeffrey Lindberg./ Photograph by Birgit Blyth.

STEPHEN HAWKING. Cover of *A Brief History of Time: From the Big Bang to Black Holes*, by Stephen Hawking. Copyright © 1988 by Stephen W. Hawking. Reprinted by permission of Bantam Books, a division of Bantam Doubleday Dell Publishing Group, Inc./ Jacket of *Black Holes and Baby Universes and Other Essays*, by Stephen Hawking. Copyright © 1993 by Stephen W. Hawking. Jacket design copyright © 1993 by One Plus One Studio. Reprinted by Bantam Books, a division of Bantam Doubleday Dell Publishing Group, Inc./ Photograph of Hawking giving lecture, AP/ Wide World Photos./ Photograph of Hawking with children and wife Jane, by Homer Sykes-Woodfin Camp &

Associates./ Photograph of Hawking's Oxford graduation, courtesy of Stephen Hawking./ Photograph of Hawking and postgraduate assistant, by Miriam Berkley./ Photograph by Stephen Shames/Visions.

MOLLIE HUNTER. Jacket of *The Stronghold*, by Mollie Hunter. Copyright © 1974 by Maureen Mollie Hunter McIlwraith. Jacket drawing by Eileen Altman. Reprinted by permission of HarperCollins Publishers, Inc./ Cover of *A Sound of Chariots*, by Mollie Hunter. Cover art copyright © 1988 by Linda Benson. Cover copyright © 1988 by Harper & Row Publishers, Inc. Reprinted by permission of HarperCollins Publishers, Inc./ Cover of *The Walking Stones*, by Mollie Hunter. Illustrations copyright © 1970 by Trina Schart Hyman. Reprinted by permission of HarperCollins Publishers, Inc./ Photographs courtesy of Mollie Hunter.

HADLEY IRWIN. Cover of *Kim/Kimi* by Hadley Irwin. Copyright © 1987 by Lee Hadley and Ann Irwin. Cover illustration copyright © 1987 by Ellen Thompson. Reprinted by permission of Ellen Thompson./ Jacket of *The Original Freddie Ackerman*, by Hadley Irwin. Copyright © 1992 by Hadley Irwin. Jacket illustration copyright © 1992 by James Hoston. Reprinted by permission of James Hoston./ Cover of *What About Grandma?*, by Hadley Irwin. Copyright © 1982 by Lee Hadley and Ann Irwin. Reprinted by permission of Avon Books, New York./ Jacket of *Can't Hear You Listening*, by Hadley Irwin. Copyright © 1990 by Hadley Irwin. Jacket illustration copyright © 1990 by Ellen Thompson. Reprinted by permission of Ellen Thompson./ Jacket of *Abby, My Love*, by Hadley Irwin. Copyright © 1985 by Lee Hadley and Ann Irwin. Jacket painting copyright © 1985 by Deborah Chabrian. Reprinted by permission of Deborah Chabrian.

JAMAICA KINCAID. Jacket of *Lucy*, by Jamaica Kincaid. Text copyright © 1990 by Jamaica Kincaid. Jacket painting by Paul Gauguin, 'Poemes Barbares,' 1896. Courtesy of The Fogg Art Museum, Harvard University, Cambridge, Massachusetts. Bequest—Collection of Maurice Wertheim, Class of 1906. Jacket design copyright © 1990 by Cynthia Krupat. Jacket design reprinted by permission of Farrar, Straus and Giroux, Inc./ Jacket of *At the Bottom of the River*, by Jamaica Kincaid. Text copyright © 1983 by Jamaica Kincaid. Jacket design copyright © 1983 by Cynthia Krupat. Jacket illustration, 'Green Summer' by Sir Edward Coley Burne-Jones, 1868. Reprinted by permission of Farrar, Straus and Giroux, Inc./ Cover of *Annie John*, by Jamaica Kincaid. Copyright © 1983, 1984, 1985 by Jamaica Kincaid. Reprinted by permission of Dutton Signet, a division of Penguin Books USA Inc./ Photograph © Jerry Bauer.

MERCEDES LACKEY. Jacket of *Winds of Change: Book Two of the Mage Winds*, by Mercedes Lackey. Copyright © 1992 by Mercedes R. Lackey. Jacket painting by Jody A. Lee. Jacket designed by George Long. Reprinted by permission of Jody A. Lee./ Jacket of *Queen's Own: Arrows of the Queen, Arrow's Flight, Arrow's Fall*, by Mercedes Lackey. *Arrows Of The Queen*, copyright © 1987 by Mercedes R. Lackey. *Arrow's Flight*, copyright © 1987 by Mercedes R. Lackey. *Arrow's Fall*, copyright © 1988 by Mercedes R. Lackey. Jacket art by Dawn Wilson. Jacket design by Jeff Brenner. Reprinted by permission of Doubleday Book & Music Clubs, Inc./ Jacket of *The Lark and the Wren: Book One of Bardic Voices*, by Mercedes Lackey. Copyright © 1992 by Mercedes R. Lackey. Jacket art by Darrell Sweet. Reprinted by permission of Baen Publishing Enterprises./ Cover of *The Oathbound, Book One: Vows and Honor*, by Mercedes Lackey. Copyright © 1988 by Mercedes R. Lackey. Cover art by Jody Lee. Reprinted by permission of Jody A. Lee./ Photograph courtesy of Glamour Shots.

HARPER LEE. Photograph of Monroe County Courthouse from *A Bridge Of Childhood: Truman Capote's Southern Years*, by Marianne M. Moates. Copyright © 1989 by Marianne M. Moates. Reprinted by permission of Aaron White Photography./ Photograph of Monroeville street scene from *A Bridge Of Childhood: Truman Capote's Southern Years*, by Marianne M. Moates. Copyright © 1989 by Marianne M. Moates. Reprinted by permission of *The Monroe Journal*. / Cover of *To Kill a Mockingbird*, by Harper Lee. Copyright © 1960 by Harper Lee. Cover printed in U.S.A. copyright © 1987 by Warner Books. Reprinted by permission of Warner Books, Inc./ Movie still from *To Kill a Mockingbird*, courtesy of Universal International./ Photograph by G. D. Hackett.

SONIA LEVITIN. Cover of *Journey to America*, by Sonia Levitin. Cover illustration copyright © 1987 by Deborah Chabrian. Cover design by Lisa Hollander. Reprinted by permission of Deborah Chabrian./ Cover of *Incident at Loring Groves*, by Sonia Levitin. Copyright © 1988 by Sonia Levitin. Reprinted by permission of Ballantine Books, a division of Random House, Inc./ Cover of *The Return*, by Sonia Levitin. Copyright © 1987 by Sonia Levitin. Cover art by Yozk. Reprinted by permission of Ballantine Books, a division of Random House, Inc./ Jacket of *The No-Return Trail*, by Sonia Levitin. Copyright © 1978 by Harcourt Brace Jovanovich, Inc. Jacket design by Loretta Trezzo./ Jacket of *Annie's Promise* by Sonia Levitin. Atheneum, 1993. Jacket illustration copyright © 1993 by Deborah Chabrian. Reprinted by permission of Deborah Chabrian./ Photograph by Rose Eichenbaum.

JACK LONDON. Illustration from *Jack London: Three Novels*, edited by Paul J. Horowitz. Introduction copyright © 1980 by Outlet Book Company, Inc./ Cover design of *The Sea Wolf*, by Jack London. Copyright © 1931 by Jack London. Cover art reprinted by courtesy of the Board of Trustees of the Victoria & Albert Museum. Cover design reprinted by permission of Bantam Books, a division of Bantam Doubleday Dell Publishing Group, Inc./ Cover of *The Call of the Wild*, by Jack London. All new material in this edition is copyright © 1986 by Tom Doherty Associates, Inc. Reprinted by permission of Tom Doherty Associates./ Cover of *White Fang*, by Jack London. Reprinted by permission of Scholastic Inc./ Movie still from *White Fang*, courtesy of Buena Vista Pictures./ Photograph of London writing outdoors, The Bettmann Archive.

MAD MAGAZINE. Illustrations from *Mad*, number 324. Entire contents copyright © 1993 by E.C. Publications, Inc. Artwork by Mort Drucker. Text by Stan Hart. Reprinted by permission of E.C. Publications, Inc./ Cover of *Mad*, number

324. Entire contents copyright © 1993 by E.C. Publications, Inc. Cover art by Richard Williams. Reprinted by permission of E.C. Publications, Inc./ Illustrations and photographs from *Completely Mad: A History of the Comic Book and Magazine,* by Maria Reidelbach. Text copyright © 1991 by Maria Reidelbach. *Mad* and E.C. Publications material copyright © 1952, 1953, 1954, 1955, 1956, 1957, 1958, 1959, 1960, 1961, 1962, 1963, 1964, 1965, 1966, 1967, 1968, 1969, 1970, 1971, 1972, 1973, 1974, 1975, 1976, 1977, 1978, 1979, 1980, 1981, 1982, 1983, 1984, 1985, 1986, 1987, 1988, 1989, 1990, 1991 by E.C. Publications, Inc. Reprinted by permission of E.C. Publications, Inc./ Photograph of Gaines by Mike Fuller.

MEREDITH ANN PIERCE. Jacket of *Birth of the Firebringer,* by Meredith Ann Pierce. Copyright © 1985 by Macmillan Publishing Company. Jacket art by Dale Gottlieb. Reprinted by permission of Four Winds Press, an imprint of Macmillan Publishing Company./ Jacket of *The Pearl of the Soul of the World,* by Meredith Ann Pierce. Copyright © 1990 by Meredith Ann Pierce. Jacket illustration by Palo Amtmann. Reprinted by permission of Little, Brown and Company./ Cover of *The Woman Who Loved Reindeer,* by Meredith Ann Pierce. Copyright © 1985 by Meredith Ann Pierce. Cover art by Dennis Nolan. Reprinted by permission of Tom Doherty Associates, Inc./ Jacket of *The Darkangel Trilogy,* by Meredith Ann Pierce. *The Darkangel:* Copyright © 1982 by Meredith Ann Pierce. *A Gathering of Gargoyles:* Copyright © 1984 by Meredith Ann Pierce. *The Pearl of the Soul of the World:* Copyright © 1990 by Meredith Ann Pierce. Jacket art by Dawn Wilson. Reprinted by permission of Doubleday Book & Music Clubs, Inc./ Photograph by Jo Ann Bell Pierce.

CHRISTOPHER PIKE. Cover of *Die Softly,* by Christopher Pike. Copyright © 1991 by Christopher Pike. Cover art by Brian Kotzky. Reprinted by permission of Pocket Books, a division of Simon & Schuster Inc./ Cover of *Spellbound,* by Christopher Pike. Copyright © 1988 by Christopher Pike. Cover art copyright © 1988 by Brian Kotzky. Reprinted by permission of Pocket Books, a division of Simon & Schuster Inc./ Cover of *The Wicked Heart,* by Christopher Pike. Copyright © 1993 by Christopher Pike. Cover art by Dru Blair. Reprinted by permission of Pocket Books, a division of Simon & Schuster Inc./ Photograph by Michael C. McFadden.

SYLVIA PLATH. Cover of *The Collected Poems: Sylvia Plath,* edited by Ted Hughes. Poems copyright © 1960, 1965, 1971, 1981 by the estate of Sylvia Plath. Editorial material copyright © 1981 by Ted Hughes. Reprinted by permission of HarperCollins Publishers, Inc./ Illustration from *Bitter Fame: A Life of Sylvia Plath,* by Anne Stevenson with additional material by Lucas Myers, Dido Merwin, and Richard Murphy. Houghton Mifflin Company, 1989. Copyright © 1989 by Anne Stevenson. Appendix I copyright © 1989 by Lucas Myers. Appendix II copyright © 1989 by Dedo Merwin. Appendix III copyright © 1989 by Richard Murphy. All unpublished material by Sylvia Plath and Ted Hughes copyright © 1989 by Ted Hughes. Reprinted by permission of the estate of Sylvia Plath./ Cover of *The Bell Jar,* by Sylvia Plath. Copyright © 1971 by Harper & Row, Publishers. Reprinted by permission of Bantam, a division of Bantam Doubleday Dell Publishing Group, Inc./ Photograph © Rollie McKenna.

ROB REINER. Movie still from *Spinal Tap,* courtesy Embassy Pictures Inc./ Photograph from the set of *The Princess Bride* by Clive Coote./ Movie still from *Stand By Me,* courtesy of Columbia Pictures./ Photograph, AP/Wide World Photos.

WILLO DAVIS ROBERTS. Cover of *The View from the Cherry Tree,* by Willo Davis Roberts. Cover illustration copyright © 1987 by Andrea Mistretta. Cover design copyright © 1987 by Lisa Hollander. Reprinted by permission of Andrea Mistretta./ Cover of *Megan's Island,* by Willo Davis Roberts. Cover illustration copyright © 1990 by Carol Newsom. Cover design by Rebecca Tachna. Reprinted by permission of Carol Newsom./ Cover of *The Girl With the Silver Eyes,* by Willo Davis Roberts. Copyright © 1980 by Willo Davis Roberts. Reprinted by permission of Scholastic Inc./ Cover of *Don't Hurt Laurie!,* by Willo Davis Roberts. Cover design by Lisa Hollander. Cover illustration copyright © 1988 by Ruth Sanderson. Reprinted by permission of Ruth Sanderson./ Photograph by Sam Watters.

RIDLEY SCOTT. Movie still from *Legend,* courtesy of Twentieth Century-Fox./ Movie still from *Alien,* courtesy of Twentieth Century Fox./ Movie still from *Thelma & Louise,* courtesy of Metro-Goldwyn-Mayer./ Movie still from *Blade Runner,* courtesy of Warner Brothers./ Photograph courtesy of Ridley Scott.

ZOA SHERBURNE. Jacket of *Girl in the Mirror,* by Zoa Sherburne. William Morrow and Company, 1966. Copyright © 1966 by Zoa Sherburne. Jacket by John Moodie. Reprinted by permission of Morrow Junior Books, a division of William Morrow and Company, Inc./ Jacket of *Too Bad about the Haines Girl,* by Zoa Sherburne. William Morrow and Company, 1967. Copyright © 1967 by Zoa Sherburne. Jacket by Cynthia Basil. Reprinted by permission of Morrow Junior Books, a division of William Morrow and Company, Inc./ Jacket of *River at Her Feet,* by Zoa Sherburne. William Morrow and Company, 1965. Copyright © 1965 by Zoa Sherburne. Jacket by Joseph Cellini. Reprinted by permission of Morrow Junior Books, a division of William Morrow and Company, Inc./ Photograph by Ann Elmo Agency, Inc.

R. L. STINE. Cover of *Silent Night,* by R. L. Stine. Copyright © 1991 by Parachute Press, Inc. Cover art by Bill Schmidt. Reprinted by permission of Pocket Books, a division of Simon & Schuster Inc./ Cover of *Broken Hearts,* by R. L. Stine. Copyright © 1993 by Parachute Press, Inc. Cover art by Bill Schmidt. Reprinted by permission of Pocket Books, a division of Simon & Schuster Inc./ Cover of *Cheerleaders: The First Evil,* by R. L. Stine. Copyright © 1992 by Parachute Press, Inc. Cover art by Edwin Herder. Reprinted by permission of Pocket Books, a division of Simon & Schuster Inc./ Photo by Richard Hutchings, courtesy of R. L. Stine.

BORIS VALLEJO. Illustrations by Boris Vallejo from *Boris Vallejo Fantasy Art Techniques,* produced, edited, and designed by Martyn Dean. Copyright © 1985 by Boris Vallejo. Reprinted by permission of Alaska Momma./ Jacket

Cumulative Index

Author/Artist Index

The following index gives the number of the volume
in which an author/artist's biographical sketch appears.